Processing and Managing Complex Data for Decision Support

Jérôme Darmont, University of Lyon 2, France

Omar Boussaïd, University of Lyon 2, France

IDEA GROUP PUBLISHING

Hershey • London • Melbourne • Singapore

Acquisitions Editor:	Michelle Potter
Development Editor:	Kristin Roth
Senior Managing Editor:	Amanda Appicello
Managing Editor:	Jennifer Neidig
Copy Editor:	Mike Goldberg
Typesetter:	Sharon Berger
Cover Design:	Lisa Tosheff
Printed at:	Yurchak Printing Inc.

Published in the United States of America by
Idea Group Publishing (an imprint of Idea Group Inc.)
701 E. Chocolate Avenue
Hershey PA 17033
Tel: 717-533-8845
Fax: 717-533-8661
E-mail: cust@idea-group.com
Web site: http://www.idea-group.com

and in the United Kingdom by
Idea Group Publishing (an imprint of Idea Group Inc.)
3 Henrietta Street
Covent Garden
London WC2E 8LU
Tel: 44 20 7240 0856
Fax: 44 20 7379 0609
Web site: http://www.eurospanonline.com

Library of Congress Cataloging-in-Publication Data

Processing and managing complex data for decision support / Jerome Darmont and Omar Boussaid, editors.
    p. cm.
  Summary: "This book provides an overall view of the emerging field of complex data processing, highlighting the similarities between the different data, issues and approaches"--Provided by publisher.
    Includes bibliographical references and index.
  ISBN 1-59140-655-2 (hardcover) -- ISBN 1-59140-656-0 (softcover) -- ISBN 1-59140-657-9 (ebook)
  1. Data warehousing. 2. Data mining. I. Darmont, Jerome, 1972- II. Boussaid, Omar.
  QA76.9.D37P76 2006
  005.74--dc22
                                2006003553

British Cataloguing in Publication Data
A Cataloguing in Publication record for this book is available from the British Library.

Processing and Managing Complex Data for Decision Support

Table of Contents

Section I: Complex Data Warehousing

Chapter I
Maria Luisa Damiani, Università di Milano, Italy and
Ecole Polytechnique Fédérale, Switzerland
Stefano Spaccapietra, Ecole Polytechnique Fédérale de Lausanne,
Switzerland

Chapter II
Vicky Nassis, La Trobe University, Melbourne, Australia
Tharam S. Dillon, University of Technology, Sydney, Australia
Wenny Rahayu, La Trobe University, Melbourne, Australia
R Rajugan, University of Technology, Sydney, Australia

Chapter III
Serge Abiteboul, INRIA-Futurs, Orsay, France
Benjamin Nguyen, Université de Versailles Saint-Quentin, France
Gabriela Ruberg, Federal University of Rio de Janeiro, Brazil

Section II: Complex Data Mining

Foreword

A data warehouse is a centralized store of enterprise information implemented specifically for query, reporting and analysis purposes. Terrabytes of data are lying around throughout company networks that need to be integrated in data warehouses or data marts for analysis. One important problem is that the data lie in all sorts of heterogeneous systems, and therefore in all sorts of formats.

To integrate data in data warehouses, companies classically use extract, transform and load (ETL) software, which includes reading data from its source, cleaning it up and formatting it uniformly and then writing it to the warehouse to be exploited. Usually, data are gathered and transformed in simple relational tables organized in stars or snowflakes around fact tables.

With the explosion of multimedia data that are semi-structured or even unstructured, such as texts, images, sounds, videos, spatial information and XML documents, data warehouses need to be extended to support complex objects. The first part of this book is an interesting collection of papers dealing with the support of complex objects in a data warehouse. Seven papers investigate the following topics:

1. Spatial data modelling.
2. Design of XML document warehouses.
3. Warehousing active documents (i.e., XML documents including Web service calls).
4. Text warehousing.
5. Object-oriented source code integration and use for reengineering and reuse.
6. Managing metadata in decision environments.

7. A modelling framework for transaction datasets entailing a partitioned storage, efficient for data mining.

   One major application of data warehouses is data mining. Data mining consists in extracting frequent patterns (tendencies, classes, rules, relationships, etc.) from databases. Storing complex objects in data warehouses requires exploring and modeling large data sets with varying composite structure or even without structure (e.g., free text). This issue of mining complex objects is addressed in the second part of this book. Six papers investigate the following topics:

8. Structural distance metrics to quantify the structural similarity between hierarchical structures, e.g., XML documents.

9. Approaches to evaluate and measure structural similarity of XML documents and schemas.

10. Storing, retrieving and manipulating patterns in an effective way using pattern models and pattern languages.

11. Multimedia database mining for visualization, using virtual reality.

12. Music data mining, including clustering, classification and pattern discovery in music.

13. Data mining for extracting meaningful biological information from genetic expressions.

Most papers include a survey of recent research and new proposals. All in all, this book is a significant collection of papers on new issues in warehousing complex data and using it for decision support. The papers have been carefully selected from a preliminary conference. Thirty three papers were submitted and 13 were selected. Altogether, the book constitutes a remarkable reference for researchers on new topics in online analysis and data mining.

Georges Gardarin
January 2006

Preface

Nowadays, the data management community acknowledges the fact that data are not only numerical or symbolic, but that they may be:

- represented in various formats (databases, texts, images, sounds, videos, etc.);
- diversely structured (relational databases, XML document repositories, etc.);
- originating from several different sources (distributed databases, the Web, etc.);
- described through several channels or points of view (radiographies and audio diagnosis of a physician, data expressed in different scales or languages, etc.); and
- changing in terms of definition or value (temporal databases, periodical surveys, etc.).

Data that fall in several of the above categories may be termed as complex data (Darmont et al., 2005). Managing such data involves a lot of different issues regarding their structure, storage and processing. However, in many decision-support fields (customer relationship management, marketing, competition monitoring, medicine, etc.), they are the real data that need to be exploited.

The advent of complex data indeed imposes another vision of decision-support processes such as data warehousing and data mining. The classic architectures of data warehouses (Inmon, 2002; Kimball & Ross, 2002) have shown their efficiency when data are "simple" (i.e., numerical or symbolic). However, these architectures must be completely reconsidered when dealing with complex data.

For instance, the concept of a centralized warehouse might not be pertinent in all cases. Indeed, the specificity of complex data and their physical location rather impose new solutions based on virtual warehousing or architecture-oriented approaches. Data integration through mediation systems may also be considered as a new approach for the ETL (extract, transform, load) process (Kimball & Caserta, 2004). Furthermore, online analytical processing, better known as OLAP (Thomsen, 2002), must surpass its initial vocation to allow more effective analyses. The combination of OLAP and data mining techniques is a new challenge imposed by complex data.

As for data mining techniques, they generally cannot apply directly onto complex data. Usual data representation spaces for classical data mining algorithms (Hand, Mannila, & Smyth, 2001; Witten & Frank, 2005) are not adapted. Either it is necessary to perform an important, often intricate, preprocessing work to map complex data into these representation spaces without losing information (Pyle, 1999), or it is necessary to substantially modify data-mining algorithms to take into account the specificity of complex data.

The complex data research topic is currently just starting to emerge. Though many people actually work on subsets of complex data, such as multimedia data, the idea of a broader field is just starting to spread. This book is designed to provide readers with an overall view of this emerging field of complex data processing by bringing together various research studies and surveys in different subfields, and by highlighting the similarities between the different data, issues and approaches. It is expected that researchers in universities and research institutions will find such discussions particularly insightful and helpful to their current and future research. In addition, this book is also designed to serve technical professionals, since many existing applications could benefit from the exploitation of other types of data than the ones they usually draw on.

This book is organized into two major sections dealing respectively with complex data warehousing (including spatial, XML and text warehousing) and complex data mining (including distance metrics and similarity measures, pattern management, multimedia and gene sequence mining).

Section I: Complex Data Warehousing

Chapter I: Spatial Data Warehouse Modelling, by Damiani and Spaccapietra, is concerned with multidimensional data models for spatial data warehouses. It first draws a picture of the research area, and then introduces a novel spatial multidimensional data model for spatial objects with geometry: the Multigranular Spatial Data warehouse (MuSD). The main novelty of the model is the representation of spatial measures at multiple levels of geometric granularity.

Chapter II: Goal-Oriented Requirement Engineering for XML Document Warehouses, by Nassis et al. discusses the need of capturing data warehouse requirements early in the design stage, and explores a requirement engineering approach, namely the goal-oriented approach. This approach is then extended to introduce the XML document warehouse (XDW) requirement model.

Chapter III: Building an Active Content Warehouse, by Abiteboul, Nguyen and Ruberg, introduces the concept of content warehousing: the management of loosely structured data. The construction and maintenance of a content warehouse is an intricate task, so the authors propose the Acware (active content warehouse) specification language to help all sorts of users to organize content in a simple manner. This approach is based on XML and Web Services.

Chapter IV: Text Warehousing: Present and Future, by Badia, is part overview of document warehouse and information retrieval techniques, part position paper. The author introduces a new paradigm, based in information extraction, for true integration, and analyzes the challenges that stand in the way of this technology being widely used. He also discusses some considerations on future developments in the general area of documents in databases.

Chapter V: Morphology, Processing, and Integrating of Information from Large Source Code Warehouses for Decision Support, by Rech, describes the morphology of object-oriented source code and how it is processed, integrated and used for knowledge discovery in software engineering in order to support decision-making regarding the refactoring, reengineering and reuse of software systems.

Chapter VI: Managing Metadata in Decision Environments, by Shankaranarayanan and Even, describes the implications for managing metadata, which is a key factor for the successful implementation of complex decision environments. Crucial gaps for integrating metadata are identified by comparing the requirements for managing metadata with the capabilities offered by commercial software products. The authors then propose a conceptual architecture for the design of an integrated metadata repository that attempts to redress these gaps.

Chapter VII: DWFIST: The Data Warehouse of Frequent Itemsets Tactics Approach, by Monteiro et al. presents the core of the DWFIST approach, which is concerned with supporting the analysis and exploration of frequent itemsets and derived patterns such as association rules in transactional datasets. The goal of this new approach is to provide flexible pattern-retrieval capabilities without requiring the original data during the analysis phase, and a standard modeling for data warehouses of frequent itemsets allowing an easier development and reuse of tools for analysis and exploration of itemset-based patterns.

Section II: Complex Data Mining

Chapter VIII: On the Usage of Structural Distance Metrics for Mining Hierarchical Structures, by Dalamagas, Cheng and Sellis, studies distance metrics that capture the structural similarity between hierarchical structures and approaches that exploit structural distance metrics to perform mining tasks on hierarchical structures, especially XML documents.

Chapter IX: Structural Similarity Measures in Sources of XML Documents, by Guerrini, Mesiti and Bertino, discusses existing approaches to evaluate and measure structural similarity in sources of XML documents. The most relevant applications of such measures, discussed throughout the chapter, are for document classification, schema extraction, and for document and schema structural clustering.

Chapter X: Pattern Management: Practice and Challenges, by Catania and Maddalena, provides a critical comparison of the existing approaches for pattern management. In particular, specific issues concerning pattern management systems, pattern models and pattern languages are discussed. Several parameters are also identified and used in evaluating the effectiveness of theoretical and industrial proposals.

Chapter XI: VRMiner: A Tool for Multimedia Database Mining with Virtual Reality, by Azzag et al. presents a new 3-D interactive method for visualizing multimedia data with a virtual reality named VRMiner. Navigating through the data is done in a very intuitive and precise way with a 3-D sensor that simulates a virtual camera. Interactive requests can be formulated by the expert with a data glove that recognizes hand gestures. The authors illustrate how this tool has been successfully applied to several real world applications.

Chapter XII: Mining in Music Databases, by Karydis, Nanopoulos and Manolopoulos provides a broad survey of music data mining, including clustering, classification and pattern discovery in music. Throughout the chapter, practical applications of music data mining are presented. This chapter encapsulates the theory and methods required in order to discover knowledge in the form of patterns for music analysis and retrieval, or statistical models for music classification and generation.

Finally, **Chapter XIII: Data Mining in Gene Expression Data Analysis: A Survey**, by Han, Gruenwald and Conway, surveys data mining techniques that have been used for clustering, classification and association rules for gene expression data analysis. In addition, the authors provide a comprehensive list of currently available commercial and academic data mining software together with their features, and finally suggest future research directions.

By gathering this collection of papers of high scientific quality, our main objective is to contribute to the emergence of already existing research in the complex data field. One ambition of this book is to become one of the first foundation references in this new and ambitious research field. We hope it will succeed.

Jérôme Darmont and Omar Boussaïd

Lyon, France

January 2006

References

Darmont, J., Boussaïd, O., Ralaivao, J. C., & Aouiche, K. (2005). An architecture framework for complex data warehouses. *Seventh International Conference on Enterprise Information Systems ICEIS '05,* Miami, FL (pp. 370-373).

Hand, D. J., Mannila, H., & Smyth, P. (2001). *Principles of data mining.* Boston: MIT Press.

Inmon, W. H. (2002). *Building the data warehouse* (2nd ed.). New York: John Wiley & Sons.

Kimball, R., & Ross, M. (2002). *The data warehouse toolkit: The complete guide to dimensional modeling* (2nd ed.). New York: John Wiley & Sons.

Kimball, R., & Caserta, J. (2004). *The data warehouse ETL toolkit.* New York: John Wiley & Sons.

Pyle, D. (1999). *Data preparation for data mining.* San Francisco: Morgan Kaufmann.

Thomsen, E. (2002). *OLAP solutions: Building multidimensional information systems* (2nd ed.). New York: John Wiley & Sons.

Witten, I. H., & Frank, E. (2005). *Data mining: Practical machine learning tools and techniques* (2nd edition). San Francisco: Morgan Kaufmann.

Acknowledgments

The editors would first like to thank the chapter authors for their insights and excellent contributions to this book, as well as Pr. Georges Gardarin, who kindly accepted to write the foreword of this book.

The editors would also like to acknowledge the help of all involved in the review process of the book, without whose support the project could not have been satisfactorily completed. Their comprehensive and constructive comments helped in improving the quality of this book and fueled very exciting discussions. We have indeed noticed that a true debate emerged during the review process, thus showing that this research field is very promising.

Finally, special thanks go to the publishing team at Idea Group Inc., and especially to Ms. Michele Rossi and Kristin Roth, who made our job as editors smooth and easy.

Reviewers list:

- Sihem Amer-Yahia, AT&T Labs – Research, USA
- Antonio Badia, University of Louisville, USA
- José Balcazar, Universitat Politecnica de Catalunya, Spain
- Yvan Bédard, Laval University, Quebec, Canada
- Zora Bellahsene, University of Montpellier II, France
- Ladjel Bellatreche, University of Poitiers, France
- Djamal Benslimane, University of Lyon 1, France
- Fadila Bentayeb, University of Lyon 2, France
- Laure Berti-Équille, IRISA Rennes, France
- Elisa Bertino, Purdue University, USA
- Henri Briand, University of Nantes, France

- Jean-Hugues Chauchat, University of Lyon 2, France
- Liming Chen, Ecole Centrale de Lyon, France
- Cristina Davino, Universita degli Studi di Macerata, Italy
- Karen Davis, University of Cincinnati, USA
- Pierre Gançarski, University of Strasbourg I, France
- Sandra Gonzalez, Buenos Aires University, Argentina
- Le Gruenwald, University of Oklahoma, USA
- Mohand-Said Hacid, University of Lyon 1, France
- Georges Hebrail, ENST Paris, France
- Stéphane Lallich, University of Lyon 2, France
- Chang-Tsun Li, University of Warwick, UK
- Sabine Loudcher, University of Lyon 2, France
- Zakaria Maamar, Zayed University, Dubai
- Anna Maddalena, University of Genova, Italy
- Yannis Manolopoulos, Aristotle University of Thessaloniki, Greece
- Florent Masseglia, INRIA Sophia Antipolis, France
- Maryvone Miquel, INSA Lyon, France
- Rokia Missaoui, Quebec University, Canada
- Amedeo Napoli, LORIA Nancy, France
- Richi Nayak, Queensland University of Technology, Australia
- Benjamin Nguyen, INRIA Futurs, France
- Nicolas Nicoloyannis, University of Lyon 2, France
- Francesca Odone, University of Genova, Italy
- Torben Bach Pedersen, Aalborg University, Denmark
- Jian Pei, New York State University, USA
- Jean-Marc Petit, University of Clermont-Ferrand II, France
- François Poulet, ESIEA Laval, France
- Joël Quinqueton, Paul Valéry University, France
- Ricco Rakotomalala, University of Lyon 2, France
- Wenny Rayahu, La Trobe University, Australia
- Jörg Rech, Fraunhofer Institute for Experimental Software Engineering, Germany
- Michel Schneider, University of Clermont-Ferrand II, France
- Florence Sèdes, University of Toulouse 3, France

- Timos Sellis, National Technical University of Athens, Greece
- Chantal Soulé-Dupuy, University of Toulouse 3, France
- David Taniar, Monash University, Australia
- Anne Tchounikine, INSA Lyon, France
- Brigitte Trousse, INRIA Sophia Antipolis, France
- Gilles Venturini, University of Tours, France
- Christel Vrain, University of Orléans, France
- Boris Vrdoljak, University of Zagreb, Croatia
- Karine Zeitouni, University of Versailles Saint-Quentin, France
- Djamel Zighed, University of Lyon 2, France

Section I:

Complex Data Warehousing

Chapter I

Spatial Data Warehouse Modelling

Maria Luisa Damiani, Università di Milano, Italy and
Ecole Polytechnique Fédérale, Switzerland

Stefano Spaccapietra,
Ecole Polytechnique Fédérale de Lausanne, Switzerland

Abstract

This chapter is concerned with multidimensional data models for spatial data warehouses. Over the last few years different approaches have been proposed in the literature for modelling multidimensional data with geometric extent. Nevertheless, the definition of a comprehensive and formal data model is still a major research issue. The main contributions of the chapter are twofold: First, it draws a picture of the research area; second it introduces a novel spatial multidimensional data model for spatial objects with geometry (MuSD – multigranular spatial data warehouse). MuSD complies with current standards for spatial data modelling, augmented by data warehousing concepts such as spatial fact, spatial dimension and spatial measure. The novelty of the model is the representation of spatial measures at multiple levels of geometric granularity. Besides the representation concepts, the model includes a set of OLAP operators supporting the navigation across dimension and measure levels.

Introduction

A topic that over recent years has received growing attention from both academy and industry concerns the integration of spatial data management with multidimensional data analysis techniques. We refer to this technology as spatial data warehousing, and consider a spatial data warehouse to be a multidimensional database of spatial data. Following common practice, we use here the term spatial in the geographical sense, i.e., to denote data that includes the description of how objects and phenomena are located on the Earth. A large variety of data may be considered to be spatial, including: data for land use and socioeconomic analysis; digital imagery and geo-sensor data; location-based data acquired through GPS or other positioning devices; environmental phenomena. Such data are collected and possibly marketed by organizations such as public administrations, utilities and other private companies, environmental research centres and spatial data infrastructures. Spatial data warehousing has been recognized as a key technology in enabling the interactive analysis of spatial data sets for decision-making support (Rivest et al., 2001; Han et al., 2002). Application domains in which the technology can play an important role are, for example, those dealing with complex and worldwide phenomena such as homeland security, environmental monitoring and health safeguard. These applications pose challenging requirements for integration and usage of spatial data of different kinds, coverage and resolution, for which the spatial data warehouse technology may be extremely helpful.

Origins

Spatial data warehousing results from the confuence of two technologies, spatial data handling and multidimensional data analysis, respectively. The former technology is mainly provided by two kinds of systems: spatial database management systems (DBMS) and geographical information systems(GIS). Spatial DBMS extend the functionalities of conventional data management systems to support the storage, efficient retrieval and manipulation of spatial data (Rigaux et al., 2002). Examples of commercial DBMS systems are Oracle Spatial and IBM DB2 Spatial Extender. A GIS, on the other hand, is a composite computer based information system consisting of an integrated set of programs, possibly including or interacting with a spatial DBMS, which enables the capturing, modelling, analysis and visualization of spatial data (Longley et al., 2001). Unlike a spatial DBMS, a GIS is meant to be directly usable by an end-user. Examples of commercial systems are ESRI ArcGIS and Intergraph Geomedia. The technology of spatial data handling has made significant progress in the last decade, fostered by the standardization initiatives promoted by OGC

(Open Geospatial Consortium) and ISO/TC211, as well as by the increased availability of off-the-shelf geographical data sets that have broadened the spectrum of spatially-aware applications. Conversely, multidimensional data analysis has become the leading technology for decision making in the business area. Data are stored in a multidimensional array (cube or hypercube) (Kimball, 1996; Chaudhuri & Dayla, 1997; Vassiliadis & Sellis, 1999). The elements of the cube constitute the facts (or cells) and are defined by measures and dimensions. Typically, a measure denotes a quantitative variable in a given domain. For example, in the marketing domain, one kind of measure is sales amount. A dimension is a structural attribute characterizing a measure. For the marketing example, dimensions of sales may be: time, location and product. Under these example assumptions, a cell stores the amount of sales for a given product in a given region and over a given period of time. Moreover, each dimension is organized in a hierarchy of dimension levels, each level corresponding to a different granularity for the dimension. For example, *year* is one level of the *time* dimension, while the sequence *day*, *month*, *year* defines a simple hierarchy of increasing granularity for the time dimension. The basic operations for online analysis (OLAP operators) that can be performed over data cubes are: *roll-up*, which moves up along one or more dimensions towards more aggregated data (e.g., moving from monthly sales amounts to yearly sales amounts); *drill-down*, which moves down dimensions towards more detailed, disaggregated data and *slice-and-dice*, which performs a selection and projection operation on a cube.

The integration of these two technologies, spatial data handling and multidimensional analysis, responds to multiple application needs. In business data warehouses, the spatial dimension is increasingly considered of strategic relevance for the analysis of enterprise data. Likewise, in engineering and scientific applications, huge amounts of measures, typically related to environmental phenomena, are collected through sensors, installed on ground or satellites, and continuously generating data which are stored in data warehouses for subsequent analysis.

Spatial Multidimensional Models

A data warehouse (DW) is the result of a complex process entailing the integration of huge amounts of heterogeneous data, their organization into de-normalized data structures and eventually their loading into a database for use through online analysis techniques. In a DW, data are organized and manipulated in accordance with the concepts and operators provided by a multidimensional data model. Multidimensional data models have been widely investigated for conventional, non-spatial data. Commercial systems based on these models are marketed. By contrast, research on spatially aware DWs (SDWs) is a step behind. The reasons are diverse: The spatial context is peculiar and complex, requiring specialized techniques for data representation and processing; the technology for spatial data management has reached maturity only in recent times with the development of SQL3-based implementations of OGC standards; finally, SDWs still lack a market comparable in size with the business sector that is pushing the development of the technology. As a result, the definition of spatial multidimensional data models (SMDs) is still a challenging research issue.

A SMD model can be specified at conceptual and logical levels. Unlike the logical model, the specification at the conceptual level is independent of the technology used for the management of spatial data. Therefore, since the representation is not constrained by the implementation platform, the conceptual specification, that is the view we adopt in this work, is more flexible, although not immediately operational.

The conceptual specification of an SMD model entails the definition of two basic components: a set of representation constructs, and an algebra of spatial OLAP (SOLAP) operators, supporting data analysis and navigation across the representation structures of the model. The representation constructs account for the specificity of the spatial nature of data. In this work we focus on one of the peculiarities of spatial data, that is the availability of spatial data at different levels of granularity. Since the granularity concerns not only the semantics but also the geometric aspects of the data, the location of objects can have different geometric representations. For example, representing the location of an accident at different scales may lead to associating different geometries to the same accident.

To allow a more flexible representation of spatial data at different geometric granularity, we propose a SDM model in which not only dimensions are organized in levels of detail but also the spatial measures. For that purpose we introduce the concept of *multi-level spatial measure*.

The proposed model is named MuSD (multigranular spatial data warehouse). It is based on the notions of *spatial fact*, *spatial dimension* and *multi-level spatial measure*. A spatial fact may be defined as a fact describing an event that occurred on the Earth in a position that is relevant to know and analyze. Spatial facts are, for instance, road accidents. Spatial dimensions and measures represent properties of facts that have a geometric meaning; in particular, the spatial measure represents the location in which the fact occurred. A multi-level spatial measure is a measure that is represented by multiple geometries at different levels of detail. A measure of this kind is, for example, the location of an accident: Depending on the application requirements, an accident may be represented by a point along a road, a road segment or the whole road, possibly at different cartographic scales. Spatial measures and dimensions are uniformly represented in terms of the standard spatial objects defined by the Open

Geospatial Consortium. Besides the representation constructs, the model includes a set of SOLAP operators to navigate not only through the dimensional levels but also through the levels of the spatial measures.

The chapter is structured in the following sections: the next section, *Background Knowledge*, introduces a few basic concepts underlying spatial data representation; the subsequent section, *State of the Art on Spatial Multidimensional Models*, surveys the literature on SDM models; the proposed spatial multidimensional data model is presented in the following section; and research opportunities and some concluding remarks are discussed in the two conclusive sections.

Background Knowledge

The real world is populated by different kinds of objects, such as roads, buildings, administrative boundaries, moving cars and air pollution phenomena. Some of these objects are tangible, like buildings, others, like administrative boundaries, are not. Moreover, some of them have identifiable shapes with well-defined boundaries, like land parcels; others do not have a crisp and fixed shape, like air pollution. Furthermore, in some cases the position of objects, e.g., buildings, does not change in time; in other cases it changes more or less frequently, as in the case of moving cars. To account for the multiform nature of spatial data, a variety of data models for the digital representation of spatial data are needed. In this section, we present an overview of a few basic concepts of spatial data representation used throughout the chapter.

The Nature of Spatial Data

Spatial data describe properties of phenomena occurring in the world. The prime property of such phenomena is that they occupy a position. In broad terms, a position is the description of a location on the Earth. The common way of describing such a position is through the coordinates of a coordinate reference system.

The real world is populated by phenomena that fall into two broad conceptual categories: entities and continuous fields (Longley et al., 2001). Entities are distinguishable elements occupying a precise position on the Earth and normally having a well-defined boundary. Examples of entities are rivers, roads and buildings. By contrast, fields are variables having a single value that varies within a bounded space. An example of field is the temperature, or the distribution, of a polluting substance in an area. Field data can be directly obtained from sensors, for example installed on satellites, or obtained by interpolation from sample sets of observations.

The standard name adopted for the digital representation of abstractions of real world phenomena is that of *feature* (OGC, 2001, 2003). The feature is the basic representation construct defined in the reference spatial data model developed by the Open Geospatial Consortium and endorsed by ISO/TC211. As we will see, we will use the concept of feature to uniformly represent all the spatial components in our model. Features are spatial when they are associated with locations on the Earth; otherwise they are non-spatial. Features have a distinguishing name and have a set of attributes. Moreover, features may be defined at instance and type level: *Feature instances* represent single phenomena; *feature types* describe the intensional meaning of features having a common set of attributes. Spatial features are further specialized to represent different kinds of spatial data. In the OGC terminology, *coverages* are the spatial features that represent continuous fields and consist of discrete functions taking values over space partitions. Space partitioning results from either the subdivision of space in a set of regular units or cells (*raster* data model) or the subdivision of space in irregular units such as triangles (*tin* data model). The discrete function assigns each portion of a bounded space a value.

In our model, we specifically consider *simple spatial features*. Simple spatial features ("features" hereinafter) have one or more attributes of geometric type, where the geometric type is one of the types defined by OGC, such as point, line and polygon. One of these attributes denotes the position of the entity. For example, the position of the state Italy may be described by a multipolygon, i.e., a set of disjoint polygons (to account for islands), with holes (to account for the Vatican State and San Marino). A simple feature is very close to the concept of entity or object as used by the database community. It should be noticed, however, that besides a semantic and geometric characterization, a feature type is also assigned a coordinate reference system, which is specific for the feature type and that defines the space in which the instances of the feature type are embedded.

More complex features may be defined specifying the topological relationships relating a set of features. Topology deals with the geometric properties that remain invariant when space is elastically deformed. Within the context of geographical information, topology is commonly used to describe, for example, connectivity and adjacency relationships between spatial elements. For example, a road network, consisting of a set of interconnected roads, may be described through a graph of nodes and edges: Edges are the topological objects representing road segments whereas nodes account for road junctions and road endpoints.

To summarize, spatial data have a complex nature. Depending on the application requirements and the characteristics of the real world phenomena, different spatial data models can be adopted for the representation of geometric and topological properties of spatial entities and continuous fields.

State of the Art on Spatial Multidimensional Models

Research on spatial multidimensional data models is relatively recent. Since the pioneering work of Han et al. (1998), several models have been proposed in the literature aiming at extending the classical multidimensional data model with spatial concepts. However, despite the complexity of spatial data, current spatial data warehouses typically contain objects with simple geometric extent.

Moreover, while an SMD model is assumed to consist of a set of representation concepts and an algebra of SOLAP operators for data navigation and aggregation, approaches proposed in the literature often privilege only one of the two aspects, rarely both. Further, whilst early data models are defined at the logical level and are based on the relational data model, in particular on the star model, more recent developments, especially carried out by the database research community, focus on conceptual aspects. We also observe that the modelling of geometric granularities in terms of multi-level spatial measures, which we propose in our model, is a novel theme.

Often, existing approaches do not rely on standard data models for the representation of spatial aspects. The spatiality of facts is commonly represented through a geometric element, while in our approach, as we will see, it is an OGC spatial feature, i.e., an object that has a semantic value in addition to its spatial characterization.

A related research issue that is gaining increased interest in recent years, and that is relevant for the development of comprehensive SDW data models, concerns the specification and efficient implementation of the operators for spatial aggregation.

Literature Review

The first, and perhaps the most significant, model proposed so far has been developed by Han et al. (1998). This model introduced the concepts of spatial dimension and spatial measure. Spatial dimensions describe properties of facts that also have a geometric characterization. Spatial dimensions, as conventional dimensions, are defined at different levels of granularity. Conversely, a spatial measure is defined as "a measure that contains a collection of pointers to spatial objects", where spatial objects are geometric elements, such as polygons. Therefore, a spatial measure does not have a semantic characterization, it is just a set of geometries. To illustrate these concepts, the authors consider a SDW about weather data. The example SDW has three thematic dimensions: {temperature, precipitation, time}; one spatial dimension: {region}; and three measures: {region_map, area, count}. While area and count are numeric measures, region_map is a spatial measure denoting a set of polygons. The proposed model is specified at the logical level, in particular in terms of a star schema, and does not include an algebra of OLAP operators. Instead, the authors develop a technique for the efficient computation of spatial aggregations, like the merge of polygons. Since the spatial aggregation operations are assumed to be distributive, aggregations may be partially computed on disjoint subsets of data. By pre-computing the spatial aggregation of different subsets of data, the processing time can be reduced.

Rivest et al. (2001) extend the definition of spatial measures given in the previous approach to account for spatial measures that are computed by metric or topological operators. Further, the authors emphasize the need for more advanced querying capabilities to provide end users with topological and metric operators. The need to account for topological relationships has been more concretely addressed by Marchant et al. (2004), who define a specific type of dimension implementing spatio-temporal topological operators at different levels of detail. In such a way, facts may be partitioned not only based on dimension values but also on the existing topological relationships.

Shekhar et al. (2001) propose a *map cube operator,* extending the concepts of data cube and aggregation to spatial data. Further, the authors introduce a classification and examples of different types of spatial measures, e.g., spatial distributive, algebraic and holistic functions.

GeoDWFrame (Fidalgo et al., 2004) is a recently proposed model based on the star schema. The conceptual framework, however, does not include the notion of spatial measure, while dimensions are classified in a rather complex way.

Pederson and Tryfona (2001) are the first to introduce a formal definition of an SMD model at the conceptual level. The model only accounts for spatial measures whilst dimensions are only non-spatial. The spatial measure is a collection of geometries, as in Han et al. (1998), and in particular of polygonal elements. The authors develop a pre-aggregation technique to reduce the processing time of the operations of merge and intersection of polygons. The formalization approach is valuable but, because of the limited number of operations and types of spatial objects that are taken into account, the model has limited functionality and expressiveness.

Jensen et al. (2002) address an important requirement of spatial applications. In particular, the authors propose a conceptual model that allows the definition of dimensions whose levels are related by a partial containment relationship. An example of partial containment is the relationship between a roadway and the district it crosses. A degree of containment is attributed to the relationship. For example, a roadway may be defined as partially contained at degree 0.5 into a district. An algebra for the extended data model is also defined. To our knowledge, the model has been the first to deal with uncertainty in data warehouses, which is a relevant issue in real applications.

Malinowski and Zimanyi (2004) present a different approach to conceptual modelling. Their SMD model is based on the Entity Relationship modelling paradigm. The basic representation constructs are those of *fact relationship* and *dimension*. A *dimension* contains one or several related levels consisting of entity types possibly having an attribute of geometric type. The *fact relationship* represents an n-ary relationship existing among the dimension levels. The attributes of the *fact relationship* constitute the measures. In particular, a spatial measure is a measure that is represented by a geometry or a function computing a geometric property, such as the length or surface of an element. The spatial aspects of the model are expressed in terms of the MADS spatio-temporal conceptual model (Parent et al., 1998). An interesting concept of the SMD model is that of *spatial fact relationship*, which models a spatial relationship between two or more spatial dimensions, such as that of spatial containment. However, the model focuses on the representation constructs and does not specify a SOLAP algebra.

A different, though related, issue concerns the operations of *spatial aggregation*. Spatial aggregation operations summarize the geometric properties of objects, and as such constitute the distinguishing aspect of SDW. Nevertheless, despite the relevance of the subject, a standard set of operators (as, for example, the operators Avg, Min, Max in SQL) has not been defined yet. A first comprehensive classification and formalization of spatio-temporal aggregate functions is presented in Lopez and Snodgrass (2005). The operation of aggregation is defined as a function that is applied to a collection of tuples and returns a single value. The authors distinguish three kinds of methods for generating the set of tuples, known as *group composition*, *partition composition* and *sliding window composition*. They provide a formal definition of aggregation for conventional, temporal and spatial data based on this distinction. In addition to the conceptual aspects of spatial aggregation, another major issue regards the development of methods for the efficient computation of these kinds of operations to manage high volumes of spatial data. In particular, techniques are developed based on the combined use of specialized indexes, materialization of aggregate measures and computational geometry algorithms, especially to support the aggregation of dynamically computed sets of spatial objects (Papadias, et al., 2001; Rao et al., 2003; Zhang & Tsotras, 2005).

A Multigranular Spatial Data Warehouse Model: MuSD

Despite the numerous proposals of data models for SDW defined at the logical, and more recently,conceptual level presented in the previous section, and despite the increasing number of data warehousing applications (see, e.g., Bedard et al., 2003; Scotch & Parmantoa, 2005), the definition of a comprehensive and formal data model is still a major research issue.

In this work we focus on the definition of a formal model based on the concept of spatial measures at multiple levels of geometric granularity.

One of the distinguishing aspects of multidimensional data models is the capability of dealing with data at different levels of detail or granularity. Typically, in a data warehouse the notion of granularity is conveyed through the notion of dimensional hierarchy. For example, the dimension *administrative units* may be represented at different decreasing levels of detail: at the most detailed level as municipalities, next as regions and then as states. Note, however, that unlike dimensions, measures are assigned a unique granularity. For example, the granularity of sales may be homogeneously expressed in euros.

In SDW, the assumption that spatial measures have a unique level of granularity seems to be too restrictive. In fact, spatial data are very often available at multiple granularities, since data are collected by different organizations for different purposes. Moreover, the granularity not only regards the semantics (semantic granularity) but also the geometric aspects (spatial granularity) (Spaccapietra et al., 2000; Fonseca et al., 2002). For example, the location of an accident may be modelled as a measure, yet represented at different scales and thus have varying geometric representations.

To represent measures at varying spatial granularities, alternative strategies can be prospected: A simple approach is to define a number of spatial measures, one for each level of spatial granularity. However, this solution is not conceptually adequate because it does not represent the hierarchical relation among the various spatial representations.

In the model we propose, named MuSD, we introduce the notion of *multi-level spatial measure*, which is a spatial measure that is defined at multiple levels of granularity, in the same way as dimensions. The introduction of this new concept raises a number of interesting issues. The first one concerns the modelling of the spatial properties. To provide a homogeneous representation of the spatial properties across multiple levels, both spatial measures and dimensions are represented in terms of OGC features. Therefore, the locations of facts are denoted by feature identifiers. For example, a feature, say p1, of type *road accident,* may represent the location of an *accident.* Note that in this way we can refer to spatial objects in a simple way using names, in much the same way Han et al. (1998) do using pointers. The difference is in the level of abstraction and, moreover, in the fact that a feature is not simply a geometry but an entity with a semantic characterization.

Another issue concerns the representation of the features resulting from aggregation operations. To represent such features at different granularities, the model is supposed to include a set of operators that are able to dynamically decrease the spatial granularity of spatial measures. We call these operators *coarsening operators.* With this term we indicate a variety of operators that, although developed in different contexts, share the common goal of representing less precisely the geometry of an object. Examples include the operators for cartographic generalization proposed in Camossi et al. (2003) as well the operators generating imprecise geometries out of more precise representations (*fuzzyfying* operators).

In summary, the MuSD model has the following characteristics:

- It is based on the usual constructs of (spatial) measures and (spatial) dimensions. Notice that the spatiality of a measure is a necessary condition for the DW to be spatial, while the spatiality of dimensions is optional;

- A spatial measure represents the location of a fact at multiple levels of spatial granularity;

- Spatial dimension and spatial measures are represented in terms of OGC features;

- Spatial measures at different spatial granularity can be dynamically computed by applying a set of coarsening operators; and

- An algebra of SOLAP operators is defined to enable user navigation and data analysis.

Hereinafter, we first introduce the representation concepts of the MuSD model and then the SOLAP operators.

Representation Concepts in MuSD

The basic notion of the model is that of *spatial fact.* A spatial fact is defined as a fact that has occurred in a location. Properties of spatial facts are described in terms of measures and dimensions which, depending on the application, may have a spatial meaning.

A *dimension* is composed of *levels*. The set of levels is partially ordered; more specifically, it constitutes a lattice. Levels are assigned values belonging to *domains*. If the domain of a level consists of features, the level is *spatial*; otherwise it is *non-spatial*. A *spatial measure*, as a dimension, is composed of levels representing different granularities for the measure and forming a lattice. Since in common practice the notion of granularity seems not to be of particular concern for conventional and numeric measures, non-spatial measures are defined at a unique level. Further, as the spatial measure represents the location of the fact, it seems reasonable and not significantly restrictive to assume the spatial measure to be unique in the SDW.

As Jensen et al. (2002), we base the model on the distinction between the intensional and extensional representations, which we respectively call *schema* and *cube*. The schema specifies the structure, thus the set of dimensions and measures that compose the SDW; the cube describes a set of facts along the properties specified in the schema.

To illustrate the concepts of the model, we use as a running example the case of an SDW of road accidents. The *accidents* constitute the spatial facts. The properties of the accidents are modelled as follows: The number of *victims* and the *position* along the road constitute the measures of the SDW. In particular, the position of the accident is a spatial measure. The *date* and the *administrative unit* in which the accident occurred constitute the dimensions.

Before detailing the representation constructs, we need to define the spatial data model which is used for representing the spatial concepts of the model.

The Spatial Data Model

For the representation of the spatial components, we adopt a spatial data model based on the OGC simple features model. We adopt this model because it is widely deployed in commercial spatial DBMS and GIS. Although a more advanced spatial data model has been proposed (OGC, 2003), we do not lose in generality by adopting the simple feature model. Features (simple) are identified by names. Milan, Lake Michigan and the car number AZ213JW are examples of features. In particular, we consider as spatial features entities that can be mapped onto locations in the given space (for example, Milan and Lake Michigan). The location of a feature is represented through a *geometry*. The geometry of a spatial feature may be of type point, line or polygon, or recursively be a collection of disjoint geometries. Features have an application-dependent semantics that are expressed through the concept of *feature type*. Road, Town, Lake and Car are examples of feature types. The *extension* of a feature type, *ft*, is a set of semantically homogeneous features. As remarked in the previous section, since features are identified by unique names, we represent spatial objects in terms of feature identifiers. Such identifiers are different from the pointers to geometric elements proposed in early SDW models. In fact, a feature identifier does not denote a geometry, rather an entity that has also a semantics. Therefore some spatial operations, such as the spatial merge when applied to features, have a semantic value besides a geometric one. In the examples that will follow, spatial objects are indicated by their names.

Basic Concepts

To introduce the notion of schema and cube, we first need to define the following notions: *domain, level, level hierarchy, dimension* and *measure*. Consider the concept of domain. A domain defines the set of values that may be assigned to a property of facts, that is to a measure or to a dimension level. The domain may be single-valued or multi-valued; it may be spatial or non-spatial. A formal definition is given as follows.

Definition 1 (Domain and spatial domain): Let V be the set of values and F the set f features with $F \subseteq V$. A domain Do is single-valued if $Do \subseteq V$; it is multi-valued if $Do \subseteq 2^V$, in which case the elements of the domain are subsets of values. Further, the domain Do is a single-valued spatial domain if $Do \subseteq F$; it is a multi-valued spatial domain if $Do \subseteq 2^F$. We denote with DO the set of domains $\{Do_1 ..., Do_k\}$.

Example 1: In the road accident SDW, the single-valued domain of the property victims is the set of positive integers. A possible spatial domain for the position of the accidents is the set $\{a4, a5, s35\}$ consisting of features which represent roads. We stress that in this example the position is a feature and not a mere geometric element, e.g., the line representing the geometry of the road.

The next concept we introduce is that of *level*. A level denotes the single level of granularity of both dimensions and measures. A level is defined by a name and a domain. We also define the notion of partial ordering among levels, which describes the relationship among different levels of detail.

Definition 2 (Level): A level is a pair < Ln, Do > where Ln is the name of the level and Do its domain. If the domain is a spatial domain, then the level is spatial; otherwise it is non-spatial.

Let Lv1 and Lv2 be two levels, dom(Lv) the function returning the domain of level Lv, and $\leq_{lv}$ a partial order over V. We say that Lv1$\leq_{lv}$ Lv2 iff for each v1 $\in$ dom(Lv1), it exists v2 $\in$ dom(Lv2) such that v1$\leq_{lv}$ v2. We denote with LV the set of levels. The relationship Lv1 $\leq_{lv}$ Lv2 is read: Lv1 is less coarse (or more detailed) than Lv2.

Example 2: Consider the following two levels: L_1=<AccidentAtLargeScale, PointAt1:1'000>, L_2=<AccidentAtSmallScale, PointAt1:50'000>. Assume that Do_1 = PointAt1:1'000 and Do2 = PointAt1:50'000 are domains of features representing accidents along roads at different scales. If we assume that Do_1 $\leq_{lv}$ Do_2 then it holds that AccidentAtLargeScale$\leq_{lv}$ AccidentAtSmallScale.

The notion of level is used to introduce the concept of *hierarchy of levels*, which is then applied to define dimensions and measures.

Definition 3 (Level hierarchy): Let L be a set of n levels L = {Lv_1, ..., Lv_n}. A level hierarchy H is a lattice over L: H =<L, $\leq_{lv}$, Lvtop, Lvbot> where $\leq_{lv}$ is a partial order over the set L of levels, and Lvtop, Lvbot, respectively, the top and the bottom levels of the lattice.

Given a level hierarchy H, the function LevelsOf(H) returns the set of levels in H. For the sake of generality, we do not make any assumption on the meaning of the partial ordering. Further, we say that a level hierarchy is of type *spatial* if all the levels in L are spatial; *non-spatial* when the levels are non-spatial; *hybrid* if L consists of both spatial and non-spatial levels. This distinction is analogous to the one defined by Han et al. (1998).

Example 3: Consider again the previous example of hierarchy of administrative entities. If the administrative entities are described by spatial features and thus have a geometry, then they form a spatial hierarchy; if they are described simply by names, then the hierarchy is non-spatial; if some levels are spatial and others are non-spatial, then the hierarchy is hybrid.

At this point we introduce the concepts of *dimensions*, *measures* and *spatial measures*. *Dimensions* and *spatial measures* are defined as hierarchies of levels. Since there is no evidence that the same concept is useful also for numeric measures, we introduce the notion of hierarchy only for the measures that are spatial. Further, as we assume that measures can be assigned subset of values, the domain of a (spatial) measure is multivalued.

Definition 4 (Dimension, measure and spatial measure): We define:

- A dimension D is a level hierarchy. The domains of the dimension levels are single-valued. Further, the hierarchy can be of type: spatial, non-spatial and hybrid;

- A measure M is defined by a unique level $< M, Do >$, with Do a multi-valued domain; and

- A spatial measure SM is a level hierarchy. The domains of the levels are multi-valued. Moreover the level hierarchy is spatial.

To distinguish the levels, we use the terms *dimension* and *spatial measure levels*. Note that the levels of the spatial measure are all spatial since we assume that the locations of facts can be represented at granularities that have a geometric meaning. Finally, we introduce the concept of *multigranular spatial schema* to denote the whole structure of the SDW.

Definition 5 (Multigranular spatial schema): A multigranular spatial schema S (schema, in short) is the tuple $S = <D1, ..Dn, M1, ...Mm, SM>$ where:

- Di is a dimension, for each i =1, .., n;

- Mj is a non-spatial measure, for each j =1, .., m; and

- SM is a spatial measure.

We assume the spatial measure to be unique in the schema. Although in principle that could be interpreted as a limitation, we believe it is a reasonable choice since it seems adequate in most real cases.

Example 4: Consider the following schema S for the road accidents SDW:
S =<date, administrativeUnit, victims, location> where:

- *{date, administrativeUnit}* are dimensions with the following simple structure:
  - date =<{year, month } , $\leq_{date}$, month, year> with month $\leq_{date}$ year
  - administrativeUnit =<{municipality, region, state}, $\leq_{adm}$, municipality, state> with municipality $\leq_{adm}$ region $\leq_{adm}$ state;

- victims is a non-spatial measure;

- location is the spatial measure. Let us call $M_1 = $ AccidentAtLargeScale and $M_2 = $ AccidentAtSmallScale, two measure levels representing accidents at two different scales. Then the measure is defined as follows: $<\{M_1, M_2\} \leq_{pos}, M_1, M_2>$ such that $M_1 \leq_{pos} M_2$.

Finally, we introduce the concept of *cube* to denote the extension of our SDW. A cube is a set of cells containing the measure values defined with respect a given granularity of dimensions and measures. To indicate the level of granularity of dimensions, the notion of *schema level* is introduced. A schema level is a schema limited to specific levels. A cube is thus defined as an instance of a schema level.

Definition 6 (Schema level): Let $S = <D_1, ..D_n, M_1, ...M_m, SM>$ be a schema. A schema level SL for S is a tuple: $<DLv_1, ..DLv_n, M_1, ...M_m, Slv>$ where:

- $DLv_i \in $ LevelsOf (D_i), is a level of dimension D_i (for each i = 1, ..., n);

- M_i is a non-spatial measure (for each i =1, ..., m); and

- $Slv \in $ LevelsOf (SM) is a level of the spatial measure SM

Since non-spatial measures have a unique level, they are identical in all schema levels. The cube is thus formally defined as follows:

Definition 7 (Cube and state): Let $SL = <DLv_1, ..DLv_n, M_1, ...M_m, Slv>$ be a schema level.

A cube for SL, C_{SL} is the set of tuples (cells) of the form: $<d_1, ..., d_n, m_1, ..., m_m, sv>$ where:

- d_i is a value for the dimension level DLv_i;

- m_i is a value for the measure M_i; and

- sv is the value for the spatial measure level Slv.

A state of a SDW is defined by the pair $<SL, C_{SL}>$ where SL is a schema level and C_{SL} a cube.

The *basic cube* and *basic state* respectively denote the cube and the schema level at the maximum level of detail of the dimensions and spatial measure.

Example 5: Consider the schema S introduced in example 4 and the schema level <month, municipality, victims, accidentAtlargeScale>. An example of fact contained in a cube for such a schema level is the tuple <May 2005, Milan, 20, A4> where the former two values are dimension values and the latter two values are measure values. In particular, A4 is the feature representing the location at the measure level accidentAtLargeScale.

Spatial OLAP

After presenting the representation constructs of the model, we introduce the spatial OLAP operators. In order to motivate our choices, we first discuss three kinds of requirements that the concept of hierarchy of measures poses on these operators and thus the assumptions we have made.

Requirements and Assumptions

Interrelationship Between Dimensions and Spatial Measures

A first problem due to the introduction of the hierarchy of measures may be stated in these terms: Since a measure level is functionally dependent on dimensions, is this dependency still valid if we change the granularity of the measure? Consider the following example: assume the cube in example 4 and consider an accident that occurred in May 2005 in the municipality of Milan, located in point *P* along a given road, and having caused two victims. Now assume a decrease in the granularity of the position, thus representing the position no longer as a point but as a portion of road. The question is whether the dimension values are affected by such a change. We may observe that both cases are possible: (a) The functional dependency between a measure and a dimension is not affected by the change of spatial granularity of the measure if the dimension value does not depend on the geometry of the measure. This is the case for the dimension *date of accident;* since the date of an accident does not depend on the geometry of the accident, the dimension value does not change with the granularity. In this case we say that the date dimension is *invariant;* (b) The opposite case occurs if a spatial relationships exists between the given dimension and the spatial measure. For example, in the previous example, since it is reasonable to assume that a relationship of spatial containment is implicitly defined between the administrative unit and the accident, if the granularity of position changes, say the position is expressed not by a point but a line, it may happen that the relationship of containment does not hold any longer. In such a case, the value of the dimension level would vary with the measure of granularity. Since this second case entails complex modelling, in order to keep the model relatively simple, we assume that all dimensions are invariant with respect to spatial measure granularity. Therefore, all levels of a spatial measure have the same functional dependency from dimensions.

Aggregation of Spatial Measures

The second issue concerns the operators for the spatial aggregation of spatial measures. Such operators compute, for example, the union and intersection of a set of geometries, the geometry with maximum linear or aerial extent out of a set of one-dimensional and two-dimensional geometries and the MBB (Minimum Bounding Box) of a set of geometries. In general, in the SDW literature these operators are supposed to be applied only to geometries and not to features. Moreover, as previously remarked, a standard set of operators for spatial aggregation has not been defined yet.

For the sake of generality, in our model we do not make any choice about the set of possible operations. We only impose, since we allow representing spatial measures as features, that the operators are applied to sets of features and return a feature. Further, the result is a new or an existing feature, depending on the nature of the operator. For example, the union (or merge) of a set of features, say states, is a newly-created feature whose geometry is obtained from the geometric union of the features' geometries. Notice also that the type of the result may be a newly-created feature type. In fact, the union of a set of states is not itself a state and therefore the definition of a new type is required to hold the resulting features.

Coarsening of Spatial Measures

The next issue is whether the result of a spatial aggregation can be represented at different levels of detail. If so, data analysis would become much more flexible, since the user would be enabled not only to aggregate spatial data but also to dynamically decrease their granularity. To address this requirement, we assume that the model includes not only operators for spatial aggregation but also operators for decreasing the spatial granularity of features. We call these operators *coarsening operators*. As previously stated, coarsening operators include operators for cartographic generalization (Camossi & Bertolotto, 2003) and fuzzyûcation operators. A simple example of fuzzyfication is the operation mapping of a point of coordinates (x,y) into a close point by reducing the number of decimal digits of the coordinates. These operators are used in our model for building the hierarchy of spatial measures.

When a measure value is expressed according to a lower granularity, the dimension values remain unchanged, since dimensions are assumed to be invariant. As a simple example, consider the position of an accident. Suppose that an aggregation operation, e.g., MBB computation, is performed over positions grouped by date. The result is some new feature, say *yearly accidents*, with its own polygonal geometry. At this point we can apply a coarsening operator and thus a new measure value is dynamically obtained, functionally dependent on the same dimension values. The process of grouping and abstraction can thus iterate.

Spatial Operators

Finally, we introduce the Spatial OLAP operators that are meant to support the navigation in MuSD. Since numerous algebras have been proposed in the literature for non-spatial DW, instead of defining a new set of operators from scratch, we have selected an existing algebra and extended it. Namely, we have chosen the algebra defined in Vassiliadis, 1998. The advantages of this algebra are twofold: It is formally defined, and it is a good representative of the class of algebras for cube-oriented models (Vassiliadis, 1998; Vassiliadis & Sellis, 1999), which are close to our model.

Besides the basic operators defined in the original algebra (LevelClimbing, Packing, FunctionApplication, Projection and Dicing), we introduce the following operators: MeasureClimbing, SpatialFunctionApplication and CubeDisplay. The *MeasureClimbing* operator is introduced to enable the scaling up of spatial measures to different granularities; the *SpatialFunctionApplication* operator performs aggregation of spatial measures; *CubeDisplay* simply visualizes a cube as a map. The application of these operators causes a transition from the current state to a new state of the SDW. Therefore the navigation results from the successive application of these operators.

Hereinafter we illustrate the operational meaning of these additional operators. For the sake of completeness, we present first the three fundamental operators of the native algebra used to perform data aggregation and rollup.

In what follows, we use the following conventions: S indicates the schema, and ST denotes the set of states for S, of the form <SL, C> where SL is the schema level <DLv_1, ..., DLv_i, ..., DLv_n, M_1, ..., M_m, Slv> and C, a cube for that schema level. Moreover, the dot notation SL.DLv_i is used to denote the DLv_i component of the schema level. The examples refer to the schema presented in Example 4 (limited to one dimension) and to the basic cube reported in Table 1.

Table 1. C_b= Basic cube

Month	Location	Victims
Jan 03	P1	4
Jeb 03	P2	3
Jan 03	P3	3
May 03	P4	1
Feb 04	P5	2
Feb 04	P6	3
Mar 04	P7	1
May 04	P8	2
May 04	P9	3
May 04	P10	1

Level Climbing

In accordance with the definition of Vassiliadis, the LevelClimbing operation replaces all values of a set of dimensions with dimension values of coarser dimension levels. In other terms, given a state S = <SL, C>, the operation causes a transition to a new state <SL', C'> in which SL' is the schema level including the coarser dimension level, and C' is the cube containing the coarser values for the given level. In our model, the operation can be formally defined as follows:

Definition 8 (LevelClimbing): The LevelClimbing operator is defined by the mapping: LevelClimbing: ST x D x LV→ ST such that, given a state SL, a dimension D_i and a level lv_i of D_i, LevelClimbing(<SL, Cb>, D_i, lv_i) = <SL', Cb > with lv_i = SL'.Dlv_i.

Example 6: Let SL be the following schema levels: SL= <Month, AccidentPoint, Victims>. Cube 1 in Table 2 results from the execution of Level_Climbing (<SL, Basic_cube>, Time, Year).

Table 2. Cube 1

Year	Location	Victims
03	P1	4
03	P2	3
03	P3	3
03	P4	1
04	P5	2
04	P6	3
04	P7	1
04	P8	2
04	P9	3
04	P10	1

Table 3. Cube 2

year	Location	#Victims
03	{P1,P2,P3,P4}	{4,2,3,1,2,1}
04	{P5,P6,P7,P8,P9,P19}	{3,3,1,3}

Packing

The Packing operator, as defined in the original algebra, groups into a single tuple multiple tuples having the same dimension values. Since the domain of measures is multi-valued, after the operation the values of measures are sets. The new state shows the same schema level and a different cube. Formally:

Definition 9 (Packing): The Packing operator is defined by the mapping: Packing: ST→ ST such that Packing(<SL, C>) = <SL, C'>

Example 7: Cube 2 in Table 3 results from the operation: Pack (SL,Cube1)

FunctionApplication

The FunctionApplication operator, which belongs to the original algebra, applies an aggregation function, such as the standard avg and sum, to the non-spatial measures of the current state. The result is a new cube for the same schema level. Let M be the set of non-spatial measures and AOP the set of aggregation operators.

Definition 10 (FunctionApplication): The FunctionApplication operator is defined by the mapping: FunctionApplication: ST×AOP×M→ ST, such that denoting with op(C, M_i) the cube resulting from the application of the aggregation operator op to the measure Mi of cube C, FunctionApplication(<DLv_1, ..., DLv_n, M_1, ...M_i, ..., M_m, op, M_i) = <SL, C'> with cube C' = op(C, M_i).

Table 4. Cube 3

year	#Victims	Location
03	13	Area1
04	10	Area2

SpatialFunctionApplication

This operator extends the original algebra to perform spatial aggregation of spatial measures. The operation is similar to the previous FunctionApplication. The difference is that the operator is meant to aggregate spatial measure values.

Definition 11 (SpatialFunctionApplication): Let SOP be the set of spatial aggregation operators. The SpatialFunctionApplication operator is defined by the mapping:

SpatialFunctionApplication: ST×SOP→ ST such that, denoting with op(C, Slv) the cube resulting from the application of the spatial aggregation operator sop to the spatial measure level Slv of cube C, SpatialFunctionApplication(<DLv_1, ..., DLv_n, M_1, ..., M_m, Slv >, sop) = <SL, C'> with C' = sop(C, Slv).

Example 8: Cube 3 in Table 4 results from the application of two aggregation operators, respectively on the measures victims and AccidentPoint. The result of the spatial aggregation is a set of features of a new feature type.

Measure Climbing

The MeasureClimbing operator enables the scaling of spatial measures to a coarser granularity. The effect of the operation is twofold: a) it dynamically applies a coarsening operator to the values of the current spatial measure level to obtain coarser values; and b) it causes a transition to a new state defined by a schema level with a coarser measure level.

Defnition 12 (MeasureClimbing): Let COP be the set of coarsening operators. The MeasureClimbing operator is defined by the mapping: MeasureClimbing : ST×COP→ ST such that denoting with:

- op(Slv): a coarsening operator applied to the values of a spatial measure level Slv

- SL =<DLv_1, ..., DLv_i, ..., DLv_n, M_1, ..., M_m, Slv>

- SL' =< DLv_1, ..., DLv_i, ..., DLv_n, M_1, ..., M_m, Slv' >

MeasureClimbing(SL, op)=SL' with Slv' = op(Slv);

Table 5. Cube 4

Year	#Victims	FuzzyLocation
03	13	Id
04	10	Id2

Example 9: Cube 4 in Table 5 results from the application of the MeasureClimbing operator to the previous cube. The operation applies a coarsening operator to the spatial measure and thus changes the level of the spatial measure, reducing the level of detail. In Cube 4, "FuzzyLocation" is the name of the new measure level.

DisplayCube

This operator is introduced to allow the display of the spatial features contained in the current cube in the form of a cartographic map. Let MAP be the set of maps.

Defnition 13 (DisplayCube): The operator is defined by the mapping: DisplayCube: ST → MAP so that, denoting with m, a map: DisplayCube(<SL, C>) =m.

As a concluding remark on the proposed algebra, we would like to stress that the model is actually a general framework that needs to be instantiated with a specific set of aggregation and coarsening operators to become operationally meaningful. The definition of such set of operators is, however, a major research issue.

Future Trends

Although SMD models for spatial data with geometry address important requirements, such models are not sufficiently rich to deal with more complex requirements posed by innovative applications. In particular, current SDW technology is not able to deal with complex objects. By complex spatial objects, we mean objects that cannot be represented in terms of simple geometries, like points and polygons. Complex spatial objects are, for example, continuous fields, objects with topology, spatio-temporal objects, etc. Specific categories of spatio-temporal objects that can be useful in several applications are diverse trajectories of moving entities. A trajectory is typically modelled as a sequence of consecutive locations in a space (Vlachos, 2002). Such locations are acquired by using tracking devices installed on vehicles and on portable equipment. Trajectories are useful to represent the location of spatial facts describing events that have a temporal and spatial evolution. For example, in logistics, trajectories could model the "location" of freight deliveries. In such a case, the delivery would represent the spatial fact, characterized by a number of properties, such as the freight and destination, and would include as a spatial attribute the trajectory performed by the vehicle to arrive at destination. By analyzing the trajectories, for example, more effective routes could be detected. Trajectories result from the connection of the tracked locations based on some interpolation function. In the simplest case, the tracked locations correspond to points in space whereas the interpolating function determines the segments connecting such points. However, in general, locations and interpolating functions may require a more complex definition (Yu et al., 2004). A major research issue is how to obtain summarized data out of a database of trajectories. The problem is complex because it requires the comparison and classification of trajectories. For that purpose, the notion of trajectory similarity is used. It means that trajectories are classified to be the same when they are sufficiently similar. Different measures of similarity have been proposed in the literature (Vlachos et al., 2002). A spatial data warehouse of trajectories could provide the unifying representation framework to integrate data mining techniques for data classification.

Conclusion

Spatial data warehousing is a relatively recent technology responding to the need of providing users with a set of operations for easily exploring large amounts of spatial data, possibly represented at different levels of semantic and geometric detail, as well as for aggregating spatial data into synthetic information most suitable for decision-making. We have discussed a novel research issue regarding the modelling of spatial measures defined at multiple levels of granularity. Since spatial data are naturally available at different granularities, it seems reasonable to extend the notion of spatial measure to take account of this requirement. The MuSD model we have defined consists of a set of representation constructs and a set of operators. The model is defined at the conceptual level in order to provide a more flexible and general representation. Next steps include the specialization of the model to account for some specific coarsening operators and the mapping of the conceptual model onto a logical data model as a basis for the development of a prototype.

References

Bedard, Y., Gosselin, P., Rivest, S., Proulx, M., Nadeau, M., Lebel, G., & Gagnon, M. (2003). Integrating GIS components with knowledge discovery technology for environmental health decision support. *International Journal of Medical Informatics, 70,* 79-94.

Camossi, E., Bertolotto, M., Bertino, E., & Guerrini, G. (2003). A multigranular spatiotemporal data model. *Proceedings of the 11th ACM International Symposium on Advances in Geographic Information Systems, ACM GIS 2003,* New Orleans, LA (pp. 94-101).

Chaudhuri, S., & Dayal, U. (1997). An overview of data warehousing and OLAP technology. *ACM SIGMOD Record, 26*(1), 65-74.

Clementini, E., di Felice, P., & van Oosterom, P. (1993). A small set of formal topological relationships suitable for end-user interaction. In *LNCS 692: Proceedings of the 3rd International Symposyium on Advances in Spatial Databases, SSD '93* (pp. 277-295).

Fidalgo, R. N., Times, V. C., Silva, J., & Souza, F. (2004). GeoDWFrame: A framework for guiding the design of geographical dimensional schemas. In *LNCS 3181: Proceedings of the 6th International Conference on Data Warehousing and Knowledge Discovery, DaWaK 2004* (pp. 26-37).

Fonseca, F., Egenhofer, M., Davies, C., & Camara, G. (2002). Semantic granularity in ontology-driven geographic information systems. *Annals of Mathematics and Artificial Intelligence, Special Issue on Spatial and Temporal Granularity, 36*(1), 121-151.

Han, J., Altman R., Kumar, V., Mannila, H., & Pregibon, D. (2002). Emerging scientific applications in data mining. *Communication of the ACM, 45*(8), 54-58.

Han, J., Stefanovic, N., & Kopersky, K. (1998). Selective materialization: An efficient method for spatial data cube construction. *Proceedings of Research and Development in Knowledge Discovery and Data Mining, Second Pacific-Asia Conference, PAKDD'98* (pp. 144-158).

Jensen, C., Kligys, A., Pedersen T., & Timko, I. (2002). Multidimensional data modeling for location-based services. In *Proceedings of the 10th ACM International Symposium on Advances in Geographic Information Systems* (pp. 55-61).

Kimbal, R. (1996). *The data warehouse toolkit.* New York: John Wiley & Sons.

Longley, P., Goodchild, M., Maguire, D., & Rhind, D. (2001). *Geographic information systems and science.* New York: John Wiley & Sons.

Lopez, I., & Snodgrass, R. (2005). Spatiotemporal aggregate computation: A survey. *IEEE Transactions on Knowledge and Data Engineering, 17*(2), 271-286.

Malinowski, E. & Zimanyi, E. (2004). Representing spatiality in a conceptual multidimensional model. *Proceedings of the 12th ACM International Symposium on Advances in Geographic Information Systems, ACM GIS 2004*, Washington, DC (pp. 12-21).

Marchant, P., Briseboi, A., Bedard, Y., & Edwards G. (2004). Implementation and evaluation of a hypercube-based method for spatiotemporal exploration and analysis. *ISPRS Journal of Photogrammetry & Remote Sensing, 59*, 6-20.

Meratnia, N., & de By, R. (2002). Aggregation and Comparison of Trajectories. *Proceedings of the 10th ACM International Symposium on Advances in Geographic Information Systems, ACM GIS 2002*, McLean, VA (pp. 49-54).

OGC--OpenGIS Consortium. (2001). *OpenGIS[â] abstract specification, topic 1: Feature geometry (ISO 19107 Spatial Schema)*. Retrieved from http://www.opengeospatial.org

OGC—Open Geo Spatial Consortium Inc. (2003). *OpenGIS[â] reference model*. Retrieved from http://www.opengeospatial.org

Papadias, D., Kalnis, P., Zhang, J., & Tao, Y. (2001). Efficient OLAP operations in spatial data warehouses. *LNCS: 2121, Proceedings of the 7h Int. Symposium on Advances in Spatial and Temporal Databases* (pp. 443-459).

Pedersen,T., & Tryfona, N. (2001). Pre-aggregation in spatial data warehouses. *LNCS: 2121, Proceedings. of the 7h Int. Symposium on Advances in Spatial and Temporal Databases* (pp. 460-480).

Rao, F., Zhang, L., Yu,X., Li,Y.,& Chen, Y. (2003). Spatial hierarchy and OLAP-favored search in spatial data warehouse. *Proceedings of the 6th ACM International Workshop on Data Warehousing and OLAP, DOLAP '03* (pp. 48-55).

Rigaux,. P., Scholl, M., & Voisard, A. (2002). *Spatial databases with applications to Gis*. New York: Academic Press.

Rivest, S., Bedard, Y., & Marchand, P. (2001). Towards better support for spatial decision making: Defining the characteristics of spatial on-line analytical processing (SOLAP). *Geomatica, 55*(4), 539-555.

Savary ,L., Wan, T., & Zeitouni, K. (2004). Spatio-temporal data warehouse design for human activity pattern analysis. *Proceedings of the 15th International Workshop On Database and Expert Systems Applications (DEXA04)* (pp. 81-86).

Scotch, M., & Parmantoa, B. (2005). SOVAT: Spatial OLAP visualization and analysis tools. *Proceedings of the 38th Hawaii International Conference on System Sciences.*

Shekhar, S. , Lu. C. T., Tan, X., Chawla, S., & Vatsavai, R. (2001). Map cube: A visualization tool for spatial data warehouse. In H. J. Miller & J. Han (Eds.), *Geographic data mining and knowledge discovery.* Taylor and Francis.

Shekhar, S., & Chawla, S. (2003). *Spatial databases: A tour.* NJ: Prentice Hall.

Spaccapietra, S., Parent, C., & Vangenot, C. (2000). GIS database: From multiscale to multirepresentation. In B. Y.Choueiry & T. Walsh (Eds.), Abstraction, reformulation, and approximation, LNAI 1864. *Proceedings of the 4th International Symposium, SARA-2000,* Horseshoe Bay, Texas.

Theodoratos, D., & Sellis, T. (1999). Designing data warehouses. *IEEE Transactions on Data and Knowledge Engineering, 31*(3), 279-301.

Vassiliadis, P. (1998). Modeling multidimensional databases, cubes and cube operations. *Proceedings of the 10th Scientific and Statistical Database Management Conference (SSDBM '98)* (pp. 53-62).

Vassiliadis, P., & Sellis, T. (1999). A survey of logical models for OLAP databases. *ACM SIGMOD Record, 28*(4), 64-69.

Vlachos, M., Kollios, G., & Gunopulos, D.(2002). Discovering similar multidimensional trajectories. *Proceedings of 18th ICDE* (pp. 273-282).

Wang, B., Pan, F., Ren, D., Cui, Y., Ding, D. et al. (2003). Efficient olap operations for spatial data using peano trees. *Proceedings of the 8th ACM SIGMOD Workshop on Research Issues in Data Mining and Knowledge Discovery* (pp. 28-34).

Worboys, M. (1998). Imprecision in finite resolution spatial data. *GeoInformatica, 2*(3), 257-279.

Worboys, M., & Duckam, M. (2004). *GIS: A computing perspective* (2nd ed.). Boca Raton, FL: CRC Press.

Yu, B., Kim, S. H., Bailey, T., & Gamboa R. (2004). Curve-based representation of moving object trajectories. *Proceedings of the International Database Engineering and Applications Symposium, IDEAS 2004* (pp. 419-425).

Zhang, D., & Tsotras, V. (2005). Optimizing spatial Min/Max aggregations. *The VLDB Journal, 14,* 170-181.

Chapter II

Goal-Oriented Requirement Engineering for XML Document Warehouses

Vicky Nassis, La Trobe University, Melbourne, Australia

Tharam S. Dillon, University of Technology, Sydney, Australia

Wenny Rahayu, La Trobe University, Melbourne, Australia

R Rajugan, University of Technology, Sydney, Australia

Abstract

eXtensible Markup Language (XML) has emerged as the dominant standard in describing and exchanging data amongst heterogeneous data sources. The increasing presence of large volumes of data appearing creates the need to investigate XML document warehouses (XDW) as a means of handling the data for business intelligence. In our previous work (Nassis, Rajugan, Dillon, & Rahayu, 2004) we proposed a conceptual modelling approach for the development of an XDW with emphasis on the design techniques. We consider important the need of capturing data warehouse requirements early in the design stage. The elicitation of requirements and their use for data warehouse design is a significant and, as yet, an unaddressed issue. For this reason, we explore a requirement engineering (RE) approach, namely the goal-oriented approach. *We will extract and extend the notion of this approach to introduce the XML document warehouse (XDW) requirement model. In order to perform this, we consider organisational objectives as well as user viewpoints. Furthermore, these are related to the XDW particularly focussing on deriving dimensions, as opposed to associating organisational objectives to the system functions, which is traditionally carried out by RE.*

Introduction

Data Warehouses

Data warehousing (DW) is an approach that has been adopted for handling large volumes of historical data for detailed analysis and management support. Transactional data in different databases is cleaned, aligned and combined to produce data warehouses. Since its introduction in 1996, the eXtensible Markup Language (XML) has become the *defacto* standard for storing and manipulating self-describing information (meta-data), which creates vocabularies to assist in information exchange between heterogeneous data sources over the Web (Pokorny, 2002). The purposes for which XML is used include electronic document handling, electronic storage, retrieval and exchange. It is envisaged that XML will also be used for logically encoding documents for many domains. Hence, it is likely that a large number of XML documents will populate the would-be repository and include several disparate XML transactional databases.

There are several distinctions instigated among data warehouses (DW) and XML data warehouses. In general, a data warehouse has two major parts:

1. **Physical store:** A database that contains all the information gathered from different sources. Operational data can be imported from various database types and once collected, the data is then structured in a uniform manner and stored in the DW. XML is well suited for representing semi-structured data. XML data originate from heterogeneous databases and are unstructured, or they have incomplete, irregular and recurrent changed structure.

2. **Logical schema:** A conceptual model that maps to the data in the physical store. This includes the following components:

    o   *Class:* Contains a collection of logically grouped attributes. For example class Customer contains attributes that describe this class.

    o   *Attributes:* A structure that stores data, for instance the attribute Full_Name of class Customer stores the full name of each customer.

    o   *Relation:* The connection between the classes. For example the class Customer is connected to class Product. In an XML data warehouse, at the logical level the components that appear differ but operate in the same manner as in conventional data warehouses. There are *XML documents* instead of classes, which have a logical collection of *elements*. As a result, data become more dimensional, forming a tree structure as opposed to atomic data records found in traditional DWs. *Relationships* also exist amongst the XML documents. In regards to data retrieval, querying the data fields of the DW fact table is a method to obtain the necessary data. In an XML DW, querying is performed on a fact repository containing XML documents, therefore a query language with XML specific syntax such as XQuery would be appropriate.

The need for managing large amounts of XML document data raises the necessity to explore the data warehouse approach through the use of XML document marts and XML document warehouses. Our purpose is to capture and represent fully XML-type semantics. The following discussion regarding the existing work on dimensional modelling of data warehouses indicates that the issue is not completely addressed. The elicitation of requirements and their use to data warehouse design is a significant and, as yet, an unaddressed issue, hence we focus on this aspect.

Since the introduction of dimensional modelling, which revolves around facts and dimensions, several design techniques have been proposed to capture multidimensional data (MD) at the conceptual level. These models feature many different characteristics, qualities and capabilities depending on their related domain. When designing a data warehouse, it is important to be able to clearly represent characteristics of the information contained within the DW, which accomplishes the aim of providing data analysis for decision support. Ralph Kimball's Star Schema (Kimball & Ross, 2002) proved very popular, from which the well-known conceptual models SnowFlake and StarFlake were derived, in which facts and dimensions are connected in a particular way. More recent comprehensive data warehouse design models are built using object-oriented concepts on the foundations of the star schema. It is evident that these models hardly capture the fundamental aspects of an application. At the conceptual level, these terms would be expressed in an abstract manner, which is considered very important when focussing on the primitive, multidimensional aspects that can be used for data analysis. In Abelló, Samos, and Saltor (2001), Lujan-Mora, Trujillo, and Song (2002) and Trujillo, Palomar, Gomez, and Song (2001), data are handled in the structure of n-dimensional cubes, which they all clearly express. They all clearly express to some extent the concepts of facts and dimensions; nevertheless the hierarchy amongst different levels of aggregation in a dimension is not fully captured by the schema. This does not convey or state clearly the meaning of each dimension to the end user. The object-relational star schema (O-R Star) model (Rahayu, Dillon, Mohammad & Taniar, 2001) concentrates on data models and object-relational data warehouses with a distinct focus on the objects' hierarchical dimensions. This model is utilized to provide support for the representation of the two types of hierarchical relationships along a dimension which are inheritance and aggregation.

Both object and relational models have a number of drawbacks if one wishes to use them for XML document warehouses (XDW), which are as follows:

(a) They are data-oriented without sufficient emphasis on capturing requirements early at the design stage. This will cause deficiencies to the resultant system and the failure to satisfy all given requirements.

(b) They are extensions of semantically-poor relational models (e.g. star and snowflake models). Provided that existing proposed conceptual models are not sufficient to capture fully multidimensional concepts, this indicates that to grasp and capture semi-structured data such as XML is an additional challenging task.

(c) There is a loss of original conceptual semantics due to the construction of the operational data source into a relational one. Data can originate from various databases with different structures. In modelling, flat relational data carry atomic values and are not semantically descriptive, such as XML data.

(d) Oversimplified dimensional modelling leads to a further loss of semantics. The central relational table denoting the FACT is where the analysis is emphasized and the surrounding tables representing the dimensions are de-normalised.

(e) Addition of data semantics to satisfy evolving requirements proves time consuming. Business is not static and therefore change in requirements is initiated. Refinements to the existing requirements are necessary to be able to accommodate the variations and fulfil the newly-formed conditions.

(f) They require complex query design and processing, therefore maintenance is troublesome. Requirements of a complex nature require compound query design for their fulfilment. The value of information is determined when data can be intelligently queried. Extracting semi-structured data, providing the highest level of accuracy, relevance and exact granularity are difficult tasks to accomplish. Based on the above arguments, it can be stated that traditional design models lack the ability to utilise or represent XML design level constructs in a well-defined abstract and implementation-independent form.

One of the early XML data warehouse implementations is the Xyleme Project (Lucie-Xyleme, 2001; Xyleme, 2001). The Xyleme project was successful in its limited objectives and it was made into a commercial product in 2002. It has a well-defined implementation architecture and proven techniques to collect and archive Web XML documents into an XML warehouse for further analysis. Another approach by Fankhauser and Klement (2003) explores some of the changes and challenges of a document-centric XML warehouse. Coupling these approaches with a well-defined conceptual and logical design methodology will help in the future design of an XML warehouse for large-scale XML systems.

In Nassis et al. (2004), we concentrated on the design of an XML document warehouse (XDW) rather than its implementation. UML, a widely-adopted standard for object-oriented (OO) conceptual models, is the foundation to build our proposed conceptual modeling approach for XDWs, considering that its graphical notation complies with the user(s) and domain experts(s)' understandings. We emphasized the design techniques to build the XDW conceptual model including an in-depth analysis of the major components, which are as follows:

(a)   design of the meaningful *XML FACT (xFACT)* repository;

(b)   use of UML package diagrams (Figures 6,7) to logically group and build hierarchical *Conceptual Views* to enhance the semantics and expressiveness of the XDW;

(c)   conceptual model and design of *Virtual Dimensions (VDims)* using logically grouped *XML Conceptual Views* to satisfy warehouse requirements (Figure 5); and

(d)   the addition of further UML constructs such as <<VDim>> (Figures 5-7) to assist with the representation of metadata. Considering the fact that we are dealing with XML documents, the task of fully capturing and representing their tree structure form through design modelling is challenging and not accomplished by existing relational and object models. Regarding the implementation of the proposed XDW conceptual modelling approach, it can be applied to native XML databases and object relational databases.

In our XDW conceptual model (Nassis et al., 2004) we regard as highly important the need for the complete capturing of the requirements early at the design stage (Nassis et al., 2005a, 2005b, 2005c). We aim to understand, define and further elicit (discover) data warehouse requirements. These are then modelled in order to generate various DW dimensions. For this reason, we will examine the use of a requirement engineering (RE) approach to discover, validate and represent requirements.

Requirement Engineering (RE)

The concept of requirement engineering (RE) actually explores the objectives of different stakeholders and the activities carried out by the system. Based on numerous studies (Lubars, Potts, & Richter, 1993; McGraw & Harbison, 1997) it is stated that a system's functionality when not successful is frequently due to the insufficient understanding of user requirements, hence RE is concerned with overcoming this inadequacy. RE relates to the elicitation and definition of system requirements. Most of the existing research focuses on deriving a surface definition of user requirements, addressing the question *"What the system is meant to do"* (Guttag & Horning, 1993; Jacobson, 1995; Jones, 1990; Rumbaugh, Blaha, Lorensen, Eddy, & Premerlani, 1991; Spivey, 1992). Recent approaches have emerged targeting user requirement elicitation, or in other words, user requirement discovery, and concentrate on the subject *"Why is the system like this?"* The following section presents facts on RE and issues encountered, particularly when focusing on the conceptual modelling for user requirements. The related literature and existing work on RE in regards to system objectives and system functionalities has raised the incentive to explore one of its existing approaches, namely the *goal-oriented approach* as illustrated in Dardenne, Van-Lamsweerde and Fickas (1993). It is important to recognise that, generally, goal-oriented approaches have been largely targeted at the development of software systems rather than focused on document data warehouses involving embedded XML structures. Given this, we will extract and extend the notion of this goal-modelling approach to XDWs, particularly in deriving requirements. This would then help guide the design of the XDW structure by identifying data warehouse dimensions and the nature of the fact repository.

Requirement Engineering Conceptual Modelling

Conceptual modelling is the conventional way of developing information systems, which is the means to accomplish an organisational intention, while requirement engineering aids in conceptualising such systems. In RE, the conceptual model of a future system is derived from the specification, which outlines the functionalities of the system. Nowadays it is becoming evident that organisational change is rapid, hence the reforms that occur in user requirements. These changes may occur at any stage in the system's development process and therefore it is essential to be able to accommodate them as they arise. Based on these facts, two important points are considered:

(a)   In order to elicit and validate a system's requirements it is important to consider their significance to the relevant organisation, and

(b)   Conceptual modelling is carried out on a system with the stated objectives (Rolland & Prakash, 2001). What remains an unsolved issue is actually understanding and recording the impact of business changes on user requirements (Lubars et al., 1993).

As is the case for data warehouses, a large number of conceptual models have also been developed to represent information systems, continuously aiming to fulfil the need to capture in greater detail real world semantics. Due to the increasing number of such models, Olle et al. (1988) developed one of the existing frameworks, arranging models based on the perception adopted to examine the *universe of discourse*. This allows information systems to be viewed from three perspectives, which include: *process oriented, data oriented* and *behaviour oriented.* In relation to developing conceptual models, one approach shows that the majority of them are based upon the integration of process-oriented and data-oriented viewpoints. The second approach as observed by Yourdon (1989) loosely connects the data flow approach (a process model) with entity-relationship (ER) modelling and state transition diagrams. The product characteristics are the focus when developing a system's conceptual model. In the early days, process models were activity-based, given that a process consists of a set of activities. As time went on more compliant models have been developed, such as the waterfall model (Royce, 1970).

As stated in Rolland and Prakash (2001), user requirements originate from two sources:

(a)   **The users:** User-defined requirements come from people in the organisation where they express their goals and intentions, and

(b)   **The domain environment:** Requirements of the domain which are related to the nature of the domain and factors that govern it. These cause the *universe of discourse* to form two worlds, namely, the *usage world*: Consists of users who will work independently with the system to meet goals and objectives, and the *subject world*: Relates to the domain where real-world objects are represented in conceptual schemas (Jarke & Pohl, 1993).

From the information presented so far, it is evident that in RE the two most important aspects are the system objectives and the user viewpoints. The modelling approaches that exist focus on these aspects and give conceptual modelling another dimension. The *goal-driven approaches* relate organisational objectives with the system functions, whereas the *scenario-based approaches* and *use-case modelling* develop a system model by putting emphasis on the user viewpoints as well as deriving useful system functions by including the role of the individuals involved.

In this chapter we will focus on the notion of one existing *goal-oriented approach* (Dardenne et al., 1993) to model requirements. In addition, with further refinements to conform to the principles of our modelling approach, we introduce the XDW requirement model, which focuses on capturing and eliciting requirements. In order to perform this, it is important to take into consideration the organisational objectives as well as the user viewpoints. Furthermore, these are related to the XDW in particular on deriving dimensions, as opposed to associating organisational objectives to the system functions, which is traditionally carried out in RE. The key issue is the principal of correspondence between the real world representation and its domain. This involves the mapping of real world entities to clearly define the corresponding entities in the system, which tends to facilitate a system's evaluation. We elect to apply a graphical representation for our XDW requirement model to initiate a dialogue between the requirement engineer and the domain expert. Our approach is distinctive, as up to now there have been no attempts to capture user requirements and the entirety of their semantic nature. It is important to note that an essential purpose of a data warehouse is to provide enhanced design support. Therefore its structure must conform to the understanding of the business organisational objectives as well as to the user queries of the data warehouse that are likely to occur.

An overview of the chapter organisation is as follows: We begin with a general outline of the essential principles that exist in data warehouses. Aspects of our previous work are then presented relating to the XML document warehouse (XDW), which includes the conceptual modelling structure of the *XML FACT (xFACT)* repository and its dimensions, referred to as *Virtual Dimensions (VDim)*, or *Conceptual Views*. In the third section we introduce the XML document warehouse (XDW) requirement model along with detailed discussions, illustrations and definitions. Finally the concepts outlined will be demonstrated using a walkthrough and a case-study example.

Prior to proceeding with the core segment of this chapter it is important to emphasize the fact that data warehousing relates with several compound modules. Therefore it is essential for us to differentiate these and clearly explain our focus.

Requirements of a Data Warehouse

The broad concept of data warehouses has several aspects, which are essential for their total creation and use. Based on the existing literature of data warehouses, the principal characteristics that have to be addressed include:

1.   design of the data warehouse structure;
2.   data assembly and population of the data warehouse repository;
3.   maintaining updates of the data warehouse; and
4.   maintaining evolution of the data warehouse.

These characteristics are illustrated in Figure 1 and are discussed in more detail as follows.

The first stage in building a data warehouse involves the design of its structure. This includes the fact repository and its associated dimensions. Then transactional data in various databases are cleaned, aligned and combined in order to populate the data warehouse repository. Data warehouse maintenance involves two processes: *update* and *evolution*. Incremental updates are conducted on the materialized views.

Transactional data develop and change as new data continue to be added and/ or old data are removed. Therefore, the information contained in the current materialized views needs to be updated. The second aspect is concerned with the evolution of the materialized views. When a user requires data, the most efficient approach is to retrieve these by querying the already created materialized views.

Figure 1. Requirements for the formation of a data warehouse

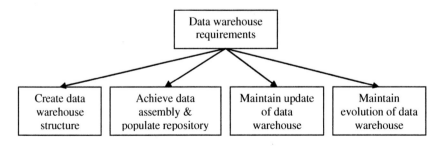

One needs to monitor user queries and trace them to determine their frequency. In order to maximise the effectiveness of querying and enable quicker information access, a materialized view is created for frequent queries that corresponds to such evolving user needs. This will result in the gradual modifications of materialized views, the dimensions and the structure of the data warehouse.

At this stage we will concentrate solely on the aspect related to the design of the data warehouse structure. This includes the design of the fact repository and deriving dimensions while considering requirements by users.

Architecture of an XML Document Warehouse (XDW)

In Nassis et al. (2004) we used UML (OMG-UML, 2003), a widely adopted standard for object-oriented (OO) conceptual models, to build a conceptual model for XML document warehouses. The main aspects of our methodology are as follows:

1. **Requirement level (RL):** Assist in determining different dimensions of the document warehouse;

2. **XML Document structure** (W3C-XML, 2004): Using XML document capability in accommodating and explicitly describing semi-structured data along with their relationship semantics (unlike flat-relational data) and

3. **XML schema:** Describes, validates and provides semantics for its corresponding instance document (XML document) at the logical level (W3C-XSD, 2004). Also, the schema has the capability to capture OO concepts and relationships (Feng, Dillon, & Chang, 2002; 2003) as well as intuitive XML specific constructs such as ordering and homogeneous aggregation relationships of components and

4. **Conceptual views** (Rajugan, Chang, Dillon & Feng, 2003, 2004, 2005): A *Conceptual view* describes how a collection of XML tags contained in an XML document relates to the direct utilisation by a domain user at the conceptual/abstract level.

The XDW model is shown in Figure 2. To our knowledge, this is unique in that it utilizes XML itself (together with XML Schema) to provide: structural constructs, metadata, validity and expressiveness (via refined granularity and class decompositions). The proposed model is composed of three levels:

Figure 2. XDW context diagram

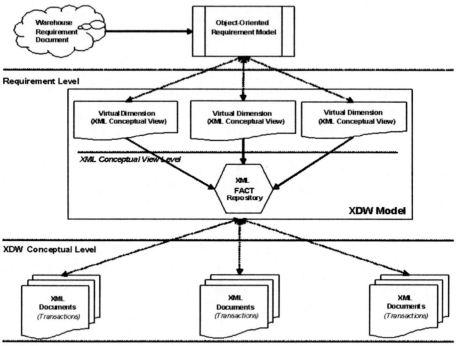

1. **The requirement level (RL):** This includes the *warehouse requirement document* and *OO requirement model*;

2. **XML document warehouse conceptual level:** Composed of an *XML FACT (xFACT)* repository (see section on XML FACT Repository) and a collection of logically-grouped *conceptual views* which translate as the dimensions that satisfy captured warehouse requirements; and

3. **Logical level:** Involves the transformation of the entire XDW's conceptual model components, which include the *xFACT* repository and *virtual dimensions (VDims)*, into XML schema.

The Requirement Level

The first level of the XDW model captures the warehouse requirements and the organisational objectives. As opposed to the classical data warehouse models, this requirement model does not consider the transactional data as the focal point for the design of the warehouse. The XDW model at the conceptual level is designed based on requirements. This level is further divided into two more sub-components, which are:

1.   **Warehouse requirement document:** Corresponds to the written, non-technical outline of the XML warehouse. This usually includes the typical or the predictable results of the XDW, and

2.   **OO requirement model:** Transforms all non-technical requirements into technical, software model-specific concepts using UML (actors, use-case and objects).

XML Document Warehouse Conceptual Level

The XML document warehouse (XDW) conceptual level includes the *XML FACT (xFACT)* repository and a collection of logically-grouped *conceptual views*. Given a *context*, the *xFACT* provides a snapshot of the underlying transactional system with semantic constructs that are needed to accommodate an XML context. The purpose of *conceptual views* is to provide the dimensions of the document warehouse stored in the *xFACT* repository. These components from our previous work (Nassis et al., 2004) will be demonstrated in the sections that follow.

Logical Level

In Nassis et al. (2005a) we used generic rules (Feng et al., 2003) to accomplish a systematic transformation of our object-oriented (OO) conceptual model into XML schema, which is the logical level. At this stage it is important to clarify the distinct meaning amongst the conceptual and logical levels in reference to the *xFACT* being a document repository. At the conceptual level, we are using UML to design the *xFACT* model. This conceptual model, when mapped at the logical level, becomes an entire, major XML schema along with its corresponding XML document. This whole XML document contains a collection of all the instances from the objects in the *xFACT*. That is to say, the *xFACT* is a document repository but the object instances are not considered as separate XML documents, but are all under the one *xFACT* XML document. On another note, it becomes clear that at the logical level the *xFACT* represents the tree structure of an XML document. In relation to transforming the *virtual dimensions (VDims)*, this is actually the translation of *conceptual views* in XML view schemas (Rajugan et al., 2005).

Having set the requirements of a data warehouse and both the conceptual model and the corresponding XML schema and XML document at the logical level have been derived, the next step would involve the implementation of the data warehouse. Querying the implemented data warehouse can be performed in a conventional way; however, in our case we are concerned with an XDW. Therefore, using a suitable query language with XML-specific syntax, such as XQuery (W3C-XQuery, 2004), allows one to extract the information needed in order to meet all the conditions of each stated requirement.

In the sections that follow, we will concentrate on the *requirement level* by introducing the XML document warehouse (XDW) requirement model. We aim to capture requirements early at the design stage of the document warehouse, as well as to fully comprehend and to further elicit these. An important task is to perform requirement validation, meaning that the information required to fulfil a given requirement must be available in the *xFACT* repository. Alternatively, in the case where the data are not obtainable, the concerned requirement needs further consideration in order to determine the best possible way to assemble the data and create a newly-refined requirement.

Before we begin to introduce the XDW requirement modelling approach, what follows is a discussion on the XDW conceptual model along with its two major components, those being the meaningful *xFACT* as well as the *virtual dimensions (VDims)*.

XML Document Warehouse
Conceptual Level

As stated in Nassis et al. (2004), the process of deriving the XDW conceptual data model involves taking the formalized requirements expressed in UML and then validating these against the XML transactional systems by checking data availability and assembling the data for the XDW. The case of lacking the necessary transactional data to assemble certain dimensional/*xFACT* data highlights an ambiguous, or non-achievable, requirement which then has to be re-defined and/or modified.

The *xFACT* is a snapshot of the underlying transactional system for a given *context*. A *context* is more than a measure (Golfarelli, Maio, & Rizzi, 1998; Trujillo et al., 2001) but instead is an aspect that is of interest for the organization as a whole. This emphasizes the need to focus on organisational objectives when designing the *xFACT*.

The role of *conceptual views* is to provide perspectives of the document hierarchy stored in the *xFACT* repository. These vews may be grouped into logical groups, where each one is very similar to that of a given *subject area* (Coad & Yourdon, 1990; Dillon & Tan, 1993) appearing in Object-Oriented conceptual modelling techniques. Each subject area in the XDW model is referred to as a *virtual dimension (VDim)* in accordance with the language of dimensional models. *VDim* is called *virtual* since it is modelled using a *conceptual view* (Rajugan et al., 2003, 2004, 2005), which is an *imaginary* XML document, behaving as a dimension to a given *xFACT*.

In reference to the preceding concept of the requirement validation process, we state that XML transactional systems are used to verify data availability. When assembling the data for the *xFACT* repository it is vital to ensure that all the required data for requirement fulfilment are available. In the case where a requirement is invalid or, in other words, cannot be satisfied with the information at hand, we are able only at the design stage to refer back to the transactional databases and obtain the data needed. For instance, when it is required to generate a report for the requirement *product sales by region* and the component *Region* has not be identified in terms of *sales* in the *xFACT*, then it is not possible to accomplish this requirement or create a dimension. This raises the argument as to whether it is possible to satisfy a requirement, given that the information is inexistent in the transactional databases. In this case the requirement needs to be excluded. It is easy to visualize the link amongst the three major components of XML: transactional databases, *xFACT* repository as well as the *virtual dimensions*, which represent data warehouse requirements. Therefore it is important to be able to move through this link from any direction to certify the correct assembly of XDW.

XML FACT (xFACT) Repository and Meaningful FACT

We emphasized that the *xFACT* repository differs from one in a traditional relational data warehouse, which is normally modelled as an ID packed, flat FACT table with its associated dimensions. But, in regards to XML, a *context* refers to the presence of embedded declarative semantics and relationships including ordered and homogeneous compositions, associations and inheritance as well as non-relational constructs such as set, list and bag (see case study section). Therefore, we argue that, a plain FACT does not provide semantic constructs that are needed to accommodate an XML *context*.

Virtual Dimensions and Packages

As discussed in Nassis et al. (2004), the requirements, which are captured in the OO Requirement Model, are transformed into one or more *conceptual views*

(Rajugan et al., 2003, 2004, 2005) also referred to as one or more *virtual dimension(s) (VDim),* in association with the *xFACT.* These are typically *views* involving aggregation or *perspectives* of the underlying stored documents of the *xFACT* document repository. A valid requirement is such that it can be satisfied by one or more XML conceptual views for a given context (e.g., *xFACT*). We introduced a new UML stereotype called <<VDim>> (Figures 5-7) to model the *Virtual Dimensions* at the XDW conceptual level. In addition to the concept of grouped conceptual views, a new view hierarchy and/or constructs can be added to include additional semantics for a given requirement. This hierarchy may form further structural or dependency relationships with existing conceptual views or view hierarchies (grouped *VDims*). Therefore, it is likely that a cluster of dimensional hierarchies can be used to model a set of requirements. In order to capture and model this logical grouping of an XML view hierarchy, we used the *package* construct (Figures 6-7) based on the OMG specification (OMG-UML, 2003). This approach is illustrated in the case study section, which shows an *xFACT* repository, *VDims* as well as the use of stereotypes and packages.

XML Document Warehouse Requirement Model

Lubars et al. (1993) and McGraw and Harbison (1997) acknowledged that a system's functionality fails due to the lack of understanding of user requirements. We choose to employ a graphical notation for our approach, which will facilitate a clear dialogue between the requirement engineer and the domain experts. This will enhance the understanding of requirements and therefore be able to critique the approach used. We adopted the central notion of the *goal-oriented approach* as illustrated in Dardenne et al. (1993) and with additional components, we built the XDW requirement model as shown in Figure 3a, while Figure 3b provides an interpretation of the graphical aspect of our model, including the symbols and notations used. The main themes of this methodology are to:

1.   capture requirements early in the design process;

2.   understand the current requirements and further elicit these to promote new requirements;

3.   illustrate the mapping of each stated requirement into a corresponding dimension of the XML document warehouse (XDW);

Figure 3a. XDW requirement model

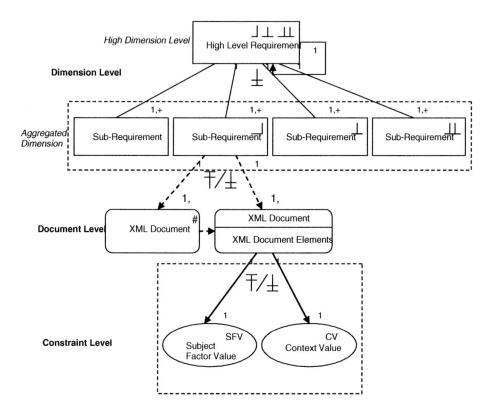

4.   certify that the information required for the *xFACT* repository can be assembled from the information available in the XDW; and

5.   ensure that the information necessary to construct a dimension is available or can be obtained from the *xFACT* repository.

The XDW Requirement model (Figure 3a) is composed of three main levels:

1.   **Dimension level:** This has two sub-levels namely the *high dimension level* and the *aggregated dimension level*;

2.   **Document level:** Includes all XML documents involved in a query based on a given requirement; and

3.   **Constraint level:** Contains parameter values with the ability to change the presentation of a query's outcome according to the corresponding

requirement's specification. What follows is a detailed discussion of each level.

1. Dimension Level

This level represents the different dimensions of the data warehouse. There are two sub-levels as shown in Figure 3a: the *high dimension level* and the *aggregated dimension level*. A high level, or an abstract requirement, indicates its wide-ranging content type. This shows that the corresponding query's result is retrieved from the entire content of one or more XML document(s) as opposed to extracting specific XML document elements. In some cases an abstract type requirement might not be sufficient to satisfy a user need and therefore it becomes necessary to aggregate the high-level requirement and form several sub-requirements. This leads to the creation of the *aggregated dimension level*.

Figure 3b. Interpretation of XDW requirement model

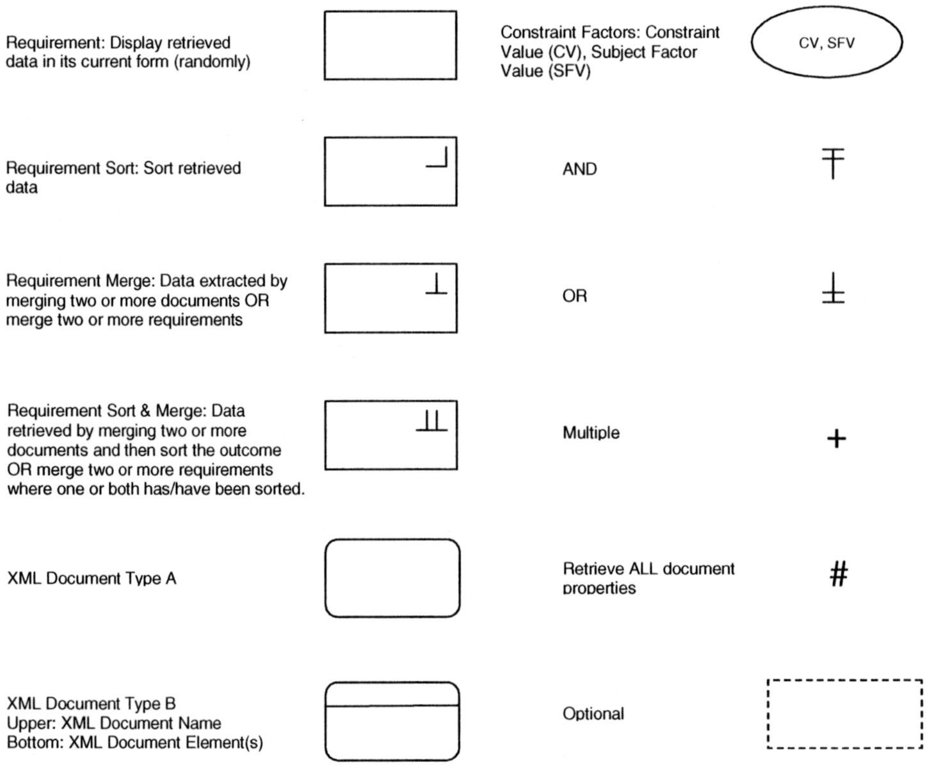

Requirement: Display retrieved data in its current form (randomly)		Constraint Factors: Constraint Value (CV), Subject Factor Value (SFV)	CV, SFV
Requirement Sort: Sort retrieved data		AND	干
Requirement Merge: Data extracted by merging two or more documents OR merge two or more requirements		OR	土
Requirement Sort & Merge: Data retrieved by merging two or more documents and then sort the outcome OR merge two or more requirements where one or both has/have been sorted.		Multiple	+
XML Document Type A		Retrieve ALL document properties	#
XML Document Type B Upper: XML Document Name Bottom: XML Document Element(s)		Optional	

Each one of the elicited sub-requirements represents an additional dimension of the XDW, and the relationship with its preceding level (high dimension level) is expressed by the cardinality (1,+) as shown in Figure 3a. This, in other words, means that when a query requires specific element attribute values and the involvement of more than one XML documents, then in itself it becomes very complex. Therefore, decomposition helps in understanding the current requirement and defines new avenues for fulfilment. Our XDW Requirement model, (Figure 3a) where the high-level requirement has an arrow pointing to itself, depicts that a requirement does not necessarily need to be decomposed but instead can remain in its current form and behave as a dimension.

This case justifies that a direct link may exist from the *high dimension level* to the *document level*. This is shown in Figure 3a where the *aggregated dimension level* component is surrounded by a dashed line indicating that it does not apply in all cases.

2. Document Level

As discussed previously, a direct connection may exist amongst the *document level* and any of the two preceding sub-levels, meaning that it can be immediately related either to: an abstract/high level requirement or a newly formed subrequirement. Regarding the *document level*, the related XML document(s) to be queried depends entirely on the specifications of the requirement in question. A query may require information that exists within one or more XML documents. It is important to note that there are two cases likely to occur in relation to the XML documents and a query outcome, which are: (a) the entire XML document(s) elements attribute values are required and extracted, and (b) only specific element(s) attribute(s) from the document(s) is/are needed. In Figure 3a at the *document level* there are two types of documents to conform to each one of these cases. In the first document type the # symbol represents that the entire document(s) properties are required. The second document type is divided into two sections, of which, the lower fragment is of significance as it shows the specific element(s) required to generate the query outcome. These two cases may be applied simultaneously as shown in Figure 3a, where the two document types are linked by a dashed arrow (dash indicates optional) pointing towards the direction of the independent/stronger component of the two. The classification of the stronger or weaker component is determined based on the developer's judgement in conjunction with the requirement specification.

3. Constraint Level

This level applies in two cases: First, to a result that needs to be arranged in a specific order (e.g., alphabetically) denoted by the *subject factor value (SFV)*. Secondly, to conduct a search and extract the necessary data based on a given value, which is indicated by the term *context value (CV)*. These two parameter values have the ability to alter the presentation of a query's result. Depending on the query context, both cases can appear and be applied simultaneously as shown in Figure 3a. To define more broadly, a *CV* is the specified value within a document which can take the form of a precise word, phrase, number or a group of values. A *SFV* can include a name, a number or it can be of any value, provided that it exists within the document(s), element(s) or attributes involved in the query.

Defining Components of the XDW Requirement Model

In the previous section we explained the different levels of our proposed model. Before we proceed in the specific and detailed terminology, it is important to first briefly state the main components of the XDW requirement model.

A component **Comp** in the XDW requirement model is an entity set, which can include a high-level/abstract requirement **R**, a sub-requirement **SR**, an XML document **D,** a constraint **C** and an attribute **A**. In other words, **Comp₁...Compₙ** aid to the formulation of the entire requirement model. There can be relationships that exist amongst these components. A relationship **Rel** links together each of the components in the model, considering the relevant purpose and cardinality amongst them. A requirement **R** expresses what we aim to achieve, meaning the expectant outcome of the data warehouse. As discussed in the *document level* section, in order to fulfil the conditions of each stated requirement, the required XML document(s) **D** is/are queried to allow one to retrieve the information needed. The query structure depends entirely on each requirement's degree of complexity. This means that a query tends to get equally compound the more precise and demanding a requirement is. In some cases a requirement can be further decomposed and form several sub-requirements **SRs**. An XML document contains a set of elements where each individually acquires a set of attributes **A**. These are single-valued attributes and are of XML schema built-in data types (eg., string or integer). Finally, the constraint **C** is a parameter of which its value can change the presentation of a query's result according to the requirement specification.

Concepts and Terminology of the XDW Requirement Model

This section provides an illustration of the previously outlined components of our XDW requirement model in greater detail through demonstrations and formal definitions.

Definition 1: Requirement = the formal definition terms of a requirement are:

R = (I) [(C)]*

where **I** = Intention and **C** = Constraint and the content within the "[ ]" (square brackets) shows that it is optional whereas the "*" (star) indicates that this component may occur multiple times.

Definition 2: Intention (I) = Phrase that states what is aimed to be achieved, in other words, the expectant outcome from the data warehouse. It is expressed in the form of natural language and can be extracted from a text-based document. This will be illustrated in more detail as sample requirements are formed in the case study section.

Definition 3: Constraint (C) = A parameter used in order to vary the way a query's outcome is displayed considering the need to conform with the user's preference and requirement needs. The two major constraints which will be used throughout are: *Context Value (CV)* and *subject factor value (SFV)*, which have been discussed in the previous section under *constraint level*. A *constraint* definition can be expressed as:

C = (CV, SFV)

In the case where there is no *CV (context value)*, meaning that the query search is conducted with no values being specified, the sign # is displayed within the document type component, as shown in the requirement model, to indicate that the search will extract all the values within that concerned document.

Definition 4: Sub-requirement = A high level requirement can often be decomposed to several sub-requirements **(SR)**. Therefore the sub-requirement set of system **S** is defined by the following function:

R: S → SR

It is important to note that the principal definition of a **requirement** stated previously, also applies when forming a **sub-requirement**.

Definition 5: Relationship = A n-ary relationship **Rel** amongst the components **Comp$_1$** ... **Comp$_N$** existing within the XDW requirement model is defined as:

Rel = (R, SR) I (R, D, [C]) I (SR, D, [C])

The previous denotes that each instance of **Rel** is equivalent to each of the above combination instances. For example, a relationship can exist between a requirement and a sub-requirement **(R, SR)**, or amongst a requirement, document and constraint **(R, D, C)**.

The cardinality of the relationship **Rel** instances among the component instances **Comp$_N$** includes the tuples (1,1) and (1,+) which express the minimum and maximum amount of possible relationships respectively. In the latter set, the **+** sign indicates a multiple connection with other components. For example, a requirement may necessitate data from multiple documents, hence the corresponding query will involve a search across several XML documents.

Definition 6: AND/OR relationships = Based on the **AND/OR** graph structures introduced by Nilsson (1971), we implement this concept into the XDW Requirement Model and note that it provides a different meaning to the components at each level. For instance, the relationship between the two *Dimension Levels* shows that a high level requirement can be further refined into several alternative or combinations of sub-requirements, where it is possible for each to be further aggregated and form smaller requirements. A requirement or sub-requirement gathers its source of data through several combinations of XML documents, of which, a query's outcome presentation varies depending on the presence of constraint value(s). An **AND/OR** relationship **Rel** of the components **Comp$_1$** and **Comp$_2$** is defined as follows (Dardenne et al., 1993):

Rel ∈ S

where **S = {AndRel,OrRel}** .

The **AND** relationship is represented by the symbol $\top$ and the **OR** relationship by the symbol $\perp$.

This means that any instance of **Rel** can take the form of an **AND** or **OR** type when linking two components. Referring to the XDW Requirement Model (Figure 3a), the **AndRel** signifies that a combination of sub-requirements as a whole can achieve a high-level requirement. Alternatively, the **OrRel** shows different ways a requirement can be achieved. Similarly, between the *dimension* and *document* levels, depending on the query, the **OR** operator means that a query can include either one of the document types. Lastly, amongst the *document* and *constraint* levels, both *CV* and *SFV* can be applied simultaneously or independently, depending on the requirement's specification. In order to enable tracking of the alternatives selected, each constraint has an attribute with a true or false value, which must be updated every time if we wish to examine another alternative (Dardenne et al., 1993).

Having the system context of our case study, we are able to formulate the necessary requirements by applying the **requirement** terminology principle. The next step is to further apply the remaining concepts in correlation with our XDW requirement model. This will be illustrated using a walk-though and a case-study example.

Case Study:
Conference Publications (CP)

Case study description:

> *The main component of a conference publication comprises a collection of papers. All the papers are documents originally written by one or more authors, which are then submitted to the appropriate conference editor to undergo review. The structure of the manuscript has three components, namely: Abstract, Content and References. In the review process, papers are distributed to two or four referees with expertise in the subject area. The given feedback will assist in the selection process of papers to be included in the proceedings book. A conference is not limited to one research area and may include several ones, hence more workshops are formed to cover each or closely-related subject topics. Usually the conference participants originate from any part of world and belong to various internationally-located institutes. The conference organisers' responsibility is to develop the conference events schedule, inform the participants and to ensure these unfold in an orderly and timely manner.*

The data warehouse of the **CP** contains data from a wide range of conferences, therefore differentiating and monitoring these is important. This can be accomplished through generating individualised reports by gathering data stored in the data warehouse, which will be used in order to measure their efficiency on a regular basis. This will involve tracing and comparing past annual outcomes.

The initial requirement is to create an entire overview of the current collection of conferences stored. Therefore it is necessary for all the conference names to appear in alphabetical order or, alternatively, in chronological order to be able to locate these in a straightforward manner. The next step is to obtain all the authors' details who are participating in each conference. When allocating papers for review, it is important to consider that a suitable reviewer is an expert in the subject area and does not come from the same institute as the author. Hence, the lists containing all authors and referees names are required, those being categorized under the institute name(s). In some cases it may be necessary to combine the already-created reports in order to establish a broader and a more enhanced overview or to promote and fulfil a new requirement.

Case Study Comments

We note that the above case study description has two main parts, which will be discussed as follows: The first part, case study description, outlines the facts of the system's context, which are captured and represented through our conceptual *xFACT* model as shown in Figure 4. The interaction amongst the objects determines the relationship configuration and cardinality, which is reflected in the conceptual design. Our complete UML conceptual model (Figure 4) emphasizes the structural complexity of the *xFACT* in which real world objects can be hierarchically decomposed into several sub-objects, where each of these can also include further aggregated objects. Such decompositions are necessary to represent a real-world object with appropriate granularity and, if needed, additional semantics are added at different levels of the hierarchy. Based on the case study of **Conference Publications (CP)**, Figure 5 shows an example of two *VDims*, namely Abstracts_By_Year and Abstracts_By_Keyword, indicating a dependant relationship among them. We show the use of packages in Figure 6 between two or more

VDims, and in Figure 7 the entire *xFACT* (Figure 4) is grouped into one logical construct and is shown in UML as one package.

The second segment of the case study focuses on the internal aspect of the XDW and is concerned with information retrieval. At this stage the requirements are specified and need to be fulfilled based on the current available information in the *xFACT* repository. Initially identified requirements might not be sufficient to be

Figure 4. The complete xFACT of the Conference Publications (CP) case study

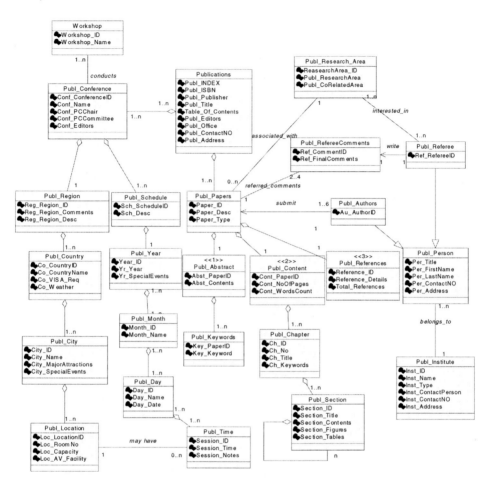

used to solve any queries. Therefore, requirement modelling is an iterative process where we ensure full comprehension of the current requirements, which will then lead to the elicitation of additional, more useful requirements that have not been initially considered.

At this stage we will be focusing on the second segment of the case study, which concerns requirements. What follows is an illustration of the requirement model with the use of identified sample requirements extracted from the text-based case study. These will be applied to the XDW requirement model (Figure 3a) in order to achieve comprehension of each requirement, especially in regards to their configuration and their equivalent association with the XDW.

Figure 5. VDim "Abstract_List" *package contents*

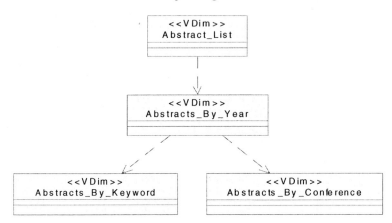

Requirements and the XDW Requirement Model

Based on the above case study facts, we can begin by extracting a number of possible requirements. What follows is a demonstration for each stated requirement, ranging from straightforward to more complex types, including modelling and implementation of actual requirement values. The proposed XDW requirement model (Figure 3a) is the foundation for building smaller requirement modelling segments to suit the structure of each formed requirement. This enables full capturing of the current requirements and encourages further elicitation of new requirements. Previously, we stated that a *VDim* corresponds to a data warehouse requirement and is a generated view of a given *xFACT*. This leads to the possibility that several *VDims* can be combined to form a newly-constructed *VDim* providing another level of meaning. The drive to instigate the combination of *VDims,* or to build a new solitary *VDim*, is initiated by the ever-changing requirements of the users and the need to fulfil these. Note, that for a full reference of the stated XML documents (object instances) in the section of requirements, illustration can be found in the complete *xFACT* conceptual model (Figure 4).

Before we progress to the actual implementation of the model with the requirements, it is important to note that based on the general characteristics that emerge from various requirements, we are able to form five main categories that portray the nature of each likely-to-occur requirement specification, which include:

Figure 6. "Conference_List," "Abstract_List" & "Author_List" *packages*

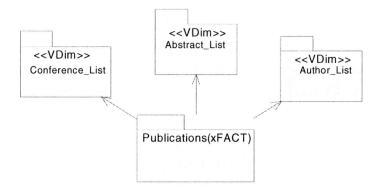

Figure 7. XDW conceptual model (in UML)

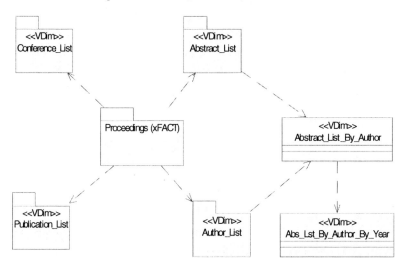

1.   Retrieve elements attributes values of an entire document.

2.   Retrieve attribute values of specified element(s) in a document.

3.   Retrieve element attribute values of a document, based on a particular *context value (CV).* The *CV* in some cases may exist in a different document, which has no direct link with the immediately-related documents involved in a given query.

4.   Sort an already-generated outcome of a query based on a *subject factor value (SFV)*.

5.   Retrieve elements attributes values by merging two or more documents.

The different types of requirements featured above are identified solely but can be combined with one another, particularly when a requirement's specification acquires a highly complex structure.

The illustration with the requirements follows where we will show three examples of possible requirements extracted from our case study. Each of these requirements represents one or a combination of the several categories presented above.

Requirement 1: List of All Conference Names

In order to generate the required list of all the conference names, the proposed query would perform a search within the document Publ_Conference and, more specifically, will extract the values of the element Conf_Name. Figure 8a shows how this specific requirement is modelled, based on our XDW requirement model, while Figure 8b shows how the actual notation is implemented according

Figure 8. Figures 8(a) and 8(b): Requirement for list of all conferences names

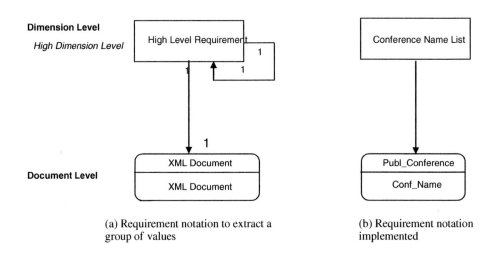

(a) Requirement notation to extract a group of values

(b) Requirement notation implemented

to the requirement's values. It is important to note the direct connection amongst the *high dimension level* and the *document level*.

Requirement 2: List of Full Authors' Details Based on Given Institute Name

It is required for all authors' details to be listed according to their associated institute, which for this requirement we use *"La Trobe University."* A simple association between the two documents, Publ_Authors and Publ_Institute, enables us to extract the required data. This case is a demonstration of an outcome derived from a query search based on a specific value from one document, and extracts all values from another document, which indicates a dependent relationship. Here both document types (Figure 3a) are implemented (section on *Document Level*) of which the Publ_Institute is the stronger component due to the fact that the list of authors to be retrieved is determined based on the given institute value. Figure 9a shows how the case of searching based on a specified value is modelled, and Figure 9b shows how the actual notation is implemented according to the requirement's values.

Figure 9. Figures 9(a) and 9(b): Requirement for list of authors' details originating from "LaTrobe University"

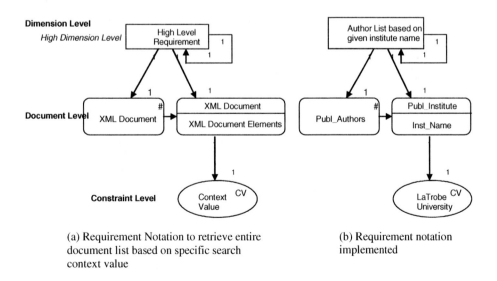

(a) Requirement Notation to retrieve entire document list based on specific search context value

(b) Requirement notation implemented

Requirement 3: List of Conference Names Sorted Chronologically With Cross-Reference to Authors' Details

This requirement is slightly more complex than the previous cases so far. This can be broken down further to simplify the process of gathering the required information. Firstly, the list of conference names (requirement 1) is a straight-forward search, which evolves within the Publ_Conference document. It is then required for the list to be displayed chronologically, which indicates that the *subject value factor (SVF)* applies in this case and takes the element value "Yr_Year" of document "Year". A third component to this requirement is to also include cross-referencing to authors' details, which are to be retrieved from the document Publ_Authors. If we refer to complete *xFACT* diagram (Figure 4), it is indicated that the search is not bound to be only within documents with direct connections amongst them. Instead, at times it may be necessary to go through several intra-connections with external documents to obtain the required values. In Figure 10a in the high-level requirement, the symbol of sort and merge

Figure 10. Figures 10(a) and 10(b): Chronological listing of conference names with cross-reference to authors' details

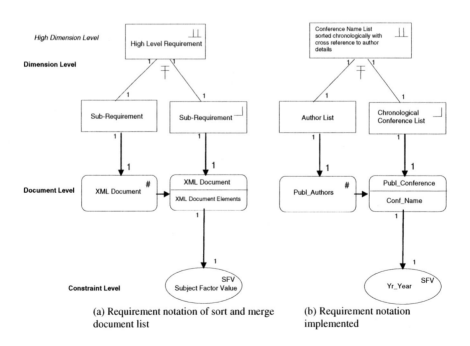

(a) Requirement notation of sort and merge document list

(b) Requirement notation implemented

appears, meaning that the outcome is a result of merging two requirements where one or both has/have been sorted. Figure 10b also shows how a document list is retrieved based on a *selected* element's attribute, then sorted based on a *SFV* and finally combined with another document list. The arrow between the documents is again present, as the extracted authors' details must correspond to the related conference.

The concept of requirement elicitation is performed in this case. We are able to decompose the high level requirement *"Conference name list sorted chronologically with cross reference to author details"* into two smaller sub-requirements, *"Author list"* and *"Chronological conference list"*, which may also prove valuable information when considered either solely or in combination with several other requirements. The approach of decomposing components aids in a better understanding of the context at hand and discovering important factors, which may have not been initially exhibited.

Conclusion and Future Work

Requirement engineering (RE) explores the objectives of various stakeholders and the activities carried out by the system. In regard to system objectives and system functionalities, in this chapter we examined one of the existing approaches — specifically the goal-oriented approach as illustrated in Dardenne et al. (1993). Generally, goal-oriented approaches until now have been mainly directed to assist in the development of software systems, as opposed to focussing on document warehouses involving XML-embedded structures. Based on this, we obtained and broadened the notion of this goal-modelling approach to XML document warehouses (XDW) to promote their structural design by identifying the data warehouse dimensions and the nature of the fact repository.

We introduced concepts from our previous work (Nassis et al., 2004, 2005a, 2005b), where we presented a coherent way to integrate a conceptual design methodology to build a native XDW, which includes the *XML FACT (xFACT)* repository and the *Virtual Dimensions (VDims)*. At this stage we concentrated only on the aspect of the data warehouse structure and design. Given the architecture of the XDW which consists of three levels: (1) Requirement level, (2) XML warehouse conceptual level and (3) Logical level, we focus on the first level by proposing the XDW requirement model.

The main themes of our methodology are to: (1) capture requirements early in the design process; (2) understand the current requirements and further elicit these to promote new requirements; (3) illustrate the mapping of each stated requirement into a corresponding dimension of the XML document warehouse

(XDW); (4) certify that the information required for the *xFACT* repository can be assembled from the information available in the XDW; and (5) ensure that the information necessary to construct a dimension is available or can be obtained from the *xFACT* repository.

We identified the main characteristics comprising the requirement model and then proceeded to the precise and detailed terminology of the components. Using as a basis the system context of our case study (Conference Publications), we extracted a number of sample requirements and applied these to our XDW requirement model in order to illustrate the concepts presented throughout.

In the chapter we emphasized the importance of requirement validation and the availability of the necessary data that aid to requirement fulfilment. A significant issue that still needs to be addressed is checking for the consistency of requirements. This can be achieved by adding an enhanced annotation that will promote a basis for verifying requirement consistency. This process involves two major factors: (a) ensuring that the requirement presentation has sufficient annotation to capture all the constraints in a precise manner, and (b) the development of an algorithm that is capable of carrying out such consistency verification, specifically dealing with inheritance and recursion. One avenue that could be pursued is the use of a language such as Object Constraint Language (OCL) to annotate the requirements.

Clearly, there are several more subject matters that deserve investigation. First, the development of formal semantics that automate the mapping between XML data and XDW schema will define views more precisely and hence support the incremental update of materialized views. Nowadays, the major challenge for any level of semi-structured data is its ability to be effectively searched. Given that the amount of content expands across an organization, locating specific resources becomes progressively more complex and time-consuming. There-fore, investigating performance issues upon query execution in relation to accessing the XDW will prove valuable. A significant aspect is the implemen-tation of the XDW requirement modelling approach, which can be achieved by building a well-formulated empirical study. Also to be explored is the construc-tion of a critical case study to evaluate and validate the application of the XDW requirement model for XML document warehouses (XDWs).

References

Abelló, A., Samos, J., & Saltor, F. (2001, November). Understanding facts in a multidimensional object-oriented model. Paper presented at the *Fourth International Workshop on Data Warehousing and OLAP (DOLAP 2001),* Atlanta, GA (pp. 32-39).

Blazewicz, J., Kubiak, W., Morzy, T., & Marek, R. (2003). *Handbook on data management in information systems*. Berlin; New York: Springer-Verlag.

Coad, P., & Yourdon, E. (1990). *Object-oriented analysis* (2nd ed.). Englewood Cliffs, NJ: Prentice Hall.

Dardenne, A., Van-Lamsweerde, A., & Fickas, S. (1993). Goal-directed requirements acquisition. *Science of Computer Programming*, 20(1-2), 3-50.

Dillon, T. S., & Tan, P. L. (1993). *Object-oriented conceptual modelling*. Australia: Prentice Hall.

Elmasri, R., & Navathe, S. B. (2000). *Fundamentals of database systems* (3rd ed.). New York: Addison-Wesley.

Fankhauser, P., & Klement, T. (2003, September 3-5). *XML for data warehousing changes & challenges (extended abstract)*. Paper presented at the Fifth International Conference on Data Warehousing and Knowledge Discovery (DaWaK 2003), Prague, Czech Republic.

Feng, L., Chang, E., & Dillon, T. S. (2002). A semantic network-based design methodology for XML documents. *ACM Transactions on Information Systems, (TOIS), 20*(4), 390-421.

Feng, L., Chang, E., & Dillon, T. S. (2003). Schemata transformation of object-oriented conceptual models to XML.*International Journal of Computer Systems Engineering (CSSE), 18*(1), 45-60.

Feng, L., & Dillon, T. S. (2003). Using fuzzy linguistic representations to provide explanatory semantics for data warehouses. *IEEE Transactions on Knowledge and Data Engineering (TOKDE), 15*(1), 86-102.

Golfarelli, M., Maio, D. & Rizzi, S. (1998). The dimensional fact model: A conceptual model for data warehouses. *International Journal of Cooperative Information Systems (IJCIS), 7*(2-3), 215-247.

Guttag, J. V., & Horning, J. J. (1993). *Larch: Language and tools for formal specification*. New York: Springer-Verlag.

Jacek, B., Wieslaw, K., Tadeusz, M., & Rusinkiewicz, M. (Eds). (2003). *Handbook on data management in information systems*. Berlin; New York: Springer.

Jacobson, I. (1995). The use case construct in object-oriented software engineering. In John M. Carroll (Ed.). *Scenario-based design: Envisioning work and technology in system development* (pp. 309-336). New York: John Wiley & Sons.

Jarke, M., & Pohl, K. (1993, December). *Establishing visions in context: Towards a model of requirements processes*. Paper presented at the Fourteenth International Conference on Information Systems, Orlando, FL.

Jones, C. B. (1990). *Systematic software development using VDM* (2nd ed.). NJ: Prentice Hall.

Kimball, R., & Ross, M. (2002). *The data warehouse toolkit: The complete guide to dimensional modelling* (2nd ed.). New York: Wiley.

Lubars, M., Potts, C., & Richer, C. (1993, January). *A review of the state of the practice in requirements modelling.* Paper presented at the First International Symposium on Requirements Engineering (RE 1993), San Diego, CA.

Lucie-Xyleme. (2001, July 16-18). *Xyleme: A dynamic warehouse for XML data of the web.* Paper presented at the International Database Engineering & Applications Symposium (IDEAS 2001), Grenoble, France.

Lujan-Mora, S., Trujillo, J., & Song I-Y. (2002a, September 30-October 4). *Extending the UML for multidimensional modelling.* Paper presented at the Fifth International Conference on the Unified Modeling Language and Its Applications (UL 2002), Dresden, Germany.

Lujan-Mora, S., Trujillo, J., & Song, I-Y. (2002b). Multidimensional modeling with UML package diagrams. Paper presented at the Twenty-First International Conference on Conceptual Modeling (ER 2002).

McGraw, K., & Harbison, K. (1997). *User centered requirements: The scenario-based engineering process.* Mahwah, New Jersey: Lawrence Erlbaum Associates.

Nassis, V., R.Rajugan, Dillon, T. S., & Rahayu, W. J. (2004, September 1-3). *Conceptual design for XML document warehouses.* Paper presented at the Sixth International Conference on Data Warehousing and Knowledge Discovery (DaWaK 2004), Zaragoza, Spain.

Nassis, V., R.Rajugan, Dillon, T.S., & Rahayu, W. (2005a). Conceptual and systematic design approach for XML document warehouses. *International Journal of Data Warehousing and Mining, 1*(3), 63-87.

Nassis, V., R.Rajugan, Rahayu, W., & Dillon, T.S. (2005b, July 25-28). *A requirement engineering approach for designing XML-View driven, XML document warehouses.* Paper presented at the Twenty-Ninth International Computer Software and Application Conference (COMPSAC 2005), Edinburgh, Scotland.

Nassis, V., R.Rajugan, Rahayu, W., & Dillon, T.S. (2005c, May 9-12). *A systematic design approach for XML-View driven web document warehouses.* Paper presented at the First International Workshop on Ubiquitous Web Systems and Intelligence (UWSI 2005), Colocated with ICCSA 2005, Singapore.

Nilsson, N. J. (1971). *Problem solving methods in artificial intelligence.* New York: McGraw Hill.

Olle, T. W., Hagelstein, J., MacDonald, I. G., Rolland, C., Sol, H. G., Van Assche, F. J. V. et al. (1988). *Information systems methodologies: A framework for understanding.* New York; Reading, MA: Addison-Wesley.

OMG-UML™ (2003). *Unified Modeling Language™ (UML) Version 1.5, Specification.* Object Management Group (OMG).

Pokorny, J. (2002, June 3-6). *XML data warehouse: Modelling and querying.* Paper presented at the Fifth International Baltic Conference (Baltic DB & IS 2002), Talinn, Estonia.

Rahayu, W. J., Dillon, T. S., Mohammad, S., & Taniar, D. (2001, August 21-24). *Object-relational star schemas.* Paper presented at the Thirteenth IASTED International Conference on Parallel & Distributed Computing and Systems (PDCS 2001), Anaheim, CA.

Rajugan, R, Chang, E., Dillon, T. S., & Feng, L. (2003, September 1-5). *XML views: Part I.* Paper presented at the Fourteenth International Conference on Database and Expert Systems Applications (DEXA 2003), Prague, Czech Republic.

Rajugan, R, Chang, E., Dillon, T. S. & Feng, L. (2004, November 2-6). *XML views, part II: Modelling conceptual views using XSemantic nets.* Paper presented at the Thirtieth Conference of the IEEE Industrial Electronics Society (IECON 2004), Workshop & Special Session on Industrial Informatics, S. Korea.

Rajugan, R, Chang, E., Dillon, T. S., & Feng, L. (2005, May 24-28). *XML views, Part III: Modeling XML conceptual views using UML.* Paper presented at the Seventh International Conference on Enterprise Information Systems (ICEIS 2005), Miami, FL.

Rahayu, W. J., Chang, E., Dillon, T. S., & Taniar, D. (2002). *Aggregation versus association in object modeling and databases.* Paper presented at the Seventh Australasian Conference on Information Systems, Hobart, Tasmania.

Rolland, C., & Prakash, N. (2000). From conceptual modelling to requirements engineering. *Special issue of Annals of Software Engineering on Comparative Studies of Engineering Approaches for Software Engineering, 10*(1-4), 51-176.

Royce, W. W. (1970, August 25-28). *Managing the development of large-scale software: Concepts and techniques.* Paper presented at the Western Electronic Show and Convention (WesCon), LA.

Rumbaugh, J. R., Blaha, M. R., Lorensen, W., Eddy, F., & Premerlani, W. (1991). *Object-oriented modelling and design.* Englewood Cliffs, NJ: Prentice Hall.

Spivey, J. M. (1992). *The Z notation — A reference manual* (2nd ed.). NJ: Prentice Hall.

Trujillo, J., Palomar, M., Gomez, J., & Song, I-Y. (2001, December). Designing data warehouses with OO conceptual models. *IEEE Computer Society, "Computer",* 66-75.

W3C-XML. (2004, February 4). *Extensible markup language (XML)* 1.0. (3rd ed.). Retrieved February 20, 2004, from http://www.w3.org/XML/

W3C-XQuery. (2004, November 2003). *XQuery 1.0: An XML query language.* Retrieved November 10, 2003, from http://www.w3.org/TR/xquery

W3C-XSD. (2004). *XML schema.* Retrieved February 5, 2004, from http://www.w3.org/XML/Schema

Xyleme. (2001). *Xyleme XML content management and business document management system.* Retrieved December 10, 2004, from http://www.xyleme.com/

Yourdon, E. (1989). *Modern structured analysis.* Englewood Cliffs, NJ: Prentice Hall.

Chapter III

Building an Active Content Warehouse

Serge Abiteboul, INRIA-Futurs, Orsay, France

Benjamin Nguyen, Université de Versailles Saint-Quentin, France

Gabriela Ruberg, Federal University of Rio de Janeiro, Brazil

Abstract

Non-quantitative content *represents a large part of the information available nowadays, such as Web pages, e-mails, metadata about photos, etc. In order to manage this new type of information, we introduce the concept of* content warehousing, *the management of loosely structured data. The construction and maintenance of a* content warehouse *is an intricate task, involving many aspects such as feeding, cleaning and enriching semi-structured data. In this chapter, we introduce the* Acware *(for active content warehouse) specification language, whose goal is to help all sorts of users to organize content in a simple manner. The problem we are faced with is the following: The data are semi-structured, and the operations to be executed on this data may be of any sort. Therefore, we base our approach on XML to represent the data, and Web Services, as generic components that can be tailored to specific applicative needs. In particular, we discuss the specification of mappings between the warehouse data and the parameters/results of services that are used to acquire and enrich the content. From the implementation point of view, an* Acware *specification of a content warehouse is compiled into a set of Active XML documents, i.e., XML documents with embedded Web service calls. These Active XML documents are then used to build and maintain the warehouse using the Active XML runtime environment. We illustrate the approach with a particular application drawn from microbiology and developed in the context of the French RNTL e.dot project.*

Introduction

The management of non-quantitative content (e-mails, legal documents, customer relationship management information, news articles, analysis reports, meta-data about audio/video/photos, and many more) that originates from various heterogeneous environments is a key issue for companies. In particular, with the broadening use of information retrieved from the World Wide Web by many applications, the integration of unstructured and unsure information with structured, proprietary data has sparked a lot of research these last years. This chapter deals with integration difficulties, and proposes a model and system to simplify related tasks. More precisely, we propose a model to design a (Web) content warehouse and tools to build and maintain it.

The focus of this chapter is non-quantitative information, since the field of data warehousing is vast. Therefore the processing of quantitative information with traditional warehousing techniques is beyond the scope of this paper. Let us introduce the term *content warehouse* (CW) (Abiteboul, 2003). We call *content warehouse* any (large) amount of non-quantitative information. The information need not be structured, nor originate from a well established source. This contrasts with traditional data warehouses (Buneman, Davidson, Fan, Hara, & Tan, 2003; Hammer, Garcia-Molina, Widom, Labio, & Zhuge, 1995), whose sources are known, have a regular format and whose data model usually is either relational or multidimensional. Many issues arise when building a content warehouse. First, it is necessary to identify and capture relevant content. This is achieved using standard services provided by ETL (extract, transform and load) tools, search engines or Web crawlers that return flows of documents. The content is extremely diverse, ranging from structured (e.g., relational and Excel tables) to very unstructured data (e.g., plain text and HTML pages), and the data need to be cleaned, classified, transformed and enriched in order to be properly used. Designing such a warehouse requires, besides the specification of the data organization, the definition of meta-data information that enables users to understand the information better and exploit the warehouse. Furthermore, the construction of the warehouse involves the use of processing tools such as crawlers and classifiers. The originality of our approach is that we view all these tools as Web services (the WC3 Web Services Activity). We will motivate further down this approach. Moreover, as content and user requirements evolve in time, a content warehouse must be maintained in order to reflect this evolution. This may be achieved, or at least facilitated, by the modularity of the system's architecture. Therefore, the connection between the warehouse data and the services used to build and maintain it is a key aspect of this approach.

In this chapter, we address the problem of designing, constructing and maintaining a content warehouse. We will discuss the following topics:

- **A state of the art:** We start the chapter with an overview of papers and systems on the topic of warehousing loosely structured data.

- **A declarative warehouse specification language:** We have defined a language that enables users to build the specification of an active (sometimes known as dynamic) warehouse. The Acware (for *active content warehouse*) language supports the description of both warehouse data and meta-data, and also provides the necessary means to define how Web services operate on the warehouse in order to perform processing tasks such as feeding, classification and transformation. The language uses XML types to describe both content elements and the interface of services.

- **A compiler and execution platform:** We have defined and implemented the Acware compiler. Starting from a warehouse specification, it generates an original instance of the warehouse, namely a set of *Active XML* (Abiteboul, Benjelloun, & Milo, 2004) documents, possibly containing some initial content. Active XML is a language based on the embedding of Web service calls inside XML documents. The warehouse is then constructed and maintained by the Active XML (AXML) system (Abiteboul, Benjelloun, Manolescu, Milo, & Weber, 2002; Active XML home page), which, in particular, controls the activation of service calls.

- **A library of basic Web services for warehouse construction:** We have identified and implemented a set of useful Web services for feeding, monitoring, classifying and enriching a warehouse. Building on new developments of AXML, we discuss pull and push services as well as synchronous and asynchronous ones. We also discuss services to monitor warehouse evolution, based on a representation of XML changes (Nguyen, Abiteboul, Cobena, & Preda, 2001).

Organization

This chapter is organized as follows: We begin with a state of the art. The *Content Warehousing* section discusses our views on content warehousing. *The Acware Model* section deals with the data and service models we propose, and addresses the problem of connecting Web services to a content warehouse. The *Interfacing Web Services* describes the *Acware* architecture and mentions basic services we implemented with regard to two particular applications: building a content warehouse for food risk assessment. We close the chapter with a conclusion.

State of the Art

General Overview

The warehousing of Web data, and in particular XML warehousing (Nassis, Rajugan, Dillon, & Rahayu, 2004), has stirred up both academia and industry in the last years. The data materialization approach of Web warehousing is opposed to the virtual integration approach that has been adopted by a number of works related to the problem of integrating heterogeneous data sources (Draper, Halevy, & Weld, 2001; Garcia-Molina, Papakonstantinou, Quass, Rajaraman, Sagiv, Ullman, Vassalos, & Widom, 1997; Halevy, Ives, Madhavan, Mork, Suciu, & Tatarinov, 2004). One of the first incursions in this area is the WIND (Warehouse of INternet Data) system, in which most of the translation and integration efforts are performed during the query processing, a key difference with the warehousing approach we follow, where integration of the information is immediate. In this regard, WIND has more of a mediator approach.

Web Warehousing

An important task of building and maintaining a content warehouse is to discover and gather relevant information. For many applications, most of the potential content has to be found on the Web, then extracted from it. In this context, content warehousing turns into *Web archiving* (Abiteboul, Cobena, Masanes, & Sedrati, 2002). This technique involves defining the perimeter of Web pages of interest to crawl and accessing the selected pages (Cho & Garcia-Molina, 2000; Pokorný, 2001), as well as calculating their importance (Abiteboul, Preda, & Cobena, 2003) and monitoring their evolution in time (Marian, Abiteboul, Cobena,

& Mignet, 2001; Nguyen, Abiteboul, Cobena, & Preda, 2001). In the domain of Web news, Maria, and Silva (2000) propose a system to generate subject-oriented data collections by exploiting a learning method called "support vector machines" to classify text documents from news Websites. Once relevant Web pages are retrieved, data transformations are often required to extract their content and finally convert it to the warehouse data format. In the XML context, the use of XSLT files that encode data transformation rules (Myllymaki, 2002) is generally widespread. It is worth noting that Web crawling consists of a time-consuming process and usually requires optimization techniques such as crawling parallelization (Cho & Garcia-Molina, 2002), and accessing some information, such as the hidden Web, is difficult (Raghavan & Garcia-Molina, 2001).

Relevant Technologies

One may also remark that although Web content is heterogeneous, XML is becoming the standard used to represent and store Web information (Mignet, Barbosa, & Veltri, 2003). This is an important observation, since it will simplify the process of feeding a content warehouse. Where once many different wrappers were needed for each standard (such as .pdf, relational data, .doc, etc.), the widespread use of XML leads us to envision that the difficulty residing in the integration of Web data is no longer the wrapping, but rather the mappings of the sources to the right location in the content warehouse, which can easily be done using XSLT, as we will show below. Rusu, Rahayu, and Taniar (2005) detail data cleaning and summarization in a systematic approach, feeding data from XML sources into an XML data warehouse. *Data cleaning* is performed by analyzing and solving several types of schema and data level conflicts, while the *data summarization* process involves creating dimensions and collecting interesting facts from the data.

As we have just seen, XML is used to store the data. However, the tools used to process it are usually proprietary tools, written in specific application languages. We believe that all content warehouses have specific tasks in common (such as feeding, cleaning, etc.). The recent interest in *Web Services* has drawn us to the conclusion that many of the previous, complicated tasks can be encapsulated and integrated using the latest technologies and standards (SOAP Version 1.2; Universal Description, Discovery and Integration of Web Services; Web Services Definition Language). There are many different sorts of Web services available, some are *synchronous*, meaning that an answer is received immediately (or, at any case, within a minute) after the call is issued. Others are *asynchronous*. The latter may be of two types: some services that have a long processing time will be invoked, and will return their results later; others will periodically send information to the warehouse, continuously feeding it with data. These different types of services can all be simply integrated by using the Active XML platform (Active XML home page). The whole point of this chapter is to show how the construction of a warehouse of XML data, using Web services to process the data, can be done in a simple and declarative way. In the rest of this chapter we will sometimes refer to Web services simply as *services*.

Multidimensional Data

Zhu, Bornhövd, Sautner, and Buchmann (2000) propose a warehousing framework based on the "metadata-based integration model for data X-change" (MIX), with a strong emphasis on converting Web data into a multidimensional model (star schema). In Hümmer, Bauer, and Harde (2003), multidimensional data are described by a family of XML document templates (called an *XCube*) that is used to exchange data cubes over a network. *XCube* enables users to efficiently download consistent chunks of warehouse data from Web servers, as well as to retrieve schema information in order to select relevant warehouse data cubes. This technique is used to avoid unnecessary data transfers. Multidimensional analysis is also used in Golfarelli, Rizzi, and Vrdoljak (2001) to build data marts from XML data sources, where *fact schemas* (defined according to a *Dimensional Fact Model*) are semi-automatically generated from the DTDs of the XML data sources.

Graphical Design Tools

Graphical tools are often used to design XML data warehouses, such as in the DAWAX (DAta WArehouse for XML) system (Baril & Bellahsene, 2003), which is based on a view mechanism for regular XML data. In Baril and Bellahsene (2003), the warehouse is defined as a set of materialized views, and subsequently XML documents are filtered and transformed according to user requirements. XML to relational mappings defined on DAWAX views are then used to store the warehouse in a relational DBMS. Views are also used by Pokorný (2001), which focus on capturing data warehousing semantics for collections of XML data, and propose a framework to model XML-star schemas. Furthermore, the traditional data-warehouse dimensions can be defined as views over the XML-warehouse, using the pattern-matching capabilities of XML query languages (Pokorný, 2002).

Content warehousing is also related to the design of Web applications. The Web Modeling Language (WebML) (Ceeri, Fraternali, Bongio, Brambilla, Comai, & Matera, 2003) consists of a high-level notation for specifying complex, data-intensive Web sites. The focus of WebML is to define the structure of Web pages and the topology of links between them. This language contributes to the development of services that can feed a content warehouse, since it enables the publication of generic specifications of Web content.

Active Databases

Research on active databases (Widom & Ceri, 1996), is also related to the topic of content warehousing. However, the context is no longer relational or object-oriented databases, but instead, semi-structured content warehouses. Here, active databases define rules and use triggers to activate SQL operations on relational data and a content warehouse invokes Web services. These Web services may be programs written in any language and perform complex tasks, using an input produced by a query on the warehouse and producing a result to be stored in it. Thus, one of the specific difficulties of our setting is interfacing services and data.

Commercial Tools

Warehousing Packages

Actual *commercial warehousing tools*, such as Oracle9i Warehouse Builder and IBM DB2 Warehouse Manager, discard key aspects of content warehousing, such as semi-structured data and continuous feeding services. For instance, they do not support data loaders that take a long time to process and return their results incrementally. Moreover, they do not enable users to intuitively connect the warehouse schema with its feeding workflows. This glue is hard-coded in stored procedures that can be sequentially composed and triggered by the database system.

WebSuite (Beeri, Elber, Milo et al., 1998) proposes independent modules that can be combined to tackle complex tasks related to Web warehousing. However, WebSuite does not provide a uniform way of specifying the warehouse and, in our opinion, lacks a high level mechanism for the automatic cooperation between different modules.

In *Data View Builder*, an application included in the BEA WebLogic package for data integration (BEA Liquid Data for WebLogic), Web services can be used as data sources for feeding the warehouse. However, this functionality is limited to the construction of views over Web service results to populate the warehouse. On the contrary, in our setting, connecting a Web service involves building not only a view over the *service result* to populate the warehouse, but also a view over the *warehouse content* to provide input to the Web service. Moreover, unlike our declarative approach, Web service invocation is performed through procedural language programming in BEA Liquid Data for WebLogic.

E.T.L. Tools

Off-the-shelf tools *for extracting, transforming and loading (ETL)* data into a warehouse, such as Business Objects Data Integrator, Reveleus and iSoft Amadea, are outstanding machinery for dealing with relational or multidimensional data. These tools emphasize the specification of workflows in a very procedural manner, thus producing complicated load scripts. We see such ETL tools as complementary to our approach, as they can be used for feeding data into an Acware warehouse.

Web Service Development

In order to develop Web service applications, our experience has shown us that the simplest method is to write traditional java programs. Once deployed on a *Tomcat* Web server via *AXIS* (AXIS Homepage), these programs are automatically transformed into Web services and the WSDL files are generated automatically. Let us stress that the development of Web services using this method has barely any overhead compared to writing and executing the Java application.

Content Warehousing

In this section, we discuss the notion of *content warehousing*. As we will see, an important distinction with classical warehouses is that it manages "content," and not only numerical data. In this chapter, we focus on the management of content, given that the many proven techniques for the management of numerical data (Widom, 1995) are beyond its scope. To illustrate our purpose, we will use the running example of the *e.dot* (*e.dot* Project) warehouse.

The e.dot Warehouse

Our case example will be the *e.dot* project (*e.dot* is a RNTL project financed by the French ministry of Research). This warehouse is used by biology experts who analyze food risk. Some of the warehouse information comes from relational databases managed by *e.dot* industrial partners. Other information comes from domain ontologies developed at *Institut National de Recherche en Agronomie*. Finally, the warehouse must also be fed with information discovered and retrieved from the Web. To this end, the Web information is analyzed, classified, enriched and stored in the warehouse, once proper links to the relational and ontological information have been constructed. The warehouse was built using the Acware system, described in the next sections.

Content Warehouse

The problem we tackle is to provide an integrated view over distributed, autonomous and heterogeneous sources of *content*. Let us first explain what we mean by content and make the notion more precise.

We introduce the term *content*, meaning *any form of interesting information*. A *content element* is the primary unit of information, but its scale is not fixed. Content elements may be documents, fragments of documents, relational tuples or any relevant piece of information. For instance, a content element may be an e-mail, a portion of e-mail, such as the *subject* field or a collection of e-mails, i.e., an e-mail folder. Some elements may stay in their original formats, such as PDF files, while other will be transformed.

Secondly, we deal with warehousing. Warehousing is one aspect of data integration, which traditionally has two approaches: (1) mediation, where the integration remains *virtual*, and (2) warehousing, where the data are stored in the integration system. Both approaches present advantages. In the warehousing approach information is fetched ahead of time. In contrast, in the mediation approach information may be cleaned and enriched before the arrival of a query. In this chapter, we adopt the warehousing approach. Our warehouse is organized logically according to a *global schema*. This is the organization that a user sees while browsing or querying the warehouse.

On the Web, content has less structure. Quite often it is stored in *semi-structured* or very loosely structured formats, such as HTML or XML. This motivates the use of XML, the Web standard for data exchange, and a semi-structured data model, as the core data model to describe content (Abiteboul, Buneman, & Suciu, 2000). With XML, one can capture plain text just as well as very structured information, such as relations. XML is also convenient for managing meta-data, an essential component of such contexts.

Why Use Web Services?

As we just mentioned, XML is the standard for data exchange on the Web, and we use it as the core format for representing information. We also want to see all processing performed in the context of the warehouse as *Web services* based on Web standards such as SOAP (SOAP Version 1.2), WSDL (Web Services Definition Language) and UDDI (Universal Description, Discovery and Integration of Web Services). Web services are the new, simple way of integrating applications. As we mentioned in Section 1, it is possible to build a Web service for virtually no cost if the program is an independent Java (or C++) application. For instance, the process of feeding information into the warehouse, a focused crawler program, is provided by the corresponding Web service. Similarly, if we want to enrich some documents by tagging key concepts, summarizing their content, classifying them, etc., by using a popular application, this may also be done by turning the application into a Web service. Web services provide a uniform interface for describing a wide range of valuable, dynamic and up-to-date sources of information (acquisition) and processing (enrichment). These are all viewed as potentially remote applications with an interface based on WSDL and XML schema, W3C standards.

Active Warehousing

We believe that a fundamental aspect of a content warehouse is to be dynamic. Warehouse content evolves when new information is acquired, enriched or when its specification is modified. This is why we use the term *Active Content Warehouse*. This means that the warehouse system provides support for controlling changes over time, such as a versioning mechanism. But it also means, for instance, that the administrator is able to request the execution at regular time intervals (e.g., weekly) of some specific tasks, such as the crawling of a site of interest in search for new, relevant information. Similarly, users may request to be notified when some particular kind of information is discovered. In our system, the versioning is performed by a versioning Web service, and the regular calls are a functionality of *Active XML*, the execution platform.

Main Functionalities

We are faced with the following problems: global schema design, content acquisition, enrichment, exploitation, storage, view management, change control and administration. See Figure 1 for an illustration of various warehouse interactions in the *e.dot* context. These tasks are not independent. For instance,

Figure 1. The e.dot *warehouse*

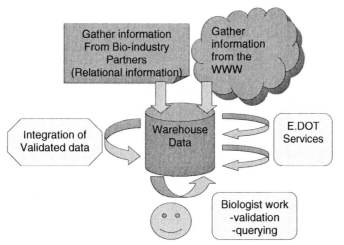

information brought from the relational DB pilot the Web search for related information, which in turn leads to the retrieval of more relational information about other food products, and so on.

We examine next the different aspects mentioned.

Global Schema Design

The design of a content warehouse consists primarily of the specification of a logical organization, i.e., which kinds of content elements belong to the ware-

Figure 2. An Acware on food-risk assessment

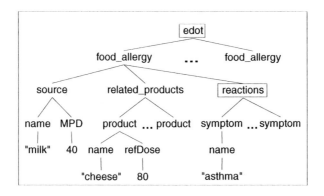

house, how they are classified, organized and what meta-information is maintained for them. A simplified structure for the e.dot warehouse is depicted in Figure 2.

Acquisition

In the spirit of ETL tools, one goal of the warehouse is to locate content elements in source information systems, obtain, transform and load them in the warehouse. The sources may be relational databases, tree-ontologies or Web sites, but one would like to be able to obtain data from virtually any system, e.g., LDAP, newsgroup, e-mails, file systems, etc. To have a uniform view of the external world, we use Web services. As we have stressed, it is easy to create a Web service, so one can easily wrap an information source into it, but this may also be done for Web crawlers or any ELT tool. Content may be acquired from external systems in *pull* or *push* mode.

In the e.dot warehouse, relational databases provide (among other things) information about allergic reactions. Documents about food products are gathered by crawling HTML and PDF documents from Web sites. These pages are obtained by alternating search phases (Google Web APIs) and focused crawling phases.

Acquisition also often involves humans, such as domain experts, who are asked to validate some information or edit meta-data: In *e.dot*, when a table is extracted from a PDF document and entered in a measurement database, an expert is asked to validate the results of the table analyzer.

Enrichment

The goal is to enrich the warehouse, in other words, add *value* to its *content*. This may involve translation to XML (XML-izers for various formats), structural transformations (using an XSLT processor), classification, summarization, concept tagging, etc. Enrichment acts at different levels:

1. enrichment of some document's meta-data, e.g., classification;

2. enrichment inside the document, e.g., extraction and tagging of concepts; and

3. discovery of various relationships between documents, e.g., tables of content or indexes.

In the *e.dot* example, a lot of measurements that interest the biologists are found in tables of document publications (typically in PDF files). An *acquisition* role would be to discover such tables. An *enrichment* role is to extract their structure and then, when possible, understand their semantics so that they may be turned into knowledge.

Storage

The warehouse must store massive amounts of XML. Additional data are stored in databases and in file systems, such as the raw PDF files. The system must also support the indexing of data and meta-data, the processing of queries over XML data and the integration with other data sources. Finally, it must provide standard repository functionalities such as recovery, access control and (to a lesser extent for the *e.dot* application) concurrency control.

Change Control

The time dimension of information is important and leads to issues such as versioning (Marian, Abiteboul, Cobena, & Mignet, 2001). On the one hand, administrators also want to monitor the evolution of the warehouse: control its size and verify that it is used properly. On the other hand, warehouse monitoring is of interest to users, for instance technology surveillance: Users want to be able to place a subscription to be notified when a newspaper article is discovered on a particular bacteria or when some group published a new article.

Exploitation

The exploitation of the warehouse involves a number of accessing and editing functionalities. Besides hypertext navigation, access is provided via full text search, canned or *ad hoc* queries (some XQuery-like language for XML). Interfaces (Web sites or dashboards) are proposed that organize the information along a variety of dimensions and classifications to facilitate the analytical processing of the content. In such a context, the user can zoom in and out in the content and query results; he or she may also use tools to sort, filter or summarize content. Let us note that such an exploitation of the warehouse is enhanced by work performed during its construction. Indeed, an important role of content enrichment is to simplify this subsequent exploitation.

The user can also enter new content, edit meta-information or annotate existing content. Such updates are performed using customized forms and standard Web browsers. Content editing may also be performed from standard editors with the WebDAV protocol.

Last, but not least, support for the generation of complex parameterized reports and on-line analysis of content is provided. In all these activities related to the exploitation of the warehouse content, the user relies on the warehouse schema and is assisted in his queries by domain ontologies.

Views and Integration

The system also provides tools for building user views. Building a view usually means restructuring some classes of documents via query language, such as XQuery, or via XSLT transformations; other views are constructed through the integration of heterogeneous collections of content elements. One should also consider proposing automatic or semi-automatic tools to analyze a set of XML schemas, integrate them and then support queries on the integration view. Ontologies play an important role in this context.

Administration

The warehouse can be administered through a Graphical User Interface or by using an Application Program Interface. This includes, in particular, the means to register acquisition and enrichment tasks, the management of users and of their access privileges as well as the control of on-going tasks such as backup and failure recovery.

We will see that an important issue in this setting is how processing relates to the warehouse. This problem leads to two questions: Where does a Web service that is used in the warehouse take its input values, and where does it store its results? These are important aspects described here.

The Acware Model

In this section, we describe the Acware model and the language used to specify active content warehouses. Our goal was not to define yet another database model. Thus, the components of our model are conventional and the warehouse organization basic. However, in the *e.dot* experiment, we found it powerful enough to satisfy the needs of a highly complex application and particularly useful to describe how relevant Web services are used.

The model may be broken into three distinct components:

- The **type system** that describes the data known about *content elements*;
- The **schema** that organizes elements in classes related by an *enrichedBy* relation; and
- The **service model**, used to declare the Web services used, as well as describing how they build their inputs and where they place their results.

We consider next these three components.

The Type System

The Acware type system is based on (i) basic types (e.g., *string*, *integer*); (ii) user-defined types obtained by compositing already defined types; and (iii) collection types. The data types follow the following abstract syntax:

t :: basic | complex
basic :: *string* | *integer* | *float* | ...
complex :: composite | collection
composite :: $[(\bullet)_1: \tau_1, \bullet_2: \tau_2, ..., \bullet_n: \tau_n]$
collection :: {composite}

The $\bullet_i$ represent attribute labels. Parentheses in composite type definitions indicate the key attributes. We impose for each composite type to have a key. We assume that the key of a basic data type is its value, while for a composite type it is recursively defined as the key of its key attributes. An attribute of type collection is not allowed to be a key attribute. There exist some restrictions in this type system; for instance, it is not possible to define *directly* a collection of collections. An element in a collection is identified by its key.

Figure 3 shows some type specifications for the *e.dot* content warehouse of Section 2 (simplified for presentation purposes). The type definitions are given in XML syntax. Observe the *key* attribute in all composite type declarations. An alternative description of *key* attributes can be given as path expressions, in the spirit of Buneman, Davidson, Fan, Hara, and Tan (2003). For example, the instances of the collection type *edot* are uniquely identified by the path *edot/ food_allergy/source/name*.

Figure 3. Some types for the e.dot *warehouse*

```
<AcwareTypes>
<type name='source' class='composite'
        key='name'>
 <child label='name' type='string' />
 <child label='MPD' type='integer' />
</type>
<type name='symptom' class='composite'
        key='name'>
 <child label='name' type='string' />
</type>
<type name='symptoms'
        class='collection' of='symptom' />
<type name='product' type='composite'
        key='name'>
 <child label='name' type='string' />
 <child label='refDose' type='integer' />
</type>
<type name='products'
        class='collection' of='product' />
<type name='food_allergy'
     class='composite' key='source'>
 <child label='source' type='source' />
 <child label='related_products'
            type='products' />
</type>
<type name='edot'
     class='collection' of='food_allergy' />
</AcwareTypes>
```

We would like to stress the importance of keys in the model. We found it essential to have such keys to identify elements in the warehouse and facilitate the use of Web services. In general, when performing a Web service call, we will often record the key of some warehouse element that we use to find where to insert the results.

The Acware Schema

The schema of a content warehouse is defined by declaring collections of elements and their *enrichedBy* relationships. The Acware system then uses these classes and their data type definitions to generate a tree-based (XML) representation of the warehouse schema.

Figure 4. The Acware schema of the e.dot *warehouse*

```
<AcwareSchema>
<collection name='edot' datatype='edot'>
 <entity name='food_allergy'
        datatype='food_allergy'>
  <entity name='source' datatype='source'>
   <basic name='name' datatype='string' />
   <basic name='MPD' datatype='integer' />
  </entity>
  <collection name='related_products'
          datatype='products'>
   <entity name='product' datatype='product'>
    <basic name='name' datatype='string' />
    <basic name='refDose'
         datatype='integer' />
   </entity>
  </collection>
  <collection name='reactions'
          datatype='symptoms' enrich='yes'>
   <entity name='symptom' datatype='symptom'>
    <basic name='name' datatype='string' />
   </entity>
  </collection>
 </entity>
</collection>
</AcwareSchema>
```

Observe in Figure 4 that the *food_allergy* entity is enriched by the collection *reactions* (of type *symptoms*). Notice that we use different tags for elements of composite, collection and basic types. This results in a better visualization of the schema in a graphical user interface.

As can be seen in Figure 4, the Acware schema forms the skeleton of the warehouse. The schema is used to generate an XML-Schema that the content warehouse is compliant with. Therefore, the warehouse becomes immediately available once the construction of the types and schema is finished.

The Service Model

The service model defines the Web services that are used in the content warehouse, and how both inputs and outputs are connected to the Acware instance. A Web service is declared by providing the URL of a WSDL file. To correctly connect a Web service to a content warehouse, three important questions must be answered:

1.   **what** are the service inputs;
2.   **where** should the service outputs be stored in the warehouse; and
3.   **when** to trigger the service calls.

The answers for the first two questions are provided by specifying service mappings between the Acware schema and the service operations. Formally, a *service mapping* consists of an association rule of the form:

service#operation := [Q_{in} U_{out}]

Q_{in} specifies how to find the input to the Web service and U_{out} where to place the results. More precisely, for each operation of a given Web service, the user must define an XQuery and an X-update statement: the input query constructs the input of the Web service, and the update statement takes the information found in the output and places it in the content warehouse.

In the next section, we will detail the construction of the input query and the update statement since these are novel ideas that turned out to be essential in the approach considered here. But first, let us briefly describe how to deal with the third aforementioned problem, i.e., the problem of *when* to call the services. The Acware system is in charge of activating the service calls when needed. For instance, when new relevant documents are discovered on the Web, one would like to automatically schedule a call to a service to classify these new documents according to the domain ontology. To control the activation of services, the warehouse relies on all the features provided by Active XML (Active XML home page). This is one aspect that motivated the use of Active XML. This control includes a number of possibilities such as activating a call:

1.   at some particular time frequency,
2.   when some event occurs (e.g., a particular document is discovered),
3.   when it is explicitly requested by the administrator,
4.   lazily when some particular data that the call may return is needed, or
5.   in push mode, i.e., when some external server decides to.

The control of service call activation, guided by parameters (attributes in the AXML incarnation) of the service calls, turned out to be greatly simplified through the use of AXML.

Interfacing Web Services

A given service may take several inputs and return several outputs, so it may be necessary to define several service mappings to connect one operation of a Web service to the content warehouse. In this section, we consider in more detail how each mapping is defined.

Overview

Quite often, the output of some service call should be stored close to, or at least at a place related to, the warehouse elements that are used as the service call inputs. For instance, in the *e.dot* warehouse, when a call to the service *GetRelatedProducts* returns the list of *products* related to a *specific allergenic source* (such as "*cheese*" is related to the source "*milk*"), the Acware system has to identify that these products are going to be *related_products* of the *food_allergy* element which *source* has *name* = "*milk*". This is achieved by

Figure 5. How service calls work in an Acware

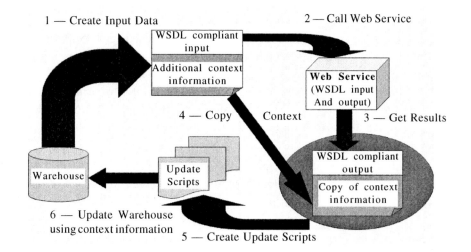

attaching in the query that is used to define the service inputs and some context information about the location of the input data. This context information is provided as an identifier using a path descriptor, as illustrated in Figure 5.

In the Acware system, we use XOQL (X-OQL Homepage), a homemade query language for XML. This is because at the time the e.dot project started, no query processor for XQuery existed. Since XOQL is similar to XQuery, we enhanced XOQL with XUpdate to capture XML updates.

The Input Query

Given a Web service and the content warehouse schema, an XOQL query Q_{in} is used to construct the input to the Web service. Additional context information, which will be needed in order to correctly place the results, is captured by the query result in *var* elements, each with a unique *name* attribute. All these elements are stored under a *context_info* element of the query result. Most of these queries can be automatically generated using a GUI.

The Update Statement

The update is described using XUpdate operations. These may be either *insert* operations, if we are adding new elements, or *update* operations, if we are modifying already existing nodes. The semantics of these operations are defined in the XUpdate specification. Clearly, one can insert a new element only in a node that already exists. To insert some new information in the Warehouse, we construct the key of the new element, then insert it using an *xupdate:insert* operation. In order to check this, we use in each XUpdate operation a *key* attribute that is used by the system to verify easily whether the update is correct with regard to the definition of keys in the data model. The update may have to use context information constructed by the query. (See Figure 5 that illustrates this mechanism.) The use of keys in order to access single elements in each collection of the warehouse is crucial for the simplicity of the model, and is a slight enhancement that we have added to XUpdate for clarity. The key attributes are used in XUpdate expression to help the update processor to check that the queries are correct in so far as they define keys when inserting values into collections.

To illustrate this, we will use the connections between the warehouse and two different Web services, namely, *GetAllergySource* and *GetRelatedProducts*.

Fetching and Transforming Data

Consider first a *GetAllergySource* service. This particular service does not use any input parameter; thus, the corresponding input query is empty. The service returns an XML element such as:

```
<output>
   <allergySource>
      <name>milk</name>
      <MPD>40</MPD>
   </allergySource>
...
</output>
```

Suppose the above *output* element has been received as an answer for the *GetAllergySource* call. The Acware system uses the following update statement, which determines where the service results should be stored in the warehouse, thanks to the use of keys. This step may also involve some data transformations. For instance, one may want to construct *food_allergy* elements from the return values of *GetAllergySource*. In this particular case, the update statement may be specified by:

```
SELECT
<xupdate:modifications>
{
SELECT
<xupdate:insert path="/edot/" key="food_allergy/source/name" >
  <food_allergy>
    <source>
     <name>$A/name</name>
     <MPD>$A/MPD</MPD>
    </source>
    <related_products />
    <reactions />
  </food_allergy>
 </xupdate:insert>
```

```
FROM
$A IN $DOC/allergySource
}
</xupdate:modifications>
FROM
  $DOC IN /output/
```

Observe that the key path (*food_allergy/source/name*) is computed relative to the end of the insert path. If the system is unable to locate the key path in the update statement, then the statement is simply discarded and an error message issued. This is the only validation that is performed on the updates. Apart from this, users are free to define any updates they want.

Managing Context Information

In the next example, we illustrate how the Acware system combines the result of a service call to the corresponding service input, thus providing location context (information). Consider a *GetRelatedProducts* service of the e.dot warehouse, which takes a single input parameter (the name of an allergenic source) and returns some related food products. Based on path expressions for the service input, one call will be activated for each existing *source* element. The issue here is that the results of each service call must be placed according to the *source* element that generates each call. To do this, we keep some context information for each call, i.e., the key of the corresponding allergenic sources. This context information is captured by the input query. In this example, the input query is:

```
SELECT
<input name="GetRelatedProducts" >
   <source>
    <name>$A/source/name</name>
   </source>
   <context_info>
    <var name='A'>$A/source/name</var>
   </context_info>
 <input>
FROM
   $A IN /edot/food_allergy/
```

The system activates one call of the *GetRelatedProducts* service for each *input* element returned by the input query. Besides that, the result of each service call is annotated with the corresponding *context_info* element that contains the key, thus indicating where the data came from. In this example, the data are equal to the key, but this is not necessarily the case. The path in the *context_info/var* element is the path of the key, whereas the path in the *source/name* element is the path of the data transferred to the service. The update statement can then use this context information.

Now suppose the following is returned by the service call with *source/name="milk"*:

```
<sc_results>
  <output>
    <product>
      <name>cheese</name>
      <percentage>80</percentage>
    </product>
    ...
  </output>
  <context_info>
    <var name='A'>milk</name>
  </context_info>
</sc_results>
```

The *output* subtree in the document represents the direct output of the Web Service, and the *context_info* subtree is inherited from the input query. The context information can then be used to define the update, i.e., append the result of the call to the proper *food_allergy* subtrees. The update statement may, for instance, be:

```
SELECT
<xupdate:modifications>
{
 SELECT
 <xupdate:insert
path="edot/food_allergy[source/name=$A/context_info/var[@name='A']/
related_products/">
    <product>
```

```
    <name>$B/name</name>
    <refDose>$B/percentage</refDose>
    </product>
  </xupdate:insert>
 FROM
  $A IN $DOC,
  $B IN $A/output/product
 }
</xupdate:modifications>
FROM
  $DOC IN /sc_results
```

In all the examples, it is important to note that with respect to the XUpdate format, the data modifications are encapsulated inside an *xupdate:modifications* element.

Automatic Generation of Queries

In the case of simple queries, where the inputs and outputs can be defined by simple path-to-path mappings, the system provides a graphical interface that automatically generates the queries. This is the case for most services we used from the Web in *e.dot*. However, the description of the algorithm that generates these queries is beyond the scope of this paper. For more complex cases, a general algorithm that generates queries that use complex restructuring remains ongoing work.

To summarize, the use of each service requires the construction and execution of a query and an update that control service invocation. The query is used to construct the input values for the Web services and the XUpdate request uses the return value of the service together with some context information to modify the warehouse.

Architecture

We discuss in this section the implementation of the Acware system. Acware specifications are compiled into Active XML (AXML) documents that are then handled by the AXML system. We briefly present AXML and then discuss our implementation of Acware. We also describe a library of basic Web services for Content Warehousing that were developed to build the *e.dot* warehouse.

We want to stress that the construction and maintenance of a content warehouse is a complex task that required the integration of many technologies. Our approach was to use emerging Web standards to take advantage of an open platform and easily reuse the software in other projects.

Active XML

We first present Active XML, a framework based on the idea of embedding calls to Web services in XML documents (Active XML home page), which is the basis of the Acware system.

In Active XML (AXML for short), parts of the data are given explicitly, while other parts consist of calls to Web services that are used to generate more data. AXML is based on a P2P architecture, where each AXML peer acts both as a client, by activating Web service calls embedded in its documents, and a server, by providing Web services that correspond to queries or updates over its repository of documents. As already mentioned, the activation of calls can be finely controlled to happen periodically, in reaction to an event (in the style of database triggers), or in a "lazy" way, whenever it may contribute data to the answer of a query.

AXML is an XML dialect. Some particular elements are used to denote embedded service calls. Data obtained by a call to a Web service may be viewed as *intensional*, because it is originally not present. It may also be viewed as *dynamic*, since the same service call might return different data when called at different times. When a service call is activated, the data it returns are inserted in the document that contains it. Therefore, documents evolve in time as a consequence of call activations. Thus, the decision to activate a particular service call or not is vital. In some cases, this activation is decided by the peer hosting the document. For instance, a peer may decide to call a service only when the data it provides are requested by a user; the same peer may choose to refresh its data returned by another call on a periodic basis, say weekly. In other cases, the service provider may decide to send data to the client because the latter registered to a subscription-based service.

A key aspect of this approach is that AXML peers exchange AXML documents, i.e., documents with embedded service calls. Let us highlight an essential difference between the exchange of regular XML data and that of AXML data. In frameworks such as Sun's JSP or PHP, dynamic data are supported by programming constructs embedded inside documents. Upon request, all the code is evaluated and replaced by its result to obtain a regular, fully materialized

HTML or XML document. But since Active XML documents embed calls to Web services, and the latter provide a standardized interface, one does not need to materialize all the service calls before sending some data. Instead, a more flexible data exchange paradigm is possible, where the sender sends an XML document with embedded service calls (namely, an AXML document) and gives the receiver the freedom to materialize the data if and when needed.

The work on Acware and the construction of the *e.dot* warehouse have been very useful for testing and improving the AXML system. The AXML system turned out to be very appropriate, primarily because it is based on XML and Web services, two key components of Acware. Furthermore, AXML provided us with a very powerful support of the activation of services. It should be noted that, motivated by *e.dot* and Acware needs, AXML was extended to support asynchronous and stream services, two functionalities that are, as we realized, essential in the context of content warehousing.

System Architecture

The Acware architecture is shown in Figure 6. There are three main components:

- **A graphical design interface** that is used to generate a specification in the declarative language defined in the *Interfacing Web Services* section;

- **A compiler** that generates AXML documents and services from the declarative specification; and

- **An execution platform** that consists of an AXML peer that manages the content warehouse.

The *Acware graphical interface* enables an intuitive design of warehouse specifications. In order to achieve this goal, the tool provides three distinct working areas: one for data-type definition, one for schema management and one for Web services and service mappings. The warehouse data types are specified in a bottom-up approach, with simpler types defined first. Simple types (such as *string*, *float* and *int*) are predefined in the system, and are used to create more complex (composite or collection-based) types. Users can graphically specify the *enrichedBy* relationship. Users can also register Web services from the Internet by providing the location of their WSDL file, which is used to import the definition of the types of services' input and output parameters. Then, users can graphically define mappings between these services' input and output parameters and the warehouse elements. Mappings on input parameters represent

Figure 6. The Acware overall architecture

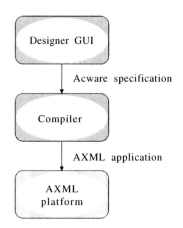

XQueries on the warehouse. By using the graphical interface, we automatically generate the mapping queries for very simple cases. However, advanced users may also write their own XQueries to connect services in a more complex manner.

The output of an Acware specification using the graphical interface consists of an XML file containing the entire warehouse specification (data types, schema and service mappings).

The *Acware compiler* takes this specification and generates an instance of the warehouse: an AXML application, i.e., some AXML documents and services (XQueries/XSLTs). In a nutshell, the AXML documents represent the skeleton of the warehouse, and the services represent the control levers of the application. The exact detail of the algorithms used to compile the *Acware* specification into the AXML application is beyond the scope of this paper. Let us now detail the documents and services produced, and what they are used for.

The AXML documents produced by the *Acware compiler* are:

- **the warehouse schema**;
- **the initial warehouse load**, which consists of user-provided data that are used to construct the initial state of the warehouse; and
- **a workspace document**, that is used by the system to keep incoming data until some transformations are performed before properly feeding them in the warehouse.

The compiler also produces specific AXML services, in this case XSLT style sheets that are used to call the services used in the application. For instance, an XSLT document is generated for the *GetAllergySources* service, which when applied to the warehouse, generates the AXML service call nodes in the workspace document. Let us stress that this operation is the *construction* of the service calls, i.e., defining what service must be called at what time, given the information found in the warehouse, and *not* the activation of their call. The activation of the service calls is controlled at runtime by the AXML system and is automatic, once the AXML service call nodes have been defined. We call these XSLT style sheets the *control levers* of the application, because it is their activation that controls which service calls are to be evaluated or not.

We want also to stress that the XSL service calls are AXML-specific service calls that *construct* the calls to the application-related services. The compiler does not directly create the service calls to the application-related services, but generates XSL services to dynamically regenerate these calls. For instance, in the case of the *GetRelatedProducts* service, this service needs as an input the value of a product, thus it is not possible to call it before having called the *GetAllergySources* service, and, moreover, the input of the *GetRelatedProducts* service is constructed with information produced by the *GetAllergySources* service. The XSL service calls' goal is to help scheduling the order and construction of these calls. The XSL services can be automatically called, or manually triggered.

Basic Web Services for Content Warehousing

Our approach strongly relies on the use of Web services. Each basic warehousing task, such as Web crawling or content classification, is associated with one or more Web services. For the purpose of *e.dot*, we have built and tested a library of common, basic Web services for Content Warehousing. Some of the services of the library were found on the Web, e.g., Google search, whereas others were developed by us or by *e.dot* partners. Some of the services are run locally whereas others run remotely and are linked to the warehouse via the SOAP protocol for Web services.

Crawling services. A first class of warehouse services consists of those related to Web crawling. These services are in charge of discovering and retrieving Web pages. In the context of *e.dot*, we used Xyleme Crawler (Xyleme, 2001), a very efficient crawler with some sophisticate monitoring of the stream of crawled pages that we developed in a previous project. This crawler was tested on over a billion Web documents, from which filtering services selected a list of approximately 22.000 URLs related to food risk.

Classification and clustering services. Once we have identified relevant Web resources, we need to classify and cluster their content. To this end, we use a clustering algorithm developed at the University of Athens in the *Thesus* system (Halkidi, Nguyen, Varlamis, & Vazirgiannis, 2003). Some functions of the Thesus system were wrapped as Web service. The services are used remotely from Athens, e.g., to cluster the 22.000 selected URLs. Thesus services were also useful to further filter Web content, by identifying and grouping together both interesting and uninteresting (unrelated to the topic of food risk) documents.

XML-izing services. An important group of services used in the *e.dot* project is related to the extraction of the "XML structure" of Web data. These services convert diverse data formats into XML. For example, a lot of work was devoted to identify table structures in PDF documents, extract their structure and semantics and represent the information in XML. In this particular context, an expert is asked to validate the data that have been extracted.

Services that transform temporary warehouse data. These are declarative, template-based services that merge Web service results into the warehouse. We have used XSLT as the programming language to implement these services in the AXML framework.

Change control. We also turned some change control tools (Marian, Abiteboul, Cobena, & Mignet, 2001; Nguyen, Abiteboul, Cobena, & Preda, 2001) into Web services to monitor and version documents in the warehouse. These tools allow transparent and automatic versioning of the warehouse. The use of deltas lets us reconstruct on the fly the contents of the warehouse.

Future Trends and Conclusion

We have presented the Acware approach for building and maintaining domain specific content warehouses: A declarative specification is constructed, using the Acware language. Then, this specification is compiled into an Active XML application that is run on an AXML system. The approach is based on a simple hierarchical organization of information and uses Web standards extensively, in particular XML. All computations that acquire information or enrich it are viewed as Web services. Our technical contributions are the declarative specification of how data from the warehouse may be used as input of the services, and how the results are inserted in the warehouse.

We have illustrated our work from one particular application from biology but many different disciplines may find a use for more loosely structured data management systems and content warehousing. In such domains, information is very often partial, incomplete and represented in various ways. Furthermore, experts of these domains are rarely computer science literate. In a recent sociological application (Dudouet, 2005) regarding the sociology of the IT standardization universe, we have also experimented with the ideas developed in this chapter. The advantages of our approach are mainly the simplicity and expressiveness of the model, even to non-experts. The problem can be reduced to the interaction of services that take input information and produce data, and, of the warehouse, whose structure must be defined in joint interaction between computer science experts and the users of the system (in our case, sociologists.)

A lot of works remain to be performed in this area. In particular, we are not satisfied with the user interfaces and believe they can be greatly improved. The library of standard Web services useful for content management is being extended. Finally, we are working on a peer-to-peer content warehousing system named KaDoP (Abiteboul, Manolescu, & Preda, 2004). The idea would be to provide similar functionalities without devoting new computer resources and while keeping full control on information (Abiteboul, 2003).

Acknowledgments

We want to thank members of the Gemo group at INRIA and of Xyleme SA for discussions on the topic. G. Ruberg is supported by Central Bank of Brazil and CNPq. The manuscript contents express the viewpoint of the authors only, and do not represent the position of these institutions.

References

Abiteboul, S. (2003). Managing an XML warehouse in a P2P context. In *Proceedings of the 15th International Conference on Advanced Information Systems Engineering, Invited Talk* (pp. 4-13).

Abiteboul, S., Benjelloun, O., Manolescu, I. Milo, T., & Weber, R. (2002). Active XML: Peer-to-Peer data and web services integration. In *Proceedings of the 28th International Conference on Very Large Databases* (pp. 1087-1090).

Abiteboul, S., Benjelloun, O., & Milo, T. (2004). Positive Active XML. In *Proceedings of the ACM Special Interest Group on the Management Of Data Conference (SIGMOD)* (pp. 35-45).

Abiteboul, S., Buneman, P., & Suciu, D. (2000). *Data on the web*. San Francisco: Morgan Kaufmann.

Abiteboul, S., Cobena, G., Masanes, J., & Sedrati, G. (2002). A first experience in archiving the French web. In *Proceedings of the 6th European Conference on Digital Libraries* (pp. 1-15).

Abiteboul, S., Manolescu, I., & Preda, N. (2004). *Constructing and querying P2P warehouses of XML resources*. Semantic Web and Databases Workshop (pp. 219-225).

Abiteboul, S., Preda, M., & Cobena, G. (2003). Adaptive on-line page importance computation. In *Proceedings of the 12th International Conference on the World Wide Web* (pp. 280-290).

Active XML home page. (n.d.). Retrieved January 5, 2005, from http://www-rocq.inria.fr/gemo/Gemo/Projects/axml/

Aguilera, V. (n.d.). X-OQL Homepage. Retrievable from http://www-rocq.inria.fr/~aguilera/xoql/

AXIS Homepage. (n.d.). Retrievable from http://ws.apache.org/axis/

Baril, X., & Bellahsene, Z. (2003). Designing and managing an XML warehouse. In *XML data management: Native XML and XML-enabled database systems*. New York: Addison Wesley.

BEA Liquid Data for WebLogic. (n.d.). Retrievable from http://www.bea.com/

Beeri, C., Elber, G., Milo, T. et al. (1998). WebSuite: A tool suite for harnessing web data. In *Proceedings of the WebDB Workshop* (pp. 152-171).

Buneman, P., Davidson, S., Fan, W., Hara, C., & Tan, W.C. (2003). Reasoning about keys for XML. *Information Systems, 28*(8), 1037-1063.

Ceeri, S., Fraternali, P., Bongio, A., Brambilla, M., Comai, S. et al. (2003). *Designing data-intensive web applications*. San Francisco: Morgan Kaufmann.

Chaudhuri, S., & Dayal, U. (1997). An overview of data warehousing and OLAP technology. *ACM SIGMOD Record, 26*(1), 65-74.

Cho, J., & Garcia-Molina, H. (2000). The evolution of the web and implications for an incremental crawler. In *Proceedings of the Very Large Databases Conference* (pp. 200-209).

Cho, J., & Garcia-Molina, H. (2002). Parallel crawlers. In *Proceedings of the World Wide Web Conference* (pp. 124-135).

Draper, D., Halevy, A., & Weld, D. (2001). The NIMBLE XML data integration system. In *Proceedings of the International Conference on Data Engineering* (pp. 155-160).

Dudouet, F-X. (2005). Sociology meets databases. *Ecole Grands Réseaux d'Interaction*. Paris.

e.dot Project. (n.d.). Retrievable from http://www-rocq.inria.fr/gemo/edot/

Faulstich, L., Spiliopoulou, M., & Linnemann, V. (1997). WIND--A warehouse for internet data. In *Proceedings of the BNCOD* (pp. 169-183).

Garcia-Molina, H., Papakonstantinou, Y., Quass, D., Rajaraman, A., Sagiv, Y., Ullman, J. et al. (1997). The TSIMMIS approach to mediation: Data models and Languages. *J. Intell. Inf. Syst. 8*(2), 117-132.

Golfarelli, M., Rizzi, S., & Vrdoljak, B. (2001). Integrating XML sources into a data warehouse environment. *IEEE SoftCOM,* 49-56.

Google Web APIs (n.d.). Retrievable from http://www.google.com/apis/

Halevy, A., Ives, Z., Madhavan, J., Mork, P., Suciu, D., & Tatarinov, I. (2004). The Piazza peer data management system. *IEEE Trans. Knowl. Data Eng., 16*(7), 787-798.

Halkidi, M., Nguyen, B., Varlamis, I., & Vazirgiannis, M. (2003). THESUS: Organizing web document collections based on link semantics. *Very Large Databases Journal, 12*(4), 320-332.

Hammer, J., Garcia-Molina, H., Widom, J., Labio, W., & Zhuge, Y. (1995). The stanford data warehousing project. *IEEE Data Engineering Bulletin, 18*(2), 41-48.

Hümmer, W., Bauer, A., & Harde, G. (2003). XCube – XML for data warehouses. In *Proceedings of the Sixth ACM International Workshop on Data Warehousing and OLAP* (pp. 33-40).

Maria, N., & Silva, M. (2000). Theme-based retrieval of web news. In *Proceedings of the WebDB Workshop* (pp. 26-37).

Marian, A., Abiteboul, S., Cobena, G., & Mignet, L. (2001). Change-centric management of versions in an XML warehouse. In *Proceedings of the 27th International Conference on Very Large Databases* (pp. 581-590).

Mignet, L., Barbosa, D., & Veltri, P. (2003). The XML web: a first study. In *Proceedings of the World Wide Web Conference* (pp. 500-510).

Myllymaki, J. (2002). Effective web data extraction with standard XML technologies. *Computer Networks, 39*(5), 635-644.

Nassis, V., Rajugan, R., Dillon, T. S., & Rahayu, J. W. (2004). Conceptual design of XML document warehouses. In *Proceedings of the 6th International Conference on Data Warehousing and Knowledge Discovery* (pp. 1-14).

Nguyen, B., Abiteboul, S., Cobena, G., & Preda, M. (2001). Monitoring XML data on the web. In *Proceedings of the ACM Special Interest Group on the Management of Data (SIGMOD)*.

Pokorný, J. (2001). Modelling stars using XML. In *Proceedings of the Fourth ACM International Workshop on Data Warehousing and OLAP* (pp. 24-31).

Pokorný, J. (2002). XML data warehouse: Modelling and querying. In *Proceedings of the Fifth International Baltic Conference on DB and IS* (pp. 267-280).

Raghavan, S., & Garcia-Molina, H. (2001). Crawling the hidden web. In *Proceedings of the S7th International Conference on Very Large Databases* (pp. 129-138).

Rusu, I., Rahayu, J., & Taniar, D. (2005). A methodology for building XML data warehouses. *Int. J. of Data Warehousing & Mining, 1*(2), 23-48.

SOAP Version 1.2: Primer. Retrievable from http://www.w3.org/TR/2003/REC-soap12-part0-20030624/

Universal Description, Discovery and Integration of Web Services (UDDI). Retrievable from http://www.uddi.org

The W3C Web Services Activity. Retrievable from http://www.w3.org/2002/ws/

Web Services Definition Language (WSDL). Retrievable from http://www.w3.org/TR/wsdl/

Xyleme, L. (2001). A dynamic warehouse for XML data of the web. *IEEE Data Engineering Bulletin, 24*(2), 40-47.

Widom, J. (1995). Research problems in data warehousing. In *Proceedings of the International Conference on Information and Knowledge Management* (pp. 25-30).

Widom, J., & Ceri, S. (1996). *Active database systems: Triggers and rules for advanced database processing*. San Francisco: Morgan Kaufmann.

Zhu, Y., Bornhövd, C., Sautner, D., & Buchmann, A. (2000). Materializing web data for OLAP and DSS. *Web-Age Information Management* (pp. 201-214).

Chapter IV

Text Warehousing: Present and Future

Antonio Badia, University of Louisville, USA

Abstract

Data warehouses, already established as the main repository of data in the enterprise, are now being used to store documents (e-mails, manuals, reports, etc.) so as to capture more domain information. In order to integrate information in natural language (so-called unstructured data) *with information in the database* (structured *and* semistructured data), *existing techniques from Information Retrieval are being used. In this chapter, which is part overview and part position paper, we review these techniques and discuss their limitations. We argue that true integration cannot be achieved within the framework of Information Retrieval and introduce another paradigm, based in Information Extraction. We discuss the main characteristics of Information Extraction and analyze the challenges that stand on the way of this technology being widely used. Finally, we close with some considerations on future developments in the general area of documents in databases.*

Introduction

Data warehouses (DWs) are already established as an important tool for understanding and improving business practices in organizations. Usually, DWs feed from smaller, transaction-oriented databases that an organization already has in place to take care of day-to-day business. Lately, however, it has been realized that this information by itself may not be enough to support decision-taking. Additional sources of information are then sought. There are two main types of sources to achieve *data enrichment*: external and internal. External data sources bring in information about the environment of the organization (state of the market, competitors, overall economical and technological trends), while internal sources bring additional insight about the workings of the organization. Often, this additional information (both external and internal) comes from documents. Consequently, interest in managing text, especially for applications within business intelligence (decision support, CRM) has grown enormously in recent years, due to the realization that a great deal of business information resides in documents like e-mail messages, memos, internal manuals, sales reports, etc. This is the basic reason to bring text into the DW: The practice of *enriching data* could be substantially improved. Furthermore, documents usually contain not only information about what happens, but about *why* things happen.

Database vendors have responded to this trend by adding to their flagship database systems modules for text management (Oracle Text in Oracle 9i — to be called Oracle Multimedia in 10g — and Text Extender in DB2 v8). These modules are based on Information Retrieval (IR) techniques, essentially creating an inverted index for a collection of documents and allowing SQL to query this index. This approach has been sanctioned by the latest SQL standard, which includes basic text search capabilities in the WHERE clause of SQL queries. However, IR approaches have clear limitations that restrict their usefulness for decision-support.

In this chapter, we overview the integration of datasets and text as is presently implemented with the use of IR technology. We then show the shortcomings of this approach, and argue that true integration of information can only happen if the information in texts is analyzed at a deeper level than IR allows. Information Extraction (IE) is a new technology that addresses this issue by doing a focused, basic analysis of document contents. While IE may be the right technology to substitute IR, its widespread use depends on the solution of some challenging technical issues which we present and discuss.

Note that we consider only the case in which the DW contains both structured or semistructured information besides documents; the case of a DW with documents alone (a *document* or *text database*) is also interesting, but we argue that the case covered here is of even more interest, and of wider applicability. Our overall goal is to integrate the information in documents with the information in the tables of a DW. Thus, our goal is different from that of document management. This field considers documents as objects with a lifecycle (creation, evolution and archive or destruction), and pays special attention to issues like editing and versioning (Sutton, 1996). While there are certainly areas of overlap (for instance, the management of document metadata), our focus is different and thus, so are our issues.

Background: Databases and Text

To incorporate documents into a data warehouse, one must design the same components as for traditional data (Kimball, 1996). In particular, all the standard elements of the ETL (extraction-transformation-load) process must be present (Kimball & Caserta, 2002): First, it is necessary to find sources of documents, and to establish the contents and capabilities of those sources; next, one must specify procedures for retrieving the documents into the warehouse. This includes querying the sources according to their capabilities (i.e., do they accept SQL?), determining when the sources offer *new* documents (not already retrieved) and physically moving the documents into the warehouse. Transformations may also be needed, as in the case of regular data: Some formats may have to be processed, some documents may need cleaning. For instance, e-mail messages may have to be stripped of headers attached to them by different programs; documents in PDF or Word may be stripped from their formatting, leaving only the text. In some cases, documents may be stored both as they originally are and in some standardized, cleaned way. Then, it is necessary to determine how documents are to be stored. Since documents may vary substantially in size (from a small Web page to a large manual) this is a complex decision. Simplifying considerably, two typical options are to store the document outside the database software that supports the warehouse, leaving pointers to the location inside the database, or to store the document inside the database. We explore this second option only, as it seems to be the most accepted nowadays. The manner in which the documents are stored depends on the options offered by the database system being used; we describe a typical scenario for a relational database. For each document, there are two parts that we need to store: the document itself, and its metadata. The document itself is usually stored as an attribute in a table, as most RDBMS now support storage of large binary objects and large character binary objects or CLOBs (Melton & Simon, 2002). Documents are very rich in metadata, and posses several types: traditional metadata (like information about sources, size, etc.), content metadata (like title, subject, description and format) plus other metadata proper of documents (for instance, information about versions, author, etc.) (Sullivan, 2001). While there is no absolute agreement on what constitutes adequate content metadata, standards like the Dublin Core are usually considered the reference (Dublin, 2004). A data warehouse would ideally capture all these different types of metadata. Note that a data warehouse usually has a metadata repository, which contains information about the data in the warehouse (Kimball, 1996; Kimball & Caserta, 2004). While some document metadata may go into that repository, other should go into tables. Thus, depending on the amount of metadata present and the degree of normalization desired, the typical option is to create one or more tables that include as attributes the document itself and all other metadata. When several tables are needed, it is usually possible to create a small star schema (Kimball, 1998), with the fact table being the one holding the documents, and different types of metadata stored in dimension tables: One dimension may correspond to content metadata, another one to storage metadata yet another one to author information (Sullivan, 2001).

However, what really characterizes a document is its content, which is in some natural language and therefore cannot be easily analyzed with traditional database tools. In order to deal effectively with document content, Information Retrieval tools are used. Information retrieval (IR) treats a document as an (unordered) bag of words and does not carry out any syntactic or semantic analysis. Each document in a collection is scanned, tokenized (i.e., divided into discrete units or tokens), stopwords (words that appear in each document and carry no meaning, like "the" or "and"') are dropped and the rest are normalized (stemmed). This involves getting rid of word inflections (prefixes, suffixes) to link several words to a common root (like "running" and "run"); it usually involves quite a few manipulations, like normalizing verbal forms. Thus, each document ends up as a list of "content" words. Each word is then substituted by a number that represents the importance of the word in the document (usually simply a count of how many times the word appears) and in the collection (usually, the inverse of the fraction of documents where the word appears). As a result, the document is seen as a vector $<t_1,...,t_n>$ where each t_i represents the weight given to the ith term in the document.

Technically, let D be a collection of documents, and let T be the collection of all terms in D. The *term occurrence frequency* (tf) is the number of times a term appears in a document. For term t in T, document d in D, we denote the occurrence frequency of t in d as tf(t,d). The intuition is that if t occurs frequently, then it is likely to be very significant to d. The *inverse document frequency* of t (in symbols, idf(t)) is computed as the fraction of documents where t appears out of all the documents. The idf tries to account for the fact that terms occurring in many documents are not good discriminators. In fact, some experiments have shown that words that occur too frequently or too infrequently are not good discriminators (the latter because they have lower probability of being used). A tf-idf weight is a weight assigned to a term t in a document d, obtained by combining tf(t,d) and idf(t). Simple multiplication may be used, but most of the time a normalization factor is also introduced in the calculation. Basically, this makes different weights comparable by neutralizing document length (without the normalization, longer documents — which tend to have higher tfs — would dominate the collection).

A query in natural language can be represented as a vector, just like a document. That is, non-content words are thrown out, stemming is used, possibly words are grouped into phrases and weights assigned to each term by the system. When the query consists simply of a list of keywords (the usual case in IR), transforming it into a vector is trivial: We simply set to 1 the terms that appear in the query, and all others to 0. Answering a query, in this context, means finding document vectors which are the closest to the query vector, where "close" is defined by some distance measure in the vector space. A possible distance measure is the dot product of two vectors. If the vectors are binary (a 0 or 1 reflecting presence/ absence of a word in a document is used instead of a tf-idf weight), this value gives the number of terms in common. However, this measure favors longer documents which will be likely to have more terms, i.e., to be represented by less sparse vectors. To remedy this, another measure called the cosine function is used. Intuitively, this measure gives the cosine of the angle between the two vectors in the vector space; in this representation, two vectors with no common terms should be orthogonal to each other. While it has been found that the cosine function favors short documents over long ones, it's still the most widely used measure (it is difficult to determine how to deal best with document length: There is a difference between a document being longer because it treats more topics, and being longer because it repeats the same message more times, i.e., redundancy).

Extensions to this basic framework abound. For instance, some systems accept phrases. Technically, phrases are n-grams (that is, n terms adjacent in the text) that together have a meaning different from the separate terms (for example, "operating system"), and hence are terms on their right. However, to discover phrases may be complicated, so not all systems support this option. Other systems use approximate string matching in order to deal with typos, misspellings, etc. which may be quite frequent on informal messages (like e-mails) due to the lack of editorial control.

One significant advantage of using a measure function as a similarity measure is that the documents retrieved can be ranked or ordered according to this measure. When the number of documents is large (which is usual), the user can focus on only the top k results (or the system may retrieve only the top k results). This is one of the most outstanding differences between IR and database systems, since in database systems the answer to a query is a set (unordered collection) of tuples or other elements (even in object-oriented databases, where ordered lists can be returned as answers, the ordering has nothing to do with a notion of ranking; all elements of the answer are equally important and fully justified to be in the answer (Catell et al., 2000)).

To support the efficient implementation of the vector-space concept, most systems rely on the idea of an *inverted index* (Belew, 2000). Given a collection of documents, each document is analyzed as explained earlier (tokenized, and perhaps other additional steps). Then, an index is built by creating a sorted list of terms; for each term, a list of document identifiers (the documents where the term appears) is kept. This is the simplest form of inverted index. One can also keep, for each term and document, the number of occurrences. Or, even more, one can keep the position(s) where the term appears (this makes it possible to support proximity queries, where the user asks that some term appears near others). These indices are very useful as they support both Boolean searches and vector-space searches. However, such an index may grow very large, and it may also be hard to maintain if the collection of documents is not static (in any sense: if the collection grows and shrinks and/or if the documents already in the collection can be edited). Note that in typical IR applications (libraries) the collection is static, but in modern applications (i.e., the Web) this is not the case at all. Therefore, a lot of research has gone into compression and maintenance of the index (Belew, 2000; Chakrabarti, 2003).

To evaluate the performance of an IR system, two main metrics are used: *recall* and *precision*. Recall is the ratio of relevant documents that are retrieved to the total number of relevant documents (in other words, the fraction of relevant documents actually retrieved). Precision is the ratio of relevant documents that are retrieved to the total number of retrieved documents (that is, the fraction of documents retrieved that is actually relevant). It is common that when recall increases, precision decreases. That is, when we retrieve more documents, we increase the probability of retrieving more relevant documents, but we also tend to retrieve more irrelevant documents. By convention, if no documents are returned precision is considered 1 but recall is considered 0. As the answer set grows bigger, recall will increase, but precision is likely to decrease.

Note that all these measures depend on knowing the set of all the documents that are truly relevant to a query. In practice, this is very problematic, as it would involve defining relevance and examining the whole collection. Relevance seems to be a subjective concept (what is relevant to one user may not be to another), and thus quite hard to formalize. Therefore, these measures are idealizations. In principle, determining all documents relevant to a query, independent of any particular user, could be achieved with a corpus carefully annotated by a set of diverse experts. However, the effort required to fully annotate large collections, and to ensure that annotations form a consensus, is so large that it is very infrequent to have such collections. Only the TREC conferences and a few research centers have managed to create collections of this nature (TREC, 2003).

Integrating IR and Databases

Most RDBMS provide integration support for Information Retrieval at several levels: at the physical level, integrating inverted indices with regular database indices, and allowing storage of documents inside the database (as stated above, most RDBMS now support storage of large binary objects, which can be used to store documents), and at the language level, allowing IR-style querying to be used within SQL. This integration allows, at the logical level, the definition of a DW where documents are an integral part of the database contents. The usual approach is to create one or several tables for documents, as explained above. Each table contains metadata (that is, information about the document, as opposed to about its contents: authors, source, size, medium and others) and the document itself. This approach allows querying of metadata and content at the same time (for instance, a query like *find all documents authored by someone in Marketing that mention "volatile items" and "revenue"* could be answered in this setup), as well as relating information in other tables with information about documents through joins. It is also a preferred setup because documents, as explained before, are rich in metadata. The latest SQL standard also strongly supports this approach by defining a FullText Abstract Data Type (ADT) that takes care of accessing the contents of the document (Melton & Simon, 2002). This ADT has two attributes: content and language. Usually, the content is a CLOB to allow for large values. The content attribute is only usable within the methods of the ADT. Casting is allowed (with functions like FullText_to_Character()). Searches can be carried out, IR style, on the content, for individual words, specific phrases, patterns and, if a thesaurus is present, broader or narrower term and synonym expansions are allowed; besides looking for the given keyword, broader terms (narrower terms, synonyms) that appear in the thesaurus are used in the search too. Searches are implemented using the CONTAINS predicate in the WHERE clause of SQL queries. CONTAINS takes as argument a character-string literal, which is used to express the pattern the user is looking for and the predicates that indicate how the pattern is to be applied to the text (some examples follow). The standard also includes additional schemes for the thesaurus (with tables like TERM_DICTIONARY, TERM_HIERARCHY, TERM_SYNONYM and TERM_RELATED), and an additional type for patterns: FT_Pattern type is a *distinct* type based on CHARACTER

VARYING. The standard contains a large number of complex patterns. One can also create a hierarchical division of the document by defining what a "section" or a "paragraph" are — useful for queries that want to focus the search on (or restrict it to) a certain part of the document.

This example is from (Melton & Simon, 2002): imagine the table created by the command:

```
CREATE TABLE DVD_info (
 title VARCHAR(100);
 stock_number INTEGER;
 notes FULLTEXT)
```

Then the following searches are allowed:

```
SELECT stock_number
FROM DVD_info
WHERE notes.CONTAINS('STEMMED FORM OF ``funny"
            IN SAME SENTENCE AS
            SOUNDS LIKE "lions") = 1
```

This query illustrates several features supported by IR-style retrieval: It searches for occurrences of any word with the root "fun" that appear in the same sentence as any word that sounds similar to "lion" (as determined by the Soundex algorithm or similar method). The next query shows an important ability of IR systems, that of ranking the results of a search:

```
SELECT score(1), stock_number
FROM DVD_info
WHERE notes.CONTAINS ("'carpet'" , 1) > 0
ORDER BY score(1) desc;
```

The CONTAINS predicate returns a number representing the rank, which is bound to the number 1; the predicate "score(1)" then retrieves this number. Note that the ORDER BY clause (which already existed in SQL) allows the result to be ranked. Finally, when a thesaurus is present, searches can be extended beyond words appearing in the document to words that are related (according to the thesaurus) to those words; the following query is an example of such conceptual search:

```
SELECT stock_number
FROM DVD_info
WHERE notes.CONTAINS('IS ABOUT ``horror''') = 1
```

This example assumes a thesaurus where the concept "horror" is linked to other, narrower terms that form a hierarchy rooted under "horror"; each word in this hierarchy would be checked against the documents.

Limitations of IR Approaches

The IR-based approach has severe limitations, since all information available is what terms appear in what document. Given that terms are (at best) second-order indicators of the content of a document, analysis of document content is very difficult in this framework. Also, the vector-space approach presents some issues of its own. We overview briefly some of the difficulties inherent to the IR approach.

One of the problems with the vector-space approach outlined before is that the number of dimensions in the space equals the number of terms in all documents. However, any given document is unlikely to contain all terms, or even a large part of them. As a result, each vector representing a document is usually sparse, with many zeroes for all the terms not appearing in a given document. Also, when we make each term a dimension, we are implicitly assuming that terms are independent of each other. However, this is rarely the case: Some terms may be highly correlated to others, and this is masked by giving each of them independent dimensions (for instance, synonyms are clearly terms that should be given a unique, shared dimension). Because of this, there are several techniques that attempt *dimensionality reduction*, that is, to reduce the number of dimensions used to represent documents by switching from terms to something else. One of the most well-known techniques for reducing dimensions is called *latent semantic indexing (LSI)* and is based on a linear algebra technique, singular value decomposition (SVD) (Berry & Browne, 1999; Belew, 2000). Without entering into technical details, SVD looks at the collection as a term-document matrix—where the dimensions are the number of documents and the number of terms, and each cell contains the number of appearances of a given term on a given document. As explained above, this matrix is bound to be sparse; SVD can be seen as a compression technique. Given n total terms in a corpus, SVD will create a matrix with k < n entries, where each document is represented by a vector in k-space, instead of n-space. Each of the k factors is uncorrelated to any other. But the factors do not correspond to the original terms exactly. Rather, they capture hidden correlations among terms and documents. Terms that were not close in the original n-space may be close now in the k-space because they co-occur frequently in documents deemed similar. Consider the terms *"car," "driver," "automobile"* and *"elephant"* (this example is from Berry and Browne, 1999). If "car" and "automobile" co-occur with many of the same words, they will be mapped very close (or to the same dimension) in the k-space. The word "driver," which has some relation, will be mapped to a somewhat close dimension. The word "elephant," which is unrelated, will be mapped to a different dimension. Thus, even though something is lost (because only k < n dimensions are retained), hopefully what is lost is noise, since we picked the most important``patterns''.

Ideally, the set of terms for a corpus should be exhaustive (have terms for all the topics any user may want to search for) and specific (have terms that help identify the relevant documents for any topic). However, both measures are in tension; there exists a trade-off between them. In effect, if an index is exhaustive, recall is high but specificity may suffer (if we associate many keywords with a document, we increase its chances of being retrieved, but precision may go down); if the index is not very exhaustive we can achieve high precision, but recall may not be very good. Note that this analysis concerns the corpus (i.e., the documents); if we look at the user's queries, the set of terms used there may be different. Thus, there may be a mismatch between terms used in queries and terms in the corpus; this is called the *vocabulary mismatch* (Belew, 2000).

Any approach based on the appearance of particular words has to deal with issues like synonyms, homonyms, ambiguity, and lack of context. One route that has been tried to attack the problem of relations among words (homonyms, synonyms and similar relations) is a *knowledge-based* approach, the use of a *thesaurus*. A thesaurus is a list of words together with a set of relationships among those words. There are some other relationships that all thesauri have: a "broader, more general term" or superclass relationships, and its inverse, the "narrower term" or "more concrete," or subclass relationship. Besides this, a "synonym" relationships may connect synonyms, and an "antonym" relationship may connect antonyms. Other semantic relationships may also exist, like "related term." Some thesauri will, at higher levels in the hierarchy of terms, have a "'theme" or "topic" relationships that relates abstract words (like "war") with words that are connected to some aspect of the topic that the abstract words represents (like "weapons," "strategy" or "history"). Note that this connection is very informal and may link words that are only somewhat related; some words are related to other words only in a particular context.

Thesauri can help deal with the issue of word relationships; but they present significant problems of their own. The most important are:

- Thesauri incorporate a classification/ontology in their relationships. There is usually more than one point of view of all but the simplest domains; different users may have different views and a given thesaurus represents but one. When a domain is standardized, this issue does not come up, but many domains are not standardized. Since most thesauri are fixed in the classification (i.e., terms cannot be changed from category to category) there is no way to overcome this problem.

- Thesauri are difficult to build and maintain. There are two main methods in building thesauri: manual (which is labor-intensive, slow and must deal with subjectivity issues) and automatic. Automatically-constructed thesauri are usually built using some machine-learning mechanism. Statistical methods are based on co-occurrence; but this approach has limitations, as it is not clear what the semantic relationship among co-occurring words is. Heuristics are usually added to such methods, but state-of-the-art procedures still require extensive supervision (Chakrabarti, 2003).

- Thesauri are limited; they cannot capture all semantic relationships for a natural language. Even on those relationships they capture, the situation may be more complex than the thesaurus indicates: Some terms, A and B, may be related only on a certain context. Most thesauri do not capture context. There are going to be failures, then, when using thesauri. However, there is no agreed-upon mechanism to deal with such failures.

From our point of view, the most important limitation of IR systems is their lack of semantic understanding, which makes it impossible to analyze the meaning of the information in the documents. This in turn harms their integration with the information in the database. As an example, assume a stockbroker database on company acquisitions. There is a table BIDS(bidder, target, date, price, character), where bidder is the company bidding to acquire another company, target is the company that is to be acquired, date and price are as expected and character is one of "hostile," "friendly" and "neutral." There is also a collection of documents, extracted from news feeds, that we use to complement the database table contents. Assume we want to query our database for all information known about a certain acquisition. We can query the information in the tables with SQL, and we can do a search with an IR system for the words "bid" and synonyms or related words (like "takeover"). However, what is returned by both searches is very different, not only in structure (rows of structured information in one case, documents in the other) but in character: The information in the database is guaranteed to be relevant to the SQL query, while the information in the document may or may not be relevant. The documents may not be about acquisitions at all, even if they contain some relevant words (note that an IR search in this same document would contain the right words, but this is not a document about takeovers). We need to extract relevant information only from the document, and if possible, we need to structure it. Another way to see this problem is to assume that our goal is to build a method that would update our database table automatically from the information in the documents (since, once in the table, all information is available to users through SQL). For this, we need more than the presence of certain words. One article may contain the following sentence: "Oracle has announced a bid to acquire PeopleSoft." For an IR system, the sentence above is indistinguishable from the following: "PeopleSoft has announced a bid to acquire Oracle" (systems that hold word offsets (positions) would be able to tell the difference, but such information is not currently used in IR systems to make these types of distinctions, only to implement the predicate NEAR). However, both sentences express clearly different content, and they should generate different tuples. Also, if we want to find out the character of a bid, it is not enough to look for certain words: "Oracle has announced a bid to acquire PeopleSoft. It is a friendly bid." and "Oracle has announced a bid to acquire PeopleSoft. It is not a friendly bid." both contain the word "friendly" but are opposite in meaning (further, note that "not" would be probably considered a stopword and ignored in most IR systems, rendering both sentences basically equivalent). Of course, the system could select documents where the right words appear, and present them to a human who could easily make such judgments. However, when the number of documents is large, this is clearly not a good solution. Also, note that some documents may be quite large, and all the relevant information may be contained in a few sentences. With the architecture sketched above, only single documents can be returned as answer to a query. To combat that, some systems offer partial solutions, like highlighting key terms in the documents (which facilitates searching for the relevant paragraphs) or summarizing it. However, these solutions are not standardized and are highly system-dependent. In fact, summarization is an active area of research, so standards are unlikely to appear any time soon.

Information Extraction

Information extraction (IE) systems are given a collection of documents, and a set of templates with slots to be filled. The templates determine what information we are looking for in the collection. Each document is analyzed using shallow parsing and other techniques like finite-state machines in order to carry out *entity extraction* (determining which entities are named or referred to in the text), *link extraction* (determining how the extracted entities are connected or related) and *event extraction* (determining what events are being described by the entities and links uncovered). The final goal is to fill in as many slots in the templates as possible using the information discovered.

An IE system is composed of a tokenizer, a morphological and lexical processor, a syntax analyzer and a domain or semantic analyzer (Patienza, 1997). The tokenizer breaks down the text into tokens (words); this is called *word segmentation* and is a similar initial step to the one taken by IR systems. The morphological and lexical analyzer (MLA) does part of speech tagging and word sense tagging: The first annotates each word with its grammatical function in a phrase (for instance, noun, adjective or verb) and thus requires shallow or light parsing. The second identifies when a word has different senses (and possibly grammatical functions), which one is being used and assigns a certain category to nouns: IE systems need not only identify names, but also to classify them as one of a certain class (e.g., company, product or organization). Usually a lexicon is used to start with: This is a simple thesaurus, a list of words with some simple information per word — inflections, possible syntactic categories, senses and real-world categories. The MLA does lookups on the lexicon to find the words in the text and tag them; at this point some ambiguity is dealt with. Part of speech taggers can be statistically- or rule-based; the best are correct about 95% of the time (Israel & Appelt, 1999). The MLA also has to give lexical features to lexical items that are not simple (composed of more than one word), like dates, times, numbers, locations and proper names. Proper numbers and spatial and temporal expressions are particularly important and difficult: These are large, open-ended classes in almost any language, and there are no simple rules as to what characterizes an item in each of the classes. To recognize names, *hidden Markov models (HMM),* as well as finite state rules, have been proposed. HMMs basically use a finite state model that incorporates probabilities in the transition function, derived from a training corpus. The underlying finite state machine is followed and the path with higher probability is chosen. For instance, the word "John" followed by the word `"Smith." has high probability of being a proper noun, but followed by "Deere" has high probability of denoting a company (Israel & Appelt, 1999).

Even after part-of-speech tagging, word sense disambiguation is still necessary; usually part-of-speech simply reduces possible readings but does not disambiguate. This is due to the multiple meanings that can be given to some nouns (i.e., interest) and verbs (i.e., run). Most techniques for word sense disambiguation are based on examining terms near the target term, their position and part-of-speech tag. Supervised learning algorithms can be used to try to distinguish word senses from such features.

The syntax analyzer tries to do shallow parsing: it only parses for main constituents of simple fragments, and only in fragments of interest; typically, it finds the verb and noun phrases of a sentence that contain recognized entities. Most prepositional phrases (starting with prepositions, conjunctions or relative pronouns) are discarded unless they fit some pattern. However, some of them (starting with prepositions "of" and "for," for instance) are usually relevant, and a second phase analysis is used sometimes to handle this more complex cases. Relative clauses (starting with "that") attached to the subject of a clause may or may not be analyzed. Coordination is hard to handle and therefore ignored most of the time: "The company invested $2 million and set up a joint venture" (VP conjunction), or "The company and the investors agreed to set up a joint venture" (NP conjunction) are simple cases and can be handled, but most IE systems do not handle disjunction. There is no attempt to organize these parts into higher-order structures (i.e., how they make up sentences and paragraphs). Usually grammars are also finite state machines. This is robust and efficient; full parsing has been tried and found slow, error prone and, many times, useless. Even though shallow parsing overlooks some parts of the text, may err and sometimes produces partial results, all systems use it instead of full parsing (Israel & Appelt, 1999).

The domain analyzer deals with some of the hardest problems in IE systems. It uses the information from previous phases to extract application-specific relationships and event descriptions and fill in the templates mentioned earlier to create the output. This is a very hard task that depends on the informational content of the documents (usually, documents created to present factual information — manuals, news — work much better than others), the complexity of the templates and the amount of knowledge available in the lexicon and other resources. This phase, like the others described before, can be attacked through a knowledge-engineering or a statistical approach. However, success on this task has been very limited so far. Rule-based strategies and learning-based strategies perform more or less the same, and neither one performs very well. Part of the problem may be that this part requires more in-depth analysis, and no good indicators are readily available with the light analysis that IE carries out. For instance, one of the hard problems the domain analyzer must deal with is that of *co-reference*: two or more expressions that refer to the same entity, or whose referents are related somehow. This is very common in natural language, especially in multi-sentence narrative. In the following example, all underlined expressions refer to the same person: "George Bush left the White House this morning. The president went to his ranch in Crawford, Texas, where he will spend the weekend." Co-reference is extremely difficult because of things like acronyms (IBM for international business machines), aliases (Big Blue), definite noun phrases ("the big computer company") and pronouns ("it"). Also, co-reference may apply to all kinds of entities, not just names but groups or collections ("The jury deliberated for only 15 minutes. It quickly decided Microsoft was a monopoly,") events (``the testimony was confusing; it didn't add to anything"), or abstract entities ("the case was interesting; it made headlines in all newspapers") (Israel & Appelt, 1999).

Another complex issue is how to use the information extracted to fill in the templates. The difficulty of this task is directly related to the structure of the templates: The simplest templates have one slot to fill and simply ask for some value for a property (for instance, a template that simply requests company names), but most templates ask for at least two values that must stand in a certain relationship; for instance, a template may ask for two values, one of them a company name, another a person name, where the person is the CEO of the company. Yet other templates involve n different values ($n > 2$), all of them related by being part of a specific event: for instance, as in our example, a template may request, for all "acquisition" events, information as to which company is the bidder, which company is the target, when the acquisition took place and what was the price paid. Note that some of the values may be temporal (like the one asking when the acquisition took place); as stated above, these may be very hard to obtain. In general, the larger the number of slots, the harder the task: Filling a template with a large number of slots may involve analyzing whole paragraphs, as the information may be disseminated among several sentences. Also, some information may simply not be present. Thus, IE systems need to get co-references right and deal with partial information.

IE does more than IR, since it pays attention to order (syntax) and other characteristics disregarded by IR. However, even though it uses some basic linguistic knowledge, IE is not full-fledged natural language processing (NLP). The difference between IE and full-fledged NLP is that in IE the task is to extract some predefined type of information from text. This implies that we can disregard all text that is determined not to be related to the target information. However, some NLP is needed because the type of information desired almost always involves a relational component, that is, two or more entities connected by some action or activity in which the entities play a certain role (for instance, in a crime there is a victim and a perpetrator). Thus, it is not enough to detect the entity, but it is necessary to look at the context to determine the role that the entity plays in a given relation (its relationship to other entities). For instance, it is relatively easy to identify people by searching for proper names, titles (Mr., etc.) and personal pronouns; thus, this search needs no context. But to identify a person as a victim of a crime (as opposed to a perpetrator, or to something else unrelated) it is necessary to pay attention to the context (Belew, 2000). Finally, IE is applied to large document collections; because of performance requirements, IE must use fast and robust techniques that perform well and deal with errors and incomplete information — many NLP techniques do not posses these characteristics.

As in the case of IR, it is very difficult to evaluate the performance of an IE system: This requires estimating, for a given collection of documents and set of templates, what is the maximum amount of information about the templates that can be obtained from the documents (that is, how many slots can be filled and in how many different ways). Even humans have difficulty with this task, and building a benchmark is difficult and time consuming (there may be no agreement among humans, e.g., some may consider the Red Cross a company, some may not). State-of-the-art seems to have stopped at around 60-80% of human performance. This assumes clean, grammatical text; text with noise (transcripts, etc.) has its own problems and may lower performance.

Combining Databases and IE in the Data Warehouse

Our ultimate goal is to integrate in depth the information in the database with the information in the documents. By "integration in depth," we mean an approach that achieves at least three things:

1. Information pieces in the database and the documents that are the same are identified and not repeated;
2. Information pieces in the database and the documents that are related are identified and linked; and
3. Answers that can be obtained from the joint content of the database and the documents are deduced.

As an illustration, we go back to our previous example: A system that could detect entities "Oracle" and "PeopleSoft," parse the phrase that contains them and find the verb and determine which company is the bidder and which one is the target would be able to integrate the information in the document with the information in table BIDS. It could also handle the problem with the sentence, "It is not a friendly takeover" — this, of course, assumes moderate reasoning capabilities, like identifying "not friendly" with "hostile." Thus, such a system could, in principle, be used to integrate the information in the documents and the information in the database. Clearly, IE systems are able to provide this functionality.

However, this integration is very difficult to achieve. A difficult issue here is that the information in documents and in databases is often of a very different nature.

A document tends to mention somewhat related but different facts, while tables in a database are collections of homogeneous facts. Moreover, text has an implicit, quite flexible structure, while the database has an explicit, rigid structure. Also, a database has mostly data (with some information in the schema), while a text may contain data, information and even knowledge[1]. Finally, determining when two entity descriptions refer to the same real-world entity (an ability required to achieve points 1 and 2 above) is an extremely difficult problem, which has generated much research but no definitive solutions so far (see the collection of papers in Elmagarmid et al. (1999) for a somewhat dated, but excellent, sample of such research).

There are two general strategies that could be followed to achieve the integration sought. The first one is to extract exactly the document information that can be added to the database and insert it into tables; this can be accomplished by limiting what is extracted from text to what fits in the database. The second one is to extract all possible information from the document (or everything the IE system can handle) and store the result somehow. However, in order to combine information fully, the information in the database should also be stored in a similar format, or a correspondence be explicitly drawn. A difficult issue that both strategies need to face is the identification of overlapping events, so as not to repeat information. For instance, if the database in our example has a tuple in the table BIDS with values ("Oracle," "PeopleSoft," "2004," "100B" and "hostile"), and one of the documents in the database contains information about this fact (as we assumed), then the information in the database and the information in the document should be combined, not repeated.

 In order to follow the first strategy, we could use an IE system with the right templates to automatically generate insertion statements into the database. Thus, templates should be generated such that they allow insertion of information in the tables of the database. This means that templates should (ideally) provide information for each attribute in the schema of a given table and nothing else. The obvious strategy here is to generate the templates from the database schema. In our example, we would generate a template called "BID" with slots for bidder, target, date, price and character. However, a disadvantage of this approach is that it may not be possible to fill such templates. Because natural language is very flexible, there may be more or less then the information requested in the text. One possibility is that there is not enough information to fill in all slots. Even if the right set of templates is developed, the document may simply not have all required information, so we must deal with a high probability of ending up with nulls in our tables (for instance, in our example there is no information about data and price, we only have values for attributes bidder and target). The use of nulls raises important questions about the semantics of SQL and is therefore highly undesirable (Date, 2003). The opposite problem happens when there is more information related to an event than the template requests. In our previous example, for instance, the sentence stating the bid of Oracle for PeopleSoft may be followed by another sentence like "On news of the bid, shares of Oracle were down, while shares of PeopleSoft went up." If our database contains no data on company shares, this information would not be sought. Thus, this approach is likely to lose some of the information present in the document. Doing so may dangerously narrow down the amount of information extracted from the documents. This is especially likely to occur, as we can see, taking into account our previous analysis of the differences between structured and unstructured data: The document is likely to contain data, information and knowledge all mixed up, while the database only has data (and hence templates generated from the database ask for data only). If the information is not ignored, though, an equally challenging issue is how to integrate it with information in the database; we discuss this point when describing the second strategy. Finally, if a single template with n slots is generated for an n-ary relation, the task of the IE system may be quite complex, especially for large values of n — and n would tend to be large in many databases. On the other hand, if several templates are generated from a single table, the information they provide must be put back together before an insertion can be made.

To explain the essence of this approach, we provide the following pseudo-code. This algorithm is quite high-level, and as such it hides several complex implementation issues, but it should provide the reader with an intuition of the overall organization of the strategy. The algorithm also introduces an extra step which would be necessary for real-life applications. We have suggested that appropriate templates could be generated from the database tables; however, in many relational databases the tables reflect not only the domain semantics, but also the result of the *normalization process* needed to convey real-world information in flat relations (Date, 2003). As a result of this process, information about real-world entities may be distributed on several tables, linked together by primary key-foreign key connections, which are a byproduct of normalization. For instance, in our previous example we used a table, BIDS, that has no such problem; but if we were to associate with each bid not just the original price, but the successive prices that offers and counteroffers would yield, we would need to split this information into two tables, BIDS(bidid, bidder, target, date, original-price, character), and BIDPRICE(bidid, price,date), where bidid is an identifier that could be system-generated. What is needed for the IE application, however, is a high-level view undisturbed by such details. This comes in the form of a *conceptual model*, like an entity-relationship (E-R) model, which underlies the database design (Thalheim, 2000). Fortunately, there are methods that, given the schema of a database, will reverse-engineer an underlying conceptual model, usually an E-R diagram. Such a method will, for instance, recognize that the two tables, BIDS and BIDPRICE, carry information about one and the same entity. The methods take as input a database schema and generate a conceptual (E-R) model as output, and also a mapping from elements in the schema of the database (tables) to elements in the model (entities and relationships). Because the mapping is reversible, it is possible to support operations in the model that can be translated then to operations in the database. In particular, the model can be populated with entities and relationships among them, and from this data and the mapping the original database can then be populated. We will use this ability in the following, where we assume that such a method is applied to the database schema, and the result is an E-R model and a mapping. The model is composed of entities (with attached attributes) and relationships among entities (possibly with attached attributes). We then generate templates from such a model, one template per entity and one per relationship (note how nicely this corresponds with the entity extraction and the link extraction tasks of an IE system).

In the algorithm, DB is the database and EM is the E-R model obtained from it; Ent(EM) is the set of entities in EM and Rel(EM) the set of relationships; Doc(DB) is the set of documents in DB. We assume that an IE system is available, that it takes as input a collection of documents and a set of templates and that it fills in slots in templates with the information found — a process called *instantiation*. Since each template may be instantiated more than once, we call the result of each instantiation an *instance* and refer to the set Ins(T) of all instances of a given template T.

1.   initialize empty set of templates T;
2.   generate E-R model EM and mapping F from the schema of DB;
3.   for each entity E in Ent(EM) do
4.   create template TR, adding a slot S for each attribute A in E;
5.   add template TR to T;
6.   for each relationship R in Rel(EM)
7.   create template TR', adding a slot S for each attribute A in E;
8.   add template TR' to T;
9.   run IE system on Doc(DB) with T;
10. for each template TR in T do
11.   for each instance I in Ins(TR) do
12.   create an entity or relationship instances appropriate from I by giving each attribute A the value in slot SA;
13. insert resulting data in DB using the inverse of the mapping F.

There are many improvements that may be added to this "naïve" approach. For instance, a thesaurus can be used in step 9 to bridge the gap between the vocabulary in the database schema (which gives the vocabulary of the E-R model) and the vocabulary in the documents.

An advantage of this approach is that it provides us with a query language (SQL) and a large body of knowledge about relational databases that can be reused in this context. Thus, such approach could be added to existing database management systems with minimal change to the database interfaces with users or applications.

The second strategy would still extract information from the documents in templates, but would then store the templates in such a way that no information is lost, regardless of database schema. As stated above, in order to combine information fully, the information in the database should also be stored in a similar format, or a correspondence be explicitly drawn. Also, this approach must determine which templates to fill, decide how to store and retrieve templates and develop a query language where structured (database) information and template information can be queried jointly. While this strategy has the potential to deliver more information than the first one, it must also face some tougher issues. The reason is that, as discussed above, content in documents freely mixes data, information and knowledge. An example of the difficult issues involved is the use of comparatives. Assume a document that says: "IBM made a bid for RedBrick on 2002; the price paid was the largest ever paid by IBM for an acquisition." Recall that one of the data items involved in our example was the price of the bid. The sentence above does not give a number, but it provides some information about the price. This information, however, cannot be captured in a relational database. And yet, it is perfectly legal in SQL to ask for the bid from IBM that has the largest price (among all IBM bids); this is easily expressible with an aggregate function.

 One of the biggest challenges for this approach, then, is to decide a representation mechanism that can handle all this information. A possible solution is to store extended templates in XML and use a schema where data (raw values) can be stored together with constraints in values and other information, perhaps in a manner similar to conditional tables (Abiteboul, Hull, & Vianu, 1995). This has the advantage of providing a very flexible data model, to which tables in the database can be easily converted. Also, it comes with a query language (Xquery) that can be used to extract the combined information. This would also solve the problem of storing and retrieving templates, as we could use the XML-handling capabilities of modern database management systems.

Another big challenge for this approach is determining which templates to fill. Since we have seen that creating templates using the database schema as guidance would fail to recognize related, but not identical, information, this solution is not satisfactory. Two strategies seem possible. One is to use the database schema as a *starting point*, but to add to the templates obtained in order to capture more information. If some source of knowledge is available, like a thesaurus or an ontology, such a source may be used to extend the templates. Another possibility is to develop an IE system that not only fills a given template, but also attempts to identify information related to the slots in the template and adds such information by adding slots and values to the given template. The second strategy would be to design an IE system that works without templates, simply capturing as much information as possible from the text. This approach would be guided by the text itself, and hence may be capable of gathering more information; however, without the initial guidance of some templates, such a system may be highly complex and inefficient. Moreover, in order to deal with large databases and large document collections, such a system should ideally not rely on manual procedures. Different learning methods are used to carry out IE tasks. Given the diversity of templates that one could generate, it is unlikely that one method proves superior to all others — as explained above, the complexity of the task depends on several factors, including template arity; different methods deal better with different levels of complexity. Therefore, such a system should be able to choose among several learning techniques and pick the one that performs better in a given scenario.

As before, we illustrate the approach with a high-level algorithmic description. In this case, we assume that the IE system being used has the ability to not only fill in the slots in a template, but also to generate additional slots (and corresponding values) when the relevant information is found in the text. Let Tab(DB) be the set of tables in the database.

1.   Steps 1-9 are as before.

2.   for each template TR in T do

3.   for each instance I in Ins(TR) do

4.   if (I has extra slots with respect to the original template)

5.   store I as an XML element;

6.   else create an entity or relationship from I as before;

7.   store all data from the E-R model into DB as before;

8.   for each relation R in Tab(DB) do

9.   store relation R in XML;

Note that this approach may store a template as a tuple in the database, but then it converts all such tuples to XML elements. The idea behind this redundant step is that it should make it easier to detect redundant information. Also, step 9 can be done in (at least) two different ways, but it presents no problems since a relation can be seen as a "flat" XML schema. The difficult part here is step 5, where an appropriate XML schema must be found to store all information coming from the IE system. In this case, the task is simplified by the fact that our templates originated within the database, and therefore are still more likely to contain data than information or knowledge. Finally, we note that in this case there is no need to worry about "denormalizing" anything, even if templates are allowed to contain sets of values, since XML can take care of such cases easily. As an example of the algorithm in action, recall the document containing the sentence: "On news of the bid, shares of Oracle were down, while shares of PeopleSoft went up." Since our database contains no data on company shares, this information would be added to the BIDS template only if the system could add slots like "bidder-shares" and "target-shares." If this were the case, the template cannot be inserted back into the entity BIDS, which originated from the table BIDS and hence has no attributes to hold this information. Thus, an XML element should be generated to hold the values for this template. In this simple case, the element would have a DTD similar to the following:

<ELEMENT BID (bidder, target, date, price, character, bidder-shares, target-shares>

In a simplified case like this, all elements are atomic, and their participation in the element BID is limited to being a single, required subelement. More complex examples would require more complex DTDs.

Finally, it must be pointed out that this second strategy opens up the possibility of developing a new query language. If all the information in documents cannot fit easily in tables, and templates must be stored as XML or as something else, the overall goal of total integration depends on having a query language which allows the user to query all the different parts of the database seamlessly. An ideal query language would allow all related information to be pulled out together, regardless of the form in which it is stored. However, in order to have good expressive power, such a language should be a superset of established languages for structured (SQL) and semistructured (Xquery) information; and on top of that the language should be able to deal with characteristics proper of documents: extensive text search facilities, integration of structure-based and text-based access, ability to rank and integrate answers, etc. Clearly, the design of such a language is extremely complex. Some initial attempts at adding full-text search capabilities to Xquery can be seen as a starting point (Amer-Yahia et al., 2004; Al-Khalifa et al., 2003); techniques aimed at supporting keyword searches in databases may also be used here (Agichtein & Gravano, 2003; Bhalotia et al., 2002). However, such languages are still based on an IR view of documents and cannot capture the extra information brought in by IE systems.

Future Trends

As stated in the previous section, there are still multiple challenges to a total integration of IE and database technologies. While there is active research in the area, commercial systems will probably evolve slowly by incorporating some features as market demands. There are already a large number of small, independent companies that offer document analysis tools based on IE techniques (Web sites like www.textanalysis.com provide information on a number of such companies). For the near future, IR technology is likely to continue dominating, especially since this is also an active area of research and therefore some of the limitations discussed earlier are being addressed — for instance, for the problem of dealing with a whole document, when only part of it is relevant (see Borkar et al., 2001; Hearts & Plaunt, 1993). At some point, though, the limits of IR will be reached and IE features will start showing up in commercial systems (a small but interesting sample of work in this direction is Agichtein and Gravano, 2003). Thus, it is likely that the market will see a smooth transition from one type of system to the other. What is not in doubt, though, is that interest in integrating databases and documents will continue to be strong and database systems will offer more and more capabilities in this respect. Research is likely to center on making IE methods more stable and offering better fallbacks for the cases not covered by any approach. Also, an increase in the quality of thesauri and dictionaries is likely to happen.

Interest in *text mining* is also going to increase considerably. Just like data mining is one frequent use of the data warehouse, text mining is also a primary consideration in gathering text information. However, true text mining (i.e., extracting previously unknown information from a set of documents) is rare; most text analysis involves feature extraction, thematic indexing, clustering and summarization. Neither of this truly qualifies as real text mining. True text mining methods, and mining methods that work on different data formats, are likely to be developed in the near future, and will fuel the demand for document warehouses (Berry, 2004).

In the end, the final goal is to control all the flow of information in the enterprise (Asprey & Middleton, 2003), so further connections among the areas of database, IR, IE, data and text mining and document management are likely to be explored in depth in the near future.

Conclusion

We have reviewed the integration of documents in data warehouses, which is currently based in the Information Retrieval paradigm. We have pointed out the limits of this approach, and proposed Information Extraction as a technology that will take systems to the next level. Challenges to this approach were sketched and discussed.

The importance of documents for databases in general, and data warehouses in particular, is bound to grow significantly in the near future. The demands of analysts will push the technology to go beyond the limitations of IR systems. Therefore, research in this area is likely to remain strong.

References

Abiteboul, S., Hull, R., &, Vianu, V. (1995). *Foundations of databases*. Boston: Addison-Wesley.

Agichtein, E., & Gravano, L. (2003). Querying text databases for efficient information extraction. In *Proceedings of the 19th International Conference on Data Engineering,* Bangalore, India. IEEE Computer Society.

Al-Khalifa, S., Yu, C., & Jagadish, H. V. (2003). Querying structured text in an XML database. In *Proceedings of the ACM SIGMOD Conference*, San Diego, CA: ACM Press.

Amer-Yahia, S., Botev, C., & Shanmugasundaram, J. (2004). Text-query: A full text search extension to Xquery. In *Proceedings of the WWW2004 Conference*. New York: ACM Press.

Asprey, L., & Middleton, M. (2003). *Integrative document & content management: Strategies for exploiting enterprise knowledge*. Hershey, PA: Idea Group Publishing.

Baeza-Yates, R., & Ribeiro-Neto, B. (1999). *Modern information retrieval*. New York: Addison-Wesley.

Belew, R. (2000). *Finding out about*. Cambridge, UK: Cambridge University Press.

Berry, M. (Ed.). (2004). *Survey of text mining: Clustering, classification and retrieval*. New York: Springer-Verlag.

Berry, M., & Browne, M. (1999). *Understanding search engines*. Philadelphia: SIAM.

Bhalotia, G., Hulgeri, A., Nahke, C., Chakrabarti, S., & Sudarshan, S. (2002). Keyword search and browsing in databases using BANKS. In *Proceedings of the 18ᵗʰ International Conference on Data Engineering (ICDE)*, New York. IEEE Computer Society.

Blair, D. C. (1984) The data-document distinction in information retrieval. *Communications of the ACM, 27*(4), 369-374.

Borkar, V., Deshmukh, K., & Sarawagi, S. (2001) Automatic segmentation of text into structured records. In *Proceedings of the ACM SIGMOD Conference*. Santa Barbara, CA. New York: ACM Press.

Catell, R. G. G. et al. (Eds.). (2000). *The object data standard: ODMG 3.0*. San Francisco: Morgan Kaufmann.

Chakrabarti, S. (2003). *Mining the web*. San Francisco: Morgan Kaufmann,

Date, C. (2003). *An introduction to database systems* (8ᵗʰ edition). Boston: Addison-Wesley.

Dublin. (2004). *The Dublin core metadata initiative*. Retrievable from http://dublincore.org/

Fellbaum, C. (1998). *WordNet: An electronic lexical database*. Boston: MIT Press.

Elmagarmid, A., Rusinkiewicz, M., & Sheth, A. (Eds.). (1999). *Heterogeneous and autonomous database systems*. San Francisco: Morgan Kaufmann.

Hearst, M. & Plaunt, C. (1993). Subtopic structuring for full-length document access. *Proceedings of ACM SIGIR Conference*. Pittsburgh, PA. New York: ACM Press.

Israel, D. , & Appelt, D. (1999). Introduction to information extraction. *Tutorial in the IJCAI-99 Conference*, available on the Web at www.ai.sri.com/~appelt/ie-tutorial/IJCAI99.pdf

Kimball, R. (1996). *The data warehouse toolkit*. Hoboken, NJ: John Wiley & Sons.

Kimball, R., & Caserta, J. (2004). *The data warehouse ETL toolkit*. Hoboken, NJ: John Wiley & Sons.

Maybury, M. (Ed.). (1996). *New directions in question answering*. Boston: AAAI Press/MIT Press.

Melton, J., & Simon, A. R. (2002). *SQL 1999: Understanding relational language components*. San Francisco: Morgan Kaufmann.

Patienza, M. T. (Ed.). (1997, July 14-18). Information extraction. In *Proceedings of the LNAI 1299, International Summer School, SCIE-97,* Frascati, Italy. New York: Springer-Verlag.

Sullivan, D. (2001). *Document warehousing and text mining.* Hoboken, NJ: John Wiley & Sons.

Sutton, M. (1996). *Document management for the enterprise: Principles, techniques and applications.* Hoboken, NJ: John Wiley & Sons.

Thalheim, B. (2000). *Entity-relationship modeling.* New York: Springer-Verlag.

TREC. (2003). *The text retrieval conference, national institute of standards and technology (NIST).* Retrievable from http://trec.nist.gov/

Endnote

[1]   Even though these terms are somewhat vague, there seems to be general agreement that a distinction exists between data (raw value, like "102"), information (data plus metadata that allows its interpretation, like "102 is someone's bodily temperature in Fahrenheit," or statements that relate several data items, like "Aconcagua is the highest mountain in the Western hemisphere") and knowledge (statements that relate information items, or provide metadata for information, like "a person's normal body temperature is about 98 degrees Fahrenheit," which would allow us to deduce that a person with 102 has a fever.

Chapter V

Morphology, Processing, and Integrating of Information from Large Source Code Warehouses for Decision Support

Jörg Rech, Fraunhofer Institute for Experimental
Software Engineering (IESE), Germany

Abstract

Source code occurs in diverse programming languages with documentation using miscellaneous standards, comments in individual styles, extracted metrics or associated test cases that are hard to exploit through information retrieval or knowledge-discovery techniques. Typically, the information about object-oriented source code for a software system is distributed across several different sources, which makes processing complex. In this chapter we describe the morphology of object-oriented source code and how we (pre-) process, integrate and use it for knowledge discovery in software engineering in order to support decision-making regarding the refactoring, reengineering and reuse of software systems.

Introduction

Traditionally, databases storing software artifacts were used to store manually classified components from in-house software systems. But as the manual classification of source code is time-consuming and costly, automated techniques for software retrieval and reuse are required to efficiently and effectively process large amounts of source code.

Today, we use *code warehouses* to store many software systems in different versions for further processing, which are very similar to the data warehouse framework described by Inmon (Inmon, 1996). Operational configuration management systems (CMS), similar to data marts, are tapped to integrate software artifacts into the code warehouse. Typically, these software repositories consist of a vast quantity of different files with interconnected source code and additional information associated with the source code (e.g., documentation). Extraction, transformation and loading processes (ETL) are used to extract the source code from different software repositories and varying languages and formats into the code warehouse. Due to the astonishing success and propagation of open source software (OSS) and large OSS repositories, such as Sourceforge (cf. http://www.sourceforge.net), many CMSs are freely available in different shapes and sizes. By tapping these operational code marts, large amounts of reusable software artifacts in diverse languages, formats and with additional information are available for further reuse, analysis and exploration.

But as code warehouses and single software systems grow larger, it becomes more complicated to decide on changes or enhancements. The complexity and dissimilarity of the source code has to be unified in order to adjust knowledge discovery (KDD) or information retrieval (IR) techniques. Tasks such as (agile) software reuse, refactoring or reengineering are increasingly more complex and intensify the need for decision support in SE (Ruhe, 2003). Techniques from artificial intelligence (AI) are being used in SE (Rech & Althoff, 2004) to support managerial decisions (e.g., where to focus testing effort) as well as design decisions (e.g., how to structure software systems). Several approaches for the discovery of knowledge to support decisions in software reuse and quality improvement have been developed (Rech et al., 2001), but support of decisions for reuse and refactoring based on large code warehouses is still unsatisfactory.

Figure 1. Data flow in the code warehouse

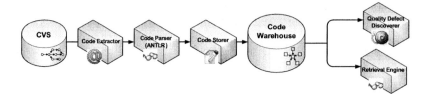

The architecture of the code warehouse as illustrated in Figure 1 depicts the flow of complex data, such as source code from a configuration management system (CMS) repository, into our code warehouse and beyond to support decisions. Data sources with source code content are typically known as configuration management systems; well-known representatives are CVS, Subversion or SourceSafe (Frühauf & Zeller, 1999). Typically, they manage several versions of a software system in order to return to previous versions if unsolvable problems occur. As shown in Figure 1, we extract source code via wrappers from a CMS, parse the code to extract structural information (e.g., classes, methods and attributes) and associated documents (e.g., license information) to finally integrate and store them in the code warehouse.

After the information is stored in the code warehouse, we use KDD and software analysis techniques to discover quality defects in a software system or retrieve source code or subsystems that might be used to build or improve a new software system. The extracted defects or similar software artifacts are then used to support decision making for refactoring, reengineering and reuse in software engineering.

In this chapter we describe the data our system is using and processing (i.e., object-oriented source code) and present the techniques to preprocess and integrate this data. The term "morphology" is used to describe the internal and external structure as well as relationships of source code elements. After a section about relevant background concerning software reuse and quality improvement (the two application areas for our system to support decisions), a section is used to describe the morphology of the used data. Furthermore, we present the techniques of how we integrate information from different sources, how we (pre-) process the data and how we use it in software engineering for defect discovery and source code retrieval. Finally, in the remainder of the chapter we give a short summary and outlook on future work.

Background

The reuse of existing knowledge and experience is a fundamental practice in many sciences. Engineers often use existing components and apply established processes to construct complex systems. Without the reuse of well-proven components, methods or tools, engineers have to rebuild and relearn these components, methods or tools again and again.

The discipline of *software engineering* (SE) was born in 1968 at the NATO conference in Garmisch-Partenkirchen, Germany (Simons et al., 2003), where the term "software crisis" was coined to describe the increasing lack of quality in software systems that were continuously growing in size. At the same conference the methodic reuse of software components was motivated by Dough McIllroy (McIllroy, 1968) to improve the quality of large software systems by reusing small, high-quality components.

Today, *reuse-oriented software engineering (ROSE)* covers the process of development and evolution of software systems by reusing existing software components. The goal is to develop complex software systems in shorter periods of time or with a higher quality by reusing proven, verified and tested components from internal or external sources. By the systematic reuse of these components and feedback about their application, their internal quality (e.g., reliability) is continuously improved. But reuse of components is only appropriate if the cost of retrieving and adapting the component is either less costly or results in higher quality than a redeveloped component.

Traditional Software Reuse

Since the eighties, the systematic reuse and management of experiences, knowledge, products and processes was refined and named *Experience Factory* (EF) (Basili et al., 1994b). This field, also known as *experience management* (Jedlitschka et al., 2002) or *learning software organization* (LSO), researches methods and techniques for the management, elicitation and adaptation of reusable artifacts from SE projects. The *component factory* (CF), as a specialization of the EF, is concerned with the capturing, managing and reuse of software artifacts (Basili et al., 1992) and builds the framework in which further knowledge discovery and information retrieval techniques are embedded.

In the beginning, only the reuse of source code was the focus of ROSE. Today, the comprehensive reuse of all software artifacts and experiences from the software development process increases in popularity (Basili & Rombach, 1991). Besides source code, artifacts such as requirements, design document, test cases, process models, quality models and best practices (e.g., design patterns) are used to support the development and evolution of software systems. These artifacts are collected during development or reengineering processes and typically stored in specific artifact-specific repositories.

Repositories for Software Reuse

In the nineties, research projects about software repositories were concerned with the development of software repositories with specific data models and interfaces for single organizations, for example: the Experience Factory of the SFB 501 (Feldmann, 1999), the "Experience Management System" (EMS) of the University of Maryland (Basili et al., 2002) and the "Repository in a Box" of the University of Tennessee under direction by the National HPCC Software Exchange (NHSE) (Browne et al., 1998). In-house products from software companies were, among others, ReDiscovery from IBM (IBM, 1994), the Workstation Software Factory (WSF) Repository from Bellcore (Shklar et al., 1994), the Semantic Hypertext Object Repository (SHORE) from sd&m (Zündorf et al., 2001) or the SEEE from Fraunhofer IESE (Althoff et al., 1999).

All of these approaches are based on manual classification of code and use either classification values or textual descriptions (e.g., manpages) for retrieval. A new approach is the Software Warehouse concept (Dai et al., 2004) that builds a framework for retrieval and mining activities but has currently only presented the software cube (i.e., data cube for software) as an innovation and needs manual classification to describe software artifacts (e.g., domain features).

Until now, relatively few approaches have exploited the information hidden in source code on a large scale. The success of open source software and the resulting availability of massive amounts of source code enabled this development. Several systems related to our research are described in the following list:

- A commercial project similar to the code warehouse has recently been introduced. The free source-code search engine, **Koders**, and its commercial subproject, KodeShare (http://www.koders.com/), offer the opportunity to search in source code of open source projects similar to the Google approach (i.e., a Web search engine). Koders has indexed the source code from tens of thousands of projects from free repositories in 15 different programming languages (e.g., ASP, C, C#, C++, Delphi, Fortran, Java, JavaScript, Perl, PHP, Python, Ruby, SQL, Tcl, VB and VB.NET) encompassing about 125 million lines of code. As no information was published about the inner working of Koders, we can only assess its offered functionality. The results presented after a free-text search indicate that

Koders not only indexes whole files containing classes but also parses their contents to identify methods and fields (a.k.a. attributes) as well as license information. Furthermore, it measures the lines of code (LOC) and calculates the cost to reproduce the code based on approximations of how many LOC are produced per month and the labor cost per month. In addition, one can browse through the file structures of the individual projects and identify or download parts of the source code .

- The research project **AMOS** (http://www.clip.dia.fi.upm.es/~amos/ AMOS/) follows a similar approach but uses a taxonomy (i.e., an ontology) for search terms defined by domain experts in order to enable the search over source code from predefined projects (Carro, 2002). The functionality of packages (e.g., source file, part of source file or collection of source files) is described manually, based on a predefined ontology (i.e., a dictionary of related terms). Interestingly, the search engine is also capable of integrating several single packages in larger packages encompassing the whole search query. As it only searches over the signature of the code, one can specify exact queries if the user knows what to look for. A more exploratory search based on code description, comments or identifiers is not possible.

- Another commercial project is DevX **Sourcebank** (http://archive.devx.com/ sourcebank/), that represents a directory of links to source code, scripts and papers from several sources around the Internet similar to the yahoo approach (i.e., a Web directory). It enables searching and browsing over these resources by a simple query interface and supports the restriction to a programming language. Results are viewable via a link to the original place (if it still exists) and typically include information such as title, author, description (e.g., the javadoc), language, URL and the date it was added to the repository. Currently, it has indexed 30,767 searchable and 12,873 browsable resources from free repositories in nine different programming languages (e.g., C, C++, Java, Perl, Assembler, JavaScript, ASP, PHP and XML) based on comments in the source code as well as several text-based sources (i.e., Web sites, research papers and articles). While this approach is great for programmers wanting to search in APIs (and one can even access the source code directly), the user gets no information on how to use it in a real context.

- Similar to the Sourcebank is DevDaily's repository search engine called the **Java Source Code Warehouse** (http://www.devdaily.com/java/ jwarehouse/). Currently, it has indexed source code from about 20 free java repositories, and its search is based on the Google™ search engine. Besides java, it supports the programming languages Ruby, PHP, Perl, C/ C++, Bourne shell scripts and CSS. The results presented after the Google-based search indicate it only indexes whole files containing classes, as filed in their subdirectories. In addition, one can browse through the file structures of the individual projects.

- Yet another code directory is **CodeArchive** (http://www.codearchive. com/), that offers topic and domain-specific browsing over 12 programming languages (Visual Basic, VB.NET, Java, JavaScript, Tcl/Tk, Linux, Delphi, PHP, Perl, C#, ASP and C/C++) and various application domains such as: controls, databases, encryption, algorithms, coding standards, applets and games. Projects and fragments were manually entered by volunteers, and the results after browsing or searching the archive include links to the source code or a compressed archive, requirements and comments.

- Finally, the project **JDocs** (http://www.jdocs.com/) is based on the open-source project **Ashkelon** (http://ashkelon.sourceforge.net/) and represents a type of repository that provides a knowledge base defined around the core Java APIs (Application Programming Interfaces). It does not include source code but gives access to a collection of 132 APIs from Java frameworks and libraries. These APIs are built from the javadoc of the projects and the search is powered by the open source search engine lucene (http://lucene.apache.org). Additionally, it is possible for users to annotate each individual project, class, field or method so that the knowledge in the javadoc API documentation can be enhanced by user-contributed questions, answers, tips, links, example code and other relevant information. While this approach is great for programmers wanting to search in APIs, two problems remain. First, one cannot directly access the source code described by an API element, and second, even if the user finds a relevant class or method, he or she has no information how to use it in a real context.

After we describe the background for software reuse and retrieval, the next subsections are focused on the background related to software quality improvement as well as quality defect and knowledge discovery.

Agile Software Development and Reuse

Agile software development methods impose as little overhead as possible in order to develop software as fast as possible and with continuous feedback from the customers. These methods (and especially extreme programming (XP)) are based upon 12 principles (Beck, 1999). We mention four of these principles as they are relevant to our work. *The Planning Game* is the collective planning of releases and iterations in the agile development process and necessary to quickly determine the scope of the next release. Knowledge about the existence of existing code elements or subsystems relevant to the project may be used to plan the scope of the next release. *Small releases* are used to develop a large system by first putting a simple system into production and then releasing new versions in short cycles. The more an engineer can reuse, the faster his work is done and the quicker the customer gets feedback. *Simple design* means that systems are built as simply as possible, and complexity in the software system is removed if at all possible. The more libraries are used and identified (via code retrieval), the less functionality has to be implemented in the real system. *Refactoring,* or the restructuring of the system without changing its behavior, is necessary to remove qualitative defects that are introduced by quick, and often unsystematic, development. Decision support during refactoring helps the software engineer to improve the system.

Traditional software reuse initiatives and approaches that were developed for process-driven software development are inadequate for highly dynamic and agile processes where the software cannot be developed for reuse, and reuse cannot be planned in advance. Teams and organizations developing with agile methods need automated tools and techniques that support their work without consuming much time. Therefore, *agile software reuse* is a fairly new area where minimally invasive techniques are researched to support software engineers (Cinneide et al., 2004). Especially in the refactoring phase, where the software is revised, automation can be used to detect *quality defects* such as code smells (Fowler, 1999), antipatterns (Brown et al., 1998), design flaws (Riel, 1996), design characteristics (Whitmire, 1997) or bug patterns (Allen, 2002). In this phase, techniques from KDD support refactoring of software systems (Rech, 2004) and techniques from knowledge management can foster experience-based refactoring (Rech & Ras, 2004).

Refactoring and Quality Defect Discovery

The primary goal of agile methods is the rapid development of software systems that are continuously adapted to customer requirements without large process overhead. Refactoring is typically done between development cycles and is a manual process to remove or weaken quality defects in order to improve the quality of software systems. Due to the fact that activities in software product maintenance account for the majority of the cost in the software lifecycle (Bennett & Rajlich, 2000), refactoring is an effective approach to prolong the software lifetime and to improve its maintainability. Especially in agile software development, methods as well as tools to support refactoring become more and more important (Mens et al., 2003).

Current research in the field of software refactoring is very active and has identified the use of metrics for refactoring as an important research issue (Mens et al., 2003). Previous research in refactoring has resulted in behavior-preserving approaches to refactor object-oriented software systems in general (Opdyke, 1992), tool support to automatically refactor or restructure applications (Griswold, 1991; Roberts, 1999) or methods for pattern-based refactoring (Cinneide, 2000).

Today, various methods for the discovery of quality defects are known. For example, inspections are used to discover defects in early development phases, code analysis is used to quantify code characteristics, testing is used to detect functional defects after implementation and coding standards are used to ensure quality attributes and prevent quality defects. Research by Simon on code smell discovery resulted in metrics-based and visually-supported quality assurance with a similarity measure (Simon, 2001) to reclassify classes and minimize inter-class coupling. Zimmermann and colleagues pursue the goal of supporting developers in maintenance activities by using a technique similar to case-based reasoning. In order to support software maintainers with related experiences in the form of association rules about changes in software systems, they mined association rules from a versioning system by collecting transactions, including a specific change (Zimmermann et al., 2004). Demeyer et al. proposed a framework to predict refactoring activities with time series analysis based on several metrics (Demeyer et al., 2000). Grant and Cordy proposed another approach to automatic code-smell detection by supporting a software developer in the rule-based discovery of code smells as well as the corresponding refactorings (Grant & Cordy, 2003). Finally, van Emden and Moonen analyzed code for two code smells and visualized them for manual discovery (Moonen, 2002).

All of the mentioned research approaches support specific kinds of manual and (semi-) automatic quality defect discovery techniques. None of these approaches are comprehensive in respect to what metrics or rules can be used to discover quality defects, or describe how refactoring experiences could be reused. In our approach, we develop models to detect quality defects with metrics or rules and support defect correction activities with tailored experiences.

Knowledge Discovery in Databases and Information Retrieval

Knowledge discovery in databases (KDD) (Klösgen & Zytkow, 2002) is concerned with the discovery of previously unknown information from large datasets. The discovery of knowledge is a process that may be divided into five sub-processes selection, preprocessing, transformation, mining and interpretation (e.g., validation and representation) (Fayyad et al., 1996). These sub-processes underpin the importance of clean data for the mining process (e.g., numerical without missing data) and the need for representation of clear, valid knowledge (e.g., visualization of clusters). The goals of KDD can be divided into the following groups:

- **cluster discovery** (e.g., answering "Are there related elements (methods in other systems)?");

- **class discovery** (e.g., answering "How to classify elements?");

- **association discovery** (e.g., answering "Do causal relations exist between elements (CMS transactions)?");

- **model discovery** (e.g., answering "Do valid causal models exist (for maintenance effects)?");

- **trend discovery** (e.g., answering "What will happen in x days (if using refactoring Y)?");

- **pattern discovery** (e.g., answering "Are there typical reoccurring structures (Are there reoccurring patterns like design patterns?)"); and

- **correlation discovery** (e.g., answering "Do correlations between measured variables (between effort and LOC) exist?").

Today, the term *data mining* (Witten & Frank, 1999) is often used as a synonym for KDD. While data mining (Witten & Frank, 1999) is the detection of previously unkown and hidden information in numerical data, various forms of mining exist that examine different types of data. For example, text mining (Berry, 2004) focuses on the extraction of knowledge from collections of long texts (e.g., books), while Web mining (Kosala & Blockeel, 2000; Hsu, 2002) specializes in typically small hypertexts (e.g., Web pages), clickstreams or log data. In this context, we classified *code mining* as a subfield of Web and text mining. Since source code may be seen as hypertext due to the fact that relations between classes or methods (e.g., function calls or inheritance relations) are analog to links, techniques from KDD, and especially Web mining, can be used in a similar way to exploit source code.

Mining in Software Repositories

Today, many application areas for KDD in SE have been established in fields such as quality management, project management, risk management, software reuse or software maintenance. Techniques, such as neural networks, evolutionary algorithms or fuzzy systems are increasingly applied and adapted for specific SE problems. They are used for the discovery of defect modules to ensure software quality or to plan software testing and verification activities to minimize the effort for quality assurance (Khoshgoftaar, 2003; Lee, 2003; Pedrycz & Peters, 1998).

For example, Khoshgoftaar et al. applied and adapted classification techniques to software quality data (Khoshgoftaar et al., 2001). Dick researched determinism of software failures with time-series analysis and clustering techniques (Dick, 2002). Cook and Wolf used the Markov approach to mine process and workflow models from activity data (Cook & Wolf, 1998). Pozewauning examined the discovery and classification of component behavior from code and test data to support the reuse of software (Pozewaunig, 2001). Michail (2000) used association rules to detect reuse patterns (i.e., typical usage of classes from libraries). As an application of KDD in software maintenance, Shirabad developed an instrument for the extraction of relationships in software systems by inductive methods based on data from various software repositories (e.g., update records and versioning systems) to improve impact analysis in maintenance activities (Shirabad, 2003). Zimmermann and colleagues pursue the same goal using a technique similar to CBR. In order to support software maintainers with related experiences in the form of association rules about changes in software systems, they mined association rules from a versioning system by collecting transactions including a specific change (Zimmermann et al., 2004). Morasca and Ruhe (2000) built a hybrid approach for the prediction of defect modules in software systems with rough sets and logistic regression based on several metrics (e.g., LOC).

Future research in this field is concerned with the analysis of formal project plans for risk discovery to acquire project information for project management, or directly mine software representations (e.g., UML and source code) to detect defects and flaws early in development.

Morphology of Object-Oriented Source Code

Until today, the functionality or semantics of a code element can not be extracted from the syntax of arbitrary source code and understood by a computer. A computer does not understand what an arbitrary algorithm like "quicksort" does. Nevertheless, valuable information may be extracted from associated and internal sources. While object-oriented source code is typically represented in a single file for every class of the system, inside these files additional blocks of information may be identified. For example, Java classes typically contain methods, attributes, comments or documentation in JavaDoc. Additional infor-

Figure 2. Structure and hierarchy of object-oriented source code

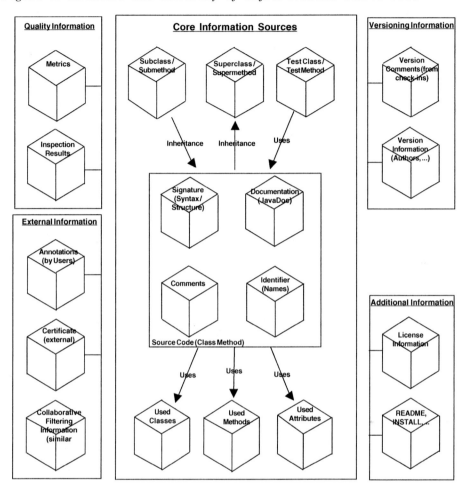

mation like introductory, readme, API or license documents is available from files residing in the project (or systems) repository. In Figure 2, every box symbolizes an individual block of information, which may be seen as a self-containing (or relatively independent) set of *features* (i.e., a "bag" of words or data). We call these sets of features *feature-spaces*. For further retrieval or mining processes, these feature-spaces have to be integrated to improve the characterization of raw source code data.

In the following description of information associated to source code, we refer to Java source code from open source projects and libraries found on the open source repositories Sourceforge (http://www.sourceforge.net/) and Freshmeat (http://www.freshmeat.net).

Object-Oriented Source Code

Object-oriented software systems consist of objects that package data and functionality together into units that represent objects of the real world (e.g., a sensor or string). These objects can perform work, report on and change their internal states and communicate with other objects in the system without revealing how their features are implemented. This ensures that objects cannot change the internal state of other objects in unexpected ways and that only the

Figure 3. Source code related structure of software projects

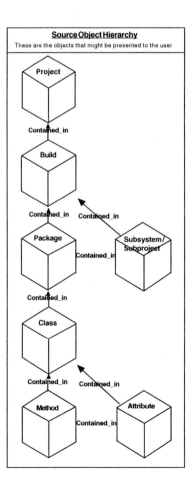

object's own internal methods are allowed to access their states. Similarly, more abstract building blocks, such as packages and projects, hide additional information that should not be visible to other resources in order to minimize maintenance effort if a unit has to be changed (e.g., if hardware such as a sensor is exchanged).

In software reuse, several of these units might be of interest to a potential user. The user might want to reuse a whole database (e.g., mySQL or PostgreSQL) or need a solution to implement a fast sorting algorithm (e.g., quicksort). Figure 3 shows several blocks that might be of interest to the user that are returned on a query. *Classes* describe these objects and group their functionality (i.e., their *methods)* and *attributes* into a single file. While every class of the system is grouped into a *package* that, in general, represents a subsystem, these subsystems are not defined in the source code. Furthermore, software *projects* are typically developed and improved over longer periods of time and stored in *builds* after specific tasks are completed (e.g., a release is finalized).

While most information blocks can be automatically extracted from the existing source code, several blocks might also be attached manually (e.g., subsystem information or annotations by (re-) users). Associated information may be integrated into retrieval and mining processes in order to improve their precision and recall.

Internal Structure of Source Code

While it is possible to write multiple classes in one file or use internal classes (i.e., a sub-class in a class) source code is typically encoded in classes that are written in single files. These files contain the description of their membership in a specific *package* and define which additional classes (beside sub-classes or package-neighbors) are needed and have to be *imported* in order to compile this class. Other information such as *method calls* or *inheritance relations* that describe external links and requirements of the code can be exploited with several techniques (e.g., the Pagerank algorithm (Brin & Page, 1998)).

Beside these external links, source code contains several internal information blocks. As depicted in Figure 2, these blocks build the core information sources to describe classes in the following order:

1. **Signature:** The signature of a method, class or attribute defines it name (i.e., an identifier), visibility (e.g., public) and inheritance relationships (i.e., used super-classes and interfaces). All these blocks represent valuable information sources but require additional processing to be useful. While relations and modifier (e.g., the visibility) are unambiguously defined for a

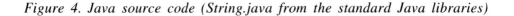

Figure 4. Java source code (String.java from the standard Java libraries)

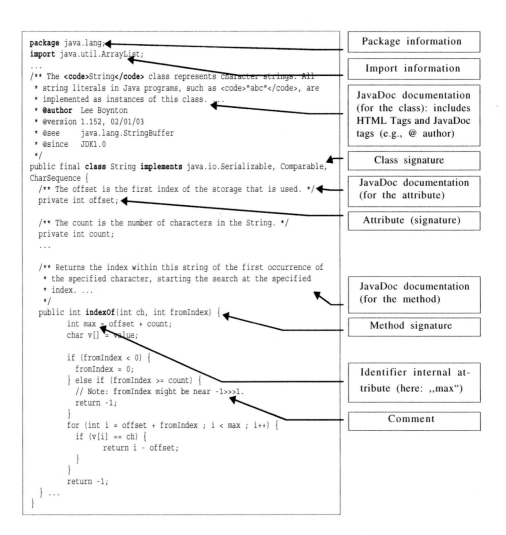

software system, the name of a class is basically free text and encoded in *camelcases* (e.g., "StringBuffer") that has to been parsed and normalized (e.g., into "string" and "buffer").

2. **Documentation:** The description of the artifact in a specific markup language (here JavaDoc with text in HTML and special tags (e.g., the @author tag is used to associate an author that created or modified (parts) of the code)). Other documentation markup languages exist for nearly every programming language (e.g., ePyDoc for Python or doxygen for

multiple languages). As the documentation is based on a specific markup language, the semantic of the text within is semi-structured and specific parsers for HTML or JavaDoc-Tag help to extract additional information (e.g., links to related documents).

3. **Comments:** Single or multiple line comments represent, in general, either notes of the developers to describe the specific code semantics or declared dead source code (that should not be executed but might be used in the future). Typically, there is no structure in comments and they can be seen as free text fields.

4. **Identifier:** Names and types of variables, constants or methods defined in a software system and used in a class represent additional information to characterize the semantics of the class or method. For example, the variable definition "public String authorName = 'Erich Gamma'" includes the information that the name about an author is stored in a string. Typically, in programming languages these identifiers are encoded in camelcases (e.g., "MalformedMessageException") or upper cases (e.g., "CLASS_NAME").

Figure 4 shows parts of the original source code of the "String" Class from the standard Java libraries.

Typical Information Associated to Source Code

Beside the internal information, additional information blocks can greatly contribute to the further processing of the source code. Software product *metrics* that are computed from the software system are used to describe the complexity (e.g., LOC or CC), coupling (e.g., CBO), cohesion (e.g., LCOM) or other characteristics of a method, class, package or project. Similarly, *inspection reports* are used to describe (potential) defects found during a manual inspection or audit. Furthermore, inspections may also be used to characterize the code on a subjective basis (e.g, rate the maintainability of a class on a scale from "very high" to "very low").

License information, typically stored in special files or in the header of class files, describes the context and conditions in which the source code might be used or reused. In general, there are three types of licence provisions: (1) gives free hand in the reuse (e.g., LGPL); (2) requires that the authors of reused code are named and license information is passed on (e.g., SISSL); and finally number (3) requires that the resulting product that uses the source code is also made open source (e.g., the GPL).

From configuration management systems, such as CVS, additional information about the exact version or change comments can be extracted. They are helpful in hiding older versions or might include helpful keywords for retrieval processes.

Processing and Integration of Source Code

As we have seen, object-oriented source code consists of textual, categorical and numerical data that may be exploited for further processing. But in order to use KDD or IR techniques on them, different information blocks must be further preprocessed and integrated.

Based on the information inside the code warehouse that was parsed and interconnected according to the source code, we create an index that stores several information blocks for every source code artifact. For example, we store the name, type, code, comments, documentation or signature after it is processed as described in the next subsection. Processing the code supports the identification, reduction and cleaning of characterizing features of the source code or an information block within. The integration is used to increase the expressiveness of features, to increase the number of similar and synonym features and to enrich the representation of results given to the end user.

Preprocessing Source Code for Retrieval Processes

In order to use retrieval or mining techniques on source code, the textual documents have to be further analyzed and processed. Source code, as many other semi-structured data sources, is enriched with special constructs and features with varying relevance.

Preprocessing of Identifiers in Source Code

In programming languages such as Java, names and identifiers of classes or methods indicate their functionality and are written in so-called camelcase (e.g., "QueryResultWrapper"; see http://en.wikipedia.org/wiki/CamelCase). To include the information enclosed in these special word constructs, filters have to be used to extract additional words (i.e., features) to further characterize the document.

The preprocessing of source code in our code warehouse is partitioned in nine phases as shown in Figure 5. First, we parse the textual data to identify tokens (i.e., everything that is not divided by whitespaces) and obtain a stream of these tokens that are processed by the following filters.

1.   The first filter decomposes identifier tokens java.sql.ResultSet into their subtokens java, sql and ResultSet before returning them to the next filter.

2.   The next Filter splits *camelcased* tokens like ResultSet into the subtokens Result and Set as well as IOException into IO and Exception. It also has the task that uppercase abbreviations like URL are not splitted, titlecase tokens like DATA_DIRECTORY are broken into DATA and DIRECTORY and that digits in tokens are associated with the previous subtoken (e.g., Index6pointer is broken into Index6 and pointer).

3.   After the camelcase filter, we change all uppercase characters in a token to *lowercase* (e.g., DATA, data or Data are all changed to data) in order to normalize different writing or coding styles (e.g., typically, constants in Java are written in titlecase).

4.   We then use the *cleaning filter* to remove unnecessary punctuation characters like commas or semicolons at the start or end of the token that might have been inserted at formulas (for example, name= or 'rech' from an expression like int name='rech' are changed to name and rech). Special

Figure 5. The processing sequence for Java source code

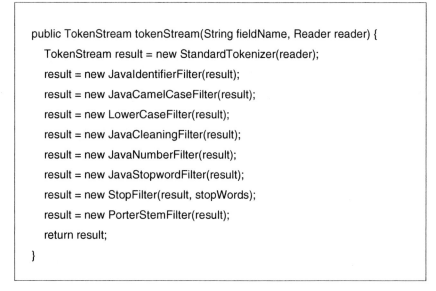

```
public TokenStream tokenStream(String fieldName, Reader reader) {
    TokenStream result = new StandardTokenizer(reader);
    result = new JavaIdentifierFilter(result);
    result = new JavaCamelCaseFilter(result);
    result = new LowerCaseFilter(result);
    result = new JavaCleaningFilter(result);
    result = new JavaNumberFilter(result);
    result = new JavaStopwordFilter(result);
    result = new StopFilter(result, stopWords);
    result = new PorterStemFilter(result);
    return result;
}
```

characters that represent multiplications, equals, additions, subtractions or divisions from formulas should be eliminated in this process (e.g., from a =b * c +d only a, b, c and d should get through).

5.   As detached *numbers* typically do not carry any meaning, the next filter identifies and removes tokens that, in the specified programming language, represent numbers like 0x000, .9 or -200 as well as Unicode characters like \u0123.

6.   After the cleaning, we use a programming-language-specific stopword filter to remove reserved words that are typically included in every code fragment of this language. For example, *Java stopwords* (a.k.a. reserved word) are abstract, package or boolean.

7.   After programming-language specific stopwords are removed, we also remove natural-language-specific stopwords from the token stream. Currently, we only remove *English stopwords* (e.g., and, into or will) as source code is almost exclusively written with English acronyms and comments.

8.   Finally, we use the standard *Porter stemmer* (Porter, 1980) to stem the remaining tokens (i.e., removing endings with ed or ing as in the words generated or billing) and reduce the number of available features with similar meanings.

Stemming and Anti-Stemming for Source Code

Beside the reduction of characterizing features from the source code, we also extract special features from the token stream during the processing phases.

Identifiers that typically name classes or methods are used in import statements to help the compiler in identifying the exact element that should be used in the program. In this context, *code stemming* is the reduction of identifiers to their stem, similar to normal language stemming (e.g., the Porter stemmer) and is used to extend the query focus. An identifier that specifies the path to the exact class in a hierarchy of packages can be used to integrate the information from classes in higher package. For example, we exploit the identifier "java.util.Arrays" that points to the class "Arrays" by looking into classes and subpackages of the "java.util" package.

Reversing the idea behind code stemming, we call the expansion of identifiers code *anti-stemming*. Multiple terms for abbreviated words are used to improve the query results by finding similar full words based on a dictionary. For example, if we have a token "calTemp" and split it into the subtokens "cal" and "temp" that do not represent valid stems of natural words, we use a dictionary to find words that might be abbreviations for the subtokens (e.g., "calculate" and "calibrate").

After this inflation we additionally use a stemmer in order to reduce the now larger set of features.

Integration of Distributed Information

In order to exploit information from several sources similar to the Pagerank algorithm Brin and Page (1998) used in Google™, the relations to superclasses, test classes or used classes are preserved to improve retrieval and mining results.

As depicted in Figure 2 and Figure 3, we use the signature, documentation, comments and identifiers to describe a source code artifact such as classes or methods. At first, we used this information to enable retrieval by matching keywords to the words in these four information blocks. But as keywords and natural text are typically very rare in source code, we use the ideas behind the Pagerank algorithm to integrate information from associated source code artifacts. In object-oriented programming languages there are several typed relations, such as inheritance, uses or calls. It is straightforward to integrate additional information from related elements as they carry additional information about the context or the functionality. For example, a method that uses the class java.awt.Graphics and calls a method drawOval might be helpful if one searches for a way to quickly learn how to draw something (especially circles) in Java.

Now, on the one hand, we have methods as drawOval that are called by many other methods that draw circles or ovals and include words that hint to their functionality (e.g., to draw something); therefore, this method would increase the bond to the words defined in the calling methods. On the other hand, we have methods that call many other methods (i.e., subfunctions) and aggregate their functionality into a higher functionality. Here, the method not only is defined by its own keywords but also by the keywords described in their subfunctions.

For retrieval, we defined and use the SourceRank (SR) and SourceScore (SS) algorithms as shown in Formula 1 and Formula 2. The SourceScore algorithm is similar to the Pagerank algorithm but does not calculate the weight from other SourceRank weights but from the SourceScore weight. In calculating the rank of an element E_0 (e.g., a class or method) it includes the sum of the SourceScore from all incoming connections (ISC) divided by the number of their outgoing connections to other source elements (OSC).

Formula 1. *The source rank algorithm:*

$$SR(E_0) \quad (1 \quad d) \quad d*(\sum_{i \ ISC(E_0)} \frac{SS(E_i)}{OSC(E_i)})$$

SR:	SourceRank
SS:	SourceScore
ISC:	Incoming Source Connections
OSC:	Outgoing Source Connections
D:	Dampening factor

Formula 2. *The source score algorithm:*

$$SS(E_0) \quad \frac{SK(E_0)}{sw} \quad \frac{DK(E_0)}{dw} \quad \frac{CK(E_0)}{cw} \quad \frac{IK(E_0)}{iw}$$

SK:	no. of Signature Keywords
DK:	no. of Documentation Keywords
CK:	no. of Comment Keywords

Other information, such as license or versioning, is only associated to the software artifact and integrated into the representation (e.g., the result list of a retrieval process). Furthermore, information about the quality of a software artifact such as metrics or inspection reports is currently not integrated into the presentation or retrieval techniques. We plan to modify the score or weight of an artifact based on its quality so that artifacts with higher quality are more dominant in the results.

Decision Support for Refactoring and Reuse

In order to support decisions about what to reuse or refactor in a software system, we developed several methods and techniques. Based on the previously described data structures, their relationships and integration strategies, we describe two environments to support decisions in software engineering.

Figure 6. Experience-based semi-automatic reuse of refactoring experiences

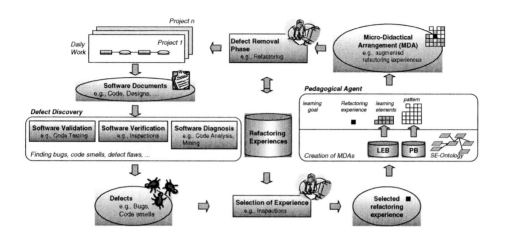

Decision Support in Software Refactoring and Reengineering

Our approach encompasses several methods in order to support the decision of where, when and in what sequence to refactor a software system as depicted in Figure 6. Beginning from the left upper corner and going counterclockwise, knowledge about quality defects from defect discovery processes is used to retrieve experiences associated to similar defects from previous refactorings. These experiences are used to handle quality defects in the defect removal phase. Additionally, suitable experiences are augmented by so-called micro-didactical arrangements (MDA) (Ras et al., 2005) that initiate learning processes and hence improve the experience's understandability, applicability and adaptability to the reuse context.

As shown in Figure 7, we define six phases, based on QIP (Basili et al., 1994a), for the continuous automatic discovery of quality defects. First, we start with the definition of qualities that should be monitored and improved. For example, this may result in different goals (i.e., quality aspects) as reusability demands more flexibility or openness while maintainability requires more simplicity. Phase two represents the application area for knowledge discovery in databases (KDD). It is concerned with the measurement and preprocessing of the source code to build a basis for quality defect discovery. Results from the discovery process (i.e., quality defects) are represented and prioritized to plan the refactoring in phase

Figure 7. Quality-driven metrics-based refactoring

three. Here, the responsible person has to decide which refactorings have to be executed in what configuration and sequence in order to minimize work (e.g., change conflicts) and maximize the effect on a specific quality. In phase four the refactoring itself is applied to the software system by the developer that results in an improved product. Phase five compares the improved with the original product to detect changes and their impact on the remaining system. Finally, in the sixth phase we report the experiences and data about the refactoring tasks, changes to the software system and other effects to learn from our work and continuously improve the model of relationship between quality, refactorings and quality defects.

As indicated previously, the KDD sub-processes are grouped in phase two. We select source code from a specific build, preprocess the code and store the results in the code warehouse, analyze the data to discover quality defects, discover deviations from average behavior, cluster code blocks with severe or multiple quality defects and represent discovered and priority-sorted quality defects to the user.

For example, suppose we detect a method in an object-oriented software system that has a length of 300 LOC. As described in (Fowler, 1999), this is a code smell called long method. A long method is a problem, especially in maintenance phases, as the responsible maintainer will have a hard time understanding the function of this method.

One suitable refactoring for the mentioned code smell might be the refactoring simply called *extract method*, wherein the source code of the Long Method is reviewed to detect blocks that can be encapsulated into new (sub-)methods. Experiences about the extract method refactoring are used to support the decisions where, when, how and if the refactoring has to be implemented. For example, the developer might remark that every block of code that has a common meaning, and could be respectively commented, could also be extracted into several smaller methods. Furthermore, the developer might note that the extraction of (sub-) methods from methods implementing complex algorithms can effect performance requirements of the software system and therefore might not be applicable.

Additionally, the generation of new methods might create another smell called "Large Class" (i.e., the presence of too many methods in a class) which might complicate the case even more. Finally, the new experiences are annotated by the developer and stored in the refactoring experience base.

While this example only touches a simple quality defect and refactoring, more complex refactorings influence inheritance relations or introduce design patterns (Fowler, 1999).

Decision Support in Reusing Software Artifacts

In software reuse, previously constructed source code is reused to save the time of redevelopment. Our goal is to support software developers, designers, analysts or testers in deciding what to reuse, to increase their options in what they could reuse and augment their decisions in reusing (parts of) software systems.

To support the reuse of such complex information as source code, we build a source code search component based on technology similar to Google™ but specialized for source code. The basic application is to find answers to questions such as "What does the quicksort algorithm looks like in C#?" or "How should the JDOM API be used?" By the integration of information about the inherited functionality, methods or licenses used, we can also support the user in the following questions:

- **May I reuse the source code found?** Based on the license information attached to the source code and a definition of the license, the user is informed if he or she may directly copy the code.

- **What do I need to make the code work in my context?** By seeing and browsing the associated relations (e.g., imports or method calls) the user can quickly oversee what libraries or functionalities have to be included in order to make the code work. Additionally, the documentation of the source code (e.g., javadoc) often describes the functionality and similar code fragments that might be used to decide the adaptation effort.

Figure 8. Screenshots from the Code Warehouse

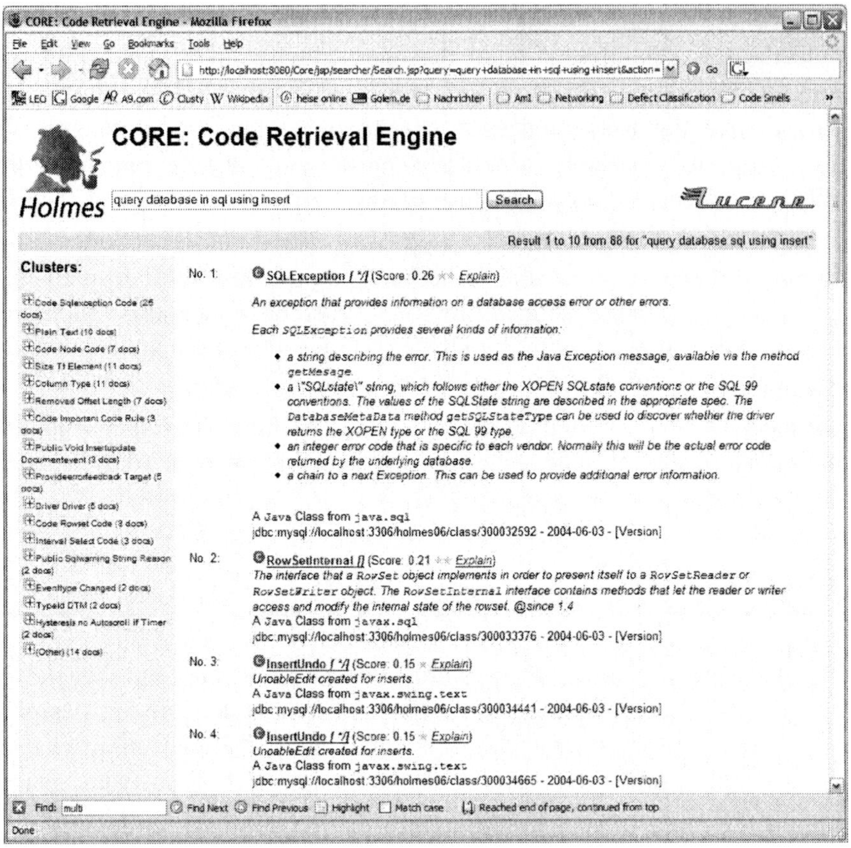

- **What is the quality of the code?** Based on the metrics data attached to the source code, the user might deduce qualities about the code. In the future, we will integrate the specification of quality models, for example, in order to calculate the maintainability of the code.

- **How do I test the functionality?** As test cases are associated with the respective source code, if they exist at all the user can easily get source code to test the reused functionality after appropriate adaptations.

As depicted in Figure 8, our system presents search results similar to Google and includes information such as the signature, license, type of language, project, version or documentation. The score is calculated by the underlying search engine and is essentially based upon the term frequency in the document and its length. Currently we also analyze techniques for the clustering of search results (e.g., see http://www.clusty.com) in order to give a better overview and discover similar elements.

Conclusion

Recapitulating, we described the morphology and complexity of object-oriented source code that we use in our approaches for decision support in software engineering. Based on the definition of our data (i.e., the source code) and its structure, we described the processes of how to integrate and (pre-) process this data from different sources. Finally, we gave two examples of how we use this base of information for decision support in quality defect discovery and software reuse.

Although we can integrate and use this complex information for several applications, we currently do not know if the system scales to large amounts of source code and how we integrate additional information, such as annotations, experiences or inspection reports. Yet another obstacle is the maintenance of source code in our warehouse, as changes to software systems are common and they invalidate the meaning of experiences with or annotations to older versions of source code. In a typical text retrieval context (i.e., Web search engine), this is similar to the question if old or defunct Web pages should be integrated into the retrieval process for current pages.

We expect to further assist software engineers and managers in their work and in decision making. One current research task is the feature selection and reduction in order to improve speed and preciseness of techniques such as self-organizing maps (SOMs) used for the clustering of the source code. One approach to enlarge the base of stopwords will be the extensive analysis of source code from Sourceforge to identify typical words used in most code artifacts (e.g., variables as temp). Planned extension to the techniques will be *trend discovery* based on system changes to detect problems in the software system as early as possible and to alert the quality and project manager about deviations from the plan. *Pattern discovery* based on the structural information of object-oriented source code will be used to detect typical patterns in the organization of source code (and maybe even new design patterns). Furthermore, we plan to use the retrieval part in order to support software architects during software design so that information about the planned system (e.g., in a class diagram) will be used to synthesize a query in order to retrieve software systems (i.e., subsystems or classes) that can be reused.

References

Allen, E. (2002). *Bug patterns in Java.* Berkeley, CA: Apress.

Althoff, K.-D., Birk, A., Hartkopf, S., Muller, W., Nick, M., Surmann, D. et al. (1999). Managing software engineering experience for comprehensive reuse. Paper presented at the SEKE'99. *Eleventh International Conference on Software Engineering and Knowledge Engineering,* Skokie, IL (pp. 10-19).

Basili, V. R., Caldiera, G., & Cantone, G. (1992). A reference architecture for the component factory. *ACM Transactions on Software Engineering and Methodology, 1*(1), 53-80.

Basili, V. R., Caldiera, G., & Rombach, D. (1994a). The goal question metric approach. In *Encyclopedia of software engineering* (1st ed., pp. 528-532). New York: John Wiley & Son.

Basili, V. R., Caldiera, G., & Rombach, H. D. (1994b). Experience factory. In J. J. Marciniak (Ed.), *Encyclopedia of software engineering* (Vol. 1, pp. 469-476). New York: John Wiley & Sons.

Basili, V., Costa, P., Lindvall, M., Mendonca, M., Seaman, C., Tesoriero, R. et al. (2002). An experience management system for a software engineering research organization. Paper presented at the *Proceedings of the 26th Annual NASA Goddard Software Engineering Workshop, 2001* (pp. 29-35).

Basili, V. R., & Rombach, H. D. (1991). Support for comprehensive reuse. *Software Engineering Journal, 6*(5), 303-316.

Beck, K. (1999). *eXtreme programming eXplained: Embrace change.* Reading, MA.

Bennett, K. H., & Rajlich, V. T. (2000). Software maintenance and evolution: A roadmap. Paper presented at the *Future of Software Engineering Track of 22nd ICSE,* Limerick, Ireland (pp. 73-87).

Berry, M. W. (Ed.). (2004). *Survey on text mining: Clustering, classification, and retrieval.* New York: Springer.

Brin, S., & Page, L. (1998, April 14-18). The anatomy of a large-scale hypertextual web search engine. Paper presented at the *7th International World Wide Web Conference,* Brisbane, Australia (pp. 107-117).

Brown, W. J., Malveau, R. C., McCormick, H. W., & Mowbray, T. J. (1998). *AntiPatterns: Refactoring software, architectures, and projects in crisis.* New York: John Wiley & Sons.

Browne, S., Dongarra, J., Horner, J., McMahan, P., & Wells, S. (1998, June 23-26). Technologies for repository interoperation and access control. In

Proceedings of Digital Libraries '98, Pittsburgh, PA (p. 408). New York: ACM.

Carro, M. (2002). *The AMOS project: An approach to reusing open source code*. Paper presented at the First CologNet Workshop on Component-Based Software Development and Implementation Technology for Computational Logic Systems, Madrid, Spain.

Cinneide, M. O. *Automated application of design patterns: A refactoring approach*. Unpublished doctoral dissertation. Trinity College, Dublin.

Cinneide, M. O., Kushmerick, N., & Veale, T. (2004). Automated support for agile software reuse. *ERCIM News*.

Cook, J. E., & Wolf, A. L. (1998). Discovering models of software processes from event-based data. *ACM Transactions on Software Engineering and Methodology, 7*(3), 215-249.

Dai, H., Dai, W. E. I., & Li, G. (2004). Software warehouse: Its design management and application. *International Journal of Software Engineering and Knowledge Engineering 14*(4), 395-406.

Demeyer, S., Ducasse, S., & Nierstrasz, O. (2000). Finding refactorings via change metrics. ACM. In *SIGPLAN Not.* (USA), 35(10), 166-177.

Dick, S. H. (2002). *Computational intelligence in software quality assurance*. Unpublished doctoral dissertation, University of South Florida.

Fayyad, U., Piatetsky, S. G., & Smyth, P. (1996). From data mining to knowledge discovery in databases. *AI Magazine, 17*(3), 37-54.

Feldmann, R. L. (1999). On developing a repository structure tailored for reuse with improvement. Paper presented at the Workshop on Learning Software Organizations (LSO) co-located with the *11th International Conference on Software Engineering and Knowledge Engineering, SEKE'99*, Kaiserslautern, Germany (pp. 51-71).

Fowler, M. (1999). *Refactoring: Improving the design of existing code* (1st ed.). New York: Addison-Wesley.

Frühauf, K., & Zeller, A. (1999, September 5-7). Software configuration management: State of the art, state of the practice. Paper presented at the *9th International Symposium on System Configuration Management (SCM 9) co-located with ESEC/FSE 99,* Toulouse (pp. 217-227).

Grant, S., & Cordy, J. R. (2003). *Automated code smell detection and refactoring by source transformation*. Paper presented at the International Workshop on REFactoring: Achievements, Challenges, Effects (REFACE), Victoria, Canada.

Griswold, W. G. (1991). *Program restructuring as an aid to software maintenance*. Unpublished doctoral dissertation, University of Washington.

Hsu, J. (2002). Web mining: A survey of world wide web data mining research and applications. *33rd Annual Meeting of the Decision Sciences Institute*. San Diego, CA, Decison Sci. Inst, 2002, CD ROM (p. 6).

IBM. (1994). *Software reuse: Overview and reDiscovery* (No. ISBN 0738405760).

Inmon, W. H. (1996). The data warehouse and data mining. *Communications of the ACM, 39*(11), 49-50.

Jedlitschka, A., Althoff, K.-D., Decker, B., Hartkopf, S., Nick, M., & Rech, J. (2002). The Fraunhofer IESE experience management system. *KI, 16*(1), 70-73.

Khoshgoftaar, T. M. (2003). *Software engineering with computational intelligence* (Vol. 731). Boston: Kluwer Academic Publishers.

Khoshgoftaar, T. M., Allen, E. B., Jones, W. D., & Hudepohl, J. P. (2001). Data mining of software development databases. *Software Quality Journal, 9*(3), 161-176.

Klösgen, W., & Zytkow, J. M. (2002). *Handbook of data mining and knowledge discovery*. New York: Oxford.

Kosala, R., & Blockeel, H. (2000). Web mining research: A survey. *SIGKDD Explorations, 2*(1), 1-15.

Lee, J. (2003). *Software engineering with computational intelligence*. New York: Berlin.

McIllroy, M. D. (1968, October 7-11). Mass-produced software components. Paper presented at the *NATO Conference on Software Engineering*, Garmisch, Germany (pp. 138-155).

Mens, T., Demeyer, S., Du Bois, B., Stenten, H., & Van Gorp, P. (2003). Refactoring: Current research and future trends. *Electronic Notes in Theoretical Computer Science, 82*(3), 17.

Michail, A. (2000). Data mining library reuse patterns using generalized association rules. Paper Presented at the *Proceedings of the 2000 International Conference on Software Engineering (ICSE 2000), Soc. Tech. Council on Software Eng*, New York (pp. 167-176).

Moonen, L. (2002). *Exploring software systems*. Unpublished doctoral dissertation, University of Amsterdam, Netherlands.

Morasca, S., & Ruhe, G. (2000). A hybrid approach to analyze empirical software engineering data and its application to predict module fault-proneness in maintenance. *Journal of Systems and Software, 53*(3), 225-237.

Opdyke, W. F. (1992). *Refactoring object-oriented frameworks*. Unpublished doctoral dissertation, University Illinois at Urbana-Champaign.

Pedrycz, W., & Peters, J. F. (1998). *Computational intelligence in software engineering*. River Edge, NJ: Singapore.

Porter, M. F. (1980). An algorithm for suffix stripping. *Program, 14*(3), 130-137.

Pozewaunig, H. (2001). *Mining component behavior to support software retrieval*. Unpublished doctoral dissertation, Universität Klagenfurt, Klagenfurt.

Ras, E., Avram, G., Waterson, P., & Weibelzahl, S. (2005). Using weblogs for knowledge sharing and learning in information spaces. *Journal of Universal Computer Science, 11*(3), 394-409.

Rech, J. (2004). Towards knowledge discovery in software repositories to support refactoring. Paper presented at the *Workshop on Knowledge Oriented Maintenance (KOM) at SEKE 2004*, Banff, Canada (pp. 462-465).

Rech, J., & Althoff, K.-D. (2004). Artificial intelligence and software engineering: Status and future trends. *Künstliche Intelligenz, 18*(3), 5-11.

Rech, J., Decker, B., & Althoff, K.-D. (2001). *Using knowledge discovery technology in experience management systems*. Paper presented at the Workshop "Maschinelles Lernen" (FGML), Universität Dortmund.

Rech, J., & Ras, E. (2004). Experience-based refactoring for goal-oriented software quality improvement. Paper presented at the *First International Workshop on Software Quality (SOQUA 2004)*, Erfurt, Germany (pp. 51-59).

Riel, A. J. (1996). *Object-oriented design heuristics*. Reading, MA: Addison-Wesley.

Roberts, D. B. (1999). *Practical analysis for refactoring*. Unpublished doctoral dissertation, University of Illinois at Urbana-Champaign.

Ruhe, G. (2003). Software engineering decision support - A new paradigm for learning software organizations. In F. Maurer (2003). *Advances in learning software organizations* (vi+2113, 2104-2013, 2024). Berlin, Germany: Springer-Verlag.

Shirabad, J. S. (2003). *Supporting software maintenance by mining software update records*. Unpublished doctoral dissertation, University of Ottawa, Ottawa, Ontario, Canada.

Shklar, L., Thattle, S., Marcus, H., & Sheth, A. (1994, October 17-20). The infoharness information integration platform. Paper presented at the the *Second International WWW Conference '94*, Chicago (pp. 809-819).

Simon, F. (2001). *Meßwertbasierte Qualitätssicherung: Ein Generisches Distanzmaß zur erweiterung bisheriger Softwareproduktmaße* (in German). Unpublished doctoral dissertation, Brandenburgische TU Cottbus, Cottbus.

Simons, C. L., Parmee, I. C., & Coward, P. D. (2003). 35 years on: To what extent has software engineering design achieved its goals? *IEE Proceedings Software, 150*(6), 337-350.

Whitmire, S. A. (1997). *Object-oriented design measurement.* New York: John Wiley & Sons.

Witten, I. H., & Frank, E. (1999). *Data mining: Practical machine learning tools and techniques with Java implementations* (1st ed.). San Francisco: Morgan Kaufmann.

Zimmermann, T., Weißgerber, P., Diehl, S., & Zeller, A. (2004). *Mining version histories to guide software changes.* Paper presented at the 26th International Conference on Software Engineering (ICSE), Edinburgh, UK, September 2003.

Zündorf, B., Schulz, H., & Mayr, D. K. (2001). *SHORE – A hypertext repository in the XML world.* Retrieved, January 3, 2005 from http://www.openshore.org/A_Hypertext_Repository_in_the_XML_World.pdf

Chapter VI

Managing Metadata in Decision Environments

G. Shankaranarayanan, Boston University School of Management, USA

Adir Even, Boston University School of Management, USA

Abstract

This chapter describes the implications for managing metadata, a higher-level abstraction of data that exists within repositories, applications, systems and organizations. Metadata is a key factor for the successful implementation of complex decision environments. Managing metadata offers significant benefits and poses several challenges, due to the complex nature of metadata. The complexity is demonstrated by reviewing different functions that metadata serves in decision environments. To fully reap the benefits of metadata, it is necessary to manage metadata in an integrated manner. Crucial gaps for integrating metadata are identified by comparing the requirements for managing metadata with the capabilities offered by commercial software products designed for managing it. The chapter then proposes a conceptual architecture for the design of an integrated metadata repository that attempts to redress these gaps. The chapter concludes with a review of emerging research directions that explore the contribution of metadata in decision environments.

Introduction

Metadata is data that describes other data. It is a higher-level abstraction of data that exists within repositories, applications, systems and organizations. Metadata is not a new concept and is typically associated with the "database catalog" or "data dictionary" — a component of database management systems that describes the database structure and constraints (Elmasri & Navathe, 2003). While the data dictionary is an important metadata component, it is only a small part of what we understand as metadata today. Metadata is more complex and has important managerial implications that are not yet well understood. Academia has examined metadata in the context of the Semantic Web (Berners-Lee, 1997) and industry experts have explored the technical requirements of metadata in data warehouses (Marco, 1998; Inmon, 2000; Imhoff, 2003). However, very few have attempted to understand and quantify the value of metadata in decision support environments. Metadata implementation in such environments is demanding, expensive and the end-result is rarely satisfactory. Investments in metadata solutions are hard to justify economically — metadata is primarily perceived as a technical necessity and its value to management is not apparent. Experts claim that metadata can improve decision making and enhance organizational knowledge (Marco, 2000; Stephens, 2004). These claims have rarely been validated.

The objective of this chapter is two-fold. First, we describe the current state of metadata in decision environments. We then highlight the changing perception of metadata as a useful tool for supporting business professionals in decision making. The section *Metadata in Complex Decision Environments* examines metadata from a functional perspective and offers a categorization of metadata that demonstrates the myriad of different functions that metadata serves. *Metadata Management in Commercial Data Warehousing Products* describes the benefits of metadata, as well as the challenges with implementing/ managing metadata. The challenges are further underscored by highlighting the mismatch between the capabilities offered by commercial products for managing metadata and the functional requirements necessary for managing metadata. An integrated metatdata repository attempts to address these challenges. A conceptual design for the integrated metadata repository is presented along with a set of alternative approaches for implementing it. The section entitled *Applications of Metadata* draws attention to recent trends that radically change the perception of metadata — from a technology component, useful for data management and integration, to a powerful aid that supports managerial decision making. Two metadata types — quality and process — are shown to aid managerial decision making, specifically in the context of analytical, data-driven decision tasks. Several interesting research questions to guide future research on metadata are raised in the last section, *Conclusion*. The chapter uses the data warehouse as an example of a complex decision environment in which metadata management is critical. However the concepts introduced in this chapter are not exclusive to data warehouses and may be generalized to other decision environments as well.

Metadata in Complex Decision Environments

This section examines metadata from a functional perspective and illustrates the different roles of metadata in a complex decision environment. Managing metadata is critical for the success of decision environments such as data warehouses (Kimball et al., 1998; Marco, 2000) and for ensuring the quality of the data within (Jarke et al., 2000). Metadata serves many different needs in complex decision environments. This has motivated attempts to classify and categorize metadata. Kimball (1998) distinguishes between metadata supporting *back-end* data processing and metadata supporting *front-end* data delivery. Marco (1998) classifies metadata as *technical* metadata useful for system and data administrators and as *business* metadata that end-users find useful when using the data, applications and systems. Imhoff (2003) classifies metadata as *business, technical and administrative*, where administrative metadata includes data necessary to manage the overall performance of the decision environment, such as audit trails and performance metrics. The above classifications do not help us completely understand the functionality of metadata.

The taxonomy presented here (first introduced in Shankaranarayanan & Even, 2004) extends the above classification schemes and classifies metadata in a more granular manner. The taxonomy is based upon functionality categories: infrastructure, data model, proisare further classified along the previously defined perspectives: business versus technical and front-end versus back-end.

- **Infrastructure metadata:** Infrastructure metadata (Table 1) contains data on system components and abstracts the infrastructure of the information system. It is used primarily for system administration, maintenance and enhancements.

- **Data model metadata:** Model metadata (Table 2), also known as data dictionary, includes definitions of the data entities maintained and the relationships among them. The data dictionary captures storage information at different levels, such as databases, tables and fields. As a data integration solution, the data dictionary includes the modules necessary for

Table 1. Infrastructure metadata

	Business	**Technical**
Back-End	• Business identification of systems • URLs	• Maintenance of hardware, OS and Database servers • Network protocols and address configuration • Database administration and configuration parameters
Front-End	Similar to the above	Similar to the above

Table 2. Data model metadata

	Business	**Technical**
Back-End	• Business interpretation of data items	• Data structure, which depends on the storage type – e.g., text files, RDBMS or data streams. • Elements specific to RDBMS storage – tables, fields, indices, views, stored procedures and triggers • Mapping source data elements to the data warehouse
Front-End	• "Semantic Layer" of naming and definitions of data items in "business" language • Reports contents and format	• Mapping data items to tables, fields,or file locations • Data extraction syntax • Syntax for joining multiple data sources • Mapping of data elements to user applications.

"vocabulary mapping" across multiple user-groups or business units. It also includes the semantic layer necessary to translate source data elements to their data warehouse representation, and the business terms needed for end-users to interpret the data elements.

- **Process metadata:** Process metadata (Table 3) abstracts information on data generation, describing how data items were transferred from sources to targets and what manipulations were applied during transfer. Process metadata serve both technical and business users — IT professionals use it for activating and managing the ETL (extraction, transformation and loading) processes, while business managers use it to assess data sources and understand the manipulations applied. Shankaranarayanan et al. (2003) propose the information product map (IPMAP) as a technique for representing the processes in the manufacture of an information product by adopting the information product approach defined by Wang et al., (1998).

Table 3. Process metadata

	Business	Technical
Back-End	• Business interpretation of data transfers: source-target mapping, new fields, integration, aggregations and filtering • Process charting (IPMAP) • Data cleansing business rules	• ETL software, engines and APIs • Implementation of business rules • Data transfer schedule and monitoring • Source/target schema adjustment • Data cleansing utilities
Front-End	N/A	N/A

Table 4. Quality metadata

	Business	Technical
Back-End	• Definition of measurements • Actual measurements	• Utilities for automated data quality assessment
Front-End	• Presentation of quality measurement • Quality dimensions and reporting	• Making quality metadata available for reporting and data analysis utilities

The IPMAP allows the decision maker to visualize not only the widespread distribution of data and data processing resources, but also the flow of data elements and the sequence by which they were processed. It is discussed in detail with an example in section 4.

- **Quality metadata:** Quality metadata (Table 4) contains quality-related information on the actual data stored and helps with assessing the quality of the data. It would include factual measurements, such as the number of records stored, as well as data quality measures along dimensions such as accuracy, completeness and timeliness, using techniques suggested in Ballou et al. (1998) and Shankaranarayanan et al. (2003).

- **Interface metadata:** Interface metadata (Table 5), also known as reporting metadata, supports the delivery of data to end users. Interface metadata includes information on report templates used for delivering data, where fields are linked to one or more data elements. It may also include the dimension hierarchies associated with the data, template files (for example, Cascade Style Sheets or CSS for Web outputs or Formula-1 templates for Excel-like outputs) used for displaying reports and configurations of reports that constitute "dashboards" — collections of data views that support managerial needs.

- **Administration metadata:** Administrative metadata (Table 6) includes data necessary for administering the decision environments and associated

Table 5. Interface metadata

	Business	**Technical**
Back-End	N/A	N/A
Front-End	• User vocabulary • Metaphors for data visualization • Personalized aggregation and other computation definitions • User-defined dimension hierarchies • Report template/layout • Template visibility and sharing • Dashboard configuration • Delivery setup	• Metadata on report templates including report fields and layouts • Physical location of template files • Mapping of report fields to data elements • Format preferences • Consolidating multiple reports into dashboards • Tracking report delivery failures • Personalizing data delivery formats and styles including metaphors for visualization

Table 6. Administration metadata

	Business	**Technical**
Back-End	• Usage privileges, usernames and passwords • Groups and roles for business functions • Legal limitation on data use • Tracking use of data elements • Documentation, on-line help and training aids	• Authentication interfaces • Application and data security
Front-End	• Users and passwords • Use privileges for data and tools • Tracking use of applications	• Tracking report delivery failures • Personalizing data delivery formats and styles

applications, supporting tasks such as security, authentication and usage tracking.

The taxonomy seen in Table 6 suggests that metadata captures the design choices and maintenance decisions associated with information systems and reflects the design of information systems. Hence, it may serve as a basis for evaluating the design of information systems and be used to evaluate the performance of complex decision environments.

Managing Metadata in Decision Environments

Well-designed and integrated metadata offers important benefits to managing complex decision environments. The complex functional requirements of metadata may cause significant challenges for integration. Commercial, off-the-shelf software products (COTS) for data warehouses offer metadata management capabilities. Each product focuses on a specific type of metadata and no one product offers the ability to comprehensively integrate and manage metadata. This motivates organizations to build a customized enterprise metadata repository.

Metadata Implementation: Benefits and Challenges

Metadata offers several benefits for managing complex decision environments:

(a)   Metadata helps manage and utilize data within data management and decision-support environments more efficiently. Organizing and cataloging data allows efficient search, preserves integrity and eases maintenance. Metadata permits data to be managed independently from applications. Cabibbo and Torlone (2001), for example, introduce a data warehouse modeling approach that adds a new layer of metadata to the traditional data warehouse model. The new "logical" layer is shown to add implementation flexibility and make end-user applications more independent from the underlying storage.

(b)   Metadata forms a semantic layer between business users and the information technology (IT). It abstracts away the complexities of IT and permits effective utilization of IT. It increases the flexibility in managing users by tracking data/resource usage patterns and proactively managing changing user requirements.

(c)   Metadata offers an abstraction layer of technical and business information promoting sharing and reuse of knowledge, expertise and application components. Set-up, maintenance and expansion of systems are made easier by explicitly documenting in-depth knowledge about the system and its components — knowledge that typically exists within programmers and administrators. Development effort and time-to-deliver new applications are reduced. Effective use of metadata makes decision environments cost-effective to manage and expand.

(d)   Metadata helps reduce the complexity of information systems. For in-
      stance, in database systems, users need to only specify "what" data they
      need, rather than "how" to get these data. The complexity of data access
      is reduced by the presence and use of metadata (catalog) as it makes the
      database structure transparent to the users (Elmasri & Navathe, 2003).

Implementing metadata solutions and fully reaping the benefits of metadata are
not easy. Without appropriate controls, metadata evolves inconsistently across
the enterprise (Marco, 1998). This creates complex, isolated and non-reusable
pockets of metadata tightly coupled with individual applications. Hence, there is
a growing frustration with attempts to implement metadata repositories. Technical challenges remain, such as the lack of a software product to comprehensively manage metadata and the lack of an accepted standard that precludes
integration of metadata, hindering implementations. Besides technical challenges, metadata implementations face cultural and financial challenges (Stephens,
2004). There are several facets to metadata, and different user-groups interpret
metadata differently. It is difficult to get all the users within an organization to
agree on the design issues and the overall metadata solution. Implementing a
metadata repository is not cheap, factoring in the time and effort required to
understand the requirements, design the repository and populate it. The benefits
gained, on the other hand, are not always apparent. Hence, investment in
metadata solutions are hard to justify. Managers often perceive metadata as a
technical necessity that has no added value beyond supporting system functionality.

The technical factors that drive up the implementation costs are the need to
support different interchangeable metadata formats and the need to support
metadata integration.

Interchangeable metadata format. Metadata may be captured and represented in different formats, depending on functional needs; each has advantages
and drawbacks. Textual flat files are inexpensive and accessible, but are less
secure and do not easily support the capture of the inter-relationships between
metadata components. Relational models are easier to centralize and integrate,
relatively secure, have a standard access method (SQL) and are equipped with
well-defined data administration utilities; however, relational implementation
may get very complex and expensive (RDBMS and administration overheads).
Graphical representations, such as entity relationship models, are more interpretable but require user training. These are also not easily integrated with metadata
in other formats. Documents allow business users to easily understand metadata
and can capture complex details. On the flip side, documents are hard to integrate
with other formats and require significant administrative overhead. Proprietary

Table 7. Summary of data formats for metadata

Method	Description	Typical Components	Pros	Cons
Text Files	Configuration files in shared directory. Information is obtained through file parsing	• Hardware and OS configuration	• Low cost • Readable • Easy to manipulate	• Hard to centralize • Less secured • Hard to capture complexity • Requires file parsing software
Relational Models	Database model implemented on RDBMS server. Access through native or ODBC drivers	• System tables in RDBMS • ETL process configuration • Semantic Layer • Security configuration	• Easier to centralize • Open architecture • Standard access method • Database administration utilities	• Relational modeling may turn too complex • Database administration overhead • Dependency on RDBMS server platform
Graphics	Graphical chart or diagram format	• ER Diagram • IPMAP • Architecture chart • Monitoring utilities	• Allow easier absorption of large volumes of information	• Hard to integrate with other components • Training and interpretation skills
Documents	Textual documentation – documents, spreadsheets and HTML	• System documentation • Semantic layer • Training materials	• Readable by business users • More flexible with capturing complexities	• Hard to integrate with technical layers
Proprietary Data Structures	Metadata are stored in internal data structures. Read/Write access via dedicated API	• Similar to Relational Modeling, vendor dependent	• Data security • Consistent access • Efficient for application use	• Access depends on API; Data is unreadable otherwise • May prevent integration with other tools

data structures are easier to customize for unique and specific organizational needs, but are hard to integrate with more standardized formats.

Table 7 summarizes the data formats for implementing metadata, along with advantages and disadvantages associated with each. Metadata implementation is likely to involve more than one format. Certain data entities may require abstraction in multiple formats, hence efficient interchangeability among formats is highly desirable. A common approach for achieving compatibility and inter-changeability is to choose one format (mostly the relational database model) as the baseline.

Metadata integration. Without appropriate controls, metadata might evolve inconsistently across the enterprise as complex, isolated and non-reusable pockets of metadata tightly coupled with individual applications (Marco, 1998). Such isolated pockets might lead to conflicting standards for business entities and disable efficient communication among sub-systems, making the system difficult to maintain (Vaduva & Veterlli, 2001). Metadata integration has important implications from different business and technical perspectives (Jarke et al., 2000). This is demonstrated by the following examples:

- **Data dictionary:** the lack of integration causes data entities to be defined differently within the data warehouse sub-systems: data storage system(s), ETL systems, reporting systems and administration systems. The result is inconsistency and lack of data integrity.

- **Single sign-on:** distributed security management is complex to manage and often causes security loopholes. Centralized user authentication and authorization, as a desired system capability, requires integration of the administrative metadata across all systems components, and

- **Aligning technical and business metadata:** typical data warehousing tools use the relational model to store technical metadata. Business metadata are hidden with textual documents associated with warehouses. Integrating the two is necessary but difficult to accomplish.

A reason for the evolution of disintegrated metadata pockets is the variety of tools used in implementation of complex systems, such as a data warehouse. Provided by different vendors, and specializing in different warehouse functions (e.g., data storage, data transfer or data presentation), each software tool manages specific types of metadata and uses different metadata representation standards. This makes metadata integration a difficult, if not impossible, task. Metadata support in commercial software tools and the related integration issues are discussed in more detail next.

Metadata Management in Commercial Data Warehousing Products

The complex requirements for managing metadata lead organizations to seek assistance from commercial off-the-shelf (COTS) software products. Since the early 90s, many of the data warehousing products offer utilities for metadata management. Based on their role in the data warehouse, these products may be grouped into three major categories:

(a) **Data storage products** (e.g., Oracle, Sybase, MS-SQL, IBM-UDB, Teradata and Essbase),

(b) **ETL — extraction, transformation and loading products** (e.g., Oracle Warehouse-Builder, MS-SQL DTS, IBM Warehouse Manager, Informatica and Hummingbird), and

(c) **Business intelligence (BI)** utilities for reporting (e.g., MicroStrategy, Business Objects and Cognos).

A major benefit of using COTS data warehousing products is that many of the required metadata management capabilities reviewed earlier are built into the products. This can reduce implementation time and effort. On the other hand, a detailed review of these products reveals a set of challenges:

(a) None of the products offers a comprehensive-enough set of capabilities needed to manage all types of metadata. Model, or data dictionary, metadata is commonly supported, and so are infrastructure and administration metadata. Process metadata is supported only by ETL products and data delivery metadata by Business Intelligence front-end tools. Quality metadata is not supported by any of the products reviewed.

(b) The products emphasize technical metadata and offer little support for business metadata. Only BI tools support business metadata as part of the data dictionary. Other essential elements of business metadata, such as interpretation of the data transformation process, linking user administration to customer management utilities or tracking the usage of data elements and systems resources are provided in a limited fashion, if at all.

(c) Storage and presentation formats of metadata are restricted to relational models or complex proprietary data structures. This may make the tool more efficient but preempts the integration and the exchange of metadata.

(d) The metadata elements are tightly coupled with one tool or a suite of tools (by the same vendor) and tailored to the specific functionality that tool supports. This tight-coupling makes metadata integration across products difficult. The ability to create a well-integrated metadata layer is needed if the data warehouse is to be successful (Marco, 1998; Inmon, 2000). Many practitioners identify the metadata integration capabilities of COTS products as an important factor for the success of metadata implementations

(Sachdeva, 1998; Seeley & Vaughan, 1999). Vendors are apparently aware of the integration issue and are making efforts to resolve it. Reasonable cross-product integration is available within a suite of tools from the same vendor (e.g., Oracle, Microsoft or IBM). A first major force for standardizing metadata exchange was the Meta Data Coalition (MDC), established in the late 90s. MDC proposed the Open Information Model (OIM), a data exchange protocol that permits each tool to maintain its own internal metadata structure and offer a uniform interface for metadata exchange. A competing standard, the Common Warehouse Model (CWM), is based on XML metadata interchange (XMI), the data interchange standard for distributed applications. CWM is championed by the Object Management Group (OMG). Seeley and Vaughn (1999) offer insights into the political struggle behind the competing metadata standards. Vaduva and Vetterli (2001) highlight the divergence of metadata exchange standards as a major obstacle for enterprise metadata implementation.

It is important to note that the above observations are based on a comprehensive study of the different tools conducted in 2004 (Shankaranarayanan & Even, 2004). For the state-of-the-art offerings and metadata capabilities, the reader is advised to consult the vendor Web sites listed in the *Reference* section

Implementing Metadata Repositories

Given the metadata implementation challenges and the limited capabilities offered by commercial products, an approach that organizations may consider is creating a customized enterprise-wide metadata repository (Sachdeva, 1998; & White, 1999). The metadata repository captures and integrates all the metadata components that are used in organizational applications and creates a single, unified source for metadata (Marco, 2000). Underlying the repository is a physical database (commonly, but not necessarily RDBMS) that implements a comprehensive metadata model and captures the actual values of all metadata characteristics and instances. The metadata repository supports every phase of IT development and operation. Organizational members, who are involved in application design and implementation, use the metadata repository to store and retrieve requirements and the resulting data and system design specifications. Once applications are implemented, these would communicate with the repository to retrieve the required metadata elements. Should organizations pursue the enterprise repository, they face several important decisions with respect to design, architectural approach and implementation alternatives.

An important decision when implementing a metadata repository is the design paradigm — top-down, bottom-up or a hybrid strategy. A top-down approach would look at the entire organizational information system schema and try to capture an overall set of metadata requirements. A bottom-up approach, on the other hand, would start from the lower granularity of subsystems and bring their metadata specifications together into one unified schema. While a top-down paradigm is more likely to ensure standardization and integration among subsystems, it might be infeasible where existing information systems with local metadata repositories are already in place. Moreover, capturing metadata requirements for an entire organization is a complex and tedious task that might not be completed within a reasonable time. The bottom-up paradigm, focusing on specific systems first, is more likely to achieve short-term results, but might fail to satisfy the larger integration needs. The "middle out" approach, as a hybrid design alternative, treats each functional type of metadata as a module or component of the larger repository. It identifies one or two key modules of metadata and builds a repository consisting of these modules. With this approach, it should be recognized that the metadata repository will not be comprehensive or exhaustive to start with. Subsequent to the "core" implementation, initial modules may be expanded and others added incrementally to grow the repository. The advantages of the middle-out approach from a business standpoint are:

(a)   it requires minimal investment initially and as the value is recognized, additional investments may be made,

(b)   it is custom-developed to meet the specific, complex requirements of the organization and its offerings, and

(c)   it can be initially built on an existing hardware and software platforms and later ported to larger, more sophisticated ones should the need arise. This approach will further ensure that the metadata and its repository remain extensible and not dependent on a single set of applications.

Another important design choice is the metadata repository architecture (Blumstein, 2003). A centralized architecture, which corresponds to a "top down" paradigm, locates the organizational metadata repository on one centralized server that becomes the only metadata source for all the front-end and back-end utilities. Alternately, a distributed architecture, which corresponds to a "bottom up" design paradigm, allows systems to maintain their own customized metadata. The hybrid architecture allows metadata to reside with applications, but keeps the control and the key components in a centralized repository. The pros and cons of these architecture alternatives are summarized in Table 8.

Table 8. Summary of metadata repository architectures

Architecture	Implementation	Pros	Cons
Centralized (Passive Repository)	Single, centralized location for metadata. All back-end (Data storage, ETL) and front-end (Business Intelligence) tools should post their metadata into the repository, which becomes the only source for pulling and using it	• Efficient access - No need to search for Metadata in multiple locations. • Better performance - No need to communicate with multiple tools • Independence from tools being activated or not • Easier to standardize and integrate • Easier to capture additional metadata not related to a specific tool	• Complex and time-consuming implementation • Data redundancy with larger chance for quality hazards • Synchronization issues • Increased maintenance efforts
Distributed (Active Repository)	Metadata are kept on the back-end and front-end tools are accessed. The users still access a single repository, which doesn't maintain copies but retrieves the metadata in real-time, as needed	• Access is still efficient - one centralized location with lightweight data requirements. • Faster application development due to higher level of independence. • No data redundancy, metadata are kept at its source. • Reduced system maintenance	• Dependency on the end-systems being active • Harder to standardize and integrate • Harder to capture and integrate in additional metadata, not supported by the end-tools
Hybrid	Pieces of metadata provided by back-end and front-end tools are kept at the tools and accessed in real-time, while additional homegrown pieces are maintained at the repository	• Efficient access • Application independence is kept • No data redundancy • Ability to integrate between 3rd-party and home-grown metadata	• Sophisticated to implement • Integration might not be achievable • Dependency on the end-systems being active

The chosen design paradigm and architectural approach are likely to be influenced by the organizational structure and the complexity of the information systems. It is unlikely that a large organization with sophisticated information needs would adopt a top-down design for metadata and implement it using a centralized server. Such organizations are likely to have many information systems already in place, hence are more likely to apply decentralized architecture, or a hybrid, using the "middle-out" design paradigm. Smaller organizations, with less complex information demands, can afford the "luxury" of a top-down approach, attempting to capture the entire set of metadata requirements and implementing a centralized architecture.

The actual implementation of the repository introduces another important choice — developing custom software for managing metadata or using commercial software products. In reality, most organizations are likely to choose a combination of the two. The process of developing customized software can be drawn out and expensive due to the complex and changing metadata requirements. On the other hand, commercial software tools might not meet the repository needs entirely (see *Metadata Management in Commercial Data Warehousing Products* for a discussion of these tools and their shortfalls). In recent years some attempts have been made by software vendors to address this gap. Microsoft's Meta Data Services (MDS), which is part of MS-SQL Server RDBMS, is an attempt to create a unified metadata infrastructure. MDS is well integrated with other Microsoft product offerings, but still has some drawbacks: it emphasizes technical metadata, pays little attention to business metadata and relies on an RDBMS with no support for other storage alternatives. In recent years, software tools that specialize in metadata management, such as Ascential, MetaCenter by the Data Advantage Group and MetaBase by MetaMatrix. These tools address the metadata repository implementation needs by supporting both technical and business metadata. They claim to be vendor and technology independent, providing interfaces to most of the leading data warehousing products and supporting both the OIM and the CWM metadata exchange models (see *Metadata Management in Commercial Data Warehousing Products* for a description of these models). At the time of writing this chapter, software products for metadata management are still emerging and have not gained significant market share. However, if the demand for metadata repository solutions continues to grow, the demand for such tools that support centralized metadata management is expected to grow as well.

Figure 1 presents a conceptual layered architecture of a homegrown repository illustrating the different modules within. This architecture is targeted for total data quality management in a data warehouse by including the process and data quality metadata within. Reporting and application-related metadata are linked with the warehouse data elements for effective communication and delivery of the data to the decision-makers. Together with formatting and vocabulary preferences of the users and personalized metaphors for data visualization, it constitutes the data delivery metadata in the warehouse. The mapping component of the data dictionary metadata, consisting of the mapping between data elements, is distributed across the conceptual layers (shown by the arrows in Figure 1). The data dictionary metadata elements used in data integration, such as the dependencies and constraints between source data elements, are captured in the middle and lower layers of the conceptual architecture.

Figure 1. Conceptual architecture for metadata repository

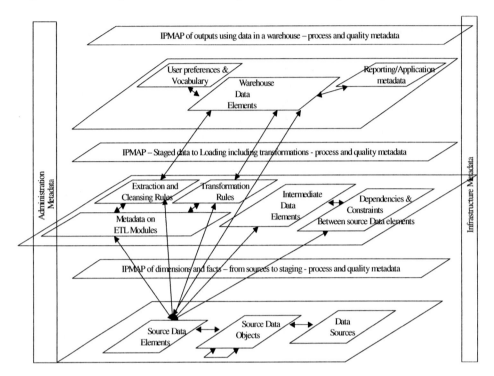

Data quality metadata is integrated with process metadata and are represented by the IPMAP in the conceptual architecture. The IPMAP stages (processes) are mapped to the extraction and transformation rules (another piece of process metadata) captured in the middle layer of the architecture. Administration and infrastructure metadata that spans the entire warehouse are shown on either side of the conceptual architecture in Figure 1. A detailed list of metadata elements corresponding to the architecture in Figure 1 is listed in Table 9.

Applications of Metadata

The preceding section described the benefits of well-managed metadata and the challenges in implementing and managing metadata repositories for decision environments. In the last decade, the benefits of metadata have been recognized in three important domains: the Semantic Web, knowledge management and

Table 9. Metadata elements for TDQM in a data warehouse

Metadata Entity	Metadata items
Warehouse Data Elements	Date loaded, Date updated, Currency (old/current) in the warehouse, associated data sources, associated extraction, cleansing, and transformation processes, whether (still) available in the data source, associated staged data elements, staged data sources
Data Sources	ID or Unique name, Format type, Frequency of update, Active Status
Source Data Objects (e.g. tables if source is relational)	Object name, Aliases, Business Entity name, Business rules associated, Owner
Source Data Elements	Element name, Units, Business rules, Computation method(s), business name/alias, data type, data length, Range-Max, Range-Min, Date/time when it was included, [Constraint and participating source elements]
Staged Intermediates /Target Objects (these are typically relational tables or object classes)	Object name, Aliases, Business Entity name, Business rules associated, Owner, Creation date, Object Status, Administrator,
Intermediate/Target Data Elements	Element name, Units, Business rules, Computation method(s), business name/alias, data type, data length, Range-Max, Range-Min, Date/time when it was included or became effective, [Constraint and participating source elements]
Source Element to Target Element Mappings & Constraints	Derivation and business rules, assumptions on default and missing values, associations between source and target data elements
ETL Process Modules	ID and/or Unique name, Creation date, Effective date, Owner, Role/Business Unit responsible, Modification date, Modified by, reason for modification, system/platform associated, location in file system, execution commands, Run Date, Error Codes/messages
Extraction Process	Applicable source data element(s), extraction rules, business restrictions/rules, Last Run Date, Error Codes/Messages, output data elements
Cleansing Process	Applicable source data element(s), sanitizing rules, business restrictions/rules, output data elements
Transformation Process	Input data element(s), transformation rules, business rules, output data elements
Load Process	Input data element(s), format/transformation rules, business rules, output warehouse data elements

decision support. The notion of a Semantic Web is one in which different applications and Web sites can exchange information and fully exploit the data/information accessible within the Web. Achieving this requires that resources (such as a Web page, a whole Web site or any item within that has data/information in some form including documents (Heery, 1998)) on the Web be augmented with metadata. The Resource Description Framework (RDF), endorsed by W3C and first created in 1997, offers a vehicle for specifying metadata for such resources to enable interoperable Web applications (Candan et al., 2002).

To enable more efficient searching and retrieval of documents within the Semantic Web, the metadata specification has to be enriched to include semantic descriptors. Users typically annotate documents (by specifying semantic metadata) to help search/retrieve information within. Ontology-based annotation systems have been proposed to assist search/retrieval of such documents: SHOE in Luke et al. (1997), Onto broker in Decker et al. (1999), WebKB in Martin and Eklund (1999) and Quizrdf in Davies et al. (2002). Corby et al. (2000) propose a model that extends the RDF to represent semantic metadata and uses concept graphs to facilitate querying and inferring capabilities by exploiting the graphs' formalisms. Understanding that maintaining semantic metadata for Semantic Web documents is not easy, techniques for extracting metadata from Web documents and using it to facilitate search/retrieval have also been proposed (Handschuh & Staab, 2003; Ding et al., 2003).

Creating metadata can be viewed as codifying data and creating a higher-level layer of knowledge for it. Similarly, codifying organizational knowledge within KM systems may be viewed as abstracting it into a metadata layer. Markus (2001) looks at three purposes for creating knowledge as elements that play a role in how knowledge is stored, processed and distributed:

1. **Self:** knowledge for self-use, where little or no attention is paid to interpretable formatting;

2. **Similar others:** knowledge for others with a similar skill set. Assuming the ability of other users to assimilate knowledge easily, knowledge reuse efforts focus on providing essential details, rather than shape and format; and

3. **Dissimilar others:** knowledge aimed for others without similar skill sets. Assuming limited ability of target users to interpret the knowledge in its raw form, more efforts will be necessary to reconstruct and formalize it. It is the last category that benefits the most from metadata.

Sheth (2003) proposes the use of metadata for capturing knowledge. His study describes a methodology for creating layers of metadata to capture not only the basic business data entities, but also to structure them into business knowledge in the form of ontology — a shared conceptualization of the world as seen by the enterprise. The ontology consists of high-level business schemas, interrelationships between entities, domain vocabulary and factual knowledge. Knowledge is stored using a structured document and not a relational model. Broekstra et al. (2001) propose a knowledge representation framework for the Web by extending the RDF, specifically, the RDF schema. This is accomplished by the Ontology Interface Language (OIL) as an extension of the RDF schema. This representation framework permits sharing of metadata on the Web and can be extended to other knowledge representation schemes.

Although the application of metadata for knowledge management and the Semantic Web are challenging and interesting, each is an extensive field in itself. In this chapter our focus is on metadata in complex decision environments, specifically, understanding and managing metadata for decision support. Recent research has explored metadata from the perspective of a decision support aid: Can the provision of metadata improve decision making? Quality and process metadata are shown to influence managerial decision making. In the remainder of this section, we first describe the current state of research in this area, then propose a theoretical model for evaluating the role of process and quality metadata in data-driven decision-making.

Contextual Assessment of Quality in Decision Tasks

Recent research has explored metadata from the perspective of a decision support aid: can the provision of metadata improve the use of data for decision making? This question is often asked in the context of data quality management. Due to the rapid growth of data volumes and their complexity, data quality is becoming a critical issue in information systems. Poor quality customer data is estimated to cost U.S. businesses $611 billion a year in printing, postage and staff overhead alone (Eckerson, 2003). Various techniques have been suggested for improving data quality, such as data cleansing (Hernandez & Stolfo, 1998), data tracking and statistical process control (Redman, 1996), data source calculus and algebra (Parssian et al., 2004), data stewardship (English, 1999) and dimensional gap analysis (Kahn et al., 2002). While these techniques are indeed useful, they are also limited in that they treat the data in isolation from the decision context in which it is used.

An important issue with respect to how people evaluate data quality is the distinction between its *impartial* and *contextual* assessments. Impartial data quality implies measurement of quality attributes based on the data element itself and independent of the context in which it is used. Contextual factors, such as the task in which the data are used, the time available for the task and the individual characteristics of the decision-maker have been shown to strongly influence perceptions of data quality (Strong et al., 1997; Jarke et al., 2000). Increasingly, researchers are taking contextual (Fisher et al., 2003) and individual differences (Yang & Strong, 2003) into account when examining data quality and acknowledge the role played by contextual assessment of data quality.

The contextual evaluation of data quality is particularly critical when the data are used for managerial decision-making. Managerial decision-making tasks are sophisticated and often relatively unstructured (Nutt, 1984). Such tasks reflect a process that is activated by business needs and incorporates multiple stages - - specifying requirements, gathering information, evaluating alternatives and forming a decision outcome (Nutt, 1994, 1998b). The efficiency of the decision-making process and the success of its outcome are influenced by organizational and individual factors, many of which have been theoretically and empirically examined (Eisenhardt & Zbaracki, 1992; Nutt, 1998a; Ford & Gioia, 2000). Although it is intuitively obvious that the quality of the data used should be a critical factor in analytical, data-driven decision-making processes, there is a paucity of research investigating this phenomenon. A few exceptions are the studies of the impact of data quality on decision-making (Chengalur-Smith et al., 1999; Fisher et al., 2003) and decision support (Wixom & Watson, 2001).

In complex datasets, the human ability to detect data quality issues associated with data is limited. In such cases, where data exceeds the absorptive capacity of the user, data quality assessment may benefit from the provision of data abstractions (Klein et al., 1997). Helpful abstractions may take the form of impartial data quality measurements (quality metadata) of the data — number of records, error rates, count of missing values or the time/date of last update. As discussed in the preceding paragraphs, decision makers must gauge data quality within the context of the decision-task. Thus providing decision makers with additional information about the data they are using, such as the size of the source sample, the extent that it was processed for error detection or the reputation of the source, can help them gauge data quality by relating this information to the decision-context.

Impartial data quality is evaluated along a set of quality dimensions (Wang & Strong, 1996). This set includes *accuracy, relevancy, representation* and *accessibility.* Reliability, believability, currency and completeness are some other dimensions of data quality that have been discussed in the literature (Ballou et al., 1998; Hufford, 1996). Empirical studies have identified that business users recognize the multi-dimensionality of data quality and evaluate data elements accordingly (Wang & Strong, 1996). The quality of data measured using quality dimensions such as accuracy and completeness is quality metadata and has been referred to as data tags (Wang et al., 1993) and as data quality information (DQI) (Fisher et al., 2003).

Chengalur-Smith et al. (1999) and Fisher et al. (2003) have shown that the provision of quality metadata does positively impact decision making. Using a structured decision-task, they have shown that in decision-tasks where the decision maker needs to find the best alternative, the provision of DQI is very valuable in improving decision outcomes. Can process metadata further improve decision outcomes in such tasks? Next, we discuss the implications for providing process metadata in decision environments.

Role of Process Metadata

Process metadata provides information about the processes that were used to generate and deliver the data (or a data set) used by the decision maker. Process abstraction, such as models or documentation, is recognized as a special form of metadata (Marco, 2000; Shankaranarayanan et al., 2003). A graphical representation that communicates process metadata is the information product map (IPMAP) (Shankaranarayanan et al., 2003). A set of constructs represents different stages of the data manufacturing process — data source, processing, storage, quality check, organizational or information system boundary and data consumer (sink). Each construct is supplemented with metadata about the corresponding stage, such as a unique identifier, the data entity composition, ownership, processing requirements and physical location where the step is performed. These help the decision maker understand *what* the output from this step is, *how* was this created, including business rules and applicable constraints,

Figure 2a. IPMAP for staging data in a data warehouse

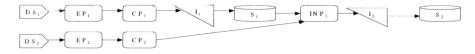

Figure 2b. IPMAP for staging of dimensions and facts in a warehouse

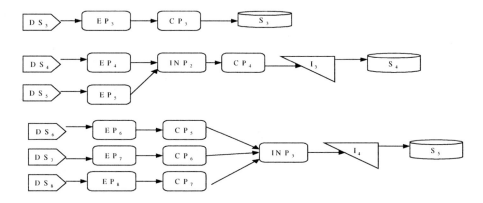

Figure 2c. IPMAP representing the transformation and loading of a warehouse

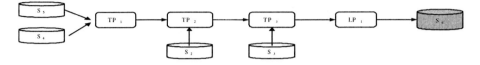

where (both physical location and the system used) and *who* is responsible for this stage in the manufacture in addition to *when* (at what stage) an operation was performed.

Figure 2 shows a generic example of an IPMAP in a data warehouse. The IPMAP modeling scheme offers six constructs to represent the manufacturing stages of an IP:

1. a data source (DS) block that is used to represent each data source/ provider of raw data used in the creation of the IP;

2. a processing (P) block that is used to represent any manipulations and/or combinations of data items or the creation of new data items required to produce the IP;

3. a storage (S) block that represents a stage where data may wait prior to being processed;

4. an information system boundary (SB) block to represent the transition of data from one information system to another (e.g., transaction data in legacy file systems transferred to a relational database after some processing);

5. a data consumer (DC) block to represent the consumer; and

6. an inspection (I) block that serves to represent predetermined inspections (validity checks, checks for missing values, authorizations, approvals, etc.). The arrows between the constructs represent the raw/component data units that flow between the corresponding stages. An input obtained from a source is referred to as a raw data unit. Once a raw data unit is processed or inspected, it is referred to as a component data unit.

Consider a warehouse having (say) three dimensions and a set of facts (or measures). A generic, high-level sequence of steps that result in the warehouse is represented by the IPMAP in Figure 2, parts **a, b,** and **c**. The data from data sources (DS_1 and DS_2) are extracted by extraction processes (EP_1 and EP_2) and cleansed (CP_1 and CP_2). The cleansed data from DS_1 is inspected (manual or automated process I_1) and stored (S_1). This is combined with the cleansed data from DS_2 by an integration process (INP_1), inspected for errors (I_2) and staged in storage S_2. The staging of the other data (dimensions and facts) may similarly be represented as shown in Figure 2. The staged fact data (in S_5) may then be combined with the staged dimension data (in S_2, S_3 and S_4) by a transformation process (TP) and loaded into the DW by the process (LP_1). Though the transformation may be a single process, it is shown as multiple stages in Figure 2c.

Iverson (2001) states that in order to improve data quality, the metadata attributes must include process documentation such as data capture, storage, transformation rules, quality metrics and tips on usage and feedback. IT practitioners acknowledge the importance of process metadata for information system professionals, who commonly use it for the design and ongoing mainte- nance of data processing and delivery systems (Redman, 1996; Marco, 2000). However, the usability of process metadata for business users has not been explored. Information processes may include a large number of stages and the resulting visual representation might be too complex for non-technical users to comprehend. It is suggested (though not explicitly shown) that that providing such metadata to business users will improve their perception of quality and hence their decision-making process (Shankaranarayanan & Watts, 2003).

How do we understand the impact of process and quality metadata on decision making? The key is to investigate the effects of process metadata in a visual form (using the IPMAP representation) — whether decision makers are likely to benefit from the availability of process metadata; if yes, to what extent does its use affect the efficiency and outcome of the decision-making process. An important aspect to explore is whether process metadata benefits the context- dependent evaluation of the data and its quality. While impartial assessment is derived from the granular details of the dataset contents, process metadata adds an extrinsic layer to the assessment — it puts the data in the context of the information processing that produced it. It is thus expected to affect users' perceptions and assessment of data quality in different ways that we seek to explore and understand.

To conclude this section, we briefly describe an empirical framework to examine how data quality assessment and the provision of metadata affect analytical, data-driven decision making. By better understanding the importance of metadata within the context of decision making, organizations can recognize the value of implementing and managing metadata. We focus specifically on process metadata and the benefits of providing it to the decision maker during the decision process. We further argue that providing process metadata will have a larger impact on decision making (both the decision process and the decision outcome).

Figure 3. The effects of quality and process metadata on the decision-making process

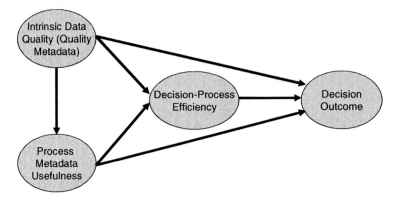

This research defines a new perspective for data quality management in decision support environments. It emphasizes the importance of contextual assessment of data quality, the provision of metadata to help this assessment and attempts to understand the impact of these two on the decision outcome. Data quality may be gauged independent of the decision-task(s) and such context-independent (impartial) assessments are captured as quality metadata (Shankaranarayanan & Even, 2004). However, impartial assessment does not always have the desired impact on the decision outcome(s), as decision makers may find impartial assessments insufficient and seek quality affirmation from additional, external sources (Shankaranarayanan & Watts, 2003). This does not overlook the importance of context-independent data quality assessment. It highlights the importance of another type of metadata, process metadata, by showing that the provision of process metadata does impact decision-making efficiency and ultimately the decision outcome. Though the link between data quality and decision outcome is understood, this research is a first step towards offering a deeper understanding of this link — one that identifies *what else* the organization must do to achieve the desired impact of improved data quality on decision outcomes.

The model presented in Figure 3 incorporates the impartial data quality assessments by the decision maker, the perceived usefulness of process metadata and the efficiency of the decision-making process into a framework for understanding how these factors influence decision outcomes. This model makes several interesting contributions. First it posits that process metadata (relevant to or associated with the data used in the decision-task), in addition to the impartial assessments (of the data used in the decision-task by the decision-maker) have a significant effect on decision outcome. Second, the model suggests that the effect of those two factors is mediated by the efficiency of the decision-making process. Earlier research (Chengalur-Smith et al., 1999; Fisher et al., 2003) suggests that quality assessment supported by metadata influences the decision outcome directly, moderated by several other factors. In this model we examine the theory that complementing the quality metadata with process metadata adds value to the decision maker. Further, the model examines the theory that both factors affect decision-making outcome, directly and indirectly. Preliminary results from testing the model show that process metadata per se does not impact decision outcomes. In combination with quality metadata, process metadata improves the efficiency of the decision process and consequently the decision outcome. The impact of the combination of the two metadata components is much more than the impacts of either metadata component alone.

Conclusion

This chapter presents a comprehensive examination of the state of metadata in decision environments such as the data warehouse. The purpose of this examination is to emphasize the need for further research on metadata by highlighting four issues:

1. the diverse and complex functionality that metadata support;
2. the challenges in successfully implementing integrated metadata repositories;
3. the roles that process and quality metadata play in improving decision outcomes; and
4. the potential contribution of metadata to management and use of organizational knowledge.

The metadata taxonomy that was introduced in this chapter highlights the different functionality that metadata serves in complex decision support environments, such as the data warehouse. It illustrates the multiple classes of metadata that support a wide spectrum of functionality in a data warehouse. This taxonomy supplements the existing metadata classification schemes and the chapter illustrates how the existing and proposed classification schemes fit together. The software industry acknowledges the importance of metadata and the difficulties with implementing metadata solutions. Software vendors now offer metadata management capabilities within data warehousing products or as separate software packages. Unfortunately, there is still a mismatch between the capabilities needed for managing metadata and capabilities that these products offer. The state of industry offerings highlights the need for a metadata standard to achieve integration and exchange of metadata across repositories. As an alternative to managing metadata using commercial products, the paper discusses the implementation of a "homegrown" integrated metadata repository and the associated challenges.

A causal model that may be used to validate the positive role of process metadata in improving decision outcomes is also described. This research model has important implications for future research in the data quality management field and for the design of complex decision-support environments. Findings support the commonsense notion that when participants perceive the quality of the input data to be good, their sense of decision-making efficiency, as well as their decision outcome, is improved. This finding, assuming further corroboration, has clear implications for user interface design — it is important not only for improving the storage and back-end processing of data, but also for communicating data quality to the end users. Having a sense of good quality will improve users' confidence in the data and in the back-end system that provides it. As a result, users ought to be able to use this data more efficiently and effectively. Findings support our assertion that the metadata layer can serve as a tool for communicating data quality to business users. The provision of process metadata in the form of the IPMAP proved to have a significant effect on both perceptions of decision process efficiency and final outcomes. Future research will investigate this link more deeply, as well as the possible effect of providing other forms of metadata to the decision maker.

An important observation is the significant difference in how technical and business metadata are perceived. Administrators, IT managers and other technical users of metadata clearly recognize the merits of metadata. Business users, however, perceive metadata as a technical necessity and do not recognize its value. Business metadata includes metadata such as the source of a data element, business rules applied to manipulate it, assumptions and models used in the manipulation and other information that helps evaluate the usefulness of that data element to the decision maker. Few business users are trained in using metadata and hence ignore or overlook it even if made available to them. This observation raises the question: "To what extent is metadata useful to business users?" Two perspectives for addressing this question are as follows:

1.   to assess the operational value of metadata; and
2.   to understand its implications for decision making.

The benefits of metadata remain largely intangible and there is a lack of models or methodologies to evaluate and quantify its operational value (Stephens, 2004). Suggestions for looking at metadata ROI have been offered by practitioners (Marco, 2000). The following issues ought to be explored to better understand the operational context of metadata in decision environments as a step towards developing such evaluation models:

- **What functional types of metadata have the most significant operational importance?** The consolidated taxonomy of metadata that was offered (see *Metadata Functionality*) can serve as a baseline for exploring this question — Are certain (functional) types of metadata more important? Other factors to look at are the data modeling method used, level of integration supported and the extent to which the metadata is exchangeable. This knowledge would assist organizations in identifying the key set of metadata modules (potentially a mix of both technical and business metadata) for the core of the metadata repository when implementing homegrown solutions.

- **Can metadata improve the performance of a data warehouse?** Dimensions for measuring data quality such as accuracy, timeliness, completeness and consistency, with specific reference to the data warehouses, have been proposed (Hufford, 1996). It is unclear, though, to what extent metadata contributes to good data quality and performance of a data warehouse. While investing in metadata is prescribed as a key factor for the success of data warehouses by several studies (Marco, 1998; Inmon, 2000; and Sachdeva, 1998), none of these studies offers theoretical quantification or empirical support for measuring such impacts. Measuring this impact is a challenging task for several reasons. First, there are many alternative approaches for measuring the performance or success of a data warehouse. Some are based on the ease of managing a data warehouse focusing on technical administration (Hufford, 1996) and others are based on evaluating the end-user experiences (Wixom & Watson, 2001). Second, there is no straightforward method for attributing costs directly to the metadata. As pointed out in the COTS product review, metadata management components are embedded within other offerings and in many cases are not priced separately. It is also practically impossible to precisely assess the software development time allocated to metadata, since it is typically part of application programming efforts. Developing measurement methods for such study is likely to require fairly sophisticated models and methods for cost and benefit attribution (Stephens, 2004).

References

Ballou, D. P., Wang, R. Y., Pazer, H., & Tayi, G. K. (1998, April). Modeling information manufacturing systems to determine information product quality. *Management Science, 44*(4), 462-484.

Berners-Lee, T. (1997). *Metadata architecture,* Retrievable from the World Wide Web Consortium, http://www.w3.org/DesignIssues/Metadata.html

Blumstein G. (2003, August 1). *Metadata management architecture. Data Management (DM) Direct Newsletter.*

Broekstra, J. Klein, M., Decker, S., Fensel, D., van Harmelen, F., & Horrocks, I. (2001). Enabling knowledge representation on the web by extending RDF schema. In *Proceedings of the 10th International World Wide Web Conference (WWW10),* Hong Kong, (pp. 467-478).

Cabibbo L., & Torlone, R. (2001). An architecture for data warehousing supporting data independence and interoperability. *International Journal of Cooperative Information Systems, 10*(3), 377-397.

Candan, K. S., Liu, H., & Suvarna, R. (2001, July). Resource description format: Metadata and its applications. *ACM SIGKDD Explorations Newsletter, 3*(1).

Chengalur-Smith I., Ballou, D. P., & Pazer, H. L. (1999, November/December). The impact of data quality information on decision making: An exploratory study. *IEEE Transactions on Knowledge and Data Engineering, 11*(6), 853-864.

Davies, J., Weeks, R., & Krohn, U. (2002). Quizrdf: Search technology for the semantic web. In *Proceedings of the 11th International World Wide Web Conference Workshop on RDF and Semantic Web Applications (WWW11).*

Decker, S., Erdmann, M., Fensel, D., & Studer, R. (1999, January). Ontobroker: Ontology-based access to distributed and semi-structured information. In R. Meersman, Z. Tari & S. M. Stevens (Eds.), *Proceedings of the 8th Working Conference on Database Semantics,* Rotorua, NZ (pp. 351-369).

Ding, L., Finin, T., Joshi, A., Pan, R., Cost, R. S. et al. (2004). Swoogle: A search and metadata engine for the semantic web. In *Proceedings of the ACM Conference on Information and Knowledge Management (CIKM),* Washington DC (pp. 652-659).

Eckerson, W. W. (2003). Achieving business success through a commitment to high quality data. *TDWI Report Series,* Data Warehousing Institute, Seattle, WA. Retrievable from http://www.dw-institute.com

Eisenhardt, K. M., & Zbaracki, M. J. (1992). Strategic decision-making. *Strategic Management Journal, 13*, 13-37.

Elmasri, R., & Navathe, S. (2003). *Fundamentals of Database Systems* (4th ed.). Redwood City, CA: Benjamin Cummings Publishing Company Inc.

English, L.P. (1999). *Improving data warehouse and business information quality: Methods for reducing costs and increasing profits*. New York: John Wiley & Sons.

Fisher, C. W., Chengalur-Smith I., & Ballou, D. P. (2003). The impact of experience and time on the use of data quality information in decision making. *Information Systems Research, 14*(2), 170-188.

Ford, C. M., & Gioia, D. A. (2000). Factors influencing creativity in the domain of managerial decision making. *Journal of Management, 26*(4), 705-732.

Handschuh, S., & Staab, S. (2003). Cream: Creating metadata for the semantic web. *Computer Networks, 42*(5), 579-598.

Heery, R. (1998, March). What is RDF. *The Ariadne Magazine*. Retrievable from http://www.ariadne.ac.uk/issue14/what-is/

Hernandez, M. A., & Stolfo, S. J. (1998). Real-world data is dirty: Data cleansing and the merge/purge problem. *Journal of Data Mining and Knowledge Discovery, 1*(2).

Hufford, D. (1996, January). Data warehouse quality. *DM Review*, Special Feature. Retrievable from http://www.dmreview.com/article_sub.cfm?articleId=1311

Imhoff, C. (2003). *Mastering data warehouse design: Relational and dimensional techniques*. Indianapolis, IN: Wiley Publications.

Inmon, B. (2000, July 7). Enterprise meta data. *Data Management Direct Newsletter*.

Iverson, D. S. (2001). *Meta-Information quality – Keynote Address in the International Conference on Information Quality by the Senior VP Enterprise Information Solutions –Ingenix*, Boston.

Jarke, M., Lenzerini, M., Vassiliou, Y., & Vassiliadis, P. (2000). *Fundamentals of data warehouses*. Heidelberg, Germany: Springer-Verlag

Kahn, B. K., Strong, D. M., & Wang, R. Y. (2002). Information quality benchmarks: Product and service performance. *Communications of ACM, 45*(4).

Kimball, R. (1998, March). Meta meta data data. *DBMS Magazine*.

Kimball, R., Reeves, L., Ross, M., & Thornthwaite, W. (1998). *The data warehouse lifecycle toolkit*. New York: Wiley Computer Publishing.

Klein, B. D., Goodhue, D. L., & Davis, G. B. (1997, June). Can humans detect errors in data? Impact of base rates, incentives and goals. *MIS Quarterly, 21*(2).

Luke, S., Spector, L., Rager, D., & Hendler, J. (1997). Ontology-based web agents. In *Proceedings of the First International Conference on Autonomous Agents (Agents97)* (pp. 59-66).

Marco, D. (1998, March). Managing meta data. *Data Management Review.*

Marco, D. (2000). *Building and managing the meta data repository: A full lifecycle guide.* New York: Wiley Computer Publishing, John Wiley & Sons.

Martin, P., & Eklund, P. (1999). Embedding knowledge in web documents. In *Proceedings of the 8th International World Wide Web Conference (WWW8)* (pp. 324-341).

Mimno, P. (2003, June). How to avoid data mart chaos using hybrid methodology. *TDWI FlashPoint.*

Nutt, P. C. (1984).Types of organizational decision processing. *Administrative Science Quarterly, 29,* 414-450.

Nutt, P. C. (1998a, March/April). Framing strategic decisions. *Organization Science, 9*(2), 195-216.

Nutt, P. C. (1998). How decision makers evaluate alternatives and the influence of complexity. *Management Science, 44*(9), 1148-1166.

Nutt, P. C. (2002, January). Making strategic choices. *Journal of Managements Studies, 39*(1), 67-93.

Parssian, A, Sarkar, S., & Jacob, V. S (2004, July). Assessing data quality for information products – Impact of selection, projection, and cartesian product.*Management Science, 50*(7).

Redman, T. C. (1996). (Ed.). *Data quality for the information age.* Boston: Artech House.

Sachdeva, S. (1998, April). Metadata architecture for data warehousing. *DM Review.*

Seeley R., Vaughan, J. (1999, August). Meta is the word. *Application Development Trends.*

Shankaranarayanan, G., & Even, A. (2004, September). Managing metadata in data warehouses: Pitfalls and possibilities. *Communications of the Association of Information Systems, 14*(13).

Shankaranarayanan, G., & Watts, S. (2003, October). A relevant believable approach for data quality assessment. *Proceedings of the MIT International Conference on Information Quality (IQ 2003)*, Boston.

Shankaranarayanan, G., Ziad, M., & Wang, R. Y. (2003, October-December). Managing data quality in dynamic decision environments: An information product approach. *Journal of Database Management, 14*(4), 14-32.

Sheth, A. (2003, July). Semantic metadata for enterprise information integration. *DM Review*.

Stephens, T. R. (2004, March). Knowledge: The essence of metadata: The meta data experience. *DM Review*.

Vaduva, A., & Vetterli, T. (2001). Metadata management for data warehousing: An overview. *International Journal of Cooperative Information Systems, 10*(3), 273-298.

Wang, R. Y., Lee, Y. W., Pipino, L. L., & Strong, D. M. (1998, Summer). Manage your information as a product. *Sloan Management Review, 39*(4).

Wang, R. Y., & Strong D. M. (1996, Spring). Beyond accuracy: What data quality means to data consumers. *Journal of Management Information Systems, 12*(4), 5-34.

White, C. (1999, February). Managing distributed data warehouse metadata. *DM Review*.

Wixom, B. H., & Watson, H. J. (2001, March). An empirical investigation of the factors affecting data warehousing success. *MIS Quarterly*, 25(1), 17-41.

Yang, W. L., & Strong, D. M. (2003, Winter). Knowing-why about data processes and data quality. *Journal of Management Information Systems, 20*(3), 13-39.

URLs for Software Products

- **Ascential**, http://www.ascential.com/
- **Business Objects**, http://www.businessobjects.com/
- **Cognos**, http://www.cognos.com/
- **Data Advantage Group**, http://www.dag.com/
- **Hummingbird**, http://www.hummingbird.com/
- **Hyperion**, http://www.hyperion.com/
- **IBM**, http://www.ibm.com/
- **Informatica**, http://www.informatica.com/

- **MetaMatrix**, http://www.metamatrix.com/
- **Microsoft**, http://www.microsoft.com/
- **MicroStrategy**, http://www.microstrategy.com/
- **Oracle**, http://www.oracle.com/
- **Sybase**, http://www.sybase.com/
- **Teradata**, http://www.teradata.com/

Chapter VII

DWFIST:
The Data Warehouse
of Frequent Itemsets
Tactics Approach

Rodrigo Salvador Monteiro,
Federal University of Rio de Janeiro, Brazil &
University of Stuttgart, Germany

Geraldo Zimbrão, Federal University of Rio de Janeiro, Brazil

Holger Schwarz, University of Stuttgart, Germany

Bernhard Mitschang, University of Stuttgart, Germany

Jano Moreira de Souza,
Federal University of Rio de Janeiro, Brazil &
University of Stuttgart, Germany

Abstract

This chapter presents the core of the DWFIST approach, which is concerned with supporting the analysis and exploration of frequent itemsets and derived patterns, e.g., association rules in transactional datasets. The goal of this new approach is to provide: (1) flexible pattern-retrieval capabilities without requiring the original data during the analysis phase; and (2) a standard modeling for data warehouses of frequent itemsets, allowing an easier development and reuse of tools for analysis and exploration of itemset-based patterns. Instead of storing the original datasets, our approach organizes frequent itemsets holding on different partitions of the original transactions in a data warehouse that retains sufficient information for future analysis. A running example for mining calendar-based patterns on data streams is presented. Staging area tasks are discussed and standard conceptual and logical schemas are presented. Properties of this standard modeling allow retrieval of frequent itemsets holding on any set of partitions, along with upper and lower bounds on their frequency counts. Furthermore, precision guarantees for some interestingness measures of association rules are provided as well.

Introduction

Some data mining tasks can produce such great amounts of data that there has arisen a new knowledge management problem (Klemettinen et al., 1994). Frequent itemset mining is long known for fitting in this category. The analysis of the results of a frequent itemset mining task is far from being trivial. The same is true for many patterns built upon frequent itemsets, such as association rules. The analyst may be easily confronted with a huge number of patterns during such an analysis. Specialized analytical and exploratory tools must be devised in order to aid analysts. The lack of a standardized way for organizing, storing and accessing frequent itemsets makes the effort of developing such tools very difficult as it avoids the reuse of general solutions for different environments.

Recent applications, such as network traffic analysis, Web clickstream mining, power consumption measurement, sensor network data analysis and dynamic tracing of stock fluctuation are some examples where a new kind of data arises, the so-called data stream. A data stream is continuous and potentially infinite. It is challenging to mine frequent patterns in data streams because this task is essentially a set of join operations, whereas join is a typical blocking operator (i.e., computation for any itemset cannot complete before seeing the past and the future data sets) (Giannella et al., 2003). Providing flexibility to mine frequent itemsets in some subset of the data stream is even more challenging, especially when the subset is not known a priori.

The research field of data warehousing has been extremely successful in providing efficient and effective ways to store and organize huge amounts of data. It has succeeded also in providing a standard modeling upon which reusable analytical tools could be designed and implemented. This chapter presents a standard modeling for frequent itemsets applicable to any transactional dataset. The product of this standard modeling is a data warehouse of frequent itemsets, which is the main component of the DWFIST approach. It organizes the whole set of transactions by disjoint partitions and stores information about the frequent itemsets holding on each partition. Different partitions may be combined to obtain the frequent itemsets with approximate support guarantees.

One particularly important application of our approach is that it can be used to leverage calendar-based pattern mining (Li et al., 2001; Ramaswamy et al., 1998) in data streams. This is an especially challenging task, as the calendar partitions of interest are not known a priori and at each point in time only a subset of the detailed data is available. Potential calendar partitions are, for example: every Monday, every first working day of each month and every holiday. We discuss how the required staging area tasks can cope with tight time constraints imposed by a data stream scenario.

Among other contributions, the DWFIST approach provides:

1.   flexible pattern-retrieval capabilities without requiring access to the detailed original data;

2.   a precision guarantee for some interestingness measures of association rules derived from frequent itemsets retrieved from the data warehouse;

3.   a conceptual view for pattern analysis that is familiar to business professionals;

4.   a standardized logical view upon which analytical tools can independently be developed; and

5.   a set of properties of the data warehouse of frequent itemsets.

This chapter covers the core of the DWFIST approach, starting with some motivation and background information on frequent itemset mining, presenting the main issues and related works, going through data staging area tasks and data warehouse modeling and, finally, reaching at the retrieval of frequent itemset based patterns. A running example for mining calendar-based patterns on data streams is presented. Analytical and explorative tools for frequent itemset based patterns are out of the scope of the chapter.

Background

The research field of data mining has provided many different techniques to explore huge amounts of data and reveal different kinds of interesting pattern or non-pattern behavior (Han & Kamber, 2001). Mining frequent patterns in transactional data, in particular the pattern domain of itemsets, is a technique that deserves special attention due to its broad applicability (Boulicaut, 2004). In the following, we present the definitions for important terms and introduce some notation that will be used throughout this chapter.

Definition 1 (transactional dataset): Let *items* be a finite set of symbols denoted by capital letters, e.g., *items* = { A, B, C, ... }. A transaction *t* is a subset of *items*. A transactional dataset *D* is a non-empty multiset $D = \{t_1, t_2, ..., t_n\}$ of transactions. ∎

Market basket data (transactions are sets of products that are bought by customers) is a classic example of a transactional dataset. Textual data (transactions are sets of keywords that characterize documents) and gene expression data (transactions are sets of genes that are over-expressed in given biological conditions) are other examples (Boulicaut, 2004).

Definition 2 (itemsets): An *itemset* is a subset of *items*. ∎

Definition 3 (frequency of itemsets): A transaction *t* supports an *itemset I* if every *item* in *I* belongs to *t*. The *frequency* of *I* over a set of transactions *T*, where $T \subseteq D$, is the number of transactions in *T* supporting *I* and is denoted by $F_T(I)$. ∎

Definition 4 (support of itemsets): Given |*T*| the number of transactions in *T*, where $T \subseteq D$, the *support* of an *itemset I* over *T* is the *frequency* of *I* divided by |*T*| and is denoted by $S_T(I)$:

$$S_T(I) = \frac{F_T(I)}{|T|} \tag{1}$$

the support of an itemset is a rate denoting the percentage of transactions in *T* supporting *I*. ∎

Definition 5 (frequent itemsets): Given a minimum support σ, an *itemset I* is considered frequent over a set of transactions *T* if $S_T(I) \geq \sigma$. Such an *itemset I* is a σ-frequent itemset over *T*. ∎

Extracting frequent itemsets that represent frequent patterns holding on some dataset is a fundamental data mining task. Many different approaches for frequent itemset mining (Agrawal & Srikant, 1994 ; Burdick et al., 2001; Han et al., 2000 ; Pasquier et al.,1999, just to mention some) were proposed since its introduction by Agrawal et al. (1993). Manku and Motwani (2002) and Giannella et al. (2003) presented algorithms to mine frequent itemsets in data streams.

Definition 6 (calendar-based frequent itemsets): Let X be a set of calendar-based constraints, Φ the set of transactions satisfying X, where $\Phi \subseteq D$, and σ a minimum support. The set of *calendar-based frequent itemsets* is defined by every *itemset I* with $S_\Phi(I) \geq \sigma$. ■

Some examples of calendar-based constraints are: weekday in {Monday, Friday}; day_period = "Morning"; holiday = "yes"; etc.

Calendar-based schemas were proposed as a semantically rich representation of time intervals and used to mine temporal-frequent itemsets (Li et al., 2001; Ramaswamy et al., 1998). An example of a calendar schema is (year, month, day, day_period), which defines a set of calendar patterns, such as *every morning of January of 1999* (1999, January, *, morning) or *every 16th day of January of every year* (*, January, 16, *).

The most widespread use of frequent itemsets is to support association rule mining (Agrawal et al., 1993). Generalized rule mining (Mannila & Toivonen, 1996) and associative classification (Liu et al., 1998) are two other examples related, respectively, to Boolean rules and classification rules.

Issues and Problems

The following issues will be addressed in this chapter:

- Mine calendar-based frequent itemsets on data streams. Let D be a transactional dataset that is provided as a data stream by some data source. Hence, only a subset of the transactions in D is available at any point in time. Nevertheless, we want to derive frequent itemsets from D based on a set of ad-hoc calendar-based constraints.

- Define a standard modeling for data warehouses of frequent itemsets. It must be applicable to any transactional dataset and be suitable for analysis tasks that rely on frequent itemsets.

Facing these issues, the challenge is to provide a standard modeling for frequent itemsets and flexible pattern retrieval capabilities without requiring the source data to be available during the analysis phase. Moreover, it must be feasible to cope with tight time constraints imposed by the data stream scenario. An overview of related works is presented in this section and major problems related to the above issues are highlighted.

Regarding storage and standard modeling for frequent itemset patterns, Kimball and Ross (2002) presented an approach for market basket analysis storing the frequency counts in a fact table. For every pair of items that appear together in any transaction, the frequency count is stored. The number of possible combinations grows exponentially with the number of items, and thus, it is likely to require more storage space than the original transactions. Furthermore, this approach does not handle information for itemsets with more than two items.

Inductive Databases introduced by Imielinski and Mannila (1996) are databases that contain inductive generalizations about the data, which are called the database theory. In such a database, the user can simply query the database theory using a conventional query language. However, the database theory relates to the data stored in the database and, therefore, we need the original data during the analysis phase. Also, it does not provide a standardized logical view for frequent itemsets representation.

The PANDA project (PANDA, 2004) studies current state-of-the-art pattern management and explores novel theoretical and practical aspects of a Pattern Base Management System. It deals with patterns in a broad sense, and does not consider predefined pattern types. The main focus is on devising a general and extensible model for patterns. As it gains in generality, it does not provide a standardized logical view for frequent itemsets representation.

The focus in data stream mining has been on stream data classification and stream clustering. Only recently has mining frequent counts in streams gained attention. An algorithm to find frequent items using a variant of classic majority algorithm was developed simultaneously by Demaine et al. (2002) and Karp et al. (2003). A framework to compute frequent items and itemsets was provided in Manku and Motwani (2002). This framework mines frequent patterns in data streams by assuming that patterns are measured from the start of the stream up to the current moment. The work presented in Giannella et al. (2003) proposes a new model for mining frequent patterns from data streams, the FP-Stream. This model is capable of answering user queries considering multiple time granularities. A fine granularity is important for recent changes whereas a coarse granularity is adequate for long-term changes. FP-Stream supports this kind of analysis by a tilted-time window, which keeps storage requirements very low but prevents calendar-based pattern analysis. An example of a tilted-time window (in minutes) is 15, 15, 30, 60, 120, 240, 480, etc. It is possible to answer queries about the last 15 minutes or the last 4 hours (15+15+30+60+120 minutes), but it is not possible to answer queries about *last Friday* or *every morning*, for example.

In order to discover temporal association rules, the work in Özden et al. (1998) states very clearly the problem of omitting the time dimension. It is assumed that the transactions in the dataset are timestamped and a time interval is specified by the user to divide the data into disjoint segments, such as months, weeks, days, etc. Cyclic association rules are defined as association rules with a minimum confidence and support at specific, regular time intervals. A disadvantage of the cyclic approach is that it does not deal with multiple granularities of time intervals. Also, an example of a calendar pattern that cannot be represented by cycles is the simple concept of the first working day of every month. Ramaswamy et al. (1998) introduces a calendar algebra, which defines a set of time intervals. A rule is called calendric if it has the minimum support and confidence over every time unit in the calendar. A disadvantage of this approach is that the user must have prior knowledge about the temporal patterns in the transactional dataset to define the calendars. The work in Li et al. (2001) tries to overcome this problem by mining the calendars. Calendar schemas are used to specify the search space for different possible calendars. The rules mined by such algorithms are presented together with their mined calendars. All these approaches are based on a calendar-based frequent itemset mining step. However, they require the transactions to be available during the calendar-based mining task. The calendars being analyzed are only defined when retrieving the patterns and thus the transactions belonging to the specified calendars must be accessible during the pattern retrieval. This feature disables these approaches from being applied to data streams because it is not possible to store the transactions for future analysis.

Partitioning methods for parallel frequent itemset mining (Zaki, 1999) aim at avoiding performance problems when the data structures involved become too large for main memory (Ahmed et al., 2004). During the parallel frequent itemset mining task, information about candidate frequent itemsets must be exchanged between the partitions in order to compute the exact frequency count. It is important to understand the distinction between this research area and the partitioning applied in our approach. The partitioning criteria applied in DWFIST are guided by analysis requirements instead of performance issues. Moreover, in the DWFIST approach there is no need for information exchange between different partitions during the mining task. The itemsets are considered frequent or not with respect to the transactions belonging to one partition.

None of the above mentioned works provides a standard way for organizing and retrieving frequent itemsets. Also, no previous approach is capable of performing calendar-based pattern mining on data streams. In the remainder of this chapter we describe the DWFIST approach and discuss how it addresses these issues.

The DWFIST Approach

The acronym DWFIST stands for data warehouse of frequent itemsets tactics. The Oxford Dictionary and Thesaurus defines tactics as: "skilful device; scheme, strategy." In this sense, the DWFIST approach aims at supporting the analysis and exploration of frequent itemsets and derived patterns, e.g., association rules in transactional datasets. The components of the approach and their relationships are presented in Figure 1.

The *pre-processing and loading* step is composed of three tasks: gather the transactions into disjoint sets (partitions) according to a pre-defined criteria (data warehouse granule); mine the frequent itemsets holding on a partition using a pre-defined mining minimum support; and load the mined frequent itemsets into the data warehouse.

The *data warehouse of frequent itemsets*, referenced simply as DW, is the main component of the approach. Its task is to store and organize the frequent itemsets into partitions. A standard modeling provides a standardized logical view.

The role of the *basic frequent itemset retrieval capabilities* component is to retrieve a set of frequent itemsets with approximate support guarantees given

Figure 1. Components of the DWFIST approach

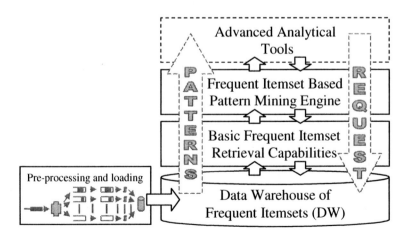

some query specifying the portion of the data warehouse to be considered. An example of such a query is: "Retrieve the frequent itemsets considering only the morning period."

The *frequent itemset based pattern mining engine* generates patterns that may be obtained from frequent itemsets. It uses a set of frequent itemsets with approximate support guarantees as input. These itemsets are provided by the basic frequent itemset retrieval capabilities component. Association rules (Agrawal et al., 1993) and Boolean rules (Mannila & Toivonen, 1996) are two examples of patterns that can be derived by this engine. Obviously, the frequent itemsets themselves are also patterns that can be "derived." This component is also responsible for computing some approximate interestingness measure guarantees related to the derived patterns, e.g., approximate confidence guarantee for association rules.

The *advanced analytical tools* component comprises analysis and exploration tools that can be built on top of the other components. It is possible to build, for example, a tool that provides a cube view of the patterns, similar to what an OLAP tool provides to conventional dimensional data. Existing automatic exploration methods, as the one presented in Sathe and Sarawagi (2001), can be adapted to explore the patterns and also new ones can be developed. This component is out of the scope of the present chapter and thus will not be further discussed.

In the following, we depict the core of the DWFIST approach, from the *preprocessing and loading* step to the frequent itemset based pattern mining engine. In order to better illustrate and explain the concepts, we introduce an example that will be used throughout the remainder of the chapter.

Running Example

We use the classical example of market basket data to illustrate the concepts of our approach. In market basket data, the transactions are sets of products that are bought by customers. As we are interested in discussing issues related to data streams, we will consider that customers' transactions arrive at an average rate of 100 transactions per second. This example was simulated in our prototype and its description follows faithfully the implementation. The simulation ran on a PC Pentium IV 1.2 GHz with 768 MB of RAM and Oracle 10g. The test data was created using the IBM synthetic market-basket data generator that is managed by the Quest data mining group. It represents a period of one week and has 60 million transactions, 1000 distinct products and an average of seven products per transaction.

Figure 2. Data source and calendar-based query examples

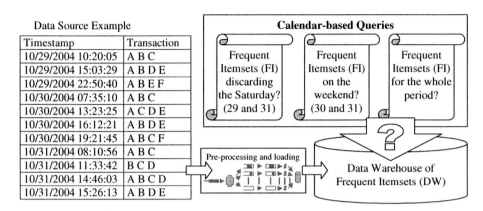

Given the above scenario, we want to retrieve calendar-based patterns holding on such a data stream. In our example the minimum slot of time that can be analyzed corresponds to a period of one hour. This corresponds to the Data Warehouse granule that will be further explained in the next section. Due to DW properties, any set of one-hour periods may be freely combined to compose a calendar partition. We may be interested, for example, in retrieving association rules valid in the morning period on weekdays. In this case, the one-hour periods, namely [08:00AM, 09:00AM), [09:00AM, 10:00AM), [10:00AM, 11:00AM) and [11:00AM, 12:00PM), belonging to weekdays will be combined.

A simplified data source example is shown in Figure 2. It also presents other calendar-based queries and sketches the retrieval of calendar-based frequent itemsets in our approach. The data warehouse of frequent itemsets receives and stores information from a transactional data source. The stored information may be used to provide approximate answers to calendar-based queries. The queries presented in Figure 2 are meant only to illustrate the calendar-based pattern retrieval. Any calendar partition that can be built using one-hour periods (e.g., afternoon, weekends, holidays, first quarter of 2004, second semester, etc.) represents a calendar-based query that can be answered by our running example.

Pre-Processing and Loading the Frequent Itemsets into the Data Warehouse

A general view of the staging area is presented in Figure 3. It presents three main tasks: separate and accumulate transactions in different partitions; mine the

Figure 3. Overview of the data staging area

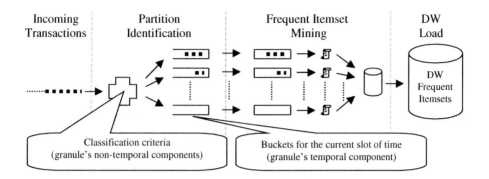

frequent itemsets holding on each individual partition; and load the frequent itemsets into the data warehouse.

First of all, one important design decision must be taken, namely, the granule definition. The granule of the DW must define a partition on the transactional data, separating it into disjoint sets. One well-known rule for conventional data warehouses says to store the data at the most granular level, in other words, it says to define the granule at the most detailed level. However, this rule must sometimes be broken in our approach. This is due to an important tradeoff that has to be taken into account when defining the granule. A more detailed granule provides more flexibility for analysis. However, the more detailed the granule of the DW, the more frequency counts need to be stored, increasing the storage requirements. Hence, analysis requirements must be considered to define the granule and storage requirement; tests have to be carried out to check the feasibility of the choice. In our running example, we define the granule as the frequent itemsets per hour. Examples of partitions defined by such a granule are "10/29/2005 [08:00AM, 09:00AM)," "10/29/2005 [09:00AM, 10:00AM)," "10/29/2005 [10:00AM, 11:00AM)" and so on. Defining such a granule avoids analyzing the pattern behavior for periods shorter than one hour. On the other hand, all possible combinations of one-hour partitions may be analyzed, providing sufficient flexibility for important calendar-based analysis. For stream data sources, the chosen granule must also be verified against imposed time constraints. Later we will discuss these time-constraint issues as well as the storage requirements in more details.

As in any data warehouse, the temporal information plays an important role in the Data Warehouse of Frequent Itemsets. The granule of the DW must have a temporal component. Even for applications where the temporal feature is not important for analysis, a temporal component must be part of the granule definition, at least in order to separate different DW loads. Other components, like spatial components, may additionally be used to define the granule. As an example, it could be defined as the frequent itemsets per store, per hour.

Once the granule of the DW is defined, the three tasks presented in Figure 3 can be implemented. The first is to separate and accumulate transactions in different partitions. When the granule has non-temporal components, such as store, a new incoming transaction has to be analyzed in order to define the partition it belongs to. Each partition for the current slot of time must have one corresponding bucket to accumulate its transactions. For example, the granule "per store per hour" requires one bucket for each store. If the granule is defined by a temporal component only, as in our running example, then one bucket will be sufficient.

The temporal component of the granule is used to identify when the set of transactions pertaining to the partitions of the current slot of time are completely collected. The complete sets of transactions are passed to the next step where the mining is performed.

The frequent itemset mining is performed on each completely collected set of transactions comprising one partition. A minimum support threshold must be specified for this task, which we call *mining minimum support*. The initial threshold value is not a definitive commitment. The mining minimum support threshold may be changed freely over time as well as customized thresholds, which can be specified for different partitions. It is only required that each partition is associated with exactly one mining minimum support threshold. The frequent itemset mining results in a list of frequent itemsets with their corresponding frequency counts holding on the transactions of a partition. The mining minimum support is set to 0.1% in the running example.

The frequent itemsets, their frequency counts, the number of transactions in the partition and the applied mining minimum support threshold must be stored in some intermediate storage area before they are finally loaded into the DW. This intermediate storage area provides isolation between the mining process and the DW load process. By this isolation, it is possible, for example, to define a daily DW load procedure having an hourly granule. As soon as one partition is mined and its information stored in the intermediate storage area, the partition's transactions may be discarded.

Finally, the information stored in the intermediate storage area will be loaded into the data warehouse periodically. Many conventional data warehouse issues arise in this step and should be treated the same way as in regular data warehouses. Some examples of such issues are assigning surrogate keys and creating new dimension instances. The isolation provided by the intermediate storage area makes it easier to take care of such issues while still having to cope with tight time constraints.

Time Constraint Issues

As far as we are able to pre-process and load the data of one slot of time before the next one is available, we are coping with data stream time constraint requirements. Let us discuss the related issues through the running example. The granule was defined as the frequent itemsets per hour. Hence, each slot of time covers data for one hour, and thus a one-hour window is available for pre-processing and load. While the transactions of the current slot of time are being gathered, the previous one is being mined and loaded. Let us discuss the mining and loading steps in more detail.

Many frequent itemset mining algorithms were proposed since the statement of this mining task in Agrawal et al. (1993). Any efficient algorithm may be applied in our mining pre-processing step. As an example of an efficient algorithm, Giannella et al. (2003) uses the FP-growth algorithm (Han et al., 2000) to mine frequent itemsets on batches of transactions from a data stream. The efficiency of this step depends mainly on the mining minimum support and the number of transactions. In our running example, a mining minimum support of 0.1% was used and the average number of transactions per partition was 360000. We used an optimized implementation of FP-growth, described in Grahne and Zhu (2003). Every partition was mined in less than one minute.

When a non-temporal component is used to define the DW granule, the different partitions of one slot of time can be processed in parallel. It is important to note that we are not talking about parallel mining. We just have to identify the frequent itemsets for each partition individually. For this purpose, a non-parallel frequent itemset algorithm could be executed on different partitions at the same time. In parallel data mining, an additional task would be to combine the frequency counts of all partitions and compute global frequent itemsets from them. As we want to keep frequent itemsets for each partition in the DW, this is not necessary in our approach.

The load step mainly comprises the insertion of new frequent itemset frequency counts and the creation of new dimension tuples. An important property of the load step is that the time required is proportional to the number of frequent itemsets to be loaded instead of the number of transactions. Also, an increase in the number of transactions for a frequent itemset mining task keeping a fixed mining minimum support does not lead to a proportional increase in the number of frequent itemsets. In most cases, the number of frequent itemsets tends to stabilize or even decrease. The partitions in the running example contain 3650 frequent itemsets (using a mining minimum support of 0.1%) on average. The average time required for the load step was 12 minutes, using a non-optimized procedure.

The definition of the granule plays a central role for coping with time constraints. First of all, it defines the time window available for processing. Second, an increase in the time window makes the task of the load step easier and the task of the mining step harder. The task of the mining step gets harder because a bigger window means a potentially higher number of transactions. Fortunately, current frequent itemset mining algorithms are able to process efficiently a considerably large number of transactions. Therefore, an increase in the time window is likely to bring more benefits for the load step than losses for the mining step.

Some scenarios may present prohibitive arrival rates even for the most efficient existing frequent itemset mining algorithm. Such fast arrival rates result in large partitions containing a large number of transactions that increases the time required for the mining task. An alternative approach for extreme scenarios is to apply the framework presented in Giannella et al. (2003), called FP-Stream, to perform our mining task. This framework is capable of answering queries such as "retrieve the frequent itemsets holding on the transactions of the last 15 minutes" or "retrieve the frequent itemsets holding on the transactions of the last 4 hours" on a stream. The important feature of this framework is that the required processing time is independent from the period being queried. This means that using this framework it is possible to increase the time window without increasing the time required for the mining step. The disadvantage of applying this framework to perform our mining task is that it introduces an error in the frequency counts. Therefore, the known frequency counts that will be loaded into the DW are not exact counts anymore. This additional error must then be considered when computing the frequency upper bound during the retrieval from the DW.

The conclusion about adjusting the temporal component of the DW granule is that it provides an effective way of coping with time constraints. Nonetheless, we cannot forget that analysis requirements must be taken into account as well, and that a more detailed temporal component provides more flexible analysis capabilities. This tradeoff must be evaluated through experimental tests to define the optimal granule for each specific scenario.

The isolation provided by the intermediate storage area helps to cope with tight time constraints as well. Using a daily load procedure, for example, it is not strictly required that the load of each one of the 24 one-hour partitions must be performed in less than one hour. It is sufficient that the set of 24 partitions can be loaded in less than 24 hours. In this way, eventual peeks of processing in the load step, caused, for example, by an extension of the DW storage area, can be handled. In the running example, even the peaks of processing in load step could be performed in less than one hour.

Storage Requirements Issues

An important observation regarding storage requirements is that the size of DW increases at a lower rate compared to the size of the considered input data stream. The reasoning that supports this assertion is two-fold. First, the frequent itemsets require less storage space than the original stream transactions; and second, the reuse of information stored in the dimensions reduces the storage requirements. The DW in the running example occupies 10MB related to the first 1GB of the data stream. It reaches 17.5MB when considering the whole test dataset of 2GB. The mentioned DW sizes include indexes structures as well.

Non-stream data sources present a less critical scenario. Nevertheless, storage requirement tests must also be carried out. In such data sources it may be interesting to build a data warehouse of frequent itemsets even if you store the original transactions. First, by pre-processing the frequent itemsets we are able to reduce the computational effort required during the analysis tasks performed by a user. Second, the redundant information can be justified as far as it provides the data in such a way that it can be more effectively analyzed (Kimball & Ross, 2002).

A similar discussion on adjusting the DW granule presented in the previous section applies to storage requirements issues. In an analogous way, the storage requirements are proportional to the number of frequent itemsets being stored.

Data Warehouse of Frequent Itemsets

The data warehouse of frequent itemsets, although presenting particularities, may be seen as a regular Data Warehouse. Therefore, many considerations presented in Kimball and Ross (2002), ranging from the use of surrogate keys to the business dimensional lifecycle, are applicable. In this section we present conceptual and logical schemas aiming at a standard modeling for data warehouses of frequent itemsets. The definition of standardized conceptual and logical schemas allows for an easier development and reuse of tools for analysis and exploration of itemset-based patterns.

Conceptual View

We present a standardized conceptual schema for data warehouses of frequent itemsets. Figure 4 shows this schema using the StarER notation (Tryfona et al., 1999). Our conceptual schema is based on a distinction between item dimensions and partition dimensions:

Figure 4. StarER standardized conceptual schema

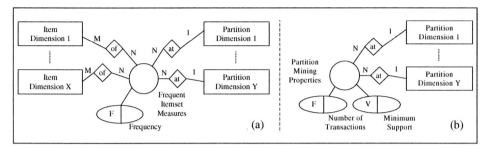

- An item dimension describes similar items that may appear as part of a frequent itemset. If there are groups of items with different features, several item dimensions should be provided in order to better describe and classify the items. In the context of medical procedures, the hospital materials could be represented in one item dimension and the medical staff in another.

- A partition dimension organizes the space of the original transactions into disjoint sets, which we call DW partitions. Each partition dimension describes one component of the DW granule. Temporal and spatial dimensions are examples of candidate partition dimensions.

Another distinction that may be observed in Figure 4 (a) is that the relationship between an item dimension and an itemset fact is an N-to-M relationship, while the relationship between a partition dimension and an itemset fact is a one-to-N relationship. The N-to-M relationship is applied because one itemset may contain different items of the same dimension.

When accessing the DW, the item dimensions are used to define features of the itemsets that must be retrieved. In the running example, it could be requested to retrieve only the itemsets containing at least one product belonging to the category "beverages." The partition dimensions are used to define the portion of the original transactions that must be considered. Retrieving the frequent itemsets holding on the transactions related to the morning period would be one possibility in the running example.

It is interesting to relate the information stored in the intermediate storage area with our conceptual schema. Figure 4 (a) represents the part of the DW that describes the frequent itemsets and their frequency counts. A frequency count is a fact attribute and a frequent itemset is represented by relationships with item dimensions. As shown in Figure 4 (b), for each partition additional information

Figure 5. StarER conceptual schema for the running example

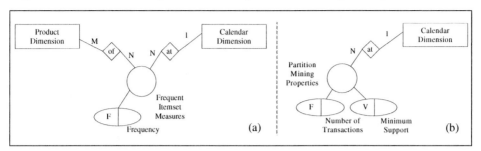

has to be stored, i.e., the number of transactions and the applied mining minimum support threshold. In the figure they are represented as fact attributes. Note, that the schema presented in Figure 4 (b) has only partition dimensions because the partition mining properties are the same for a complete partition, thus independent from a specific frequent itemset.

The dimensions should conform to the data warehouse bus architecture (Kimball & Ross, 2002). This allows for crossover operations that relate the attributes of the two different facts presented in Figure 4 through the corresponding partition dimensions.

Figure 5 presents the conceptual schema for our running example. A calendar dimension plays the role of a partition dimension organizing the space of the original transactions into disjoint sets representing non-overlapping one-hour periods. The schema in Figure 5 (b) represents the number of transactions on each one-hour period and the minimum support used for mining the frequent itemsets in the pre-processing step. A product dimension describes the products that may appear as part of a frequent itemset, thus playing the role of an item dimension. The schema in Figure 5 (a) represents, for each one-hour period, the frequency counts of each set of products mined as frequent. The attributes of the product and calendar dimensions are not presented in Figure 5 for the sake of a clear presentation. Just to mention a few: product name, category and sales department are examples of attributes of the product dimension; period of the day (morning, afternoon, etc.), weekday and holiday (yes or no) are some attributes of the calendar dimension.

Logical View

A standardized logical schema is presented in Figures 6. In the logical design we introduce one itemset dimension for each item dimension as can be seen in Figure

Figure 6. Standardized logical schema

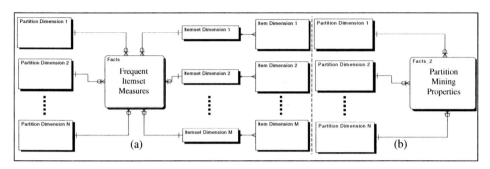

(a)   (b)

Figure 7. Logical schema for the running example with some instance samples

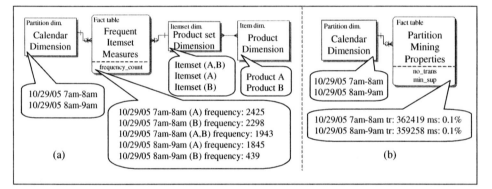

(a)   (b)

6 (a). The itemset dimension works as a bridge table representing the n-to-m-relationships between the item dimensions and the facts in the conceptual schema. Analytical tools usually hide the existence of bridge tables. An analytical tool developed upon a data warehouse of frequent itemsets should know about the item dimensions and the corresponding itemset dimensions in order to provide such a transparency and perform the required mappings.

The itemset dimensions contain one identifier for each distinct itemset, which will be used as a foreign key in the fact table and to group the items into itemsets as well. The logical schema presented in Figure 6 (b) is derived straightforward from the conceptual schema presented in Figure 4 (b).

The logical schema for the running example is presented in Figure 7, together with some sample data for each table. Two instances representing one-hour periods are shown in the calendar dimension. In Figure 7 (a) two products are listed in the product dimension and some related itemsets are presented in the itemset dimension. The frequency counts of the itemsets for the two one-hour periods are presented in the frequent itemset frequency measures fact table. Note that there is no frequency count for the itemset (A, B) related to the partition "10/29/2005 [08:00AM, 09:00AM)." This means that the itemset (A, B) was not frequent in this partition. In Figure 7 (b) the number of transactions of the two one-hour periods is presented along with the mining minimum support (0.1%) in the partition mining properties fact table.

Relying on the standard modeling presented above, analytical and explorative tools can independently be developed. The standard modeling provided plays the same role for frequent itemsets as star and snowflake schemas play for regular data.

Basic Frequent Itemset Retrieval Capabilities

This section describes how the information stored in the data warehouse of frequent itemsets may be used to retrieve frequent itemsets holding on original transactions represented by any arbitrary set of DW partitions. The basic frequent itemset retrieval capabilities component is responsible to perform this task, which is formalized as follows:

Frequent itemset retrieval task: Given a set of DW partitions ρ and a query minimum support σ_q, retrieve the set Φ of all itemsets I with $S_\rho(I) \geq \sigma_q$. The set Φ must also contain approximate frequency counts for each I represented by intervals $[\text{LB\_}F_\rho(I), \text{UB\_}F_\rho(I)]$. Therefore, if I is a σ_q-frequent itemset holding on the original transactions represented by ρ with frequency count $F_\rho(I)$, then:

$$I \in \Phi \text{ and } \text{LB\_}F_\rho(I) \leq F_\rho(I) \leq \text{UB\_}F_\rho(I) \qquad (2) \ \blacksquare$$

In other words, the set Φ of retrieved σ_q-frequent itemsets must be complete, not missing any σ_q-frequent itemset holding on the original transactions represented by ρ, and lower and upper bounds on the frequency counts must be provided as well. This task cannot be accomplished for all values of σ_q, as the DW does not contain every itemset frequency count. Instead, it contains only the ones that were mined as frequent. Also, the completeness of Φ must be checked and the frequency lower and upper bounds computed. The following properties will help to address these issues.

Property 1 (Disjoint partitions): The DW partitions represent completely disjoint sets of transactions and thus the frequency counts of a specific itemset can be summed over any set of partitions. ∎

Property 2 (Error upper bound): Given $|\rho_i|$, the number of original transactions in partition ρ_i, and σ_{mi}, the mining minimum support used on partition ρ_i, the product $|\rho_i|\sigma_{mi}$ provides a strict upper bound on the number of missed frequencies over partition ρ_i. Moreover, a strict error upper bound UBe_ρ for a set of DW partitions ρ, is provided by simply summing the upper bounds of the individual partitions:

$$UBe_\rho = \sum_{\rho_i \in \rho} |\rho_i|\sigma_{mi} \tag{3}$$

In the special case where σ_{mi} is constant over ρ we have:

$$UBe_\rho = \sum_{\rho_i \in \rho} |\rho_i|\sigma_{mi} = \sigma_m \sum_{\rho_i \in \rho} |\rho_i| = \sigma_m |\rho| \tag{4} \ \blacksquare$$

Property 3 (Frequency count bounds): Lower and upper bounds on the frequency count of an itemset I over a set of DW partition ρ can be calculated using properties 1 and 2 as follows:

$$LB\_F_\rho(I) = \sum_{\rho_i \in \rho_{known}} F_{\rho_i}(I) \qquad UB\_F_\rho(I) = LB\_F_\rho(I) + UBe_{\rho-\rho_{known}} \tag{5}$$

where ρ_{known} represents the subset of partitions from ρ, where the itemset I was mined as frequent, and thus its frequency count is known. The expression $\rho - \rho_{known}$ represents the complementary subset from ρ, where the frequency count of I is unknown.

Properties 1 and 2 provide the building blocks for property 3. Property 3 is used in practice to compute and retrieve from the DW the approximate frequency of an itemset over a set of original transactions. The set of original transactions is represented by any arbitrary set of DW partitions.

The samples presented in Figure 7 may be used to exemplify how the frequency count bounds are computed. Considering ρ equal to the two sample partitions presented in Figure 7, we can depict how the frequency bounds would be computed for the itemsets (A), (B) and (A,B) using property 3. The frequency

Figure 8. SQL query for the frequent itemset retrieval task on the running example

```
Select
  S.itemset_id,
  S.LB_Frequency,
  ( S.LB_Frequency + G.Global_Error - S.Known_Part_Error) as UB_Frequency
From ( Select
          FIM.itemset_id,
          sum(FIM.frequency_count) as LB_Frequency,
          sum(PMP.no_trans*PMP.min_sup) as Known_Part_Error,
       From Calendar_Dimension CD,
            Frequent_Itemset_Measures FIM,
            Partition_Mining_Properties PMP
       Where  CD.CD_id = PMP.CD_id and
              CD.CD_id = FIM.CD_id and
              CD.day_period = 'Morning'
       Group by FIM.itemset_id) S,
     ( Select
          sum(PMP.no_trans) as Total_no_trans,
          sum(PMP.no_trans*PMP.min_sup) as Global_Error
       From Calendar_Dimension CD,
            Partition_Mining_Properties PMP
       Where  CD.CD_id = PMP.CD_id and
              CD.day_period = 'Morning') G
Where ( S.LB_Frequency + G.Global_Error - S.Known_Part_Error) >=
      ( G.Total_no_trans * :query_minimum_support)
```

lower bound is simply computed by summing the known frequency counts. Therefore, we have 4270 (2425+1845) for (A); 2737 (2298+439) for (B); and 1943 for (A,B). The frequency upper bound is computed using the frequency lower bound and the information stored on the partition mining properties fact table. As the frequency counts of itemsets (A) and (B) are known in both partitions, the exact frequency is known and thus, the frequency upper bound is equal to the frequency lower bound. The frequency of the itemset (A,B) is unknown in partition "10/29/2005 [08:00AM, 09:00AM)." The error upper bound for this partition is calculated using equation (3) and is 359.258 (0.1% of 359258). Therefore, the frequency upper bound for itemset (A,B) is 2302.258 (1943+359.258). The decimal part may be discarded at the end, as frequency counts are integer measures. Finally, the computed frequency count bounds are [1943,2302] for itemset (A,B), [4270,4270] for itemset (A) and [2737,2737] for itemset (B).

Based on the schema of our running example presented in Figure 7, an SQL query to perform the frequent itemset retrieval task is presented in Figure 8. It retrieves the frequent itemsets holding on the morning period and thus is an example of calendar-based frequent itemset mining. A tool that provides an interface for specifying conditions on the dimensions and accesses the frequent itemsets through the presented standardized logical schema can automatically build such a query.

Let us now discuss under which conditions the completeness of Φ can be guaranteed.

Property 4 (Completeness 1): If $F_\rho(I)$ is equal or greater than UBe_ρ then I is represented in at least one partition $\rho_i \in \rho$.

Proof: Considering that no partition $\rho_i \in \rho$ has any information about I means that $F_{\rho i}(I) < |\rho_i|\sigma_{mi} \ \forall \ \rho_i \in \rho$. Using property 1 and 2, and comparing with (3):

$$\sum_{\rho_i \in \rho} F_{\rho_i}(I) < \sum_{\rho_i \in \rho} |\rho_i|\sigma_{mi} = \text{UBe}_\rho \qquad (6) \ \blacksquare$$

Property 5 (Completeness 2): Let Φ be a list of σ_q-frequent itemsets retrieved from a set of DW partitions ρ. The completeness of Φ can be guaranteed for any σ_q such that:

$$\sigma_q \geq \frac{\text{UBe}_\rho}{|\rho|} \qquad (7)$$

Proof: In order to be considered a σ_q-frequent itemset over a set of DW partitions ρ, an itemset I must have a minimum frequency count of $\sigma_q|\rho|$. From property 4 we have that all itemset I with $F_\rho(I) \geq \text{UBe}_\rho$ will be present in at least one partition $\rho_i \in \rho$. If the minimum frequency count $\sigma_q|\rho|$ is equal or greater than the error upper bound UBe_ρ then the completeness of Φ can be guaranteed:

$$|\rho|\sigma_q \geq \text{UBe}_\rho \qquad (8)$$

Equation (7) is directly obtained from (8). Also, in the special case where σ_{mi} is constant over ρ, from equation (4), we have:

$$|\rho|\sigma_q \geq |\rho|\sigma_m \qquad\qquad \sigma_q \geq \sigma_m \qquad (9) \ \blacksquare$$

Properties 4 and 5 tell us in practice that the retrieved set of patterns is guaranteed to be complete as far as we request the frequent itemsets using a query minimum support equal or greater than the mining minimum support. In other words, given this condition on σ_q, we are not missing any σ_q-frequent itemset holding on a set of original transactions. Once again, the set of original transactions is represented by any arbitrary set of DW partitions.

The above set of properties, together with a proper definition of the DW granule, allows performing calendar-based frequent itemset mining on data streams.

Frequent Itemset Based Pattern Mining Engine

Once we have retrieved a list of frequent itemsets and their corresponding approximate frequency counts holding on a set of DW partitions ρ, using a query minimum support σ_q, we can build other patterns upon it. In doing so, the uncertainty about the exact frequency counts must be taken into account. This is the task of the frequent itemset based pattern mining engine component. We exemplify this task by discussing how association rules and some related interestingness measures may be obtained from frequent itemsets retrieved from the DW. Furthermore, analyzing the worst-case, we can derive theoretical bounds providing a precision guarantee for these measures.

Association rules were first discussed in Agrawal et al. (1993) and may be defined as follows:

Definition 7 (association rules): An association rule is denoted as $\alpha \rightarrow \gamma$, where α and γ are itemsets and $\alpha \cap \gamma = \varnothing$; α is the body of the rule, also called antecedent, and γ is the head of the rule, also called consequent. Semantically, an association rule expresses a tendency of having γ whenever α is present. ∎

Extracting association rules based on a list of frequent itemsets is a well-known and solved problem. An efficient algorithm is presented in Agrawal et al. (1996). As far as the completeness of the set of frequent itemsets is guaranteed by properties 4 and 5, the completeness of the set of association rules is also guaranteed. The relevant issue in our context is how to compute measures related to association rules using the approximate frequency counts of itemsets. Two measures are discussed in the following, namely confidence and gain. For both, we present how specific bounds for individual rules can be computed. Afterwards, a precision guarantee is provided.

Confidence

The confidence of a rule $\alpha \rightarrow \gamma$ represents the probability of having the consequent (γ) in a transaction, given that the antecedent (α) is present. Given a set of DW partitions ρ, it can be computed as follows:

$$\text{conf}_\rho(\alpha \rightarrow \gamma) = \frac{F_\rho(\alpha \cup \gamma)}{F_\rho(\alpha)} \tag{10}$$

Lower and upper bounds on the confidence for an individual rule can be computed as:

$$\text{LBconf}_\rho(\alpha \to \gamma) = \frac{\text{LB\_}F_\rho(\alpha \cup \gamma)}{\text{UB\_}F_\rho(\alpha)} \qquad \text{UBconf}_\rho(\alpha \to \gamma) = \frac{\text{UB\_}F_\rho(\alpha \cup \gamma)}{\text{LB\_}F_\rho(\alpha)}(11) \blacksquare$$

The reasoning is quite simple. We select the frequency lower bound or upper bound in the numerator or denominator in order to minimize or maximize the result. Using the sample data in Figure 7, we can compute the confidence bounds for the rule A→B. Remembering the retrieved frequency counts from itemset (A) [4270,4270] and itemset (A,B) [1943,2302], and applying equation (11), we have LBconf_ρ(A→B) as 45% and UBconf_ρ(A→B) as 54%. Therefore, an approximate confidence of 49.5% ± 4.5 percentage points can be retrieved.

As we raise the query minimum support (σ_q) for the frequent itemset retrieval task, the ratio $\text{UBe}_\rho/\text{LB\_}F_\rho(\alpha)$ between the frequency count errors and the itemsets' lower bound frequency is reduced. The simple reasoning is that the error is kept constant and the itemsets' lower bounds are increased. Therefore, it can be expected to get lower confidence errors when raising σ_q.

The following property provides a precision guarantee for the confidence measure of every association rule retrieved from a set of DW partitions ρ using a query minimum support σ_q. For the sake of simplicity, and without loss of generality, we consider that a constant minimum support σ_m was used for mining during the pre-processing step of all partitions ρ_i belonging to ρ. If this is not the case, we can simply assume σ_m as the maximum σ_{mi} used for all ρ_i.

Property 6: Given a set of DW partitions ρ, σ_m, a mining minimum support used over ρ, σ_q a query minimum support and taking the central value of the interval [LBconf,UBconf] as the confidence approximate value, we have a worst-case error on the confidence expressed by:

$$\text{Worst\_Case\_conf\_error}_\rho = \frac{\sigma_m}{\sigma_q - \sigma_m} \qquad (12)$$

Proof: Taking the central value of the interval [LBconf,UBconf], we have a maximum error of half of the interval's length for one individual association rule. Maximizing the error we have:

$$\mathrm{conf\_error}_\rho(\alpha \to \gamma) = \frac{\mathrm{UBconf}_\rho(\alpha \to \gamma)\,\text{-}\,\mathrm{LBconf}_\rho(\alpha \to \gamma)}{2} =$$

$$\left(\frac{\mathrm{UB\_}F_\rho(\alpha \cup \gamma)}{\mathrm{LB\_}F_\rho(\alpha)} - \frac{\mathrm{LB\_}F_\rho(\alpha \cup \gamma)}{\mathrm{UB\_}F_\rho(\alpha)} \right)\frac{1}{2} \leq$$

$$\left(\frac{\mathrm{LB\_}F_\rho(\alpha \cup \gamma) + \mathrm{UBe}_\rho}{\mathrm{LB\_}F_\rho(\alpha)} - \frac{\mathrm{LB\_}F_\rho(\alpha \cup \gamma)}{\mathrm{LB\_}F_\rho(\alpha) + \mathrm{UBe}_\rho} \right)\frac{1}{2} =$$

$$\frac{\mathrm{UBe}_\rho\left(\mathrm{LB\_}F_\rho(\alpha) + \mathrm{UBe}_\rho\right) + \mathrm{UBe}_\rho\mathrm{LB\_}F_\rho(\alpha \cup \gamma)}{2\mathrm{LB\_}F_\rho(\alpha)\left(\mathrm{LB\_}F_\rho(\alpha) + \mathrm{UBe}_\rho\right)} =$$

$$\frac{1}{2\mathrm{LB\_}F_\rho(\alpha)}\left(\mathrm{UBe}_\rho + \frac{\mathrm{UBe}_\rho\,\mathrm{LB\_}F_\rho(\alpha \cup \gamma)}{\left(\mathrm{LB\_}F_\rho(\alpha) + \mathrm{UBe}_\rho\right)} \right) <$$

$$\frac{\mathrm{UBe}_\rho + \mathrm{UBe}_\rho}{2\mathrm{LB\_}F_\rho(\alpha)} = \frac{\mathrm{UBe}_\rho}{\mathrm{LB\_}F_\rho(\alpha)} < \frac{\mathrm{UBe}_\rho}{\sigma_q|\rho| - \mathrm{UBe}_\rho} = \frac{\sigma_m|\rho|}{\sigma_q|\rho| - \sigma_m|\rho|} = \frac{\sigma_m}{\sigma_q - \sigma_m}$$

The graph in Figure 9 was drawn using equation (12). The values on the horizontal axis refer to the σ_q/σ_m ratio between the query minimum support and the mining minimum support. In the running example, we used a mining minimum support of 0.1%. Therefore, Figure 9 refers to values ranging from 0.2% to 2%

Figure 9. Precision guarantee for confidence of association rules

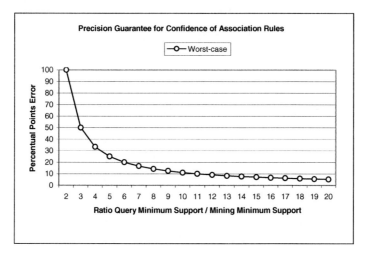

for the query minimum support when considering our running example. If we retrieve the association rules from the DW using a query minimum support of 1.1% in our example, a precision of 10 percentage points is guaranteed for the confidence measure.

The graph in Figure 9 may be used to adjust the DW configuration. We may look at it from a different point of view and use it to aid at the choice of the mining minimum support. For example, if we expect to mine association rules using a query minimum support of $S\%$ and want to guarantee a maximum confidence error of 11 percentage points, Figure 9 tell us that we should use a mining minimum support of one-tenth of S.

Gain

The gain function of Fukuda et al. (1996) is given below. The parameter θ is a fractional constant between 0 and 1:

$$\text{gain}_\rho(\alpha \to \gamma) = F_\rho(\alpha \cup \gamma) - \theta \, F_\rho(\alpha) \tag{13}$$

Lower and upper bounds of the gain for an individual rule may be computed as:

$$\text{LBgain}_\rho(\alpha \to \gamma) = \text{LB\_}F_\rho(\alpha \cup \gamma) - \theta \, \text{UB\_}F_\rho(\alpha) \tag{14} \blacksquare$$
$$\text{UBgain}_\rho(\alpha \to \gamma) = \text{UB\_}F_\rho(\alpha \cup \gamma) - \theta \, \text{LB\_}F_\rho(\alpha)$$

The following property provides a precision guarantee for the gain measure of association rules retrieved from a set of DW partitions ρ:

Property 7: Using the central value in the interval [LBgain,UBgain] as the gain approximate value, we have a worst-case error on the gain expressed by:

$$\text{Worst\_Case\_gain\_e}_\rho(\alpha \to \gamma) = \text{UBe}_\rho \tag{15}$$

Proof: Taking the central value of the interval [LBgain,UBgain], we have a maximum error of half of the interval's length:

$$gain\_e_\rho(\alpha \to \gamma) = \frac{UBgain_\rho(\alpha \to \gamma) - LBgain_\rho(\alpha \to \gamma)}{2} =$$

$$\frac{UB\_F_\rho(\alpha \cup \gamma) - \theta\, LB\_F_\rho(\alpha) - \left(LB\_F_\rho(\alpha \cup \gamma) - \theta\, UB\_F_\rho(\alpha)\right)}{2} =$$

$$\frac{LB\_F_\rho(\alpha \cup \gamma) + UBe_\rho - \theta\, LB\_F_\rho(\alpha) - LB\_F_\rho(\alpha \cup \gamma) + \theta\left(LB\_F_\rho(\alpha) + UBe_\rho\right)}{2} = \blacksquare$$

$$\frac{UBe_\rho + \theta\, UBe_\rho}{2} \leq UBe_\rho \qquad max(\theta) = 1$$

The worst-case error on the gain measure is exactly the same as the upper bound on the frequency count error and is completely independent of the query minimum support.

Similar precision guarantees can be provided for other interestingness measures of association rules. Precision guarantees for other patterns, such as Boolean and classification rules, can be provided as well and are not presented in this chapter due to space constraints.

Conclusion and Future Trends

This chapter presented the core of the DWFIST approach focusing on two issues: (1) provide a standard modeling for frequent itemsets; and (2) mine calendar-based frequent itemsets on data streams. A data warehouse plays a central role in our approach. It stores frequent itemsets holding on different partitions of the original transactions retaining information for future analysis. We discussed staging area tasks that must be performed. Time constraints and storage requirements issues were considered in a data stream scenario. A tradeoff between analysis capabilities and the time window available for pre-processing must be taken into account for defining the DW granule. A running example for mining calendar-based frequent itemsets was provided. This example was implemented in a prototype and some measurements were presented to illustrate how the proposed approach works in practice. The standard modeling presented for frequent itemset warehousing provides a standardized logical view upon which analytical and explorative tools may independently be developed. A set of properties of the data warehouse of frequent itemsets allows for a flexible retrieval of frequent itemsets holding on any set of DW partitions. Using the running example, we exemplified how the flexibility provided for pattern retrieval may be used for calendar-based pattern mining. Finally, the retrieval of frequent itemset-based patterns from the DW was exemplified by association rules and two related interestingness measures, namely confidence and gain.

As future trends, we would like to highlight the development of analytical and exploratory tools to exploit large sets of patterns. Such tools can rely on the standardized logical schema provided by our approach to access and retrieve patterns. Evaluating the applicability and usage of different condensed representations for representing the frequent itemsets on a DW partition is an interesting topic as well. The use of condensed representations for frequent itemsets, such as closed frequent itemsets, can reduce the storage requirements and also bring benefits to the DW load process. However, an overhead will be introduced for the retrieval of patterns from the DW. This tradeoff must be further explored and analyzed. At last, deploying other frequent itemset-based patterns is an additional issue for future research.

Acknowledgments

This work was partially supported by CNPq as a Sandwich Program, during which Monteiro was a visiting PhD student at University of Stuttgart.

References

Agrawal, R., Imielinski, T., & Swami, A. (1993). Mining association rules between sets of items in large databases. In *Proceedings of the 1993 Int'l Conference on Management of Data ACM SIGMOD,* Washington, DC (pp. 207-216).

Agrawal, R., Mannila, H., Srikant, R., Toivonen, H., & Verkamo, A. I. (1996). Fast discovery of association rules. In U. Fayyad, G. Piatetsky-Shapiro, P. Smyth, & R. Uthurusamy (Eds.), *Advances in knowledge discovery and data mining* (pp. 307-328). AAAI/MIT Press.

Agrawal, R., & Srikant, R. (1994). Fast algorithms for mining association rules in large databases. In *Proceedings of the 20th International Conference on Very Large Data Bases*, Santiago de Chile, Chile (pp. 487-499).

Ahmed, S., Coenen, F. & Leng, P. (2004). A tree partitioning method for memory management in association rule mining. In *Proceedings (LNCS),*

DAWAK 2004 Conference, Zaragoza, Spain (Vol. 3181, pp. 331-340). Springer.

Boulicaut, J. (2004). Inductive databases and multiple uses of frequent itemsets: The cInQ approach. In R. Meo et al. (Eds.), *Database support for data mining applications (LNCS)*. (Vol. 2682, pp. 3-26). Springer.

Burdick, D., Calimlim, M., & Gehrke, J. E. (2001). MAFIA: A maximal frequent itemset algorithm for transactional databases. In *Proceedings of the 17th International Conference on Data Engineering*, Heidelberg, Germany.

Demaine, E. D., López-Ortiz, A., & Munro, J. I. (2002). Frequency estimation of internet packet streams with limited space. In *Proceedings of the 10th Annual European Symposium on Algorithms*, Rome, Italy (pp. 348-360).

Fukuda, T., Morimoto, Y., Morishita, S., & Tokuyama, T. (1996). Data mining using two-dimensional optimized association rules: Scheme, algorithms, and visualization. In *Proceedings of the 1996 ACM-SIGMOD Int'l Conf. on the Management of Data*, Montreal, Canada (pp. 13-23).

Giannella, C., Han, J., Pei, J., Yan, X., & Yu, P.S. (2003). Mining frequent patterns in data streams at multiple time granularities. In H. Kargupta, A. Joshi, K. Sivakumar, & Y. Yesha (Eds.), *Data mining: Next generation challenges and future directions*. AAAI/MIT Press.

Grahne, G., & Zhu, J. (2003). Efficiently using prefix-trees in mining frequent itemsets. In *Proceeding of the First IEEE ICDM Workshop on Frequent Itemset Mining Implementations (FIMI'03)*, Melbourne, FL.

Han, J., & Kamber, M. (2001). *Data mining: concepts and techniques*. Academic Press.

Han, J., Pei, J., & Yin, Y. (2000). Mining frequent patterns without candidate generation . In *Proceedings of the 2000 ACM-SIGMOD Int'l Conf. on the Management of Data*, Dallas, TX (pp. 1-12).

Imielinski, T., & Mannila, H. (1996). A database perspective on knowledge discovery. *Communications of the ACM, 39*, 58-64.

Karp, R. M., Papadimitriou, C. H., & Shenker, S. (2003). A simple algorithm for finding frequent elements in streams and bags. *ACM Transactions on Database Systems, 28*(1), 51-55.

Kimball, R., & Ross, M. (2002). *The data warehouse toolkit: The complete guide to dimensional modelling* (2nd ed.). New York: Wiley Publishers.

Klemettinen, M., Mannila, H., Ronkainen, P., Toivonen, H., & Verkamo, A. I. (1994). Finding interesting rules from large sets of discovered association rules. In *Proceedings of the Third International Conference on Information and Knowledge Management*, Gaithersburg, MD (pp. 401-407).

Li, Y., Ning, P., Wang, X.S., & Jajodia, S. (2001). Discovering calendar-based temporal association rules. In *Proceedings of the 8ᵗʰ International Symposium on Temporal Representation and Reasoning*, Cividale de Friuli, Italy (pp. 111-118).

Liu, B., Hsu, W., & Ma, Y. (1998). Integrating classification and association rule mining. In *Proceedings of the Fourth Int'l Conf. on Knowledge Discovery and Data Mining (KDD'98)*, New York (pp. 80-86). AAAI Press.

Manku, G., & Motwani, R. (2002). Approximate frequency counts over data streams. In *Proceedings of the International Conference on Very Large Data Bases*, Hong Kong, China (pp. 346-357).

Mannila, H., & Toivonen, H. (1996). Multiple uses of frequent sets and condensed representations . In *Proceedings of the Second International Conference on Knowledge Discovery and Data Mining (KDD'96)*, Portland, Oregon (pp. 189-194). AAAI Press.

Özden, B., Ramaswamy, S., & Silberschatz, A. (1998). Cyclic association rules. In *Proceedings of the 14ᵗʰ Int'l Conf. on Data Engineering*, Orlando, FL (pp. 412-421).

PANDA Project (2004). Retrievable from http://dke.cti.gr/panda/

Pasquier, N., Bastide, Y., Taouil, R., & Lakhal, L. (1999). Discovering frequent closed itemsets for association rules . In *Proceedings of ICDT Int. Conf. on Database Theory*, Jerusalem, Israel (pp. 398-416).

Ramaswamy, S., Mahajan, S., & Silberschatz, A. (1998). On the discovery of interesting patterns in association rules. In *Proceedings of the 24ᵗʰ International Conference on Very Large Data Bases*, New York (pp. 368-379).

Sathe, G., & Sarawagi, S. (2001). Intelligent rollups in multidimensional OLAP data. In *Proceedings of the 27ᵗʰ International Conference on Very Large Data Bases*, Rome, Italy (pp. 531-540).

Tryfona, N., Busborg, F., & Christiansen, J. G. B. (1999). StarER: A conceptual model for data warehouse design. *Proceedings of the Second Int. Workshop on Data Warehousing and OLAP*, Kansas City, MO (pp. 3-8).

Zaki, M. J. (1999). Parallel and distributed association mining: A survey. *IEEE Concurrency*, *7*(4), 14-25.

Section II:

Complex Data Mining

Chapter VIII

On the Usage of Structural Distance Metrics for Mining Hierarchical Structures

Theodore Dalamagas, National Technical University of Athens, Greece

Tao Cheng, University of Illinois at Urbana-Champaign, USA

Timos Sellis, National Technical University of Athens, Greece

Abstract

The recent proliferation of XML-based standards and technologies demonstrates the need for effective management of hierarchical structures. Such structures are used, for example, to organize data in product catalogs, taxonomies of thematic categories, concept hierarchies, etc. Since the XML language has become the standard data exchange format on the Web, organizing data in hierarchical structures has been vastly established. Even if data are not stored natively in such structures, export mechanisms make data publicly available in hierarchical structures to enable its automatic processing by programs, scripts and agents. Processing data encoded in hierarchical structures has been a popular research issue, resulting in the design of effective query languages. However, the inherent structural aspect of such encodings has not received strong attention till lately, when the requirement for mining tasks, like clustering/classification methods, similarity ranking, etc., on hierarchical structures has been raised. The key point to perform such tasks is the design of a structural distance metric to quantify the structural similarity between hierarchical structures. The chapter will study distance metrics that capture the structural similarity between hierarchical structures and approaches that exploit structural distance metrics to perform mining tasks on them.

Introduction

Hierarchical structures have been widely used in the past in the form of tree or graph structures to organize data in thematic categories, taxonomies, catalogs, SGML files, etc. Since the XML language is becoming the standard data exchange format on the Web, the idea of organizing data in hierarchical structures to enable its automatic processing by programs, Web scripts and agents has been re-visited. Vast amounts of data from many knowledge domains are available or processed to be available on the Web, encoded in hierarchical structures under the XML format.

While the processing and management of data encoded in such structures have been extensively studied (Abiteboul, Buneman, & Suciu, 2000), operations based on the structural aspect of such an encoding have received strong attention only lately. Structural distance metrics is a key issue for such operations. A structural distance metric can quantify the structural similarity between hierarchical structures. Thus, it is a tool that can support mining tasks for such structures. Examples of these tasks are clustering methods, classification methods and similarity ranking. For instance, a clustering task can identify sets of structures such that each set includes similar structures (in terms of their form or the way that they organize data). A similarity ranking mechanism can detect hierarchical structures which are similar to a hierarchical structure given as a test pattern, and also quantify such a similarity.

In this chapter we will first study distance metrics that capture the structural similarity between hierarchical structures. Then we will present approaches that exploit structural distance metrics to perform mining tasks on hierarchical structures. We concentrate on hierarchical structures encoded as XML documents due to the proliferation of the XML language for encoding data on the Web.

The chapter is organized as follows: The *Background* section gives examples of mining tasks for hierarchical structures and discusses background issues; *Structural Distance Metrics* presents various ways of defining and calculating structural distance metrics; *Mining Tasks* discusses approaches that exploit structural distance metrics to perform mining tasks for hierarchical structures; and, finally, *Conclusions and Future Perspectives* concludes the chapter and discusses future perspectives.

Background

Vast amounts of data from various knowledge domains have been encoded in hierarchical structures and become available on the Web. This is due to the enormous growth of the Web and the establishment of the XML language as the standard data exchange format. The XML language provides a simple syntax for data that is human- and machine-readable, and its model is perfectly suited for organizing data in hierarchical structures (see next subsection). Mining these structures is a useful task for many domains, as the examples in the following paragraphs show.

Spatial data are often organized in data model catalogs expressed in hierarchical structures. For instance, areas that include forests with lakes, rivers and farms may be represented as tree-like structures. Clustering by structure is a mining task that can identify spatial entities with similar structures, e.g., entities with areas that include forests with lakes. For example, in Table 1, areas encoded by D_1 and D_2 are structurally similar, since D_2 only misses the *river* element. On the other hand, areas encoded by D_3 are organized in a different way than D_1 and D_2. Examples on using XML representation for organizing geographical data in hierarchical structures are presented in Wilson et al. (2003).

Bioinformatics is another application area where mining hierarchical structures may be applied. The main concern in this domain is the discovery of structurally similar macromolecular tree patterns. The detection of homologous protein structures (i.e., sets of protein structures sharing a similar structure) is such an example (Sankoff & Kruskal, 1999). Nowadays, such structures have been also encoded as XML documents. Such encodings, as well as general hierarchical encodings for life sciences, are presented in Direen and Jones (2003).

But even for the XML data management itself, mining hierarchical structures is an important issue. XML documents may optionally have a Document Type Descriptor (DTD). A DTD serves as a grammar for an XML document, determining its internal structure and enabling exchange of documents through common vocabulary and standards. However, many XML documents are

Table 1. Examples of spatial information hierarchically structured in the form of XML documents

(D1)	(D2)	(D3)
---	---	---
<?xml version="1.0"?>	<?xml version="1.0"?>	<?xml version="1.0"?>
<area type="rectangle"	<area type="rectangle"	<area type="rectangle"
x1="100" y1="200">	x1="130" y1="210">	x1="300" y1="500">
<forest type="rectangle"	<forest type="rectangle"	<forest type="rectangle"
x1="20" x2="20">	x1="30" x2="10">	x1="50" x2="70">
<lake type="circle"	<lake type="circle"	<lake type="circle"
x1="5" y1="10" r1="5">	x1="2" y1="15" r1="10">	x1="35" y1="14"
The lake	The lake	r1="30">
</lake>	</lake>	The lake
<farm	<farm type="rectangle">	</lake>
type="rectangle">	The farm	<river type="line">
The farm	</farm>	The river
</farm>	</forest>	</river>
</forest>	</area>	</forest>
<river type=line>		<farm type="rectangle">
The river		The farm
</river>		</farm>
</area>		</area>

constructed massively from data sources like RDBMSs, flat files, etc., without DTDs. XTRACT (Garofalakis, Gionis, Rastogi, Seshadri, & Shim, 2000; Garofalakis, Gionis, Rastogi, Seshadri, & Shim, 2003) and IBM AlphaWorks emerging technologies (http://www.alphaworks.ibm.com) provide DTD discovery tools that automatically extract DTDs from XML documents. Such tools fail to discover meaningful DTDs in the case of diverse XML document collections (Garofalakis et al., 2003). Consider, for example, news articles from portals, newspaper sites, news agency sites, etc., hierarchically structured in the form of XML documents. Such documents, although related, may have such a different structure that one cannot define a meaningful DTD for all of them. See, for example, the four XML documents in Table 2. A unique DTD for these documents should define an element, which might be either *article* or *news_story*. This element should contain a *title* element, and then either an *author* or a *picture* element. However, *picture* in D_3 doc is identical to *image* in *D1*. Also, *picture* in D_3 comes before the *author* element, while the equivalent *image* in D_1 comes after the *author* element. Such irregularities make the construction of a unique, meaningful DTD a hard task. For this reason, identifying groups of XML documents that share a similar structure is crucial for DTD discovery systems. If a collection of XML documents that encode hierarchical data is first grouped into sets of structurally similar documents, then a meaningful DTD may be assigned to each set individually. For example, the XML documents in Table

Table 2. Examples of news articles hierarchically structured in the form of XML documents

(D1)	(D2)
---	---
<?xml version="1.0"?>	<?xml version="1.0"?>
<article>	<article>
<title>...</title>	<title>...</title>
<author>	<author>
<first_name>...</first_name>	<first_name>...</first_name>
<last_name>...</last_name>	<last_name>...</last_name>
</author>	</author>
<image>...</image>	<summary>...</summary>
<summary>...</summary>	<main>...</main>
<main>...</main>	</article>
</article>	

(D3)	(D4)
---	---
<?xml version="1.0"?>	<?xml version="1.0"?>
<news_story>	<news_story>
<title>...</title>	<title>...</title>
<picture>...</picture>	<author>
<author>	<name>...</name>
<name>...</name>	</author>
</author>	<summary>...</summary>
<summary>...</summary>	<body>...</body>
<body>...</body>	</news_story>
</news_story>	

2 can be grouped in two sets: The first set includes documents D_1 and D_2, and the second one includes documents D_3 and D_4.

Documents in each set are structurally similar. For example, D_2 misses only the element *image* (inside *article*), compared to D_1. On the other hand, D_1 and D_3 are not structurally similar: *Picture* in D_3 comes before the *author* element, while the equivalent *image* in D_1 comes after the *author* element.

We next show how hierarchical structures are used to organize data on the Web.

Semistructured Data

In the context of the Web, the notion of *semistructured data* has been introduced to capture schemaless, self-describing and irregular data. The term *semistructured* indicates that there is not a clear distinction between the organization of data (i.e., their structure) and data itself. To capture this

Figure 1. (a) OEM example, (b) XML data model example

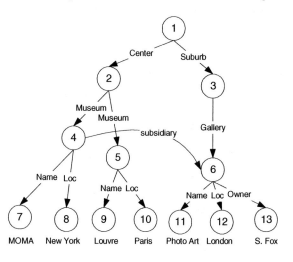

(a)

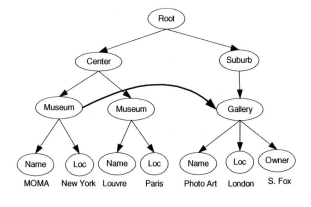

(b)

characteristic, models for semistructured data have been introduced (Abiteboul et al., 2000). Such models are simple, flexible and describe data as one entity with graph-based or tree-based hierarchical structures. The *object exchange model* (*OEM*) and the *XML data model* are examples of semistructured data models.

The object exchange model (OEM) is a graph representation of a collection of objects, introduced in the TSIMMIS project (Garcia-Molina et al., 1997). Every OEM object has an identifier and a value, atomic or complex. An atomic value is an integer, real, string or any other data, while a complex value is a set of oids, each linked to the parent node using a textual label. Objects with atomic values are called atomic objects and objects with complex values are called complex objects. The XML data model is another graph representation of a collection of atomic and complex objects. However, while the OEM model denotes graphs with labels on edges, the XML data model denotes graphs with labels on nodes. The XML data model provides a mechanism to define references that are unique. Using references, one can refer to an element by its identifier.

Figure 1(a) presents an example of an OEM database with six complex objects (i.e., objects 1, 2, 3, 4, 5 and 6) and seven atomic objects (i.e., 7, 8, 9, 10, 11, 12 and 13). In Figure 1(b), the example of Figure 1(a) is re-expressed using the XML data model. Without references (e.g., like the thick line in Figure 1(b)), the XML data model becomes a rooted ordered labeled tree.

Structural Distance Metrics

A structural distance metric quantifies the structural similarity between hierarchical structures. Since such structures are actually tree or graph structures, a popular way to define distances is by using tree/graph edit sequences or graph-matching techniques. For example, the minimum number of operations needed to transform one tree to another is an indication of how similar these trees are. Or, the number of common edges between two graphs is an indication of how similar the graphs are.

Distance metrics generally fulfill certain algebraic properties compared to distance or similarity measures:

1. $d(A, B) \geq 0$ (positivity)
2. $d(A, B) = d(B, A)$ (symmetry)
3. $d(A, B) + d(B, C) \leq d(A, C)$ (triangular equation)

Such properties are considered important, since the metrics are exploited in mining tasks like clustering and classification, where the quality of those metrics clearly affects the quality of the results obtained. To this extent, we do not consider measures used in change detection methods (see Cobena, Abiteboul and Marian (2002) for a comparative study). These methods can detect sets of edit operations with cost close to the minimal and significantly reduced computation time. However, minimality is important for the quality of any measure to be used as a distance metric.

In the next two subsections we discuss in detail methods to define and calculate structural distance metrics based on tree-edit distances and on graph/subgraph isomorphism.

Structural Distances Based on Tree Edit Distances

This subsection introduces tree edit distances and shows how they may be used to define and calculate structural distance metrics.

Background

The notion of tree edit operations is central in all approaches that utilize tree edit distances to define structural distance metrics. An *atomic tree edit operation* on a tree structure is an operation that manipulates a node as a single entity, for example, deletion, insertion and replacement of a node. A *complex tree edit operation* is a set of atomic tree edit operations treated as one single operation. An example of a complex tree edit operation is the insertion of a whole tree as a subtree in another tree, which is actually a sequence of atomic node insertion operations. We next present variations of tree edit operations.

1. insert node
    a. Variation I ($Ins^l(x,y,i)$): In this variation, a new node x is inserted as the i_{th} child of node y. All children of y should be leaf nodes.
    b. Variation II ($Ins(x,y,i)$): The restriction that new nodes are inserted only as a leaf node is relaxed. A new node x, which is inserted as the i_{th} child of node y, takes a subsequence of the children of y as its own children. Thus, given p, node y will have $y_1 \ldots y_j, x, y_{p+1}, \ldots y_n$ as children and x will have $y_{j+1}, y_{j+2}, \ldots y_p$ as children.
2. delete node
    a. Variation I ($Del(y)$): Deletion may be applied to any node. The children of the deleted node become the children of its parent.
    b. Variation II ($Del^l(y)$): Only leaf nodes can be deleted.
3. replace node ($Rep(x,y)$): Node y replaces node x.
4. move subtree ($Mov(x,y,k)$): The subtree rooted at node x is moved to become the k_{th} child of node y.

Figure 2. An example of tree edit sequence

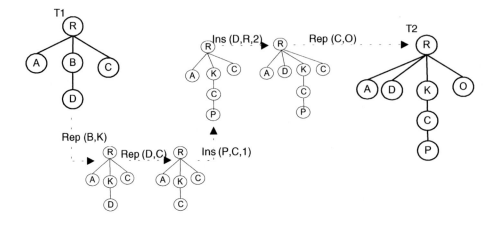

A *tree edit sequence* is a sequence of tree edit operations that transforms T_1 to T_2. Assuming a cost model to assign costs for tree edit operations, the *tree edit distance* between T_1 and T_2 is the minimum cost between the costs of all possible tree edit sequences that transform T_1 to T_2. Based on the notion of tree edit distance, we can now define the structural distance between tree structures.

Definition 3.1.1. *Let T1 and T2 be two tree structures, $D(T_1,T_2)$ their tree edit distance and $D'(T_1,T_2)$ the cost to delete all nodes from T_1 and insert all nodes from T_2. The structural distance S between T_1 to T_2 is defined as $S(T_1,T_2)=D(T_1,T_2) / D'(T_1,T_2)$.*

The structural distance is (a) *0* when the trees have exactly the same structure and the same labels in their matching nodes; (b) *1* when the trees have totally different structure and not even two pairs of matching nodes with the same ancestor/descendant relationship; (c) low when the trees have similar structure and a high percentage of matching nodes; and (d) high when the trees have different structure and a low percentage of matching nodes. Figure 2 presents the sequence of tree edit operations to transform tree T_1 to T_2 with minimum cost, assuming unit cost for every tree edit operation. In this example, $D'(T_1,T_2)=12$, since five nodes must be deleted from T_1 and seven nodes must be inserted from T_2. Also, $D(T_1,T_2)=5$, since five unit-cost operations are needed to transform tree T_1 to T_2.

The next subsection gives a detailed survey of tree edit techniques that may be used to define structural distance metrics.

Related Techniques and Algorithms

Selkow (1977) suggests a recursive algorithm to calculate the tree edit distance between two rooted ordered labeled trees. An *insert node* or *delete node* operation is permitted only at leaf nodes. Any node can be updated using the *replace node* operation. So, the set of permitted tree edit operations is $\{Ins^l(x,y,i), Del^l(y), Rep(x,y)\}$. The cost to delete a whole subtree rooted at node y is denoted by $W_d(y)$, and is the sum of the costs spent to delete all nodes of the subtree, starting from the leaves. Similarly, $W_i(x)$ denotes the cost to insert a whole subtree.

The algorithm to compute the edit distance D between the two trees, T_1 and T_2, calculates recursively the distance between their subtrees. The idea of the main recursion is that the calculation of the distance between two (sub)trees, t_1 and t_2 requires the calculation of four distances: (a) t_1 without its last subtree and t_2; (b) t_1 and t_2 without its last subtree; (c) t_1 without its last subtree and t_2 without its last subtree; and (d) last subtree of t_1 and last subtree of t_2. If M and N are the total number of nodes for T_1 and T_2, respectively, then the complexity of the algorithm is exponential (4min(N,M)).

Let r be the root of current subtree t_1 of T_1, k the number of subtrees in r and i the last node of the last subtree of t_1 ($i=i_k$) according to the preorder sequence. Similarly, let s be the root of current subtree t_2 of T_2, l the number of subtrees in s and j the last node of the last subtree of t_2 ($j=j_l$). $D(r,i:s,j)$ denotes the tree edit distance between t_1 and t_2. Analytically, the algorithm proceeds as follows:

1. if (r==i) and (s==j) then D=0:

    If t_1 and t_2 consist only of one node each (their roots), then the cost to transform t_1 to t_2 is equal to 0 (roots are the same).

2. if (s==j) then D=$W_d(i_{k-1}+1)$ + D(r,i$_{k-1}$:s,j):

    If t_2 consists only of one node, then the cost to transform t_1 to t_2 is equal to the cost to delete the k_{th} subtree of t_1 (which is the last subtree of the root of t_1) plus the cost to transform $t_{1''}$ (which is t_1 without its k_{th} subtree) to t_2.

3. if (r==i) then D=$W_i(j_{l-1}+1)$ + D(r,i:s,j$_{l-1}$):

    If t_1 consists only of one node, then the cost to transform t_1 to t_2 is equal to the cost to insert the l_{th} subtree of t_2 (which is the last subtree of the root of t_2) in t_1 plus the cost to transform t_1 to $t_{2''}$ (which is t_2 without its l_{th} subtree).

4. In any other case, find the minimum between the following three costs D=min(d_1,d_2,d_3):

a. $d_1 = W_d(i_{k-1}+1) + D(r,i_{k-1}:s,j)$:

the cost to delete the k_{th} subtree of t_1 (which is the last subtree of the root of t_1) plus the cost to transform $t_{1''}$ (which is t_1 without its k_{th} subtree) to t_2.

b. $d_2 = Wi(j_{l-1}+1) + D(r,i:s,j_{l-1})$:

the cost to insert the l_{th} subtree of t_2 (which is the last subtree of the root of t_2) in t_1 plus the cost to transform t_1 to $t_{2''}$ (which is t_2 without its l_{th} subtree).

c. $d_3 = D(r,i_{k-1}:s,j_{l-1}) + c_r(i_{k-1}+1,j_{l-1}+1) + D(i_{k-1}+1,i_k:j_{l-1}+1,j_l)$:

the cost to transform $t_{1''}$ (which is t_1 without its k_{th} subtree) to $t_{2''}$ (which is t_2 without its l_{th} subtree) plus the cost (i.e., c_r) to replace the root of the k_{th} subtree of t_1 with the root of the l_{th} subtree of t_2 plus the cost to transform the k_{th} subtree of t_1 to the l_{th} subtree of t_2.

Zhang and Shasha (1989) suggest a recursive algorithm to calculate the tree edit distance between two rooted ordered labeled trees, permitting tree edit operations anywhere in the trees. So, the set of permitted tree edit operations is $\{Ins(x,y,i), Del(y), Rep(x,y)\}$. The algorithm is based on the notion of mappings. A *tree mapping M* between two trees T_1 and T_2 is a one-to-one relationship between nodes of T_1 and nodes of T_2. A mapping M includes a set of pairs (i,j). For any two pairs (i_1,j_1) and (i_2,j_2) in M: (a) $i_1 = i_2$ iff $j_1 = j_2$; (b) $t_1[i_1]$ is to the left of $t_1[i_2]$ iff $t_2[j_1]$ is to the left of $t_2[j_2]$; and (c) $t_1[i_1]$ is an ancestor of $t_1[i_2]$ iff $t_2[j_1]$ is an ancestor of $t_2[j_2]$ ($t[i]$ refers to the node i of T, according to the postorder sequence). Every mapping M corresponds to a sequence of edit operations. Nodes in T_1 which are untouched by M correspond to $Del(y)$ operations in T_1. Nodes in T_2 which are untouched by M correspond to $Ins(x,y,i)$ operations in T_1. Nodes in T_1 related to nodes in T_2 by M correspond to $Rep(x,y)$ operations.

The algorithm calculates the minimum cost between the costs of the sequences of edit operations that transform a tree T_1 to the tree T_2, produced by all possible valid mappings on T_1 and T_2. Let $D(T_1[i'':i], T_2[j'':j])$ be the distance between trees $T_1[i'':i]$ and $T_2[j'':j]$ (a tree T is denoted as $T[i:j]$, where i is the label of its root and j is the label of its rightmost leaf, according to the postorder sequence). We note that $t[i]$ refers to the node i of T, and $l[i]$ refers to the postorder number of the leftmost leaf of the subtree rooted at $t[i]$, according to the postorder sequence. Then:

1. $D(0, 0) = 0$ (one-node trees, roots are labeled as 0)

2. $D(T_1[l(i_1):i],0) = D(T_1[l(i_1):i-1],0) + \text{cost\_to\_delete\_node}(t_1[i])$

3. $D(0,T_2[l(j_1):j]) = D(0,T_2[l(j_1):j-1]) + \text{cost\_to\_insert\_node}(t_2[j])$

4. $D(T_1[l(i_1):i], T_2[l(j_1):j]) = \min(d_1, d_2, d_3)$:

   a. $d_1 = D(T_1[l(i_1):i-1], T_2[l(j_1):j]) + \text{cost\_to\_delete\_node}(t_1[i])$

   b. $d_2 = D(T_1[l(i_1):i], T_2[l(j_1):j-1]) + \text{cost\_to\_insert\_node}(t_2[j])$

   c. $d_3 = D(T_1[l(i_1):l(i)-1], T_2[l(j_1):l(j)-1]) + D(T_1[l(i):i-1], T_2[l(j):j-1]) + \text{cost\_to\_replace\_node}(t_1[i], t_2[j])$ (where i and j are descendants of $t_1[i_1]$ and $t_2[j_1]$, respectively)

The recursion is similar to the one in Selkow's algorithm presented before. However, deletions and insertions are permitted anywhere in the tree. If *M* and *N* are the total number of nodes for T_1 and T_2 and *b* and *d* are their depths, respectively, then the complexity of the algorithm is *O(MNbd)*.

Chawathe, Rajaraman, Garcia-Molina, and Widom (1996) and Chawathe (1999) suggest algorithms to calculate tree edit distances. An *insert node* ($Ins^l(x,y,i)$) or *delete node* ($Del^l(y)$) operation is permitted only at leaf nodes. Any node can be updated using the *replace node* ($Rep(x,y)$) operation. In (Chawathe et al., 1996), a *move subtree* ($Mov(x,y,k)$) operation is also available. However, the distance calculation needs a predefined set of matching nodes between the trees. On the other hand, the distance calculation in Chawathe (1999) is based on shortest path detection on an *edit graph*. An edit graph can represent tree edit sequences. The edit graph for two trees T_1 and T_2 is an *(M+1)*x*(N+1)* grid of nodes, having a node at each (x,y) location, *x* in *[0… (M+1)]* and *y* in *[0… (N+1)]*. Directed lines connect the nodes. A horizontal line $((x-1,y), (x,y))$ denotes deletion of $T_1[x]$, where $T_1[x]$ refers to the x_{th} node of T_1 in its preorder sequence. A vertical line $((x,y-1), (x,y))$ denotes insertion of $T_2[y]$, where $T_2[x]$ refers to the x_{th} node of T_2 in its preorder sequence. Finally, a diagonal line $((x-1,y-1), (x,y))$ denotes update of $T_1[x]$ by $T_2[y]$.

Figure 3. An example of an edit graph

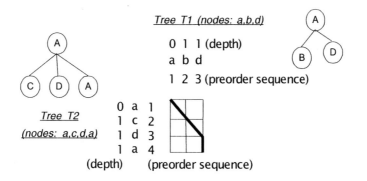

Figure 3 shows an example of an edit graph which represents an edit sequence to transform tree T_1 to tree T_2. Notice that T_1 becomes T_2 by ($Rep(T_1[2],c)$, $Rep(T_1[3],d)$, $Ins(T_2[4],T_1[1],3)$. Every edit sequence that transforms T_1 to T_2 can be mapped to a path in an edit graph. The tree edit distance between two rooted ordered labeled trees is the shortest of all paths to which edit sequences are mapped in an edit graph. An edit graph G is constructed as a $(M+1)\times(N+1)\times3$ matrix, whose cells contain the cost of the corresponding edit operation. The third dimension is used to determine the direction of the line drawing, that is, the type of the operation; for example, [0] for horizontal lines, i.e., *delete node*, [1] for vertical lines, i.e., *insert node* and [2] for diagonal lines, i.e., *replace node*. If a line is missing from the edit graph, the corresponding cell contains the infinite value. For example $G[4][6][0]= \infty$ means that there is no horizontal line from node *4* to node *6* in the edit graph.

Consider any path that connects the node *(0,0)* to node n *(x,y)* in an edit graph. Node n *(x,y)* is the last node in the path. The distance D of n from *(0,0)* cannot be greater than that distance of its left node plus the cost of the line connecting that node to n. Similarly, D can neither be greater than that distance of n's top node plus the cost of the line connecting that node to n, nor greater than that distance of n's diagonal node plus the cost of the line connecting that node to n. Based on the above remarks, the following recurrence calculates the shortest path $D[x,y]$ from *(0,0)* to *(x,y)* in an edit graph G:

$$D(x,y)=\min(m_1,m_2,m_3)$$

Where:

1. $m_1 = D[x-1,y-1] + \text{cost\_to\_replace\_node}(T_1[x], T_2[y])$, if $((x-1,y-1),(x,y))$ in G (the distance of *(x,y)*'s diagonal node in G plus the cost to replace $T_1[x]$ with $T_2[y]$), or ∞ otherwise,

2. $m_2 = D[x-1,y] + \text{cost\_to\_delete\_node}(T_1[x])$, if $((x-1,y),(x,y)$ in G (the distance of *(x,y)*'s left node in G plus the cost to delete $T_1[x]$), or ∞ otherwise,

3. $m_3 = D[x,y-1] + \text{cost\_to\_insert\_node}(T_2[y])$, if $((x,y-1),(x,y))$ in G (the distance of *(x,y)*'s top node in G plus the cost to insert $T_2[y]$), or ∞ otherwise.

In the algorithm, $D[i,j]$ keeps the tree edit distance between tree T_1 with only its i nodes, assuming preorder traversal, and tree T_2 with only its j nodes, assuming preorder traversal. If M and N are the dimensions of the matrix that represents the edit graph, then the complexity of the algorithm is $O(MN)$.

Overview

All of the algorithms for calculating the edit distance for tree structures are based on dynamic programming techniques related to the string-to-string correction problem (Wagnera & Fisher, 1974). The key issue of these techniques is the detection of the set of tree edit operations which transform a tree to another one with the minimum cost (assuming a cost model to assign costs for every tree edit operation). Selkow's algorithm (Selkow, 1977) allows insertion and deletion only at leaf nodes, and relabel at every node. Its main recursion leads to increased complexity. Chawathe's (II) algorithm (Chawathe, 1999) allows insertion and deletion only at leaf nodes, and relabel at every node, too. It is based on the model of edit graphs, which reduces the number of recurrences needed compared to Selkow's. This algorithm is the only one that has been extended to efficiently calculate distances in external memory in case tree sizes are prohibitively large, as presented in Chawathe (1999). Chawathe's (I) algorithm (Chawathe et al., 1996) is based on a different set of tree edit operations than Chawathe's (II). It allows insertion and deletion only at leaf nodes. Its main characteristic is the need of a pre-defined set of matching nodes between the trees. This set acts like a seed for the algorithm. Zhang's algorithm (Zhang & Shasha,1989) permits operations anywhere in the tree and uses a similar recurrence as Selkow's algorithm (Selkow, 1977).

We note that permitting insertion and deletion only at leaves prevents the destruction of membership restrictions of tree structures. For example, in the case of a deletion, we can avoid deleting a node and moving its children up one level. Actually, the deletion of an internal node requires deletions of all nodes in its path, starting from the leaf node and going up to the internal node, a task which is assigned a high cost due to the deletion of all these nodes.

Finally, we note that tree edit distances can satisfy positivity, symmetry and triangular equation, and therefore they can be metrics under certain conditions, for example having equal weights for all allowed tree edit operations.

Structural Distances Based on Graph Matching

This subsection discusses how graph and subgraph isomorphism may be used to define structural distance metrics.

Background

An alternative to view hierarchical structures is to regard them as graphs. Therefore, we could leverage the existing powerful graph-matching algorithms.

Graph isomorphism (Read & Corneil, 1977), subgraph isomorphism (Ullman, 1976) and maximum common subgraph (Bunke, Jiang, & Kandel, 1983; Levi, 1972) are basic concepts for graph matching. In Bunke and Shearer (1998), a graph similarity measure based on the maximum common subgraph of two graphs is proposed. A relatively new concept, minimum common supergraph is introduced in Bunke, Jiang and Kandel (2000), together with a graph similarity measure based on it. In Fernandez and Valiente (2001), another approach comes up with a graph distance metric by combining both maximum common subgraph and minimum common supergraph. In this subsection, we will mainly focus on these three methods (Bunke & Shearer, 1998; Bunke et al., 2000; Fernandez & Valiente, 2001). Another way to measure the similarity of two graphs is by defining graph edit distances. A graph edit distance is a generalization of tree edit distance. Algorithms for graph edit distances and related similarity measures have been discussed in Tsai and Fu (1979); Shapiro and Haralick (1981); Sanfeliu and Fu (1983); and Bunke et al. (1983). An advantage of distance metrics based on graph matching over edit distances is the independency on edit costs. Using those new distance metrics, we can avoid the intensive calculations needed for obtaining edit costs.

Related Techniques and Algorithms

For the ease of introducing the three methods for deriving distance measures, we first give some basic graph definitions (we use the definitions from Fernandez and Valiente (2001)).

Definition 3.2.1. *Let L be a finite alphabet of vertex and edge labels. A graph is a tuple, $G = (V, E, \alpha)$, where V is the finite set of vertices, $E \subseteq V \times V$ is the finite set of edges and $\alpha: V \cup E \rightarrow L$ is the vertex and edge labeling function.*

Let $|G| = |V| + |E|$ denote the size of G. The empty graph such that $|G| = 0$ will be denoted by ϕ.

Definition 3.2.2. *A graph $G = (V_1, E_1, \alpha_1)$ is a subgraph of a graph $G = (V_2, E_2, \alpha_2)$, denoted by $G_1 \subseteq G_2$, if $V_1 \subseteq V_2$, $E_1 \subseteq E_2$, and $\alpha_1(x) = \alpha_2(x)$ for all $x \in V_1 \cup E_1$. A graph G_2 is called a supergraph of G_1 if $G_1 \subseteq G_2$.*

Definition 3.2.3. *Let $G = (V, E, \alpha)$ be a graph, V_2 a set of vertices and $f: V_1 \rightarrow V_2$ a bijective function, where $V_1 \subseteq V$ and $V_1 \cap V_2 = \phi$. A renaming*

of G by f, denoted by f(G), is the graph   Gf = (V_f, E_f, α_f) defined by V_f = V_2
∪ (V\\V_1),E_f = {(f'(u), f'(v))| (u, v) ∈ E} ,α_f(f'(v)) = α(v) for all v ∈ V, α_f(e)=
α(e) for all e ∈ E, where f' : V → V_f is defined by:

$$f\ (v) \qquad \begin{array}{ll} f(v), & \text{if } v \quad V_1 \\ v, & \text{otherwise} \end{array}$$

Definition 3.2.4. *Two graphs G_1 and G_2 are isomorphic, denoted by $G_1 \cong G_2$, if there is a renaming f of G_1 such that f(G_1) = G_2, and in this case it is said that f : $G_1 \to G_2$ is a graph isomorphism.*

Definition 3.2.5. *A graph $\hat{G}$ is a common subgraph of two graphs G_1 and G_2 if there exist subgraphs $\hat{G}_1 \subseteq G_1$ and $\hat{G}_2 \subseteq G_2$ such that $\hat{G} \cong \hat{G}_1 \cong \hat{G}_2$. It is maximum if there is no other common subgraph of G_1 and G_2 larger than $\hat{G}$.*

Definition 3.2.6. *A graph $\breve{G}$ is a common supergraph of two graphs G_1 and G_2 if there exist graphs $\breve{G}_1 \subseteq \breve{G}$ and $\breve{G}_2 \subseteq \breve{G}$ such that $\breve{G}_1 \cong G_1$ and $\breve{G}_2 \cong G_2$. It is minimum if there is no other common supergraph of G_1 and G_2 smaller than $\breve{G}$.*

All the three graph distance measures we are going to show below are proved to satisfy positivity, symmetry and triangular equation, and therefore are metrics.

In Bunke and Shearer (1998), a graph distance based on a maximum common subgraph is proposed. The distance of two non-empty graphs and is defined as:

$$d(G_1, G_2) \quad 1 \quad \frac{|\hat{G}|}{\max(|G_1|, |G_2|)}, \tag{1}$$

where $\hat{G}$ is the maximum common subgraph of G_1 and G_2. Notice that given G_1 and G_2, their maximum common subgraph is not unique.

The relationship between graph edit distance, maximum common subgraph and the minimum common supergraph is discussed in Bunke et al. (2000). It is observed that under certain assumptions of the cost function (used for graph edit distance), the graph edit distance and the size of both maximum common subgraph and minimum common supergraph are equivalent to each other. More specifically, knowing one of them together with the cost function and the size of the two underlying graphs, the other can be immediately calculated. If the cost function is restricted, such that the insertion and deletion of nodes are unit operations, we could rewrite equation (1) and have the following graph similarity measure based on minimum common supergraph:

$$d(G_1, G_2) = 1 - \frac{|G_1| + |G_2| - |\breve{G}|}{\max(|G_1|, |G_2|)}, \tag{2}$$

where $\breve{G}$ is the minimum common supergraph of G_1 and G_2. Notice that given G_1 and G_2, their minimum common supergraph is not unique.

In (Fernandez & Valiente, 2001), the authors further study the relationship between the maximum common subgraph and the minimum common supergraph of two graphs. Simple constructions allow obtaining the maximum common subgraph from the minimum common supergraph, and visa versa. The maximum common subgraph and the minimum common supergraph are combined into a new graph distance metric.

$$d(G_1, G_2) = |\breve{G}| - |\hat{G}|, \tag{3}$$

where $\hat{G}$ is the maximum common subgraph of G_1 and G_2, and $\breve{G}$ is the minimum common supergraph of G_1 and G_2.

Overview

In this subsection we examined how graph matching algorithms can be used to calculate structural distance metrics for hierarchical structures. More specifically, we investigated three techniques which use maximum common subgraph, minimum common supergraph and a combination of both. Maximum common subgraph tries to eliminate the superfluous structural information, whereas minimum common supergraph takes into account the missing structural information. Superfluous and missing structural information are both taken into consideration when the measure is based on both maximum common subgraph and minimum common supergraph. Graph matching methods to calculate structural distance metrics scale well compared to methods based on tree edit distances. The latter needs the calculation of tree edit sequences, which is a quite intensive task.

The Approach of IR Community

This subsection introduces approaches used in IR community to detect the similarity between hierarchical structures encoded as XML documents. Bitmap indexing (Chan & Ioannidis, 1998) has been introduced to improve performance of information retrieval. Similarity measures could be defined using bitmap indexes on hierarchical structures.

Related Techniques and Algorithms

In Yoon, Raghavan, and Chakilam (2001), an XML document is regarded as a sequence of ePaths (Element Path) associated with content. An ePath is defined as the path leading to the content information associated with leaf nodes from the XML root in the hierarchical structure. A set of XML documents in a database may be indexed by a document-ePath bitmap index. In such a bitmap index, a column represents a unique ePath, and a row represents an XML document.

Below we show an example to describe such a bitmap index (Yoon et al., 2001). All the possible ePaths in the three XML documents in Table 3 are: P_0=/e0/e1, P_1=/e0/e2/e3, P_2=/e0/e2/e4, P_3=/e0/e2/e5, P_4=/e0/e2/e4/e6, P_5=/e0/e2/e4/e7, P_6=/e0/e8 and P_7=/e0/e9

In a document-ePath bitmap index, if a document has a certain ePath, then the corresponding bit is set to 1, otherwise it is set to 0. By examining the three documents in Table 3, we could see that D_1 contains paths P_0, P_1, P_2, P_3; D_2 contains paths P_0, P_1, P_2, P_4, P_5, P_6; D_3 contains paths P_0, P_1, P_2, P_3, P_7.

Table 3. A set of simple XML documents

(D₁)	(D₂)	(D₃)
`<e0>`	`<e0>`	`<e0>`
`<e1>V1</e1>`	`<e1>V1</e1>`	`<e1>V11</e1>`
`<e2>`	`<e2>`	`<e2>`
`<e3>V2 V3 V4</e3>`	`<e3>V3 V7</e3>`	`<e3>V2 V7</e3>`
`<e4>V3 V8</e4>`	`<e4>V9`	`<e4>V3 V9</e4>`
`<e5/>`	`<e6>V4</e6>`	`<e5/>`
`</e2>`	`<e7>V6</e7>`	`</e2>`
`</e0>`	`</e4>`	`<e9>V5</e9>`
	`</e2>`	`</e0>`
	`<e8>V6 V12</e8>`	
	`</e0>`	

Figure 4. A bitmap index for documents in Table 3

	P_0	P_1	P_2	P_3	P_4	P_5	P_6	P_7
D_1	1	1	1	1	0	0	0	0
D_2	1	1	1	0	1	1	1	0
D_3	1	1	1	1	0	0	0	1

The bitmap index for the three documents in Table 3 is shown below in Figure 4. The rows represent the three XML documents, and the columns represent all eight possible ePaths in these three documents.

Once we have the bitmap index, the distance (Hamming Distance) between two documents is defined as follows:

$$d(D_i, D_j) = | XOR(D_i, D_j) |, \tag{4}$$

where *XOR* is a bit-wise exclusive *OR* operator. The operator ‖ denotes the number of 1s in a vector. For example, the distance between two documents D_1 and D_2 is 4.

In the above distance measure, only structural information is taken into consideration and content information is not used. In Carmel, Maarek, Mandelbrod, Mass, and Soffer (2003), XML documents are compared by combining both structural and content information together. Although the similarity measure introduced is intended to find the relevance score between a query and a document, it could be naturally used for finding the similarity between two documents. This is because the queries are represented as XML fragments, which are essentially XML documents.

In the regular vector space model, documents are represented by vectors in a space whose dimensions each correspond to a distinct unit. Typical units are words and phrases, which are all content information. The term $w_x(t)$ stands for the "weight" of term *t* in document *x* within the given collection. The weight is typically calculated from the document and collection statistics. One effective measure that could be used for calculating the similarity between two documents is the cosine measure (Salton & McGill, 1983), where:

$$\rho(D_i, D_j) = \frac{\sum_{t \in Di \cap Dj} w_{Di}(t) * w_{Dj}(t)}{\| D_i \| * \| D_j \|}, \tag{5}$$

This model works well with plain documents, but for structural documents, the structural information is lost. By introducing distinct indexing units, not as single terms but as pairs of the form (t, c) where t is qualified by the context c in which it appears, structural information is included. The context of appearance of a term is represented by the path leading to the term from the XML root in the hierarchical structure of the document. This way, the weight of individual terms in Formula (5) should be replaced by the weight of terms in context, denoted as $w_t(t, c)$. Context matching is also relaxed by introducing a function cr that calculates the context resemblance between contexts. Formula (5) becomes:

$$\rho(D_i, D_j) = \frac{\sum_{(t,c_m) \in D_i} \sum_{(t,c_n) \in D_j} w_{Di}(t, c_m) * w_{Dj}(t, c_n) * cr(c_m, c_n)}{\| D_i \| * \| D_j \|}, \qquad (6)$$

Various instantiations could be used to measure the context resemblance. Four examples of cr functions are introduced in the paper.

Perfect match:

$$cr(c_m, c_n) = \begin{cases} 1 & c_m = c_n \\ 0 & \text{otherwise} \end{cases}$$

Only (t,c) pairs that appear in both in of the two documents will be counted.

Partial match:

$$cr(c_m, c_n) = \begin{cases} \dfrac{1 + | c_m |}{1 + | c_n |} & c_m \text{ subsequence of } c_n \\ 0 & \text{otherwise} \end{cases}$$

This measure requires context c_m be contained in context c_n. $|c_m|$ is the number of tags in context c_m and $|c_n|$ is the number of tags in context c_n. For example,

$$cr("/article/bibl", "/article/bm/bib/bibl/bb") = 3/6 = 0.5$$

Fuzzy match:

This type of matching allows for even finer grain similarity between contexts, such as treating context as strings and using string-matching techniques.

Flat:

$$\forall c_m, c_n. \, cr(c_m, c_n) = 1$$

This model completely ignores contexts by regarding all the contexts as the same context.

Overview

This subsection discussed the existing techniques used in IR community to find the similarity between hierarchical structured text databases. In Yoon et al. (2001), bitmap indexing is used to index XML documents based on their structural information. A distance measure based on the bitmap index is derived. The advantage of this approach is efficiency by using the bit-wise operations (such as) once the bitmap index is calculated. The authors in Carmel et al. (2003) extend the regular vector space model for plain documents. Structural information and content information are used simultaneously to derive the new model and a similarity measure based on this new model is defined. The similarity function depends on the weighting function as well as the context matching scheme.

Mining Tasks

Structural distance metrics (either based on tree edit distances, graph matching or on IR approaches) can be used in mining tasks on hierarchical structures, and specifically on their inherent structural aspect. Specifically, we explore clustering, classification and similarity ranking.

Clustering is a statistical technique that generates groups of data. Members of the same group should have a high degree of association (i.e., similar to each other), while members of different groups should have a low degree of association. In particular, clustering of hierarchical structures results in groups of structurally similar hierarchical structures. Structural similarity is captured by the structural distance metrics discussed in the previous section.

Classification differs from clustering, since, in the former, the groups are known a priori. In particular, classification assigns new hierarchical structures to pre-defined groups of structurally similar hierarchical structures. As in clustering, structural similarity is captured by the structural distance metrics discussed in the previous section.

In a similarity ranking task, a type of test pattern that describes data is provided and data similar to that pattern is retrieved. Retrieved data are presented in an order according to their degree of similarity with the test pattern. In particular, similarity ranking for hierarchical structures retrieves structures which are similar to a pre-defined one. Again, structural similarity is captured by structural distance metrics.

From those mining tasks, clustering hierarchical structures is quite popular in the research literature. Most of the approaches presented actually deal with clustering. For this reason we first give an overview of clustering methods.

Clustering Methods

Clustering methods are divided into two broad categories. Non-hierarchical methods group a data set into a number of clusters. They have low computational requirements ($O(kn)$, if, for example, n documents need to be grouped into k clusters), but certain parameters like the number of formed clusters must be known a priori. A popular example of such a method is the *K-Means* algorithm (MacQueen, 1967; Rasmussen, 1992). Given a pre-defined number of clusters c, the algorithm creates c cluster centers which correspond to c clusters. Then, each object from the data set to be clustered is assigned to the cluster whose center is the nearest. The cluster centers are then re-computed, and the process is continued until the cluster centers do not change.

Hierarchical methods produce nested sets of data (hierarchies), in which pairs of elements, or clusters, are successively linked until every element in the data set becomes connected. They are computationally expensive ($O(n^3)$) if n documents need to be clustered. However, hierarchical methods have been used extensively as a means of increasing the effectiveness and efficiency of retrieval (Voorhees, 1985). *Single link*, *complete link* and *group average link* are known as hierarchical clustering methods. All these methods are based on a similar idea. Each element of the data set to be clustered is considered to be a single cluster. The clusters with the minimum distance (i.e., maximum similarity) are merged and the distance between the remaining clusters and the new, merged one is recalculated. The process continues until there is only one cluster. In single link (complete link), the distance between two non-single clusters is defined as the minimum (maximum) of the distances between all pairs of

238   Dalamagas, Cheng & Sellis

elements so that one element is in the first cluster and the other element is in the second cluster. In group average link, the distance between two non-single clusters is defined as the mean of the distances between all pairs of elements so that one element is in the one cluster and the other element is in the other cluster. For a wide ranging overview of clustering methods, one can refer to Rasmussen (1992) and Halkidi, Batistakis, and Vazirgiannis (2001).

We next describe approaches that exploit structural distance metrics to perform mining tasks on hierarchical structures.

Related Techniques and Algorithms

In Nierman and Jagadish (2002), tree structures encoded as XML documents are clustered using the group average link hierarchical method. The distance metric used to quantify structural similarity is a variation of the tree edit distance suggested in Chawathe (1999). Specifically, the set of tree edit operations used to calculate the tree edit distance includes two new ones which refer to whole trees (*insert_tree* and *delete_tree* operations) rather than nodes. Trees are pre-processed to determine whether a subtree is contained in another tree. Such pre-processing is needed to precalculate costs for sequences of single *insert_tree* operations, or combinations of *insert_tree* operations and *insert node* operations. Their experiments on real and synthetic structures show low numbers of misclustered documents.

In Dalamagas, Cheng, Winkel, and Sellis (2004), clustering of hierarchical structures encoded as XML documents is performed exploiting tree structural summaries. These summaries maintain the structural relationships between the elements of hierarchical structures and at the same time have minimal processing requirements instead of the original structures. To this extent, structural summaries are representatives of the original structures. Figure 5 presents an example

Figure 5. Structural summary extraction

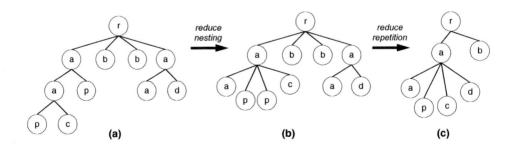

of structural summary extraction. The extraction task is based on a nesting reduction phase followed by a repetition reduction phase. The phases eliminate nested and repeated nodes that provide the same structural information, causing redundancy. The distance metric used to quantify structural similarity is a variation of the tree edit distance suggested in Chawathe (1999) that avoids the pre-computation of the edit graph (see Section 3.1.2). Experiments with single link hierarchical clustering on real and synthetic data show high quality clustering. The results are confirmed with non-hierarchical clustering algorithms as well as with the kNN classification algorithm.

The notion of representative structures, but for clusters and not for the original hierarchical structures, is introduced in Costa, Manco, Ortale, and Tagarelli (2004). Clustering is performed on tree structures encoded as XML documents. The structural distance metric exploited in the clustering algorithm is not based on tree edit distances but on the percentage of common paths between the structures. Matching trees and merge trees are used to extract cluster represen-

Figure 6. (a)/(b) example tree structures, (c) lower-bound, (d) upper-bound and (e) representative tree

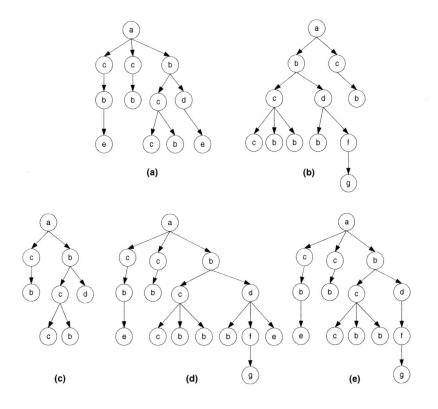

tatives. A matching tree for two tree structures is defined as the tree that includes only their common nodes and maintains their structural relationships (i.e., a lower-bound structure). A merge tree for two tree structures is defined as the tree that includes all their nodes and maintains their structural relationships (i.e., an upper-bound structure). A cluster representative is constructed from the cluster merge tree by deleting nodes in such a way that the distance between the refined merge tree and the other members of the cluster is minimized. Figure 6(e) presents an example of a representative tree structure for trees in (a) and (b). Note that tree in (c) is the lower-bound tree (i.e., matching tree) and the tree in (d) is the upper-bound tree (i.e., merge tree) (originally taken from Costa et al. (2004)).

In Lian, Cheung, Mamoulis, and Yiu (2004), the graph distance metric introduced in Bunke and Shearer (1998) and Bunke et al. (2000) (see section *Related Techniques and Algorithms*), is used in a hierarchical clustering algorithm to group together structurally similar XML documents. Such grouping is then used to improve the cost of query processing and evaluation in case these documents are stored in tables of relational database systems. Specifically, the grouping decreases the number of join operations needed between tables during the query evaluation. The approach is highly scalable, compared to the approaches based on tree edit distances presented before. The actual distance calculation between two XML documents is done on *s-graphs,* which includes all distinct nodes and edges appearing in either document.

Similarity ranking techniques among XML documents and DTDs are presented in Bertino, Guerrini, and Mesiti (2004). It differs from the previous approaches since it explores to what extent a hierarchical structure satisfies constraints imposed by grammars like DTDs. The similarity measure does not consider the structural aspect directly (as those based on tree edit distances) but only through the number of so-called *plus, common* and *minus* elements. Plus elements are those that appear in an XML document but not in the DTD used to rank the document. Common elements are those that appear in an XML document and in that DTD. Minus elements are those that do not appear in an XML document but appear in that DTD. The level of each element is also taken into account: Elements at higher levels are given higher weight compared to elements at lower levels.

Overview

From the approaches presented, it is clear that the key issue in mining hierarchical structures using structural distance metrics is not the design and study of new mining tools, such as new clustering tools. The strong technical background established in the past concerning such tools is directly exploited and applied in the context of hierarchical structures. Most of the approaches use a type of hierarchical clustering algorithm with a structural distance metric based on variations of tree-edit distances. All approaches result in high quality clustering, indicating that structural distance metrics can really capture similarities and dissimilarities between different hierarchical structures.

An interesting point is the way that most of the approaches evaluate their methods. Since it is quite a hard task to manually examine the results of a clustering procedure, evaluation is based on a priori knowledge of the cluster that a hierarchical structure belongs to. The XML technology provides the means for such a task. XML documents that encode hierarchical structures are generated automatically from DTDs. Clustering is performed for these documents, and the clusters detected should ideally correspond (one-by-one) to the DTDs used. In the case that real documents are used, it is enough to know the DTDs that these documents conform to.

Finally, we note that some methods introduce structures which summarize the original hierarchical structures. This speeds up the mining tasks but, on the other hand, different hierarchical structures might have the same summary structure, posing difficulties in capturing fine structural dissimilarities.

Conclusion and Future Perspectives

Hierarchical structures is a popular means of organizing data, especially after the proliferation of the XML language. Management of data encoded in such structures has been a popular research issue. However, the structural aspect has received strong attention only lately with the usage of structural distance metrics. A structural distance metric can quantify the structural similarity between hierarchical structures. For example, it can estimate how similar two spatial entities (e.g., spatial configurations with forests, lakes, etc.) are. Since hierarchical structures are tree or graph structures, structural distance metrics may be defined using the notion of tree edit distance or graph matching. Actually, the majority of the approaches suggested in the research literature, and presented in detail in this chapter, are based on variations of tree edit distances to define structural distance metrics.

Structural distance metrics can be used in clustering algorithms, classification algorithms and similarity ranking mechanisms to support mining tasks for hierarchical structures. For instance, clustering by structure is a mining task that can identify spatial entities with similar structures, e.g., entities with areas that include forests with lakes. The chapter presented approaches that exploited structural distance metrics to perform such mining tasks.

Structural distance metrics based on tree edit distances are quite popular, and they can capture fine structural dissimilarities. However, their calculation is quite intensive. On the other hand, structural distance metrics, for example, based on maximum and minimum common subgraphs (Bunke et al., 2000; Lian et al., 2004), are scalable enough. However, they cannot capture fine structural dissimilarities. Vector-based approaches that capture the hierarchical relationships of tree structures should be extensively explored as a basis to design appropriate indexes for the efficient calculation of structural distance metrics. For example, in Flesca, Manco, Masciari, Pontieri, and Pugliese (2002), tree structures are linearized into numerical sequences, and then discrete Fourier transform compares the encoded structures in the domain of frequencies.

An important issue is that certain applications may restrict the context of interest for calculating structural distance metrics to specific parts instead of the entire hierarchical structure. Thus, flexible models to manipulate hierarchical structure taking into consideration their granularity should be examined. Such models have been used for calculating distance metrics to estimate content similarity in older works for structured text database retrieval (Baeza-Yates & Navarro, 1996).

Concerning the definition of structural distance metrics, there are certain requirements that should be taken into account. An example is the need for ordering in the objects of hierarchical structures. For instance, the ordering of two objects A and B which are children of the object C might be important if A, B and C encode macromolecular tree patterns, but might be of no interest if they encode entities from other knowledge domains. Another example is the difference in the importance of the objects as structural primitives in a hierarchical structure. In Bertino et al. (2004), for instance, the level of each XML element is taken into account: Elements at higher levels are given higher weight compared to elements at lower level.

In any case, mining hierarchical structures using structural distance metrics is a problem which does not require the design and study of new mining tools, like new clustering tools. Mining tasks like clustering/classification algorithms and similarity ranking have been widely studied in the research literature. The strong technical background established can be directly exploited and applied in the context of hierarchical structures. The key issues for successful application are the definition of an appropriate structural distance metric and its efficient calculation.

References

Abiteboul, S., Buneman, P., & Suciu, D. (2000). *Data on the web.* Morgan Kaufmann Publishers.

Baeza-Yates, R., & Navarro, G. (1996). Integrating contents and structure in text retrieval. *ACM SIGMOD Record, 25*(1).

Bertino, E., Guerrini, G., & Mesiti, M. (2004). A matching algorithm for measuring the structural similarity between an XML document and a DTD and its applications. *Information Systems, 29*(1).

Bunke, H., Jiang, X., & Kandel, A. (1999). A metric on graphs for structural pattern recognition. In H.W. Schüssler (Ed.), *Signal processing II: Theories and applications.* North Holland: Elsevier Science Publishers B.V.

Bunke, H., Jiang, X., & Kandel, A. (2000). On the minimum common supergraph of two graphs. *Computing, 65*(1).

Bunke, H., & Shearer, K. (1998). A graph-distance metric based on the maximal common subgraph. *Pattern Recognition Letters, 19*, 3-4.

Carmel, D., Maarek, Y., Mandelbrod, M., Mass, Y., & Soffer, A. (2003). Searching XML documents via XML fragments. *Proceedings of the International Conference on Research and Development in Information Retrieval (SIGIR 2003)*, Toronto, Canada.

Chan, C. &, Ioannidis, Y. (1998). Bitmap index design and evaluation. *Proceedings of* the *International Conference on Management of Data* (ACM SIGMOD'98), Seattle, WA, USA.

Chawathe, S.S. (1999). Comparing hierarchical data in external memory. *Proceedings of the International Conference on Very Large Databases (VLDB'99)*, Edinburgh, Scotland, UK.

Chawathe, S.S., Rajaraman, A., Garcia-Molina, H., & Widom, J. (1996). Change detection in hierarchically structured information. *Proceedings of the International Conference on Management of Data (ACM SIGMOD'96)*, Montreal, Canada.

Cobena, G., Abiteboul, S., & Marian, A. (2002). Detecting changes in XML documents. *Proceedings of the International Conference on Data Engineering (ICDE'02)*, San Jose, California, USA.

Costa, G., Manco, G., Ortale, R., & Tagarelli, A. (2004). A tree-based approach to clustering XML documents by structure. *Proceedings of the European Conference on Principles and Practice of Knowledge Discovery in Databases Knowledge (PKDD'04)*, Pisa, Italy.

Dalamagas, T., Cheng, T., Winkel, K.J., & Sellis, T. (2004). Clustering XML documents using structural summaries. *Proceedings of the EDBT Workshop on Clustering Information over the Web* (ClustWeb'04), Heraklion, Greece.

Direen, H.G. & Jones, M.S. (2003). Knowledge management in bioinformatics. In A.B. Chaudhri, A. Rashid, & R. Zicari (Eds.), *XML data management.* New York:Addison Wesley.

Fernandez, M.-L., & Valiente, G. (2001). A Graph distance metric combining maximum common subgraph and minimum common supergraph. *Pattern Recognition Letters,* 22(6-7).

Flesca, S., Manco, G., Masciari, E., Pontieri, L., & Pugliese, A. (2002). Detecting structural similarities between XML documents. *Proceedings of the Workshop on The Web and Databases (WebDB'02),* Madison, Wisconsin, USA.

Garcia-Molina, H., Papakonstantinou, Y., Quass, D., Rajaraman, A., Sagiv, Y., Ullman, J. D. et al. (1997). The TSIMMIS approach to mediation: Data models and languages. *Journal of Intelligent Information Systems,* 8(2).

Garofalakis, M., Gionis, A., Rastogi, R., Seshadri, S., & Shim, K. (2000). XTRACT: A system for extracting document type descriptors from XML documents. *Proceedings of the International Conference on Management of Data (ACM SIGMOD'00),* Texas, USA.

Garofalakis, M., Gionis, A., Rastogi, R., Seshadri, S., & Shim, K. (2003). XTRACT: learning document type descriptors from XML document collections. *Data Mining and Knowledge Discovery,* 7.

Halkidi, M., Batistakis, Y., & Vazirgiannis, M. (2001). Clustering algorithms and validity measures. *Proceedings of the Scientific and Statistical Databases Management Conference (SSDBM'01),* Virginia, USA.

Levi, G. (1972). A note on the derivation of maximal common subgraphs of two directed or undirected graphs. *Calcolo,* 9.

Lian, W., Cheung, D. W., Mamoulis, N., & Yiu, S. M. (2004). An efficient and scalable algorithm for clustering XML documents by structure. *IEEE Transactions on Knowledge and Data Engineering (TKDE),* 16(1).

MacQueen, J.B. (1967). Some methods for classification and analysis of multivariate observations. *Proceedings of the Symposium on Math. Statistics and Probability,* University of California Press, Berkeley.

McGregor, J.J. (1982). Backtrack search algorithms and the maximal common subgraph problem. *Software Practice and Experience,* 12.

Nierman, A., & Jagadish, H. V. (2002). Evaluating structural similarity in XML documents. *Proceedings of the Workshop on The Web and Databases (WebDB'02),* Madison, Wisconsin, USA.

Rasmussen, E. (1992). Clustering algorithms. In Frakes, W. & Baeza-Yates, R. (Eds.), *Information retrieval: Data structures and algorithms.* NJ: Prentice Hall.

Read, R.C., & Corneil, D.G. (1977). The graph isomorphism disease. *J. Graph Theory,* 1.

Salton, G.,& McGill, M. J. (1983). *Introduction to modern information retrieval.* New York: McGraw-Hill.

Sanfeliu, A., & Fu, K.S. (1983). A distance measure between attributed relational graphs for pattern recognition. *IEEE Transactions on Systems, Man, and Cybernetics,* 13.

Sankoff, D., & Kruskal, J. (1999). *Time warps, string edits and macromolecules: The theory and practice of sequence comparison.* CSLI Publications.

Selkow, S. M. (1977). The tree-to-tree editing problem. *Information Processing Letters,* 6.

Shapiro, L.G. & Haralick, R.M. (1981). Structural descriptions and inexact matching. *IEEE Trans. On Pattern Analysis and Machine Intelligence,* 3.

Tsai, W. H., & Fu, K. S. (1979). Error-correcting isomorphisms of attributed relational graphs for pattern analysis. *IEEE Transactions on Systems, Man, and Cybernetics,* 9(12).

Ullman, J.R. (1976). An algorithm for subgraph isomorphism. *Journal of ACM,* 23(1).

Voorhees, H. (1985). *The effectiveness and efficiency of agglomerative hierarchic clustering in document retrieval.* Unpublished doctoral dissertation, Cornell University, Ithaca, New York.

Wagner, R., & Fisher, M. (1974). The string-to-string correction problem. *Journal of ACM, 21*(1).

Wilson, R., Cobb, M., McCreedy, F., Ladner, R., Olivier, D., Lovitt, T. et al. (2003). Geographical data interchange using XML-enabled technology within the GIDB system. In A.B. Chaudhri, A. Rashid, & R. Zicari (Eds.), *XML data management.* New York: Addison Wesley.

Yoon, J., Raghavan, V., & Chakilam, V. (2001). Bitmap indexing-based clustering and retrieval of XML documents. *Proceeding of the ACM SIGIR Workshop on Mathematical/Formal Methods in IR,* New Orleans, Louisiana, USA.

Zhang, K., & Shasha, D. (1989). Simple fast algorithms for the editing distance between trees and related problems. *SIAM Journal of Computing, 18.*

Chapter IX

Structural Similarity Measures in Sources of XML Documents

Giovanna Guerrini, Università di Genova, Italy

Marco Mesiti, Università degli Studi di Milano, Italy

Elisa Bertino, Purdue University, USA

Abstract

This chapter discusses existing approaches to evaluate and measure structural similarity in sources of XML documents. A relevant peculiarity of XML documents, indeed, is that information on the document structure is available in the document itself. In the chapter we present different approaches aiming at evaluating structural similarity at three different levels: among documents, between a document and a schema, and among schemas. The most relevant applications of such measures are for document classification and schema extraction, and for document and schema structural clustering, though other interesting applications such as document change detection and structural querying can be devised, and will be discussed throughout the chapter.

Introduction

Sources of XML documents (W3C, 1998) are today proliferating on the Web. A peculiarity of XML documents is that information on document structures is available on the Web together with the document contents. This information can be exploited to improve document handling and query processing. A relevant feature of XML document sources on the Web is that they are highly dynamic, both in document content and schema source structures. Documents can be moved among sources and schemas can require changes, ranging from minimal updates to integration with other schemas, in order to adhere to the actual documents in the source. Moreover, documents with similar structure can be clustered in order to infer new schemas and thus implementing more effective indexing structures and efficient access. The complex structure, size and the dynamicity of the data and schema information of a source, together with its heterogeneity, require exploiting database tools for managing them. There is, therefore, a strong need for methodologies and tools supporting the following functionalities:

- **XML document classification with respect to schemas.** An XML document that enters a source and partially adheres to the structure of a local schema may be considered a *weak instance* of such a schema and thus, the access, indexing and protection policies specified on the schema can be propagated to the "*matching parts*" of the document.

Figure 1. Different levels in computing the structural similarity

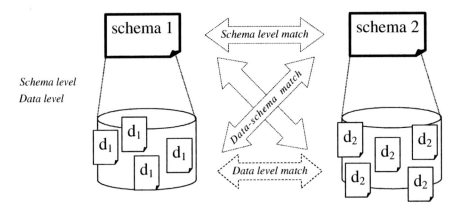

- **Grouping together documents with similar structures.** As clustering assembles together related documents, that is, documents with similar content, structural clustering assembles together documents with similar structures. This can be the first step for the individuation of a concise schema, so that documents may be stored and retrieved more efficiently, but it may also be useful for Web site structural analysis, through which the information provided by the site can be better understood and presented.

- **Grouping together schemas with similar structures.** This is particularly meaningful for heterogeneous data integration and specifically for the development of scalable integration techniques.

In addition to previously outlined applications, a new and interesting scenario in which the approaches presented in this chapter can be effectively applied is for XML database service providers (Hacigümüs et al., 2002), where storage and retrieval facilities are offered to different organizations. Even if more than one organization deal with the same kind of data, each organization may be not aware of that and thus data could be structured differently. Approaches for clustering together similar documents and schemas are needed to an effective storage and retrieval of data the service provider should handle. We remark that in this context, asking organizations to exploit a single standard schema for the representation of their data is not feasible.

In order to provide all these functionalities, measures for evaluating the structural similarity among documents and schemas are required. Many factors should be taken into account in the evaluation. Among them, let us mention the hierarchical and complex structure of XML documents and schemas together with the tags labelling their elements.

In this chapter, we discuss the main efforts of the research community towards the definition of structural similarity measures for sources of XML documents at three different levels, graphically depicted in Figure 1: among documents; between a document and a schema; and among schemas. At each level we also discuss additional applications of the developed measures.

The chapter starts by introducing the commonly adopted representation of XML documents and schemas, and the starting points of most existing proposals for measuring structural similarity, namely, tree edit distance and tag/content similarity. The existing proposals for measuring XML structural similarity at the data, data and schema and schema levels are then presented, in turn. Future trends in measuring structural similarity in XML sources are finally discussed.

Background

In this section we first introduce the representation of XML documents and schemas, then we present the basics of tree similarity and the best known approaches to compute tree edit distance. Finally, the problem of evaluating syntactic and semantic term similarity is discussed.

Document and Schema Representations

An XML document, as shown in Figure 2, simply consists of a sequence of nested, tagged elements. An element contains a portion of the document delimited by a start tag (e.g., <nameprod>) at the beginning and an end tag (e.g., </nameprod>) at the end. Empty elements of the form <*tagname/*> are also possible. The outermost element containing all the elements of the document, element order in Figure 2, is referred to as a document element. Each element may be characterized by one or more attributes that are name-value pairs appearing just after the element name in the start/empty tag (e.g., idprod="1"), and by a textual content, that is the portion of text appearing between the start tag and the end tag (e.g., Post-It Notes and Dispenser).

A set of rules, collectively known as the *document type definition* (DTD), can be attached to XML documents specifying the schema that the document may follow. Figure 2 also shows an example of DTD. A DTD is composed of two sections, the *element declarations* and the *attribute list declarations*. The

Figure 2. XML document and DTD

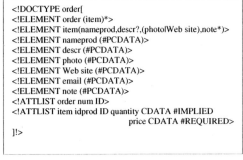

Figure 3. Tree representation of an XML document and a DTD

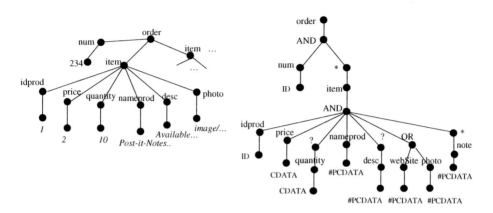

element declaration section specifies the structure of the elements contained in the document. For each element, it specifies its subelements (if any) and/or the type of its data content. This type may be EMPTY if no content is allowed, ANY, if all kinds of content are allowed or #PCDATA if only textual content is allowed. Moreover, it is possible to specify the order of subelements and, for each subelement, whether it is optional (?), whether it may occur several times (* for 0 or more times and + for one or more times), whether some subelements are alternative with respect to each other (|) or constitute a sequence (,).

The attribute list declaration section specifies, for each element, the list of its attribute names, types, optionality clauses (#IMPLIED to denote an optional attribute, #REQUIRED to denote a mandatory one, and #FIXED to denote a mandatory attribute with constant value), and (optional) default values. Attributes can have different types allowing one to specify an element identifier (type ID), links to other elements (type IDREF, referring to a single target or IDREFS, referring to multiple targets) or additional information about the element (e.g., type CDATA for textual information).

Both XML documents and DTDs are conveniently represented as labelled trees. In trees representing documents, internal nodes are labelled by tag names and leaves are labelled by data content, whereas in trees representing schemas, internal nodes are labelled either by tag names or by *operators* (i.e., sequence AND, choice OR or optionality and repeatability ?,+ and * constraints) and leaves are labelled by simple (atomic) data types. In the tree representation, attributes are not distinguished from elements; both are mapped to the tag name set. Thus, attributes are handled as elements, attribute nodes appear as children of the element they refer to and, for what concerns the order, they are sorted by attribute name and appear before all sub-element "siblings." XML document and schema elements may actually refer to, that is, contain links to, other elements. Including these links in the model gives rise to a graph rather than a tree. Such links can be important in the use of XML data. However, they are not meaningful for what concerns describing the structure of the document, thus most approaches disregard them and simply model documents and schemas as trees.

Figure 3 depicts the tree representations of the document and DTD in Figure 2, pointing out relationships among elements that are considered for structural similarity:

- father-children relationship, that is, the relationship between each element and its direct subelements;
- ancestor-descendant relationship, that is, the relationship between each element and its direct and indirect subelements; and
- order relationship among siblings.

Some of the approaches described in the chapter are not specifically tailored for XML documents, rather they are developed for semi-structured data and data guides. Semi-structured data and data guides are normally represented through an object exchange model (OEM) which essentially is an edge-labelled graph in which nodes represent objects and edges represent relationships between objects.

Tree Similarity: Basics

The problem of computing the distance between two trees, also known as a *tree editing problem*, is the generalization of the problem of computing the distance between two strings (Wagner & Fischer, 1974) to labelled trees. The editing operations available in the tree editing problem are changing (i.e., relabelling), deleting and inserting a node. To each of these operations a cost is assigned that can depend on the labels of the involved nodes. The problem is to find a sequence of such operations transforming a tree T_1 into a tree T_2 with minimum cost. The distance between T_1 and T_2 is then defined to be the cost of such a sequence. Applications of the tree editing problem are in the comparison of RNA secondary structures and in syntax theory, where to compare two sentential forms, the distance between their parse trees can be computed.

The best known and referenced approach to compute edit distance for ordered trees is by Zhang and Shasha (1989). They consider three kinds of operations for

Figure 4. Mapping

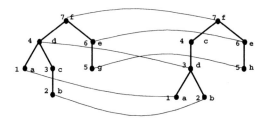

ordered labelled trees. *Relabelling* a node *n* means changing the label on *n*.
Deleting a node *n* means making the children of *n* become the children of the
parent of *n* and then removing *n*. *Inserting n* as the child of *m* will make *n* the
parent of a consecutive subsequence of the current children of *m*. Let Σ be the
node label set and let λ be a unique symbol not in Σ, denoting the null symbol. An
edit operation is represented as $a \rightarrow b$, where *a* is either λ or the label of a node
in T_1 and *b* is either λ or the label of a node in T_2. An operation of the form $\lambda \rightarrow$
b is an insertion, an operation of the form $a \rightarrow \lambda$ is a deletion. Finally, an operation
of the form $a \rightarrow b$, with $a, b \neq \lambda$ is a relabelling. Each edit operation $a \rightarrow b$ is
assigned a cost, that is, a nonnegative real number $\gamma(a \rightarrow b)$ by a cost function
γ. Function γ is a distance metric, that is:

1. $\gamma(a \rightarrow b) \geq 0, \gamma(a \rightarrow a) = 0$;

2. $\gamma(a \rightarrow b) = \gamma(b \rightarrow a)$;

3. $\gamma(a \rightarrow c) \leq \gamma(a \rightarrow b) + \gamma(b \rightarrow c)$.

Function g is extended to a sequence of edit operation $S = s_1, \dots s_k$ by letting:

$$\gamma(S) = \sum_{i=1}^{k} \gamma(s_i).$$

The edit distance between the two trees T_1 and T_2 is defined as the minimum cost
edit operation sequence that transforms T_1 to T_2, that is:

$$D(T_1, T_2) = min_S \{\gamma(S) \mid S \text{ is an edit operation sequence taking } T_1 \text{ to } T_2\}.$$

The edit operations give rise to a mapping which is a graphical specification of
which edit operations apply to each node in the two trees. Figure 4 is a mapping
example showing a way to transform T_1 to T_2. It corresponds to the edit sequence

$c \rightarrow \lambda ; g \rightarrow h; \lambda \rightarrow c$. The figure also shows a left-to-right postorder of nodes, which is commonly used to identify nodes in a tree.

For a tree T, let $t[i]$ represent the *ith* node of T. A *mapping* (or *matching*) from T_1 to T_2 is a triple *(M, T_1, T_2)* where M is a set of pairs of integers *(i,j)* such that:

- $1 \leq i \leq |T_1|$, $1 \leq j \leq |T_2|$;
- for any pair *(i_1, j_1)* and *(i_2, j_2)* in M:
    - $i_1 = i_2$ iff $j_1 = j_2$ (one-to-one),
    - $t_1[i_1]$ is to the left of $t_1[i_2]$ iff $t_2[j_1]$ is to the left of $t_2[j_2]$ (sibling order preserved),
    - $t_1[i_1]$ is an ancestor of $t_1[i_2]$ iff $t_2[j_1]$ is an ancestor of $t_2[j_2]$ (ancestor order preserved).

The mapping graphically depicted in Figure 4 consists of the pairs: $\{(7,7), (4,3), (1,1), (2,2), (6,6), (5,5)\}$. Let M be a mapping from T_1 to T_2, the cost of M is defined as:

$$\gamma(M) = \sum\nolimits_{(i,j) \in M} \gamma(t_1[i] \rightarrow t_2[j]) + \sum\nolimits_{\{i | \neg \exists j s.t.(i,j) \in M\}} \gamma(t_1[i] \rightarrow \lambda) + \sum\nolimits_{\{j | \neg \exists i s.t.(i,j) \in M\}} \gamma(\lambda \rightarrow t_2[j])$$

There is a straightforward relationship between a mapping and a sequence of edit operations. Specifically, nodes in T_1 not appearing in M correspond to deletions; nodes in T_2 not appearing in M correspond to insertions; nodes that participate to M correspond to relabellings if the two labels are different, to null edits otherwise.

The dynamic programming approach adopted by Zhang and Shasha to compute the tree-to-tree edit distance is based on computing, as subroutines, the distance between certain pairs of subtrees and between certain pairs of ordered subforests. An ordered subforest of a tree T is a collection of subtrees of T appearing in the same order they appear in T, and is obtained by considering all the children of a given node of T. In determining the distance between a source tree T_1 and a destination tree T_2, indeed, the key to formulating the problem using dynamic programming is to first determine the cost of inserting every subtree of T_2 and the cost of deleting every subtree of T_1. Moreover, suffix trees are exploited as follows. In order to compute the edit distance between the T_1 subtree rooted at $t_1[i]$ and the T_2 subtree rooted at $t_2[j]$, almost all the distances between subtrees rooted at $t_1[i']$ and $t_2[j']$, with i',j' descendants of i,j, respectively, are needed in advance. This suggests a bottom-up procedure for computing all subtree pairs. Moreover, denoting with $l(n)$ the leftmost leaf descendant of the subtree rooted at n, when i' is in the path from $l(i)$ to i and j' is in the path from $l(j)$ to j, there is no need to compute the distance between the subtrees rooted at $t_1[i]$ and $t_2[j]$ separately, since they can be obtained as a byproduct of computing the distances between $t_1[i']$ and $t_2[j']$. Intuitively, separate computations are needed only for tree T and for the subtrees of T rooted at nodes that have a left sibling. Referring to the trees in Figure 4, this means that out of the 36 subtree distances, only the nine corresponding to the subtrees rooted at the following nodes are computed: (3,2), (3,5), (3,6), (5,2), (5,5), (5,6), (6,2), (6,5) and (6,6).

Given two ordered trees T_1 and T_2, the algorithm finds an optimal edit script in time $O(|T_1| \times |T_2| \times min\{depth(T_1), leaves(T_1)\} \times min\{depth(T_2), leaves(T_2)\})$, where $|T|$ denotes the number of nodes in a tree T, $depth(T)$ denotes the depth of a tree T and $leaves(T)$ denotes the number of leaves of a tree T.

Edit distance for unordered trees, i.e., trees in which the left-to-right ordering among siblings is not significant, has been considered in Zhang et al. (1992). Specifically, they proved that the problem for unordered trees is NP-complete. Zhang (1993) proposed a polynomial time algorithm for unordered trees based on a restriction that matching is only allowed between nodes at the same level.

Syntactic and Semantic Tag and Content Similarity

In evaluating the structural similarity among two labelled trees, an important issue is how to evaluate the similarity among labels. This entails XML-specific problems for labels that are operators, whereas it is a better addressed problem when labels are data content or user-defined element tags. Two strings (either element tags or element content) may be considered similar if they are identical, or if they are likely to represent the same concept, that is, they are *semantically similar*, or if they are similar as strings, that is, they are *syntactically similar*. Semantic similarity may be detected on the basis of terminological relationships that can be tested relying on a given Thesaurus, such as WordNet (Miller, 1995). Examples of relevant terminological relationships among terms include synonyms, that is, terms denoting the same class of real world objects (e.g., 'Client' and 'Customer'); broader and narrower terms, or hypernyms-hyponyms, that is, terms denoting classes of real world objects included one in the other (e.g., 'Person' and 'Client'); terms having a common lexical root (e.g., 'Person' and 'Personnel'); terms that are morphological variants, such as an acronym and its expansion or a singular term and its plural. By contrast, syntactic similarity disregards the term meaning and simply relies on a string edit distance function (Wagner & Fischer, 1974), that is, two terms are syntactically similar if the string edit function returns a number of edit operations less than a given threshold. The string edit distance between two strings s_1 and s_2 is the minimum number of operations to transform string s_1 to s_2. Allowable operations are character insert, delete and modify, and all are assumed to have unit cost. Thus, the edit distance between 'sting' and 'string' is 1. Dynamic programming algorithms to compute the edit distance between two strings in $O(n^2)$ for strings of length n are well known. Variants allowing for additional operations such as block moves (so that the edit distance between 'John Smith' and 'Smith John' becomes 1) or assigning different relative weights to operations have also been proposed.

Though semantic similarity seems more appropriate, a problem with semantic similarity applied to tags is that often tags employed in real XML documents are not present in the Thesaurus because they are not nouns. Often a tag is a combination of lexemes (e.g., ProductList, SigmodRecord, Act_number), a shortcut (e.g., coverpg, CC), a single letter word (e.g., P for paragraph, V for verse) or a preposition or a verb (e.g., from, to, related). Thus, while for document content, semantic similarity is generally preferable to syntactic similarity, for what concerns tags in many cases, syntactic tag similarity could be more reliable than semantic tag similarity. Otherwise, new Thesauri should be generated tailored to disambiguate tags and containing nouns, verbs and frequent shortcuts commonly used as tags for XML documents.

Similarity at Data Level

In this section we deal with approaches for measuring the structural similarity among XML documents, emphasizing the peculiarities with respect to the general tree similarity problem discussed above. Specifically, we present ad hoc approaches for document clustering, change detection in documents and approximate querying of documents.

We focus on approaches matching a document against another one or against a query, though, more in general, as outlined in Guha et al. (2002), there could be also the problem to match all pairs of documents from two data sources that requires techniques for efficiently reporting all pairs with matching cost less than a given threshold.

Document Structural Clustering

The goal of these approaches is to exploit the structural similarity between two XML documents as the metric in clustering algorithms. By focusing on the structure of the documents, disregarding their content, the obtained clusters contain structurally homogeneous documents. As clustering assembles together documents with similar terms, structural clustering assembles together documents with a similar structure. Grouping together documents with similar structures has interesting applications in the context of information extraction, heterogeneous data integration, personalized content delivery and Web site structural analysis. As we will discuss in the following section, approaches have been proposed to extract schema information from a set of structurally similar documents. Preliminary to this schema extraction process is the creation of structurally homogeneous subsets of the documents in the source through the creation of structural clusters. The need to group heterogeneous data in structurally homogeneous collections arises each time DBMS facilities would be used for handling these data, thus taking advantage of the homogeneous structure for indexing and query processing. Clustering data relying on their structural similarity may be also useful in semistructured data integration for recognizing different sources providing the same kind of information. In Web site structural analysis, structural clustering can help in understanding and presenting the information provided by the site. The identification of structurally similar documents conforming to a specific schema can serve as the input for wrappers working on structurally similar Web pages.

Nierman and Jagadish (2002) measure the structural similarity among XML documents. Documents are represented as ordered labelled trees, as discussed in the previous section, but, since the focus is on structural similarity, the actual values of document elements and attributes are not represented in the tree (i.e., leaf nodes of the general representation are omitted from the tree). They suggest to measure the distance between two ordered labelled trees relying on a notion of tree edit distance. However, two XML documents produced from the same DTD may have very different sizes due to optional and repeatable elements. Any edit distance (as the ones discussed in the previous section) that permits changes to only one node at a time will necessarily find a large distance between such a pair of documents, and consequently will not recognize that these documents should be clustered together as being derived by the same DTD. For instance, referring to the document in Figure 2, the distance with respect a document containing a single item with the required structure can be high because of the missing of the two structured item elements, though both documents are valid for the same DTD. Thus, they develop an edit distance metric that is more indicative of this notion of structural similarity. Specifically, in addition to insert, delete and relabel operations of Zhang and Shasha (1989), they also introduce the insert subtree and delete subtree editing operations, allowing the cutting and pasting of whole sections of a document. Specifically, operation $insertTree_T(A,i)$ adds A as a child of T at position $i+1$ and operation $deleteTree_T(T_i)$ deletes T_i as the i-th child of T. They impose, however, the restriction that the use of the $insertTree$ and $deleteTree$ operations is limited to when the subtree that is being inserted (or deleted) is shared between the source and the destination tree. Without this restriction, one could delete the entire source tree in one step and insert the entire destination tree in a second step, thus making completely useless insert and delete operations. The subtree A being inserted/deleted is thus required to be *contained in* the source/destination tree T, that is, all its nodes must occur in T, with the same parent/child relationships and the same sibling order; additional siblings may occur in T (to handle the presence of optional elements), as graphically shown in Figure 5. A second restriction imposes that a tree that has been inserted via the *insertTree* operation cannot subsequently have additional nodes inserted, and, similarly, a tree that has been deleted via the *deleteTree* operation cannot previously have had nodes deleted. This restriction provides an efficient means for computing the costs of inserting and deleting the subtrees found in the destination and source trees, respectively. The resulting algorithm is a simple bottom up algorithm obtained as an extension of Zhang and Shasha's basic algorithm, with the difference that any subtree T_i has a *graft* cost which is the minimum among the cost of a single *insertTree* (if allowable) and of any sequence of insert and (allowable) *insertTree* operations, and, analogously, any subtree has a *prune* cost. At each node $v \in T_1$, the cost of inserting the single node v is computed and added to the graft cost of each child of v, obtaining a value d. If the tree rooted at v is contained in the source tree T_1, the insert tree cost d' for the tree is computed. The graft cost for the subtree rooted at v is then the minimum between d and d'. Prune costs are computed analogously.

The obtained algorithm has overall $O(|T_1| \times |T_2|)$ complexity. A good question is whether this tree structure-based measure is needed. An alternative would be to simply count tag occurrences in the two documents and add the absolute values of the differences. By using a simple hash data structure, the tag frequency distance can be computed in $O(|T_1| + |T_2|)$. Experiments (Nierman & Jagadish, 2000) show that the number of mis-clusterings with this tag frequency distance is much higher than with their distance.

Flesca et al. (2002) perform structural clustering that does not rely on matching algorithms. They represent the structure of an XML document as a time series in which each occurrence of a tag corresponds to a given impulse. Thus, they take into account the order in which tags appear in the documents. They interpret an XML document as a discrete-time signal in which numeric values summarize some relevant features of the elements enclosed within the document. If, for instance, one simply indents all tags in a given document according to their nesting level, the sequence of indentation marks, as they appear within the document rotated by 90 degrees, may be looked at as a time series whose shape roughly describes the document structure. These time-series data are then analysed through their discrete Fourier transform (DFT), leading to abstract from structural details which should not affect the similarity estimation (such as different number of occurrences of an element or small shift in its position). More precisely, during a preorder visit of the XML document tree, as soon as a node is visited, an impulse is emitted containing the information relevant to the tag.

Figure 5. Contained in relationship

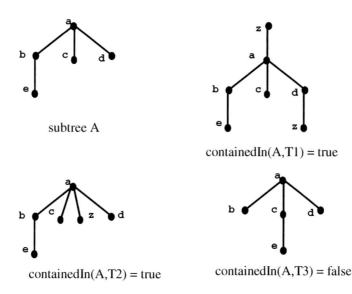

subtree A

containedIn(A,T1) = true

containedIn(A,T2) = true   containedIn(A,T3) = false

Thus:

- each element is encoded as a real value;
- the substructures in the documents are encoded using different signal shapes; and
- context information can be used to encode both basic elements and substructures, so that the analysis can be tuned to handle in a different way mismatches occurring at different hierarchical levels.

Once having represented each document as a signal, document shapes are analysed through DFT. Some useful properties of this transform, namely, the concentration of the energy into few frequency coefficients, its invariance of the amplitude under shifts, allow the revelation of much about the distribution and relevance of signal frequencies without the need of resorting to edit distance based algorithms, thus, more efficiently. As the encoding guarantees that each relevant subsequence is associated with a group of frequency components, the comparison of their magnitudes allows the detection of similarities and differences between documents. With variable-length sequences, however, the computation of the DFT should be forced on M fixed frequencies, where M is at least as large as the document sizes, otherwise the frequency coefficients may not correspond. To avoid increasing the complexity of the overall approach, the missing coefficients are interpolated starting from the available ones. The distance between documents d_1 and d_2 is then defined as:

$$\text{dist}(d_1, d_2) = \left(\sum_{k=1}^{M/2} (|[\widetilde{DFT}(enc(d_1))](k)| - |[\widetilde{DFT}(enc(d_2))](k)|)^2 \right)^{1/2}$$

where *enc* is the document encoding function, $\widetilde{DFT}$ denotes the interpolation of DFT to the frequencies appearing in both d_1 and d_2 and M is the total number of points appearing in the interpolation. Comparing two documents using this technique costs $O(n \log n)$, where n is the maximum number of tags in the documents, that is, $n = max(|d_1|, |d_2|)$. The developed approach is demonstrated to be practically as effective as approaches based on tree edit distance.

Document Change Detection

The goal of these approaches is to detect and represent changes to hierarchically structured information. A relevant application, in the context of the Web, is that of a user repeatedly visiting certain documents and thus interested in knowing how each document has changed since the last visit. Changes are detected by comparing the old and new versions of the documents. Since documents may be represented as trees, the hierarchical change detection problem can be formulated as the problem of finding a minimum cost edit script that transforms one data tree to another. The focus here, however, is not only to produce a number (distance) quantifying the similarity between the documents, rather to also identify the mismatching portions of the documents. The problem is thus to match a pair of documents approximately, that requires:

- techniques for approximate match of a document pair,
- deriving a cost for matching the pair.

The interest, moreover, is in mismatches both in content and structure, whereas approaches considered in the previous section completely disregard document content.

The problem has been first addressed by Chawathe et al. (1996), who formulated the change detection problem on hierarchically structured documents, modelled as ordered labelled trees. They do not employ the general tree edit distance

Figure 6. move *operation*

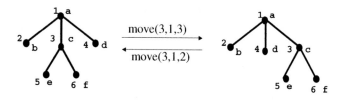

algorithm (Zhang & Shasha, 1989), rather they develop a different algorithm to achieve better performance.

Edit operations are assumed to be unit cost operations, with the exception of the relabelling operation, whose cost is assumed to be represented by a *compare* function that evaluates how different old and new values are. The cost of an edit script is the sum of the costs of its individual operations. The algorithm they propose is based on the key assumption that the number of tree duplicate nodes is limited; more specifically: given two labelled trees T_1 and T_2 the matching function *compare* is "good," in that, given any leaf s in T_1, there is at most one leaf in T_2 close enough to match s. In addition to "classical" insert, delete and relabel edit operations, they also consider a *move* operation, allowing to move a subtree as a single edit operation, as illustrated in Figure 6.

The approach they propose is a two-step approach. First, matching nodes are identified and then the edit script is derived. The complexity of deriving the matching is improved by heuristically limiting the number of pairs considered during the match. Intuitively, the heuristic aims at identifying how structurally different two subtrees are and they then consider matching nodes with not too dissimilar subtrees. Once matching is derived, the algorithm derives the edit script given the matching by updating labels; aligning leaf nodes by assessing the longest common subsequence between sets of ordered leaves; and inserting, moving and deleting nodes.

The complexity is linear in the number of nodes of the trees; more precisely the algorithm runs in $O((leaves(T_1)+leaves(T_2))*e+e^2)$, where $leaves(T)$ denotes the number of leaves of a tree T and e is the "weighted edit distance," that is, the sum over the edits in the edit script transforming T_1 to T_2 of 1 if the edit is an insert or a delete, of $|x|$ if the edit is a move of a subtree x, of 0 if the edit is a relabelling. (Typically, $e << leaves(T_1) + leaves(T_2)$). The problem with this approach is that the key assumption holds well for many SGML documents that do not contain duplicate or similar objects, but it may not hold for many XML documents. If the assumption does not hold, the algorithm is not guaranteed to find the minimal edit script.

In a subsequent work, Chawathe et al. (1997) raise the assumptions of the previous algorithm of ordered nodes and few duplicate node labels and, in addition to the move operation, they also offer the *copy* and *glue* operations that are similar to the *insertTree* and *deleteTree* operations considered in Nierman and Jagadish (2000). The idea is to report changes in a succinct and descriptive way. The obtained *MH-Diff* algorithm operates on unordered trees and the resulting approach, like the previous one, is a heuristic approach, that is, it is not guaranteed to find the optimal solution. The problem is reduced to a minimum cost edge cover in a bipartite graph. Each operation is given a user-defined fixed cost except for the relabel operation, whose cost is determined by a user-provided function that compares the values of two nodes. The complexity of this heuristic solution is $O(n^3)$, reduced to $O(n^2)$ in many practical scenarios, where $n = |T_1| + |T_2|$ is the total number of nodes of the two trees.

The problem of document change detection has also been addressed for XML documents modelled as unordered trees by Wang et al. (2003). They argue that an unordered model is more suitable for most database applications, though change detection (as a tree-to-tree matching problem) is substantially harder than using the ordered model. The *X-Diff* algorithm they propose integrates key XML structure characteristics with the standard edit distance technique, thus resulting in an efficient algorithm, whose time complexity is in $O(|T_1| \times |T_2| \times max\{deg(T_1), deg(T_2)\} \times log_2(max\{deg(T_1), deg(T_2)\})))\}$, where $deg(T)$ denotes the maximum outdegree in a tree T, that is, the maximum number of child nodes of nodes in T. The algorithm computes the optimal difference between two versions of an XML document and is obtained by relying on specific XML domain characteristics, such as node signatures. Specifically, when looking for the match of corresponding nodes in the two trees, they do not match every node in the first tree against every node in the second tree, rather they take into account that each node in XML has its own context. Thus, they only match nodes that have the same signature, where, intuitively, the signature of a node is obtained by concatenating the tags of all its ancestors with its own tag and type. For instance, referring to the document of Figure 3, the signature of the leftmost item leaf is order/item/idprod/Text.

In Table 1, the considered approaches for measuring structural similarity at data level are summarized and compared along a number of dimensions. The first column states whether the approach considers order among sibling elements. The second column lists the edit operations considered in tree matching. The third and fourth columns specify the relationship among data content and tags, respectively. The fifth column specifies whether the proposed algorithm is optimal or heuristic, whereas the sixth column mentions restrictions or assumptions made by the approaches.

Table 1. Structural similarity at data level

	Order	Edit operations	Content relationship	Tag relationship	Optimal/ heuristic	Restrictions or assumptions
Nierman & Jagadish, (2000)	Y	insert, delete, relabel, insertTree, deleteTree		Equality	O	
Flesca, et al. (2000)	Y			Equality		
Chawathe, et al. (1996)	Y	insert, delete, relabel, moveTree	equality	Equality	H	few duplicate node labels
Chawathe, et al. (1997)	N	insert, delete, relabel, moveTree, insertTree, deleteTree	equality		H	
Wang, et al. (2003)	N	insert, delete, relabel	equality	Equality	O	match of nodes with same signature

Approximate Queries

The need of shifting from exact queries with Boolean answers to proximity queries with ranked approximate results is a relevant requirement of XML query languages for searching the Web, and several approaches in this direction have been developed. These approaches share the goal of integrating structural conditions typical of database queries with weighted and ranked approximate answers typical of information retrieval.

The first step is to allow approximate matching in data content (tree leaves), and to rank the results according to the matching degree. An approach in this direction is ELIXIR (Chinenyanga & Kushmerick, 2002). Here, the document structure is not taken into account. A first step to take document structure into account is that made by approaches like XIRQL (Fuhr & Grossjohann, 2001) and XXL (Theobald & Weikum, 2000) that accept approximate matching at nodes, and then discuss how to combine weights depending on the structure. Thus, approximate answers are accepted for content and element tags, but conditions on document structure are interpreted as filters, thus they need to be satisfied exactly. XXL supports a similarity operator and, to use this operator, the user must know that similar keywords or element tags exist.

A different perspective is that of approaches looking for partial, that is, approximate, structural matches allowing the structure of the document and query trees to partially match. The first approaches in this direction, however, identify the matches but do not measure them. Specifically, Kilpelainen (1992) discusses 10 different kinds of tree inclusion problems, that is, 10 different variations of the problem of locating instances of a query tree Q in a target tree T. He orders these different problems, ranging from unordered tree inclusion to ordered subtrees, highlighting the inclusion relationships among them. Moreover, he gives a general schema of solution and instantiates it for each problem, discussing the resulting complexities. The unordered tree inclusion problem, for instance, means relaxing all parent-child relationships to ancestor-descendant in the matching process. His goal, however, is not to measure the distance, but rather to find all the instances of the pattern in the data tree. At the algorithmic level in the approaches in Kilpelainen (1992), the query drives the algorithm, since the query is always included. This, together with the fact that the query dimension is assumed to be small, allows some precomputation.

Analogously, Kanza and Sagiv (2001) advocate the need of more flexible query evaluation mechanisms in the context of OEM semistructured data. They model both queries and data as graphs and they propose to weaken rigid matchings to semiflexible and flexible matchings. In semiflexible matchings, query paths are mapped to data paths in which nodes are not necessarily in the same order. In flexible matchings, query edges are mapped to data paths. No notion of similarity evaluation and ranking is proposed.

Some approaches have, however, been proposed that combine the two requirements, thus allowing partial structural matches and ranking documents according to their structural (and content) similarity to the query.

In the approach proposed by Damiani and Tanca (2000), both XML documents and queries are modelled as graphs and then a fuzzy labelling is applied to those graphs in which information is fuzzy weighted according to its relative relevance. They propose to employ both structure-related weighting (weight on an edge) and tag-related weighting (weight on a node). Some criteria for weighting are proposed, such as: weight decreases in moving away from the root and the weight depends on the dimension of the subtree. Shortcut edges are considered, thus allowing the insertion of nodes, the weight of which is a function of the weights of edges. The match score is a normalized sum of the weight of edges.

In the relaxation tree approach by Amer-Yahia et al. (2002), exact and relaxed weights are associated with query nodes and edges. The score of a match is computed as the sum of the corresponding weights, and the relaxed weight is the function of the transformations applied to the tree. The considered transformations are:

- relax node: replacing the node content with a more general concept;
- delete node: making a leaf node optional by removing the node and the edge linking it to its parent;
- relax edge: transforming a parent/child relationship to an ancestor/descendent relationship; and
- promote node: moving up in the tree structure a node (and the corresponding subtree).

The approXQL (Schlieder, 2002) approach can also handle partial structural matchings. A variation of the tree similarity problem is considered, which is restricted to a subset of classical tree edit operations and thus results in a polynomial complexity. All the paths in the query are required to be present in the document, thus the algorithms can be driven by the query structure. The considered edit operations are delete node, insert intermediate node and relabel node, and the score of match is function of the number of transformations, each one of which is assigned a user-specified cost.

The main differences among the considered approaches are summarized in Table 2, inspired and adapted from Amer-Yahia et al. (2003). The first column states whether the approach considers order among sibling elements. The second and third columns specify the relationship among data content and tags, respectively, which can be equality or semantic similarity. Semantic relaxation means substituting a concept with a more general one. The fourth column mentions the captured mismatches between the two structures, whereas the last column distinguishes approaches producing a numerical evaluation of the similarity between the document and the query.

Referring to the XML document in Figure 2, this means that ELIXIR considers the first item element of that document as an answer to the query:

order/item/nameprod/"Post it Dispenser"

where the structural constraints are exactly met and there is a partial match of textual content, whereas XXL considers it as an answer also for the query:

order/ordereditem/prodname/"Post it Dispenser"

where there is a partial matching also of tag names. The approach by Kanza and Sagiv identifies in the document tree all the (approximate) occurrences of a tree like the one in Figure 7(a), in which nodes appear in a different order and tag

Table 2. Structural similarity in approximate queries

	Order	Content relationship	Tag Relationship	Edit operations	Score ranking
ELIXIR		Semantic similarity			Y
XIRQL	Y	Semantic similarity	Equality	relabel	Y
XXL	N	Semantic similarity	Semantic similarity	relabel	Y
Tree inclusion (Kilpailanen, 1992)	both	Equality	Equality	insert	N
Kanza & Sagiv (2001)	N	Equality	Equality	Insert/permute node order in paths	N
Damiani & Tanca (2000)	N	Semantic similarity	Semantic similarity	insert, relabel	Y
Tree relaxation	N	Semantic relaxation	Semantic relaxation	insert,delete,relabel	Y
approXQL	N	Semantic similarity	Semantic similarity	insert, delete, relabel	Y

Figure 7. Approximate queries as trees

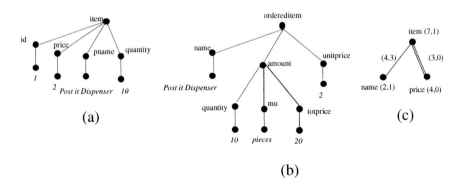

names slightly differ, approXQL, like the one in Figure 7(b) allowing for the insertion of intermediate nodes, whereas tree relaxation considers queries as weighted trees like the one in Figure 7(c), where // denotes a path rather than an edge and weights on nodes and edges specify the score to be assigned to exact and approximate matches, respectively.

Similarity between Data and Schema

For what concerns similarity between data and schema, existing approaches either address approximate conformance of data to a schema or the extraction of schema information from data relying on their structural similarities. Other related topics we do not consider in this section are frequent subtree mining (Termier et al., 2002; Zaki, 2002) and structural classification of XML documents (Zaki & Aggarwal, 2003), where structural rules are mined in a training phase and are then exploited for document structural classification.

Approximate Conformance

Few approaches attempt measuring the structural similarity between data and schema at the intensional level, despite the practical relevance of the problem, both from a data modelling and a querying perspective. The only approaches we are aware of are by Grahne and Thomo (2001) and by us (Bertino et al., 2004). Grahne and Thomo (2001) face the problem of determining whether semi-structured data, represented as edge-labelled graphs, approximately conform to a data guide. The focus of this approach is on approximate querying: starting from a regular path query and a regular transducer specifying the allowed sequences of elementary "distortions" together with their costs, the answers that are within an approximation of the original query are determined. A transducer (S, I, O, τ, s, F) is a finite set of states S, an input alphabet I, an output alphabet O, a starting state s, a set of final states F *and* a transition-output function t from finite subsets of $S{\times}I^*$ to finite subsets of $S{\times}O^*$. The transducer also defines a distance function, based on the concept of edit distance and on the cost of the elementary distortions, for computing the distance from the original query. The authors also discuss how the approach may be used for detecting whether data instances approximately satisfy a schema such as a data guide. A basic assumption in this work is that users specify a distortion transducer, through which they can distort the data guide by allowed elementary distortions (e.g., by specifying alternatives to the name of an element) and then test if the database conforms to the distorted data guide. A notion of k-satisfaction is also introduced meaning that k is the bound of the distance between the database and the data guide, thus providing a quantitative measure of approximate satisfaction. The approach is thus based on the assumption that the possible deviations from the original schema specification and their importance (weight) are specified by users through the distortion transducer. We remark that it is seldom possible to know in advance the distortion between the data and the schema because tags exploited in the schema and the structure of the schema itself may be unknown.

The approach by Grahne and Thomo (2001), moreover, has not been developed for XML documents and DTDs, but for generic semi-structured data and data guides represented as edge-labelled graphs. A data guide, however, is simpler than a DTD since it does not contain constraints on the repeatability or alternativeness of elements.

In Bertino et al. (2004), the structural similarity between a document D and a DTD T is "extensionally" defined as the highest structural similarity between D and one of the valid documents for the DTD (say it is D'). The similarity between D and D' is computed as the ratio between their common elements and the total number of elements by taking several factors into account. A matching algorithm is defined for the intensional computation of the structural similarity, that is, without generating the set of valid documents for a DTD T. Documents and DTDs are represented through labelled trees and a function *Match* is introduced in order to identify and properly evaluate the common and divergent elements/ attributes between the two structures. In the match, the following factors are taken into account:

- Some attributes and subelements specified for an element in the DTD can be missing from the corresponding element of the document, and vice versa, the document can contain some additional attributes and subelements not appearing in the DTD.

- Elements at higher levels of the hierarchical structures of the document and the DTD are more relevant than deeply-nested elements.

- Order of sibling elements is not considered because the focus is on data-centric documents.

- Both semantic and syntactic tag similarity between document and DTD tags is considered.

In the algorithm, the DTD rules constraining the element contents are exploited for determining the best match. By following this intensional approach, an algorithm that is much faster in common situations is obtained.

Extraction of Schema Information from Data

A related problem that has been investigated for semi-structured data and XML is that of structure extraction, that is, discovering of schema information (in the form of a data guide or of a DTD, respectively) from a set of documents. The proposed approaches that we discuss in this section require the application of data mining techniques for identifying commonalities among the complex structures of XML documents. This information is then exploited for the definition of an approximate schema of the documents. The generated schema in general, with the exception of Bertino et al. (2002), contains all the elements that are present in the set of documents. However, it is approximate in the sense that the DTD rules for an element can also consider valid elements that do not belong to the set of documents. The purpose of the similarity measure is thus to determine the most concise combination of operators in the DTD rules or, in other words, to rank the possible DTD rules for an element and to choose the most concise and minimal one for the considered documents. For example, if an element presents the sequence of subelements "ababbbd", possible DTD rules can be (a,b,a,b,b,b,d),((a|b)*,d), ((a,b*)+,d), ((a,b)*,b+,d). Here the similarity measure is employed to identify the best DTD rule.

Nestorov et al. (1998) propose a technique for extracting implicit schema information, in the form of an *approximate type assignment*, from semi-structured data. The type assignment is approximate since data are not required to exactly conform to the type assigned to them. The approach is based on the idea of defining Datalog programs to type a set of semi-structured objects. Semi-structured data are represented as facts, and types are represented as monadic Datalog programs. A class defined on such a type is a Datalog rule, whose head represents the class name and whose body represents the internal structure of objects instances of the class. The maximal fixpoint semantics of the Datalog program corresponds to the class extent. Starting from a perfect typing (that is, a type for any distinct object), the number of types is then reduced by collapsing the types with a slightly different structure. To determine which types to collapse, some measures are used. The measures compare the number of object properties that fit the type with the number of exceeding and missing object properties with respect to the type. This evaluation is combined with the number of type instances and the Manhattan distance between types is exploited in order to obtain a more accurate evaluation. A final peculiarity of this approach is the fact that an object may be associated with more than one type. This is particularly important to avoid the proliferation of composite types (e.g., PersonEmployeePlayer type) and allow an object to belong to several simple types (e.g., Person AND Employee AND Player type).

The Road Map approach proposed by Wang and Liu (1998) is based on the idea of extracting, from a set of semi-structured documents on the same topic, a structure which is common to the majority of the documents. The approach relies on three concepts: *tree expression, weaker than* relationship between tree expressions and *support* of a tree expression. A tree expression is a tree extracted from a graph representation of semi-structured data in which some edge can be labelled by the wildcard *?,* denoting that any label can match it. A tree expression te_1 is weaker than a tree expression te_2 when, intuitively, all the structural information contained in te_1 is found in te_2. Given a tree expression te, the support of *te* is the number of root documents *d,* such that *te* is weaker than *d.* The problem of discovering the common structure of a set of semi-structured documents is specified as finding a tree expression *te* whose support is greater than a user defined minimal support (that is, it is *frequent*) and no other tree expression with higher support exists. The approach may be thought as a generalization of the data mining association rules in which frequent sets of structures are considered instead of frequent sets of items. Even if a specific similarity measure is not specified in this approach, it is implicitly used in the weaker than relationship by considering the frequencies of tree expressions.

XTRACT (Garofalakis et al., 2000) is based on an algorithm for extracting, given a set of XML documents, a DTD being at the same time concise (that is, small) and precise (that is, capturing all the document structures). The algorithm works element by element. For each element that appears in the set of documents, the goal is to derive a regular expression (that is, a DTD rule) that subelement sequences for the element (in the XML documents) conform to. The algorithm is based on three steps:

- heuristic algorithms are used for finding patterns in subelements sequences and replacing them with appropriate regular expressions to produce more general candidate DTD rules;

- common subexpressions are factored out from the generalized candidate DTD rules obtained from the previous step in order to make them more concise; and

- among the candidate DTD rules, those providing the most concise representation of subelement sequences in terms of the DTD are chosen.

In this process, a measure to evaluate among different DTD rules the one that best fits the subelement structures is thus required. This is realized in two steps. First the subelement sequences and the candidate DTD rules are encoded in bit sequences. Then, the minimum description length (MDL) principle is exploited to rank each candidate DTD depending on the number of bits required to describe the subelement sequences in terms of the DTD (DTD requiring fewer bits are ranked higher).

Moh et al. (2000) develop an approach for re-engineering structures of Web documents. The starting point is the extraction of each document structure, in the form of a document tree, and the grouping of documents with similar structure in clusters. This grouping is performed through pattern matching algorithms applied to document trees. Then, a general structure is extracted for each cluster of documents through a data structure referred to as *spanning graph*, which is a DAG containing information on the structures of the original document trees and is incrementally built while document trees are analysed. From this structure, a DTD is finally obtained by considering for each element the longest common subsequence in order to group together child nodes. Moreover, the frequencies of subelements and of subelement groups are considered in order to determine whether they are optional or repeatable (zero or more times/ one or more times). Finally, some heuristic rules have been identified in order to reduce the complexity of the pattern describing the structure of subelements.

Bertino et al. (2002) face the problem of discovering a new schema from a set of XML documents assuming the presence of a DTD and of documents that are similar but not identical to the DTD. With respect to other schema extraction approaches, this one may be referred to as schema *update* approach. Guided by *exceptions*, that is, data that are not captured by the current DTD, the DTD itself is updated by means of heuristic policies. The goal is thus to evolve the previous DTD structure in a new one so that deviations in the structures of documents in the source are taken into account. The evolution process consists of two phases: a *recording phase* in which structural information of the portions of documents not conforming to the corresponding DTD is acquired, and an *evolution phase*, in which the recorded information is used to update the DTD and adapt it to the actual population of the source. The heuristic policies exploited in the evolution phase are based on both positive and negative data mining association rules (Antonie & Zaiane, 2004) to find frequent structural patterns in documents as well as alternative structures.

Table 3 presents a comparison of the approaches for measuring structural similarity at the data-schema level. The first and second columns report whether the approach has been specifically tailored to XML or it has been developed for semistructured data (SSD). Then, the kind of representation of data and schema is reported in the third column, together with the main approach followed in solving the problem. The fourth column reports whether the approach considers the order of sibling elements. The fifth column states the relationship holding between data and schema: *contained* means that all the elements appearing in data are also present in the schema, *contains* means that all the elements appearing in the schema are present in data, and *intersection* means that data can contain elements that do not appear in the schema and the schema can contain elements not present in data. The relationship among tags, namely, equality, similarity or equality extended with the possibility to specify alternatives or use wildcards, is specified in the sixth column. The last column specifies whether the father-children (F/C) relationship is preserved or it is relaxed, i.e., only ancestor-descendant relationship (A/D) is preserved.

Table 3. Structural similarity between data and schema elements appearing in the schema

	Data	Schema	Representation/ Approach	Order	Inclusions	Tag relationship	A/D / F/C
Grahne & Thomo (2001)	SSD	Data guide	Edge labeled graph/ Transducer	N	contained	equality + alternatives	A/D
Bertino et al. (2004)	XML doc.	DTD	Node labeled tree/ Match beteewn trees	N	intersection	similarity (syntactic and semantic)	F/C
Nestorov et al. (1998)	SSD	Data guide	Datalog facts and inference rules/ Maximal fixpoint semantics	N	intersection	equality	F/C
Wang & Liu (1998)	SSD	Data guide	Tree expression/ Frequencies of tree expressions	Both	contained	equality + wildcard	F/C
Garofalakis et al. (2000)	XML doc.	DTD	Sequences + regular expressions/ Heuristics + MDL principle	Y	contained	equality	F/C
Moh et al. (2000)	XML doc.	DTD	Node labeled trees + spanning Graph/Frequencies of elements	Y	contained	equality	F/C
Bertino et al. (2002)	XML doc.	DTD	Node labeled trees/ Heuristics +association rules	N	intersection	equality	F/C

Similarity at Schema Level

The issue of measuring the structural similarity between two schemas has been extensively investigated in the context of heterogeneous data integration and, recently, in the context of XML DTD clustering.

Heterogeneous Data Integration

The problem of heterogeneous data integration is that of identifying corresponding components in different schemas, keeping in account both names and structures of schema elements. Thus, the need arises also in that context of analysing structure similarity. Rahm and Bernstein (2001), in a recent survey on automatic schema matching, propose a taxonomy of individual approaches that can be used to classify the different matching algorithms (called matchers): schema-and-instance level, element-and-structure level and language-and-constraint-based matching approaches. Matchers may be exploited for the evaluation of particular properties (schema names, schema structures and instances of a schema), and can be combined through hybrid and composite combination approaches. A hybrid approach consists in the integration of many matchers in an integrated system, whereas a composite approach exploits different matchers and combines their results in a single evaluation. Cupid (Madhavan et al., 2001), LSD (Doan et al., 2001) and COMA (Do & Rahm, 2002) are prototypes of data integration systems supporting the integration of schemas for XML documents. These approaches map a DTD into an internal schema. This internal schema is more similar to a data guide for semi-structured data (Godman & Widom, 1997) than to a DTD. Therefore, constraints on the occurrences of elements (such as optionality and repeatability of elements) are not considered in performing the integration process. Some of these approaches consider such constraints afterward to tune the obtained similarity.

Cupid (Madhavan et al., 2001) is a hybrid approach that considers both tag names and hierarchical structures of schema. The similarity between an element of the first schema and an element of the second schema relies on the similarity of their components, hereby emphasizing the name and type similarities present at the finest granularity level (leaf level). Starting from a tree representation of two DTDs, their structural similarity is based on the following principles:

1. Elements that are leaves of the two trees are similar if their tags are similar, and the elements in their respective vicinities (ancestors and siblings) are similar;

2. Two non-leaf elements are similar if their tags are similar, and the subtree rooted at the two elements are similar; and

3. Two non-leaf elements are structurally similar if their leaf sets are highly similar, even if their immediate children are not. This is because the leaves represent the atomic data the schema ultimately describes.

The structural similarity between two elements $e1$ and $e2$, belonging respectively to the first and second schema, is specified as:

$$ssim(e_1, e_2) = \frac{\left| \begin{matrix} \{x \mid x \in leaves(e_1) \wedge \exists y \in leaves(e_2), stronglink(x, y)\} \\ \cup \{x \mid x \in leaves(e_2) \wedge \exists y \in leaves(e_1), stronglink(x, y)\} \end{matrix} \right|}{\left| leaves(e_1) \cup leaves(e_2) \right|}$$

where, *leaves(e)* is the set of leaves in the subtree rooted at *e*, and *stronglink(x,y)* is true when their similarity exceeds a given threshold.

Finally, COMA (Do & Rahm, 2002) is a composite approach, which provides an extensible library for the application of different approaches, and supports various ways for combining matching results. Two COMA matchers have been developed for measuring the structural similarity between two DTD elements. The first matcher determines the similarity between two inner elements based on the combined similarity between the child elements, which in turn can be both inner and leaf elements. The similarity between the inner elements is thus recursively computed from the similarity between their respective children. The similarity between the leaf elements is obtained from another matcher (the leaf level matcher) which matches elements based on a combination of their name and data type similarity. The second matcher only considers the leaf elements to estimate the similarity between two inner elements. The authors argue that the second matcher is more stable when the structures are particularly heterogeneous (e.g., there is a missing level between the two DTDs). Rahm et al. (2003) extend the COMA system in order to deal with XML schema of big dimension by exploiting a fragment-oriented approach to decompose a large match problem into several smaller ones and to reuse previous match results at the level of schema fragments.

Clustering of XML DTDs

Lee et al. (2002) propose XClust, an integration strategy that involves the clustering of DTDs. A matching algorithm based on the semantics, immediate descendent and leaf-context similarity of DTD elements is developed to compute the similarity between two DTDs. The similarity between a pair of DTDs T_1 and T_2 is computed in three steps:

1. T_1 and T_2 are normalized by replacing OR operators in the DTD rules with AND operators. This operation is performed through transformation rules like (a|b)*→(a*,b*) and ((a|b)+)?→(a*,b*).

2. The set of best matches *BestMatch* between elements of T_1 and T_2 is computed. For each element $e_1 \in T_1$, $e_2 \in T_2$, $(e_1, e_2) \in$ *BestMatch* if the element similarity of e_1 with e_2 is higher than with any other $e \in T_2$ (and above a given threshold).

3. The similarity between T_1 and T_2 is computed as the sum of the element similarity of pairs in *BestMatch*, normalized by the maximal number of nodes of the two DTDs:

$$DTDSim(T_1, T_2) = \frac{\sum\limits_{(e_1, e_2) \in BestMatch} sim(e_1, e_2)}{\max(|T_1|, |T_2|)}$$

In the evaluation of the similarity between two elements, many factors are taken into account. First, their tag similarity (both syntactic and semantic tag similarity); then, the cardinality of the elements (optional, repeatable or mandatory); and finally, the context in which e_1 and e_2 appear in the hierarchical structures of the DTDs. A context is composed by the element father, the immediate descendant and the leaf descendant. These factors are evaluated and combined in order to determine the similarity of two elements.

The XClust approach for computing the structural similarity between two DTDs is much more sophisticated than the approaches developed for schema integration. They consider a higher number of DTD properties. However, they do not consider DTDs that specify alternative elements, and they simplify element structures.

Future Trends

Several future trends can be devised in measuring structural similarity at the three levels we have discussed. Though there are several approaches and many measures tailored for different applications, what we believe could be extremely useful is a systematic comparison of different similarity measures in order to identify those more adequate depending on the application context and the heterogeneity of the considered data. Such measures can be collected in a framework of functions that a user can select, compose and apply depending on his or her needs.

There is, moreover, the need of allowing more flexible tag matching, keeping tag semantics into account. It is not reasonable, indeed, to weaken the structural constraint by imposing that the tag names employed are exactly the same. Semantic term equivalence approaches specifically tailored to tags should be devised. A related issue is the multilingual requirement arising in many applicative contexts.

At the schema level, there is the need to consider semantically richer schemas than DTDs, thus moving towards XML Schemas (W3C 2000), that allow the representation of the type of values different elements can assume as well as numerical cardinality constraints. Work at the schema level would surely be of benefit to similar developments undergoing in the field of ontology alignment.

At the data level, an interesting direction could be that of defining composite and hybrid approaches, following the same way as adopted at the schema level. Particularly challenging, from the applicative viewpoint, is the combination of structural clustering approaches with content-based and link-based approaches, thus developing clustering techniques that can group documents relying on their structure, content and on their mutual relationships.

Finally, at all the discussed levels, the approaches suffer from some problems in experimental validation, due to the lack of repository of real XML data showing some degree of structural similarity. Many approaches are validated on synthetic data, or on real data whose structure is artificially manipulated or distorted in some way. The INEX evaluation initiative is currently under way to overcome this lack of real XML data (Kazai et al., 2003). The main goal of INEX is to promote the evaluation of XML retrieval by providing a large test collection of XML documents, uniform scoring procedures and a forum for organizations to compare their results. Content and structure based retrieval evaluation is one of the goals of the INEX initiative.

References

Amer-Yahia, S., Cho, S., & Srivastava, D. (2002). Tree pattern relaxation. In *Proceedings of the Eighth International Conference on Extending Database Technology (LNCS)* (Vol. 2287, pp. 496-513).

Amer-Yahia, S., Koudas, N., & Srivastava, D. (2003). Approximate matching in XML. In *Proceedings of the Nineteenth International Conference on Data Engineering* (p. 803).

Antonie, M. L., & Zaiane, O. R. (2004). Mining positive and negative association rules: An approach for confined rules. In *Proceedings of the Eighth European Conference on Principles and Practice of Knowledge Discovery in Databases (LNCS)* (Vol. 3202, pp. 27-38).

Bertino, E., Guerrini, G., & Mesiti, M. (2004). A matching algorithm for measuring the structural similarity between an XML document and a DTD and its applications. *Information Systems, 29*(1), 23-46.

Bertino, E., Guerrini, G., Mesiti, M., & Tosetto, L. (2002). Evolving a set of DTDs according to a dynamic set of XML documents. In *Proceedings of EDBT workshop XMLDTD (LNCS)* (Vol. 2490, pp. 45-66).

Chawathe, S. S., & Garcia-Molina, H. (1997). Meaningful change detection in structured data. In *Proceedings of the ACM SIGMOD International Conference on Management of Data* (pp. 26-37).

Chawathe, S. S., Rajaraman, A., Garcia-Molina, H., & Widom, J. (1996). Change detection in hierarchically structured information. In *Proceedings of the ACM SIGMOD International Conference on Management of Data* (pp. 493-504).

Chinenyanga, T., & Kushmerick, N. (2002). An expressive and efficient language for XML information retrieval. *Journal of the American Society for Information Science and Technology, 53*(6), 438-453.

Damiani, E., & Tanca, L. (2000). Blind queries to XML data. In *Proceedings of the International Conference on Database and Expert Systems Applications* (pp. 345-356).

Do, H. H., & Rahm, E. (2002a). COMA—A system for flexible combination of schema matching approaches. In *Proceedings Twenty-eighth International Conference on Very Large Databases.*

Do, H. H., Melnik, S., & Rahm, E. (2002b). Comparison of schema matching evaluations. In *Proceedings GI-Workshop Web and Databases.*

Doan, A., Domingos, P., & Halevy, A. (2003). Learning to match the schemas of data sources: A multistrategy approach. *Machine Learning, 50*, 279-301.

Flesca, S., Manco, G., Masciari, E., Pontieri, L., & Pugliese, A. (2002). Detecting structural similarities between XML documents. In *Proceedings of the Fifth International Workshop on the Web and Databases* (pp. 55-60).

Fuhr, N., & Grossjohann, K. (2001). XIRQL: A query language for information retrieval in XML documents. In *Proceedings of the International Conference on Research and Development in Information Retrieval* (pp. 172-180).

Garofalakis, M. N., Gionis, A., Rastogi, R., Seshadri, S., & Shim. K. (2000). XTRACT: A system for extracting document type descriptors from XML documents. In *Proceedings of the ACM SIGMOD International Conference on Management of Data* (pp. 165-176).

Grahne, G., & Thomo, A. (2001). Approximate reasoning in semi-structured databases. In *Proceedings of the Eighth International Workshop on Knowledge Representation Meets Databases (CEUR Workshop)* (Vol. 45).

Guha, S., Jagadish, H. V., Koudas, N., Srivastava, D., & Yu, T. (2002). Approximate XML joins. In *Proceedings of the ACM SIGMOD International Conference on Management of Data* (pp. 287-298).

Hacigümüs, H., Mehrotra, S., & Iyer B. R. (2002). Providing database as a service. In *Proceeding of the IEEE ICDE International Conference on Data Engineering* (p. 29).

Kanza, Y., & Sagiv, Y. (2001). Flexible queries over semistructured data. *Proceedings of the Twentieth ACM SIGACT-SIGMOD-SIGART Symposium on Principles of Database Systems.*

Kazai, G., Gövert, N., Lalmas, M., & Fuhr, N. (2003). The INEX evaluation initiative. In *Intelligent Search on XML Data, Applications, Languages, Models, Implementations, and Benchmarks (LNCS)* (Vol. 2818, pp. 279-293).

Kilpelainen, P. (1992). *Tree matching problems with applications to structured text databases.* Unpublished doctoral dissertation, University of Helsinki, Finland.

Lee, M. L., Yang, L. H., Hsu, W., & Yang, X. (2002). XClust: Clustering XML schemas for effective integration. In *Proceedings of the Eleventh ACM International Conference on Information and Knowledge Management (CIKM).*

Madhavan, J., Bernstein, P. A., & Rahm, E. (2001). Generic schema matching with Cupid. In *Proceedings of the Twenty-Seventh International Conference on Very Large Databases.*

Miller, G. (1995). WordNet: A lexical database for English. *Communications of the ACM, 38*(11), 39-41.

Moh, C., Lim, E., & Ng, W. (2000). Re-engineering Structures from web documents. In *Proceedings of the Fifth ACM International Conference on Digital Libraries* (pp. 67-76).

Nestorov, S., Abiteboul, S., & Motwani, R. (1998). Extracting schema from semistructured data. In *Proceedings of the ACM SIGMOD International Conference on Management of Data* (pp. 295-306).

Nierman, A., & Jagadish, H. V. (2002). Evaluating structural similarity in XML documents. In *Proceedings of the Fifth International Workshop on the Web and Databases* (pp. 61-66).

Rahm, E., & Bernstein, P. A. (2001). A survey of approaches to automatic schema matching. *VLDB Journal, 10*(4).

Rahm, E., Do, H. H., & Mabmann, S. (2004). Matching large XML schemas. *Sigmod Record, 33*(4).

Schlieder, T. (2002). Schema-driven evaluation of approximate tree-pattern queries. In *Proceedings of the Eighth International Conference on Extending Database Technology (LNCS)* (Vol. 2287, pp. 514-532).

Termier, A., Rousset, M.-C., & Sebag, M. (2002). TreeFinder: A first step towards XML data mining. In *Proceedings of the IEEE International Conference on Data Mining* (pp. 450-457).

Theobald, A., & Weikum, G. (2000). Adding relevance to XML. In *Proceedings of the International Workshop on the Web and Databases (LNCS 1997)* (pp. 105-124).

W3C (1998). *Extensible markup language* (XML).

W3C (2000). *XML schema.*

Wagner, R., & Fischer, M. (1974). The string-to-string correction problem. *Journal of the ACM, 21*(1), 168-173.

Wang, K., & Liu, H. (1998). Discovering typical structures of documents: A road map approach. In P*roceedings of the Twenty-first Annual International ACM SIGIR Conference On Research and Development in Information Retrieval* (pp. 146-154).

Wang, Y., DeWitt, D. J., & Cai, J.-Y. (2003). X-Diff: An effective change detection algorithm for XML documents. In *Proceedings International Conference on Data Engineering* (pp. 519-530).

Zaki, M. J. (2002). Efficiently mining frequent trees in a forest. In *Proceedings of the Eighth ACM SIGKDD International Conference on Knowledge Discovery and Data Mining* (pp. 71-80).

Zaki, M. J., & Aggarwal, C. C. (2003). XRules: An effective structural classifier for XML data. In *Proceedings of the Ninth ACM SIGKDD International Conference on Knowledge Discovery and Data Mining* (pp. 316-325).

Zhang, K. (1993). A new editing based distance between unordered labeled trees. In *Proceedings of the Fourth Annual Symposium on Combinatorial Pattern Matching* (pp. 254-265).

Zhang, K., & Shasha, D. (1989). Simple fast algorithms for the editing distance between trees and related problems. *SIAM Journal of Computing, 18*(6), 1245-1262.

Zhang, K., Statman, R., & Shasha, D. (1992). On the editing distance between unordered labeled trees. *Information Processing Letters, 42*(3), 133-139.

Chapter X

Pattern Management: Practice and Challenges

Barbara Catania, University of Genoa, Italy

Anna Maddalena, University of Genoa, Italy

Abstract

Knowledge intensive applications rely on the usage of knowledge artifacts, called patterns, to represent in a compact and semantically rich way huge quantities of heterogeneous raw data. Due to pattern characteristics of patterns, specific systems are required for pattern management in order to model, store, retrieve and manipulate patterns in an efficient and effective way. Several theoretical and industrial approaches (relying on standard proposals, metadata management and business intelligence solutions) have already been proposed for pattern management. However, no critical comparison of the existing approaches has been proposed so far. The aim of this chapter is to provide such a comparison. In particular, specific issues concerning pattern management systems, pattern models and pattern languages are discussed. Several parameters are also identified that will be used in evaluating the effectiveness of theoretical and industrial proposals. The chapter is concluded with a discussion concerning additional issues in the context of pattern management.

Introduction

The huge quantity of heterogeneous raw data that we collect from modern, data-intensive applicational environments does not constitute knowledge by itself. A knowledge extraction process and data management techniques are often required to extract from data concise and relevant information that can be interpreted, evaluated and manipulated by human users in order to drive and specialize business decision processing. Of course, since raw data may be heterogeneous, several kinds of knowledge artifacts exist that can represent hidden knowledge. Clusters, association rules, frequent itemsets and symptom-diagnosis correlations are common examples of such knowledge artifacts, generated by data mining applications. Equations or keyword frequencies are other examples of patterns, relevant, for example, in a multimedia context. All those knowledge artifacts are often called *patterns*. In a more concise and general way, patterns may be defined as compact and rich in semantics representation of raw data. The semantic richness of a pattern is due to the fact that it reveals new knowledge hidden in the huge quantity of data it represents. Patterns are also compact, since they represent interesting correlations among data providing, in many cases, a synthetic, high level description of some data characteristics. Patterns are therefore the knowledge units at the basis of any knowledge intensive application

Due to their specific characteristics, ad hoc systems are required for pattern management in order to model, store, retrieve, analyze and manipulate patterns in an efficient and effective way.

Many academic groups and industrial consortiums have devoted significant efforts towards solving this problem. Moreover, since patterns may be seen as a special type of metadata, pattern management has also some aspects in common with metadata management.

In general, scientific community efforts mainly deal with the definition of a pattern management framework providing a full support for heterogeneous pattern generation and management, thus providing back-end technologies for pattern management applications. Examples of these approaches are the 3W model (Johnson et al., 2000), the inductive databases approach — investigated in particular in the CINQ project (CINQ, 2001) and the PANDA framework (PANDA, 2001; Catania et al., 2004). In the context of inductive databases, several languages have also been proposed supporting the mining process over relational (or object-relational) data by extending the expressive power of existing data query languages with primitives supporting the mining process. Examples of such approaches are MSQL (Imielinski & Virmani, 1999), Mine-Rule (Meo et al., 1998), DMQL (Han et al., 1996) and ODMQL (Elfeky et al., 2001). On the other hand, industrial proposals mainly deal with standard representation purposes for patterns resulting from data mining and data warehousing processes, in order to support their exchange between different architectures. Thus, they mainly provide the right front end for pattern management applications. Examples of such approaches are: the Predictive Model Markup Language (PMML, 2003), the common warehouse metamodel (CWM, 2001) and the Java Data Mining API (JDM, 2003).

In general, existing proposals can be classified according to the following aspects:

(a)   the chosen architecture to manage patterns together with data;

(b)   the pattern characteristics supported by the data model; and

(c)   the type of operations and queries supported by the proposed languages.

As far as we know, even if several proposals exist, no critical comparison of the existing approaches has been proposed so far. We believe that such a comparison would be very useful in order to determine whether the existing approaches are sufficient to cover all pattern requirements and to guide application developers in the choice of the best solution in developing knowledge discovery applications.

The aim of this chapter is to provide such a comparison. We first present a definition of patterns and pattern management. Then, specific issues concerning pattern management systems, pattern models and pattern languages are discussed, pointing out possible alternative solutions in the context of a given scenario. Several parameters relevant to the pattern management context will also be identified and then used to evaluate the effectiveness of various theoretical and industrial proposals. Moreover, relationships between pattern and general metadata management will also be identified, and some existing approaches for metadata representation discussed. Finally, we will briefly discuss solutions for pattern management, supported by some popular commercial DBMSs. The chapter concludes with a discussion of additional issues and possible future trends in the context of pattern management.

Pattern Management: Background

In many different modern contexts, a huge quantity of raw data is collected. A usual approach to analyze such data is to generate some compact knowledge artifacts (i.e., clusters, association rules, frequent itemsets, etc.) through data processing methods that reduce the number and size of data, to make them manageable for humans while preserving as much as possible their intrinsic information or discovering new interesting correlations. Those knowledge artifacts that constitute our knowledge unit are called *patterns*.

Definition 1: *A* pattern *is a compact and rich in semantics representation of raw data.*

Patterns may be regarded as knowledge units that effectively describe entire subsets of data (in this sense, they are compact). The quality of the representation achieved by a pattern can be quantified by using some statistical measures. Depending on their measures, patterns can describe relevant data properties (in this sense, they are rich in semantics).

Pattern management is an important issue in many different contexts and domains. The most important contexts in which pattern management is required are business intelligence and data mining. Business intelligence concerns a broad category of applications and technologies for gathering, storing, analyzing and providing access to data to help enterprises in business decisions. Data mining is one of the fundamental activities involved in business intelligence applications besides querying and reporting, OLAP processing, statistical analysis and forecasting. The knowledge units resulting from the data mining tasks may be quite different.

As an example, in the context of the market-basket analysis, association rules involving sold items derived from a set of recorded transactions are often generated. In addition, in order to perform a market segmentation, the user may also be interested in identifying clusters of customers, based on their buying preferences, or clusters of products, based on customer buying habits. In financial brokerages, users cope with stock trends derived from trading records. In epidemiology, users are interested in symptom-diagnosis correlations mined from clinical observations.

Pattern management is a key issue also in many other domains not involved directly with a data mining process. For instance, in information retrieval, users are interested in extracting keyword frequencies and frequent sets of words appearing in the analyzed documents in order to specialize searching strategies and to perform similarity analysis. Content-based music retrieval is another domain in which patterns have to be managed in order to represent and query rhythm, melody and harmony (Conklin, 2002). In image processing, recurrent figures in shapes may be interpreted as specific types of patterns (Nakajima et al., 2000). In machine learning (Mitchell, 1997), predictions and forecasting activities are based on classifiers, which can be interpreted as specific types of patterns.

Recently, pattern management is becoming much more important, not only in centralized architectures but also in distributed ones. Indeed, the diffusion of the Web and the improvement of networking technologies speed up the requirement for distributed knowledge discovery and management systems. For instance, in the Web context, sequences of clicks collected by Web servers are important patterns for clickstream analysis. Moreover, knowledge representation and management, in terms of patterns, is a fundamental issue in the context of the Semantic Web and in agent-based intelligent systems where metadata have to be shared among different parties.

Depending on the specific domain, different processes may be used for pattern extraction, e.g., knowledge discovery processes for data mining patterns, feature extraction processes in multimedia applications or manual processes when patterns are not extracted but directly provided by the user or the application (for example, a classifier not automatically generated from a training set).

Patterns share some characteristics that make traditional DBMSs unable to represent and manage them. As discussed above, patterns may be generated from different application contexts resulting in very heterogeneous structures. Moreover, heterogeneous patterns often have to be managed together. For instance, in a Web context, in order to better understand e-commerce buying habits of a certain Web site's users, different patterns can be combined, for example:

(a) **navigational patterns** (identified by clickstream analysis) describing their surfing and browsing behaviour;

(b) **demographic and geographical clusters**, obtained with market segmentation analysis based on personal data and geographical features;

(c) **frequencies of the searching keywords** specified by the user when using a search engine (typical information treated in information retrieval); and

(d) **metadata used by an intelligent agent-based crawling system** (typical of the artificial intelligence domain) the user may adopt.

Additionally, patterns can be generated from raw data by using some data mining tools (*a posteriori* patterns) but also known by the users and used, for example, to check how well a data source is represented by them (*a priori* patterns).

Since source data change with great frequency, another important issue consists in determining whether existing patterns, after a certain time, still represent the data source from which they have been generated, possibly being able to change pattern information when the quality of the representation changes. Finally, all types of patterns should be manipulated (e.g., extracted, synchronized, deleted) and queried through dedicated languages.

All of the previous reasons motivate the need for the design of ad hoc Pattern management systems (PBMSs), i.e., according to (Rizzi et al., 2003), systems for handling (storing/ processing/retrieving) patterns defined over raw data.

Definition 2: *A* pattern base management system (PBMS) *is a system for handling (storing/processing/retrieving) patterns defined over raw data in order to efficiently support pattern matching and to exploit pattern-related operations generating intensional information. The set of patterns managed by a PBMS is called a* pattern base.

The pattern base management system is therefore not a simple repository for the extracted knowledge (patterns); rather it is an engine supporting pattern storage (according to a chosen logical model) and processing (involving also complex activities requiring computational efforts).

The design of a PBMS relies on solutions developed in several disciplines, such as: data mining and knowledge discovery for *a posteriori* pattern extraction; database management systems for pattern storage and retrieval; data warehousing for providing raw datasets; artificial intelligence and machine learning for pattern extraction and reasoning; and metadata management. Pattern management can therefore be seen as a relatively new discipline lying at the intersection of several well-known application contexts.

Key Features in PBMS Evaluation

In the following we first present a typical data mining scenario and then, based on it, we present useful parameters in comparing existing pattern management solutions. In particular, we consider three different aspects:

(a) architecture for a pattern management system;
(b) pattern models; and
(c) pattern languages.

The Scenario

The market-basket analysis is a typical data mining application concerning, in our example, the task of finding and handling *association rules* and *clusters* concerning customer's transactions. Given a domain D of values and a set of transactions, each corresponding to a subset of D, an association rule takes the form $B \Rightarrow H$, where $B \subseteq D$, $H \in D$ and $H \cap B = \varnothing$. H is often called the head of the rule, while B is its body. The informal meaning of the rule is that, given a transaction T, it often happens that when T contains B then it also contains H. This qualitative information can be quantified by using two measures: the *support* (i.e., the ratio between the number of transactions satisfying the body of the rule and the total number of transactions) and the *confidence* (i.e., the ratio between the number of transactions satisfying both rule body and head and the number of transactions satisfying just the body).

Suppose a commercial vendor traces shop transactions concerning milk, coffee, bread, butter and rice, and applies data mining techniques to determine how he can further increase his sales. The vendor deals with different kinds of patterns: association rules, representing correlations between sold items; clusters of association rules, grouping rules with respect to their similarity; and clusters of products, grouping products with respect to their type and price. Now, we suppose the vendor wants to execute the following operations, or steps:

1. **Modeling heterogeneous patterns.** Since the vendor deals with (at least) three different types of patterns, he would like to generate and manage those patterns together, in the same system, in order to be able to manipulate all this knowledge in an integrated way.

2. **Periodic pattern generation.** At the end of every month, the vendor mines from his transaction data association rules over sold products by filtering interesting results with respect to certain thresholds. He assumes the reliability of rules extracted from the instant in which they have been generated until the last day of the month. The vendor then groups the rules into clusters.

3. **Pattern querying.** The vendor may be interested in analyzing patterns stored in the system, i.e., to retrieve patterns satisfying certain conditions, to combine them in order to construct new patterns, to establish whether a pattern is similar to another and to correlate patterns and raw data. For instance, the vendor may be interested in retrieving all association rules mined during March 2005 involving "bread" or similar items, or in identifying all association rules extracted from a certain set of transactions with a reasonable level of detail (i.e., with quality measures higher than specified

thresholds). In order to solve the last query, both the data management and the pattern management system have to be used.

4. **Promotion of a new product.** From April 2005, the vendor will start to sell a certain product P. To promote P in advance, he may promote some other products he already sells, for which there exists a correlation with P, in order to stimulate the demand for P. In this way, it is possible that customers will start to buy P without the need for a dedicated advertising campaign. In order to know, for example, whether "bread" may stimulate the sale of P, he may insert in the system an association rule such as 'bread → P' (not automatically generated) and verify whether it holds or not with respect to the recorded transactions.

5. **Pattern update, synchronization and deletion.** Patterns may have to be updated. For instance, the user may know that the quality of the representation that a pattern achieves with respect to its data source has been changed because source data have been changed, thus the pattern quality measures (evaluated at insertion time) have to be updated, since the pattern may no longer be semantically valid, i.e., it may not correctly represent the updated source data. As an example, when on April 1, 2005, the vendor starts to sell a new product P, new raw data concerning sales are collected, new patterns are generated and, at the same time, patterns previously extracted may not correctly represent source data. Thus, a synchronization is required between data and patterns to reflect patterns changes occurring in raw data. In this case, the measures may change as well. Finally, there is the need for pattern deletion operations. For example, the vendor may be interested in deleting all patterns that are no longer semantically valid or in removing from the system all rules having "rice" as value in their head or its body.

Architecture for a Pattern Base Management System

The architecture of a PBMS may be integrated or separated. In an *integrated architecture*, raw data and patterns are stored together by using the same data model and managed in the same way. On the other side, in a *separated architecture*, raw data are stored and managed in a traditional way by a DBMS, whereas patterns are stored and managed by a dedicated PBMS.

Since in the integrated architecture a unique data model is used for both data and patterns, design of the pattern base is simplified. For example, an association rule can be represented in the relational model by using a set of relational tuples, each containing the head of the rule and one element in the body. However, traditional data models may not adequately represent all pattern characteristics, thus making manipulation operations more complex. Further, by storing patterns with data, we rely on traditional DBMS capabilities for what concerns query expressive power and query optimization. In particular, under an integrated architecture, the mining process is usually seen as a particular type of query. However, patterns may require sophisticated processing that, in traditional systems, can only be implemented through user-defined procedures.

Separated architectures manage data and patterns by using two distinct systems. Thus, two models and languages have to be used to deal with pattern-based applications. The usage of a specific pattern data model guarantees a higher and more tailored expressive power in pattern representation. Moreover, operations over data are activated by the PBMS only by demand, through the so-called *cross-over queries*. The PBMS can therefore support specific techniques for pattern management and retrieval. Mining operations are not part of the query language; rather, they are specific manipulation operators. Finally, specific query languages can be designed providing advanced capabilities, based on the chosen pattern representation.

Pattern Models

We can define a pattern model as a formalism by which patterns are described and manipulated inside the PBMS. In defining a pattern model, we believe that the following aspects should be taken into account.

User-defined pattern types support. The ability to model heterogeneous patterns is very important to make the PBMS flexible and usable in different contexts. Most of the systems allow the user to manipulate different types of patterns (see Step 1 of the scenario) that usually correspond to different data mining results, such as association rules, clusters, etc. However, in many cases they cannot be used "together" in a unified framework. Moreover, often it is not possible for the user to define new pattern types, which are therefore predefined.

Relation between raw data and patterns. Often patterns are generated from raw data through the application of some mining technique; it may be useful to store the relation between patterns and raw data in order to make the pattern richer in semantics and provide additional, significant information for pattern retrieval. Most of the systems recognize the importance of this aspect and provide a mechanism to trace the source data set from which a pattern has been generated. In the proposed scenario, this corresponds to maintain information concerning the dataset from which association rules have been extracted. Such information may then be used to solve some of the queries pointed out in Step 3 of the scenario. Besides the source dataset, it may be useful to exactly know the subset of the source dataset represented by the pattern. For example, to generate rule 'bread $\rightarrow$ milk', only transactions containing "bread" and "milk" are considered from the overall set of transactions in the source dataset. This subset can be represented in a precise way by listing its components, or in an approximate way by providing a formula satisfied by the elements of the source dataset from which the pattern probably has been generated. Most of the systems do not support the representation of this relationship or support it only in an approximated way.

Quality measures. It is important to be able to quantify how well a pattern represents a raw data set by associating each pattern with some quantitative measures. For example, in the identified scenario, each association rule mined from data is associated with confidence and support values. Most of the systems allow the user to express this quality information, which is generally computed during pattern generation and never modified.

Temporal features. Since source data change with high frequency, it is important to determine whether existing patterns, after a certain time, still represent the data source from which they have been generated. This happens when, given a pattern p extracted at time t, the same pattern p can be extracted at time $t' > t$ from the same raw dataset, with the same or better measure values. In this case, we say the pattern is semantically valid at time t'. When this happens and measures change, the system should be able to change pattern measures. In practice, it may be useful to assign each pattern a validity period, representing the interval of time in which it may be considered reliable with respect to its data source.

Hierarchies over types. Another important feature that a pattern management system should provide is the capability to define some kind of hierarchy over the existing pattern types in order to introduce relationships, such as specialization or composition, that increase expressivity, reusability and modularity. For instance, in the proposed scenario, the vendor deals with association rules and with more complex patterns that are clusters of association rules (see Step 1). Thus, a composition relationship is exploited.

Pattern Languages

Similar to a DBMS, a PBMS must provide at least two different types of languages: the *Pattern Manipulation Language* (PML), providing the basic operations by which patterns may be manipulated (e.g., extracted, synchronized and deleted), and the *Pattern Query Language* (PQL), supporting pattern retrieval. PQL queries take as input patterns and data sets and return patterns. On the other hand, PML operations take as input a pattern set and return a new pattern set, which replaces the input one in the pattern base. Aspects concerning both manipulation and query languages for patterns will be evaluated by means of several parameters introduced in the following.

Pattern Manipulation Language Parameters

Automatic extraction. This is the capability of a system to generate patterns starting from raw data using a mining function. It corresponds to the data mining step of a knowledge data discovery process and generates *a posteriori* patterns. In the proposed scenario, association rules generated in Step 2 of the scenario represent *a posteriori* patterns.

Direct insertion of patterns. There are patterns that the user knows *a priori* and wishes to verify over a certain data source. They are not extracted from raw data, but inserted directly from scratch in the system. Ad hoc primitives are therefore needed to perform this operation. In the proposed scenario, patterns described in Step 4 are examples of *a priori* patterns.

Modifications and deletions. Patterns can be modified or deleted. For example, users may be interested in updating information associated with patterns (such as their validity in time or the quality of raw data representation they achieve, represented in terms of measures) or in removing from the system patterns satisfying (or not satisfying) certain characteristics. For instance, in the proposed scenario (Step 5), the user is interested in removing an association rule when it does not correctly represent the source data set any longer. Not all the systems guarantee both deletion and update operations over patterns; in many cases, only pattern generation and querying are provided.

Synchronization over source data. Since modifications in raw data are very frequent, it may happen that a pattern extracted at a certain instant of time from a certain data source does not correctly represent the data source after several modifications occur (Step 5). Thus, the need for a synchronization operation arises in order to align patterns with the data source they represent. This operation is a particular type of update operation for patterns. For instance, in the proposed scenario (Step 5), the user is interested in updating the measure values associated with a certain rule (such as 'bread $\rightarrow$ P') when the source data change. Synchronization may also be executed against a different dataset in order to check whether a pattern extracted from a certain data source holds also for another data source. In this case, we call it "recomputation." For example, suppose the vendor receives a data set DS concerning sales in the month of January 2005 in another supermarket. He may be interested in checking whether the association rules mined from his data set represent reasonable patterns for the new data set DS. Unfortunately, synchronization between raw data and patterns (Step 5) is rarely supported

Mining function. Patterns are obtained from raw data by applying some kind of mining function, e.g., the APriori (Agrawal & Srikant, 1994) algorithm may be used to generate association rules (Step 2). The presence of a library of mining functions and the possibility to define new functions if required makes pattern manipulation much more flexible.

Pattern Query Language Parameters

Queries against patterns. The PBMS has to provide a query language to retrieve patterns according to some specified conditions. For example, all association rules having "bread" in their body may need to be retrieved (Step 3). In general, pattern collections have to be supported by the system in order to be used as input for queries. Similar to the relational context where a relation contains tuples with the same schema, patterns in a collection must have the same type. Moreover, it is highly desirable for the language to be closed, i.e., each query over pattern must return a set of patterns of the same type over which other queries can be executed.

Pattern combination. Operations for combining patterns together should be provided as an advanced form of reasoning. Combination may be seen as a sort of "join" between patterns. For example, transitivity between association rules may be seen as a kind of pattern join.

Similarity. An important characteristic of a pattern language is the ability to check pattern similarity based on pattern structure and measures. Only a few general approaches for pattern similarity have been provided that can be homogeneously applied to different types of patterns. Moreover, few existing PQLs support such an operation.

Queries involving source data. According to the chosen architecture and the logical model, a system managing patterns has to provide operations not only for querying patterns but also data. Such queries are usually called *cross-over queries*. When the system adopts a separated architecture, cross-over operations require the combination of two different query processors in order to be executed. In our scenario, the second query of Step 3 is a cross-over query.

Theoretical Proposals

As we have already stressed, the need for a unified framework supporting pattern management is widespread and covers many different contexts and domains. Thus, great effort has been put into the formalization of the overall principles under which a PBMS can be developed, providing the background for the development of back-end technologies to be used by pattern-based applications. In the following we briefly present and compare the following proposals by considering all the parameters previously introduced:

- **Inductive databases approach** (Imielinsky & Mannila, 1996; De Raedt, 2002; CINQ, 2001): an inductive framework where both data and patterns are stored at the same layer and treated in the same manner;

- **3-Worlds model** (Johnson et al., 2000): a unified framework for pattern management based on the definition of three distinct worlds: an intensional world (containing intensional descriptions of patterns), an extensional world (containing an explicit representation of patterns); and a world representing raw data; and

- **Panda Project** (PANDA, 2001): a unified framework for the representation of heterogeneous patterns, relying on a separated architecture.

Inductive Databases Approach

Inductive databases (Imielinsky & Mannila, 1996; De Raedt, 2002) rely on an integrated architecture. Thus, patterns are represented according to the underlying model for raw data. More precisely, the repository is assumed to contain both datasets and pattern sets. Within the framework of inductive databases, knowledge discovery is considered as an extended querying process (Meo et al., 2004; De Raedt et al., 2002). Thus, a language for an inductive database is an extension of a database language that allows one to:

(a)   select, manipulate and query data as in standard queries;

(b)   select, manipulate and query patterns; and

(c)   execute cross-over queries over patterns.

Queries may then be stored in the repository as views, in this way datasets and pattern sets are intensionally described.

Inductive databases have been mainly investigated in the context of the CINQ project of the European Community (CINQ, 2001), which tries to face both theoretical and practical issues of inductive querying for the discovery of knowledge from transactional data. CINQ covers several different areas, spreading from data mining tasks to machine learning. The considered data mining patterns are itemsets, association rules, episodes, data dependencies, clusters, etc. In the machine learning context, interesting patterns considered by the project are equations describing quantitative laws, statistical trends and variations over data.

From a theoretical point of view, a formal theory is provided for each type of pattern, providing:

(a)   a language for pattern description;

(b)   evaluation functions for computing measures and other significant data related to patterns; and

(c)   primitive constraints for expressing basic pattern properties (e.g., minimal/ maximal frequency and minimal accuracy).

By using primitive constraints, extraction and further queries (seen as postprocessing steps in the overall architecture) can be interpreted as constraints and executed by using techniques from constraint programming, using concepts from constraint-based mining. Other manipulation operations, such as the insertion of *a priori* patterns, are delegated to the underlying DBMS, since an integrated architecture is exploited. Note that since a theory is provided for each type of pattern, integration is not a project issue. Moreover, no support for temporal management and pattern hierarchies is provided.

From a more practical point of view, extension of existing standard query languages, such as SQL, have been provided in order to query specific types of patterns, mainly association rules. The combination of a data mining algorithm, usually some variation of the Apriori algorithm (Agrawal & Srikant, 1994), with a language such as SQL (or OQL) offers some interesting querying capabilities. Among the existing proposals, we recall the following:

- **DMQL (Data Mining Query Language)** (Han et al., 1996) is an SQL-based data mining language for generating patterns from relational data. An object-oriented extension of DMQL based on Object Query Language (OQL) (Cattell & Barry, 2000), has been presented in Elfeky et al. (2001).

  Discovered association rules can be stored in the system, but no post-processing (i.e., queries over the generated patterns) is provided. Indeed, they are simply presented to the user and a further iterative refining of mining results is possible only through graphical tools. The obtained rules can be specialized (generalized) by using concept hierarchies over source data. Besides association rules, other patterns can be generated, such as: data generalizations (a sort of aggregate), characteristic rules (assertions describing a property shared by most data in certain data set, for example the symptoms of a certain disease), discriminant rules (assertions describing characteristics that discriminate a dataset from another one) and data classification rules (patterns for data classification). For each type of pattern, a set of measures is provided (confidence and support for association rules) and conditions governing them can be used in order to generate only patterns with a certain quality level (Figure 1(a)).

- **MINE RULE** (Meo et al., 1998) extends SQL with a new operator, MINE RULE, for discovering association rules from data stored in relations. By using the MINE RULE operator, a new relation with schema (BODY, HEAD, SUPPORT, CONFIDENCE) is created, containing a tuple for each generated association rule. The body and head itemsets of the generated rules are stored in dedicated tables and referred to within the rule-base table by using foreign keys. The cardinality of the rule body as well as minimum support and confidence values can be specified in the MINE RULE statement. MINE RULE is very flexible in specifying the subset of raw data from which patterns have to be extracted as well as conditions that extracted patterns must satisfy. However, no specific support for post-processing (queries) is provided, even if standard SQL can be used since rules are stored in tables. Similar to DMQL, hierarchies over raw data may be used to generalize the extracted association rules, or more specifically, to extract only association rules at a certain level of generalization. A similar operator called XMine, for extracting association rules from XML documents, has been presented in Braga et al. (2002).

- **Mine-SQL (MSQL)** (Imielinsky & Virmani, 1999) is another SQL-like language for generating and querying association rules. Similar to MINE RULE, only association rules are considered. Also, in this case input transactions and resulting rules are stored in relations. With respect to MINE RULE, it supports different types of statements; one for rule extraction (*GetRules*), one for rule post-processing (*SelectRules*) and some predicates for cross-over queries (*Satisfy*, *Violate*). Concerning extraction, MSQL is less flexible in specifying the source data set; indeed, it must be an existing table or view. However, similarly to MINE RULE, constraints over the rules to be generated may be specified. Extracted queries can be queried using the *SelectRules* operator. Various conditions can be specified, depending on the body and the head of the rules. By using the *SelectRules* statement, it is also possible to recompute measures of already extracted rules over different datasets. In order to explicitly support cross-over queries, MSQL proposes the operators *Satisfy* and *Violate*. They determine whether a tuple satisfies or violates at least one or all the association rules in a given set, specified by using either *GetRules* or *SelectRules* commands.

Figure 1. Inductive languages: examples

```
                          MINE RULE MarketAssRules        GetRules(Transactions)
                          AS                              into MarketAssRules
                          select distinct                 where confidence > 0.9
                                  1..n item as Body,          and support > 0.3
Find association rules            1..n item as Head,                  (c)
from Transactions                 Support,
with support                      Confidence            SelectRules(MarketAssRules)
  threshold=0.3           from Transactions             where body has {(bread=yes)}
with confidence           group by tr#                            (d)
  threshold=0.9           extracting rules with
                                  Support:0.3,          select *
          (a)                     Confidence:0.9         from Transactions
                                                         where VIOLATES ALL (
                                     (b)                   GetRules(Transactions)
                                                           where body has {(bread=yes)}
                                                           and confidence > 0.75 )
                                                                    (e)
```

Figure 1 presents a usage example of the just presented languages for extracting association rules from transactions stored in relation Transactions and storing them, when possible, in relation MarketAssRules.

Finally, we recall that results achieved in the context of the CINQ project have been experimented with in the context of machine learning in the implementation of a molecular fragment discovery demo system (MOLFEA, 2004). In the context of association rule mining, they have been experimentally used in the demo version of the Minerule Mining System (Minerule System, 2004).

3-Worlds Model

The 3-Worlds (3W) model (Johnson et al., 2000) is a unified framework for pattern management based on a separated architecture. Under this approach, the pattern model allows one to represent three different worlds: the intensional world (I-World), containing the intensional description of patterns; the extensional world (E-World), containing an extensional representation of patterns; and the data world (D-World), containing raw data. In the I-World, patterns correspond to (possibly overlapping) regions in a data space, described by means of linear constraints over the attributes of the analyzed data set. For example, a cluster of products based on their price in dollars can be described by the following constraint "10<=price<=20" (call this region "cheap_product"). More complex regions can be defined, composed of a set of constraints. In the E-World, each region is represented in its extensional form, i.e., by an explicit enumeration of the members of the source space satisfying the constraint characterizing the region. Thus, the extension corresponding to region "cheap_product" (contained in the I-world) contains all source data items with price between 10 and 20. Finally, the D-World corresponds to the source data set in the form of relations, from which regions and dimensions can be created as result of a mining process. Note that regions in the I-World are not predefined, thus user-defined patterns are allowed. Each region can be associated with a number of attributes, including measures, which do not have a special treatment. Additionally, the framework does not support *a priori* patterns. Indeed, operations to directly insert patterns in the system are not supported. Moreover, no pattern temporal management is provided.

Query languages for all the worlds have been proposed. In particular, for the D-World and the E-World, traditional relational languages can be used (with some minor extensions for the E-World). On the other hand, dimension algebra has been defined over regions in the I-World, obtained by extending relational languages. The main operations of this language are described in the following:

- the **selection** operation allows pattern retrieval by invoking various spatial predicates such as overlap (||), containment ($\subset$), etc. between regions;

- the **projection** operation corresponds to the elimination of some property attributes; this amounts to setting their value to "true" in every region;

- a **purge** operator, returning inconsistent regions, i.e., regions whose constraint cannot be satisfied by any data point (thus, with an empty extensional representation). For instance, a region with constraint "price>20 AND price<10" is clearly inconsistent, since the constraint is intrinsically unsatisfiable; and

- traditional relational operators (**cartesian product**, **union**, **minus** and **renaming**) have then been extended to cope with sets of regions.

The following cross-over operators are also provided, allowing the user to navigate among the three worlds:

- automatic extraction of patterns (**mine**);

- the assignment of an extension to a region (**populate**), given a certain data source;

- the detection of the regions corresponding to a certain extension (**lookup**); and

- a sort of synchronization, providing the computation of new extensions starting from combinations of regions and a given dataset (**refresh**).

Note that all the previous operators but mine can be interpreted as cross-over query operators. We remark that, even if no PML is explicitly provided, some of the proposed operators can be interpreted as PML operations when attempting to change the three worlds according to the query result. For example, the mine operator can be seen as a PML operator when the result of the mining is made persistent in the I-World.

PANDA Project

The purposes of the PANDA (PAtterns for Next-generation DAtabase systems) project of the European Community (PANDA, 2001) are:

1.   to lay the foundations for pattern modeling;
2.   to investigate the main issues involved in managing and querying a pattern-base; and
3.   to outline the requirements for building a PBMS.

The PANDA approach relies on a separated architecture. The proposed model provides the representation of arbitrary and heterogeneous patterns by allowing the user to specify his or her own pattern types. It provides support for both *a priori* and *a posteriori* patterns and it allows the user to define ad-hoc mining functions to generate *a posteriori* patterns.

Under this modeling approach, pattern quality measures are explicitly represented, as well as relationships between patterns and raw data that can be stored in an explicit or approximated way. For example, a cluster of products based on their price in dollars can be described in an approximate way by the following constraint: "10<=price<=20". However, not necessarily all products with a price between 10 and 20 belong to this cluster. Thus, an explicit representation of the relationship between patterns and raw data will list the exact set of products belonging to the cluster. Moreover, the definition of hierarchies involving pattern types has been taken into account in order to address extensibility and reusability issues. Three types of hierarchies between pattern types have been considered: specialization, composition and refinement. Specialization is a sort of inheritance between pattern types. On the other hand, composition is a sort of aggregation. Finally, refinement allows patterns to be used as source data. As an example, in the proposed scenario, clusters of association rules rely on a refinement relationship with association rules. If the representative of such clusters is an association rule, then there exists also a composition relation between them.

In this context, languages for pattern manipulation and querying have also been defined. In particular, the pattern manipulation language supports the main manipulation operations involving patterns, such as pattern insertion and deletion. Both *a priori* and *a posteriori* patterns can be manipulated by using the language proposed. On the other hand, by using the proposed pattern query language patterns inserted in the system (directly or mined by applying a mining function) patterns can be retrieved and queried by specifying filtering conditions involving all pattern characteristics supported by the model. Additionally, it allows the user to combine different patterns and to correlate them with raw data, i.e., it supports cross-over operations. An approach for pattern similarity has also been provided by Bartolini et al. (2004).

Starting by the PANDA approach, an extended model for patterns has been proposed (Catania et al., 2004). Such a model addresses the need for temporal information management associated with patterns. In this way, it becomes possible to exploit and manage information concerning pattern semantics and temporal validity, including synchronization and recomputation. Furthermore, the previously proposed PML and PQL have been extended in order to cope with temporal features during pattern manipulation and querying.

Concluding Discussion

Table 1 summarizes the features of the frameworks presented above according to the previously introduced parameters. In the table, the PANDA approach refers to the extended temporal model (Catania et al., 2004).

Concerning the architecture, only inductive databases adopt an integrated approach. On the other hand, 3W and PANDA rely on a separated PBMS. For what concerns the model, the more general approach seems to be PANDA, where there is no limitation on the pattern types that can be represented. PANDA is also the only approach taking into account temporal aspects, hierarchies and providing both a precise and an approximated relationship of patterns with respect to source data. In particular, it can be shown that the approximated representation in PANDA is quite similar to the region representation in 3W.

Concerning the manipulation language, 3W and CINQ do not support direct insertion of patterns or deletion and update operations. On the other hand, all the proposals take into account synchronization (recomputation) issues. Concerning the query language, all the approaches propose either one (or more) calculus or algebraic languages, providing relational operators.

Specific characteristics of languages provided in the context of inductive databases are summarized in Table 2. Concerning extracted patterns, MINE

Table 1. Features comparison: theoretical proposals

		Inductive Databases	**3W Model**	**PANDA**
Model & Architecture	*Type of architecture*	Integrated	Separated. Three layers: source data, mined data and intermediate data.	Separated. Three levels: database, pattern base and intermediate data
	Predefined types	-Itemsets -Association Rules -Sequences -Clusters -Equations	Users can define their own types that must be represented as sets of constraints	Users can define their own types
	Link to source data	Yes. Datasource is part of the architecture	Yes. Datasource is one of the layers of the architecture. Relationship is precise	Yes. Datasource is one of the layers of the architecture. Relationship can be either precise or approximated
	Quality measures	Yes	Yes, but not explicit	Yes
	Mining function	Yes. The mining process is a querying process	Yes	Yes
	Temporal features	No	No	Yes
	Hierarchical types	No	Yes	Specialization, composition, and refinement
Manipulation Language	*Manipulation language*	Manipulation through constraint-based querying and SQL	Yes	Yes
	Automatic extraction	Yes. Constraint-based queries	Yes	Yes
	Direct insertion	No	No	Yes
	Modifications and deletions	Yes (SQL)	No	Yes
	Synchronization over source data	Yes, recomputation	Yes, recomputation	Yes, recomputation & synchronization
	Mining function	No	No	Yes
Query Language	*Queries against patterns*	Constraint-based calculus	Algebra	Algebra & Calculus
	Pattern combination	No	Yes, Cartesian product	Yes, join
	Similarity	No	No	Yes
	Queries involving source data	Yes	Yes	Yes

Table 2. Features comparison: theoretical proposals (query language)

		DMQL & ODMQL	MINE RULE	MSQL
Model	*Predefined types*	-Association rules -Data generalizations -Characteristic rules -Discriminant rules -Data classification rules	Association rules	Association rules
Manipulation Language	*Manipulation language*	Only extraction, but no storage	Only extraction	Yes
	Automatic extraction	Yes	Yes	Yes
	Direct insertion	No	Using standard SQL	Using standard SQL
	Modifications and deletions	No	Using standard SQL	Using standard SQL
	Synchronization over source data	No	No	Yes, recomputation
Query Language	*Queries over patterns*	Only visualization and browsing	Using standard SQL	SQL-like
	Pattern combination	No	No	No
	Similarity	No	No	No
	Queries involving source data	No	Using standard SQL	Yes

RULE and MSQL deal only with association rules, whereas DMQL and ODMQL deal with many different types of patterns. When patterns are stored, SQL can be used for manipulation and querying (including cross-over queries). Among the proposed languages, however, only MSQL proposes ad-hoc operators for pattern retrieval and post-processing.

As a final consideration, we observe that when dealing with applications managing different types of patterns (this is the case of advanced knowledge discovery applications), the 3W and PANDA theoretical frameworks are the best solutions, since they provide support for heterogeneous patterns in a unified way. On the other side, the inductive databases approach provides better solutions for specific data mining contexts, such as association rules management, with a low impact on existing SQL-based applications.

Standards

The industrial community has proposed standards to support pattern representation and management in the context of existing programming languages and database (or data warehousing) environments in order to achieve interoperability and (data) knowledge sharing. Thus, they provide the right front-end for pattern management applications.

In general, they do not support generic patterns and, similar to the inductive database approach, specific representations are provided only for specific types of patterns. Moreover, they do not provide support for inter-pattern manipulation.

Some proposals, such as Predictive Model Markup Language (PMML, 2003) and common warehouse metamodel (CWM, 2001), mainly deal with data mining and data warehousing pattern representation, respectively, in order to support their exchange between different architectures. Others, such as Java Data Mining (JDM, 2003) and SQL/MM Data Mining (ISO SQL/MM part 6, 2001), provide standard representation and manipulation primitives in the context of Java and SQL, respectively. In the following, all these proposals will be briefly presented and compared with respect to the parameters previously introduced.

Predictive Model Markup Language

PMML (PMML, 2003) is a standardization effort of DMG (Data Mining Group) consisting of an XML–based language to describe data mining models (i.e., the mining algorithm, the mining parameters and mined data) and to share them between PMML compliant applications and visualization tools. Figure 2 shows an extract of a PMML association rule mining model. Since PMML is primary

Figure 2. PMML example

```
<PMML>
...
<!--items in input data for the mining of association rule #1 -->
  <Item id="1" value="milk"/>
  <Item id="2" value="coffe"/>
  <Item id="3" value="bread"/>
  ...
<!-- definition of the mining model used -->
<AssociationModel modelName="mba"
<!-mining algorithm used -->
    algorithmName="Apriori"
<!-- tuples in Transactions -->
    numberOfTransactions="10"
<!-- thresholds for support and confidence -->
    minimumSupport="0.3"
    minimumConfidence="0.9"
...
<!-- item sets involved in association rule #1 -->
  <!-- item set containing the item corresponding to 'coffee' -->
  <Itemset id="1" numberOfItems="1"> <ItemRef itemRef="2"/> </Itemset>
  <!-- item set corrsponding to 'bread' -->
  <Itemset id="2" numberOfItems="1"> <ItemRef itemRef="3"/> </Itemset>
...
<!-- association rules -->
<AssociationRule support="0.3" confidence="1.0" antecedent="1" consequent="2"/>
...
</AssociationModel>
</PMML>
```

aimed at the exchange of data between different architectures, no assumptions about the underlying architecture are done.

PMML traces information concerning the data set from which a pattern has been extracted by allowing the user to specify the data dictionary, i.e., the collection of raw data used as input for the mining algorithm. Concerning the mining function, it is possible to express the fact that a certain pattern has been mined from a certain raw data set by using a specified mining algorithm. However, no assumption is made about the existence of a mining library. For instance, in the example shown in Figure 2, the represented association rule is the result of the application of the APriori algorithm (algorithmName = "Apriori").

Moreover, PMML does not allow the user to define its own types. Indeed, one can only define models of one of the predefined types that cover a very large area of the data mining context (see Table 3). It is also important to note that PMML allows the user to represent also information concerning quality measures associated with patterns.

Due to its nature, PMML does not provide temporal features. Even if no general support for pattern hierarchies is provided, PMML 3.0 supports refinement for decision trees and simple regression models. More general variants may be defined in future versions of PMML.

All major commercial products supporting data knowledge management and data mining attempt to be compliant with PMML standard. Among them we recall Oracle Data Mining tool in Oracle 10g (Oracle DM), DB2 Intelligent Miner tools (DB2) and MS SQL Server 2005 Analysis Services (MS SQL).

Common Warehouse Metamodel

The common warehouse metamodel (CWM, 2001) is a standardization effort of the ODM (Object Management Group) and it enables easy interchange of warehouse and business intelligence metadata between warehouse tools, platforms and metadata repositories in distributed heterogeneous environments. CWM is based on three standards:

(a) **UML (Unified Modeling Language)** (UML, 2003), an object oriented modeling language used for representing object models;

(b) **MOF (Meta Object Facility)** (MOF, 2003), which defines an extensible framework for defining models for metadata and provides tools with programmatic interfaces to store and access metadata in a repository; and

(c) **XMI (XML Metadata Interchange)** (XMI, 2003), which allows metadata compliant with the MOF meta-model to be interchanged as streams or files with a standard XML-based format.

CWM has been defined as a specific metamodel for generic warehouse architectures. Thus, it is compliant with the MOF metamodel and relies on UML for object representation and notation. Since MOF is a metamodel for metadata, UML metamodels may also be represented in MOF. This means that both CWM metadata and UML models can be translated into XML documents by using XMI through the mapping with MOF.

CWM consists of various metamodels, including a metamodel for data mining (CWM-DM), by which mining models and parameters for pattern extraction can be specified.

Unfortunately, CWM has been designed to analyze large amounts of data, where the data mining process is just a small part. Only few pattern types can be represented: clustering, association rules, supervised classification, approximation and attribute importance. The user does not have the capability to define its own pattern types and no temporal and hierarchical information associated with patterns can be modeled.

Finally, no dedicated languages for query and manipulation are proposed, since it is assumed manipulation is provided by the environment importing CWM-DM metadata.

Due to the complexity of the model, CWM is supported to some extent by most commercial systems providing solutions for data warehousing, such as Oracle, IBM (within DB2), Genesis and Iona Technologies (providing e-datawarehouse solutions) and Unisys (providing backbone solutions for UML, XMI and MOF core tools for CWM development). However, CWM-DM is rarely integrated in specific solutions for data mining where often only import/export in PMML, providing a much more simple pattern representation, is supported.

SQL/MM — DM

The International Standard ISO/IEC 13249 (ISO SQL/MM part 6, 2001) "Information technology — Database languages — SQL Multimedia and Application Packages (ISO SQL/MM)" is a specification for supporting data management of common data types (text, spatial information, images and data mining results) relevant in multimedia and other knowledge intensive applications in SQL-99. It consists of several different parts. Part number 6 is devoted to data mining aspects. In particular, it attempts to provide a standardized interface to data mining algorithms that can be layered at the top of any object-relational database system and even deployed as middleware when required, by providing several SQL user-defined types (including methods on those types) to support pattern extraction and storage.

Differently from PMML and CWM, SQL/MM does not only address the issue of representation but also of manipulation. Thus, it can be used to develop specific data mining applications on top of an object-relational DBMS (ORDBMS).

Four types of patterns are supported (thus, the set of pattern types is not extensible and no support for user-defined pattern types is provided): association rules, clusters, regression (predicting the ranking of new data based on an analysis of existing data) and classification (predicting which grouping or class new data will best fit based on its relationship to existing data). For each pattern type, a set of measures is provided. For each of those models, various activities are supported:

- **Training:** the mining task (also called the model) is specified by choosing a pattern type, setting some parameters concerning the chosen mining function, and then applying the just configured mining function over a given dataset.

- **Testing:** when classification or regression is used, a resulting pattern can be tested by applying it to known data and comparing the pattern predictions with that known data classification or ranking value.

- **Application:** when clustering, classification or regression are used, the model can then be applied to all the existing data for new classifications or cluster assignment.

All the previous activities are supported through a set of SQL user-defined types. For each pattern type, a type DM_*Model (where the "*" is replaced by a string identifying the chosen pattern type) is used to define the model to be used for data mining. The models are parameterized by using instances of the DM_*Settings type, which allows various parameters of a data mining model, such as the minimum support for an association rule, to be set. Models can be trained using instances of the DM_ClassificationData type and tested by building instances of the DM_MiningData type that holds test data and instances of the DM_MiningMapping type that specify the different columns in a relational table that are to be used as a data source. The result of testing a model is one or more instances of the DM_*TestResult type (only for classification and regression). When the model is run against real data, the obtained results are instances of the DM_*Result type. In most cases, instances of DM_*Task types are also used to control the actual testing and running of your models.

Since SQL/MM is primary aimed at enhancing SQL with functionalities supporting data mining, no specific support is provided for *a priori* patterns. Advanced modeling features, such as the definition of pattern hierarchies and temporal information management, are not taken into account. However, queries over both data and patterns can be expressed through SQL. In the same way, the specified mining model and patterns can be modified or deleted.

Java Data Mining API

The Java Data Mining (JDM) API (JDM, 2003) specification addresses the need for a pure Java API to facilitate the development of data mining applications. While SQL/MM deals with representation and manipulation purposes inside an ORDBMS, Java Data Mining is a pure Java API addressing the same issues. As any Java API, it provides a standardized access to data mining patterns that can be represented according to various formats, including PMML and CWM-DM. Thus, it provides interoperability between various data mining vendors by applying the most appropriate algorithm implementation to a given problem without having to invest resources in learning each vendor's API.

JDM supports common data mining operations, as well as the creation, storage, access and maintenance of metadata supporting mining activities under an integrated architecture, relying on three logical components:

(a) **Application programming interface (API)**, which allows end-users to access to services provided by the data mining engine (DME);

(b) **Data mining engine (DME)**, supporting all the services required by the mining process, including data analysis services; and

(c) **Mining object repository (MOR)**, where data mining objects are made persistent together with source data.

Various technologies can be used to implement the MOR, such as a file-based environment or a relational/object database, possibly based on SQL/MM specifications. The MOR component constitutes the repository against which queries and manipulation operations are executed.

Through the supported services, *a posteriori* patterns of predefined types (see Table 3) can be generated by using several different mining functions. Similarly to SQL/MM, pattern extraction is executed through tasks, obtained by specifying information concerning the type of patterns to be extracted, the source dataset, the mining function and additional parameters. Each generated pattern is associated with some measures, representing the accuracy with respect to raw data. Patterns are then stored in the MOR and then used for mining activities. JDM supports various import and export formats, including PMML.

Concluding Discussion

Table 3 summarizes the features of the presented standards, according to the previously introduced parameters. From the previous discussion, it follows that

Table 3. Feature comparison: Industrial proposals

		PMML	JDM API	SQL/MM	CWM
Model & Architecture	*Type of architecture*	Only representation of patterns. No Architecture	Integrated	Integrated	Only representation of patterns. No architecture
	Predefined types	-Association Rules -Decision Trees -Center/ Distribution Based Clustering -(General) Regression -Neural Networks -Naive Bayes -Sequences	-Clustering -Association Rules -Classification -Approximation -Attribute Importance	-Clustering -Association Rules -Classification -Regression	-Clustering -Association Rules -Supervised -Classification -Approximation -Attribute Importance
	Link to source data	Yes	Yes	Yes	Yes
	Quality measures	Yes	Yes	Yes	Yes
	Temporal features	No	No	No	No
	Hierarchical types	Partial	No	No	No
Manipulation Language	*Manipulation language*	No	Java API	SQL	No
	Automatic extraction	No	Yes	Yes	No
	Direct insertions	No	Yes	Yes	No
	Modifications and deletions	No	Possible through direct access to objects via Java	Possible through direct access to objects via SQL	No
	Synchroniz-ation over source data	No	No	No	No
	Mining function	Yes	Yes	Yes	Yes
Query	*Query language*	No	Java-API	SQL	No

all the proposals described above rely on an integrated architecture. Among them, PMML and CWM-DM simply address the problem of pattern representation. On the other hand, SQL/MM and JDM cope with both pattern representation and management.

All standards provide a support for the representation of common data mining patterns. Among them, PMML provides the largest set of built-in pattern types.

No user-defined patterns can be modeled, i.e., the set of pattern types is not extensible.

All standards allow users to specify the mining function/algorithm they want to apply. However, in PMML it is just a string used only for user information purposes. Furthermore, all considered approaches support measure computation and description of the source dataset, which is used in SQL/MM and JDM for pattern extraction.

None of the standards supports advanced modeling features concerning patterns such as temporal information management associated with patterns and definition of hierarchies involving patterns. Moreover, no specific support for *a priori* patterns is provided by such approaches even if imported patterns in JDM may be seen as a sort of *a priori* patterns.

Concerning pattern management, no dedicated languages for pattern manipulation are supported. In ISO SQL/MM and JDM, since raw data and patterns are stored together, manipulation and querying are possible by using typical languages used for accessing data.

Finally, we outline that since PMML and CWM simply address the issue of pattern representation, they can be used in any PBMS architecture. As we will see later, most commercial systems support PMML, which guarantees a clear XML representation that can be easily integrated with other XML data; on the other hand, due to its complexity, CWM-DM is rarely supported. SQL/MM and JDM can be used to develop specific data mining applications on top of existing technologies. In particular, SQL/MM can be put on top of an ORDBMS environment, whereas JDM works in a JAVA-based environment, providing an implementation for the proposed API.

Metadata Management

Patterns may be interpreted as a kind of metadata. Indeed, metadata in general represent data over data and, since patterns represent knowledge over data, there is a strong relationship between metadata management and pattern management. However, as we have already stressed, pattern management is a more complex problem since patterns have some peculiar characteristics that general metadata do not have. Indeed, metadata are usually provided for maintaining process information, as in data warehousing, or for representing knowledge in order to guarantee interoperability, as in the Semantic Web and intelligent agent systems. Specific pattern characteristics, such as quantification of importance through quality measures, are not taken into account. Usually, metadata are not used to improve and drive decision processes. Since metadata management has nonetheless influenced pattern management, in the following we briefly describe some approaches defined in this context.

In the artificial intelligence area, many research efforts have been invested in the *Knowledge Sharing Effort* (KSE, 1997), a consortium working on solutions for sharing and reuse of knowledge bases and knowledge based systems. Standards proposals of such a consortium are computer-oriented, i.e., they are not dedicated to human users, even if in some cases they can take advantage of using the proposed standard languages. The most important contributions developed by the consortium are *Knowledge Interchange Format* (KIF) and *Knowledge Query and Manipulation Language* (KQML) specifications. The first is a declarative language to express knowledge about knowledge and is used to exchange knowledge units among computers. It does not provide support for internal knowledge representation, thus each computer receiving KIF data translate them into its internal logical model in order to be able to apply some computation process. The second contribution proposes a language and a protocol supporting interoperability and cooperation among collections of intelligent agents involved in distributed applications. KQML can be used as a language by an application to interact with an intelligent agent system or by two or more intelligent systems to interact cooperatively in problem solving.

Concerning the emerging Semantic Web research area, Web metadata management problems have been taken into account by the W3C and a framework for representing information in the Web, Resource Description Framework (RDF, 2004), has been proposed. One of the essential goals of *RDF* (and *RDF-schema*) is to allow — in a simple way — the description of Web metadata, i.e., information about Web resources and how such resources can be used by a third-party in order to make them available not only for human users but also for machines and automatic processes. RDF uses an XML-based syntax and it exploits the URI identification mechanism. Recently, an emerging research field coping with the integration of ontology management and Web data management has emerged. In this context, W3C proposes a recommendation for a dedicated language: the *Web Ontology Language* (OWL, 2004). OWL is primarily dedicated to applications that need to process the content of information instead of just presenting information to human users. OWL supports better machine interpretability of Web content than XML, RDF or RDF Schema (RDF-S) solutions since it provides an extended vocabulary along with a more precise semantics.

Issues concerning metadata management have also been extensively considered in the context of the *Dublin Core Metadata Initiative* (DCMI, 2005), "an organization dedicated to promoting the adoption of interoperable metadata standards and developing specialized metadata vocabularies for describing resources that enable more intelligent information discovery systems." The main aim of DCMI is to support Internet resources identification through the proposal of metadata standards for discovery across domains and frameworks (tools, services and infrastructure) and for metadata sharing.

Pattern Support in Commercial DBMSs

Since the ability to support business intelligence solutions enhances the market competiveness of a DBMS product, all the most important DBMS producers supply their products with solutions for business intelligence supporting data mining and knowledge management processes. Pattern management in commercial DBMSs is provided in the context of such environments. In the remainder of this section we will briefly discuss data mining solutions proposed by three leading companies in database technology: Oracle, Microsoft and IBM.

Oracle Data Mining Tool

Starting from release 9i, Oracle technology supports data mining processing (Oracle DM, 2005). In the Oracle Data Mining server, basic data mining features have been specialized and enhanced. Oracle Data Mining (ODM) is a tool tightly integrated with Oracle 10g DBMS, supporting basic data mining tasks such as classification, prediction and association, and also clustering and ranking attribute importance. By using ODM, the user can extract knowledge (in the form of different kinds of patterns) from corporate data in the underlying Oracle databases or data warehouses. Supported patterns include categorical classifiers (computed by applying naïve Bayes network or support vector machines), continuous/numerical classifiers relying on linear or non-linear regression models (obtained by Support Vector Machines), association rules and clusters (produced by the K-Means algorithm or a proprietary clustering algorithm). Mining algorithms and machine learning methods are built into ODM, but the user may change some settings and/or define new parameters for the mining model through the ODM Java API. Statistical measures can be associated with classifiers and association rules.

In the latest release (i.e., ODM 10g-Release 1), ODM's functionalities can be accessed in two ways: through a Java-based API or through the PL/SQL interface. Up to now, Java API and PL/SQL API are not interoperable, i.e., a model created in Java cannot be used in PL/SQL and vice versa. To overcome this limitation, the next ODM release (10g-Release 2) will adhere to the JDM standard specification, a JDM API will be implemented as a layer on top of ODM PL/SQL API and the current Java API will be abandoned.

Concerning other data mining standards, ODM supports PMML import and export, but only for naïve Bayes and association rule models. Exchanges through PMML documents are fully supported between Oracle database instances, but the compatibility with PMML models produced by other vendors can be achieved only if they use core PMML standard.

Microsoft SQL Server 2005

The business solutions proposed by Microsoft SQL Server exploit OLAP, data mining and data warehousing tools (MS SQL, 2005). The pioneer data mining functionalities appeared in SQL Server 2000 (only two types of patterns were supported: decision trees and clusters), but they have been consolidated and extended in the recent SQL Server 2005 beta release. Within the SQL Server environment, there are tools supporting data transformation and loading, pattern extraction and analysis based on OLAP services.

SQL server 2005 allows the user to build different types of mining models dealing with traditional mining patterns (such as decision tree, clusters, naïve Bayes classifier, time series, association rules and neural networks) and to test, compare and manage them in order to drive the business decision processes. Seven mining algorithms are provided by SQL Server 2005. The entire knowledge management process is performed through a mining model editor to define, view, compare and apply models. Besides this editor, additional tools are provided to exploit other mining phases (for example, data preparation). Within the SQL Server 2005, through OLE DB for Data Mining (OLEDB, 2005), it is possible to mine knowledge from relational data sources or multi-relational repositories. OLE DB for Data Mining extends SQL to integrate data-mining capabilities in other database applications. Thus, it provides storage and manipulation features for mined patterns in an SQL style. Using OLE DB for Data Mining, extracted patterns are stored in a relational database. Thus, in order to create a mining model, a CREATE statement quite similar to the SQL CREATE TABLE statement can be used; to insert new patterns in your mining model, the INSERT INTO statement can be used; finally, patterns can be retrieved and predictions made by using the usual SQL SELECT statement. For the sake of interoperability and compatibility with standards, OLE DB for Data Mining specification incorporates PMML.

IBM DB2 Intelligent Miner

DB2 database management environment provides support for knowledge management by means of a suite of tools, DB2 Intelligent Miner (DB2, 2005),

dedicated to the basic activities involved in the whole data mining process. Thus, users may use data mining functionalities as they use any other traditional relational function provided by the DBMS.

The interaction between DB2 Intelligent Miner's tools takes place through PMML standard.

In particular, an ad-hoc DB2 Extender for data mining allows the automatic construction of mining models within DB2/SQL applications and their update with respect to changes occurring in the underling raw data. The generated mining models are PMML models and are stored as binary large objects (BLOBs). The other DB2 tools supporting training, scoring (or prediction) and visualization of a model work on PMML models, thus they can manage third-party PMML models without additional overhead. It is quite important to note that the scoring tool has the ability to score a mining model over data recorded not only on DB2 databases but also on Oracle ones. This capability has a great impact in applications development since it may reduce design and building costs.

Since DB2 Intelligent Miner's tools are tightly integrated with the database environment and the mining results are stored as BLOBs, the user may interact with the system through an SQL API. In particular, by using SQL it is possible to perform association rules discovery, clustering and classifications techniques provided by the DB2 environment.

Moreover, through ODBC/JDBC or OLE DB, data mining results can be integrated within business applications developed using an external powerful programming language.

Concluding Discussion

As we have seen, commercial DBMSs do not provide a comprehensive framework for pattern management, yet. Rather they support business intelligence by providing an applicational layer offering data mining features in order to extract knowledge from data, and by integrating mining results with OLAP instruments in order to support advanced pattern analysis. For this reason, in general, they do not provide a dedicated logical model for pattern representation and querying, since these aspects are demanded to the applications using the mined results. An exception is represented by SQL Server 2005, where pattern storage, manipulation and querying are made through OLE DB for Data Mining, which can be considered an SQL-based language for pattern management.

None of the systems allow the user to define its pattern types. Moreover, mining functions are built into the system; however, the user can modify some settings, specializing the algorithm to the case he or she is interested in. Finally, none of the DBMSs takes into account advanced modelling aspects involving patterns,

Table 4. Features comparison: commercial DBMSs

	Oracle Data Mining (10g)	Microsoft SQL Server 2005	IBM DB2
Predefined types	-Association rules -Discrete and continuous classifier -Clusters -Attribute importance	-Association rules and itemsets -Clusters -Decision trees -Naïve Bayes classifier -Time series -Neural Networks	-Association rules -Clusters -Classifiers
Quality measures	Yes	Yes	Yes
Mining function	Built-in (user-defined settings)	Built-in (user-defined settings)	Built-in (user-defined settings)
Temporal features	No	No	Yes (scoring phase)
Hierarchical types	No	No	No
Supported standards	PMML JDM (ODM 10g-Release2)	PMML	PMML

such as temporal information management and the existence of hierarchical relationships between patterns. Only DB2 considers patterns-data synchronization issues, through a scoring mechanism that can be started up by some triggers monitoring raw data changes.

Table 4 summarizes the features of the described commercial DBMSs by considering a subset of the previously introduced parameters.

Additional Issues

In order to make PBMSs a practical technology, besides issues concerning architectures, models, and languages, additional topics have to be taken into account when developing a PBMS. Among them, pattern reasoning, physical design, query optimizations and access control are fundamental issues that have only been partially taken into account by existing proposals. In the following, such topics will be discussed in more detail.

Pattern reasoning. Pattern reasoning is supported only in few theoretical proposals, in the form of similarity check (PANDA) or pattern combination (3W-model and PANDA). However, an overall approach for reasoning about possibly

heterogeneous patterns needs more sophisticated techniques describing the semantics of pattern characteristics. As an example, consider measures. In general, various approaches exist for measure computation (general probabilities, Dempster-Schafer and Bayesian Networks — see, for example, Silberschatz and Tuzhillin, 1996). It is not clear how patterns, possibly having the same type but characterized by different measures, can be compared and managed together. Probably, measure ontologies could be used to support such quantitative pattern reasoning.

Physical design. Since patterns are assumed to be stored in a repository, specific physical design techniques must be developed. Unfortunately,up to now it is not clear what constitutes a reasonable physical layer for patterns. Most commercial DBMSs store patterns as BLOBs that are then manipulated using specific methods. However, in order to provide a more efficient access, specific physical representations, clustering, partitioning, caching and indexing techniques should be developed. Concerning theoretical proposals, as we have already seen in the context of the 3W model, patterns are represented as regions, thus techniques developed for spatial databases can be used for their physical management.

Query optimization. Query optimization for pattern queries has been only marginally investigated. Some preliminary work, concerning query rewriting, has been proposed in the context of the 3W framework. An overall query optimization approach, taking into account choices concerning physical design, has not been defined yet. Assuming the necessity of dealing with a separated architecture, the main issue is how to perform data and patterns computations in an efficient way. An important issue here is how it is possible to use patterns to reduce data access in data and cross-over queries and how data and pattern query processors can be combined. On the other side, under an integrated architecture, where extraction is a kind of query, the main issue is the optimization of pattern generation. Some work has been done in the context of inductive databases, where approaches to optimize pattern extraction, based on constraints over pattern properties (Ng et al., 1998), or refine the set of generated patterns (Baralis & Psaila, 1999), have been proposed. Techniques for reducing the size of the generated pattern sets by representing them using condensed representations have also been proposed for itemsets and association rules (CINQ, 2001).

Access control. Patterns represent highly-sensitive information. Their access has therefore to be adequately controlled. The problem is similar to that of access control in the presence of inference (Farkas & Jajodia, 2002). In general, assuming a user has access to some non-sensitive data, the inference problem arises when, through inference, sensitive data can be discovered from non-sensitive ones. In terms of patterns, this means that users may have the right to access some patterns, for example some association rules, and starting from them they may infer additional knowledge over data upon which they may not have the access right.

Techniques already proposed in the inference context should be adapted and extended to cope with the more general pattern management framework. Some of these approaches rely on pre-processing techniques and check through mining techniques whether it is possible to infer sensitive data; others can be applied at run-time (i.e., during the knowledge discovery phase), releasing patterns only when they do not represent sensitive information; finally, modifications over original data, such as perturbation and sample size restrictions, that do not disturb data mining results can be also applied in order to encrypt the original data and to prevent unauthorized user data access.

Conclusion

Patterns refer to knowledge artifacts used to represent in a concise and semantically rich way huge quantities of heterogeneous raw data or some of their characteristics. Patterns are relevant in any knowledge intensive application, such as data mining, information retrieval or image processing. In this chapter, after presenting a sample scenario of pattern usage, specific issues concerning pattern management have been pointed out in terms of the used architecture, models and languages. Several parameters have also been identified and used in comparing various pattern management proposals.

From the analysis proposed in this chapter, it follows that there is a gap between theoretical proposals and standard/commercial ones that spans from a lack of modelling capabilities (such as no support for user-defined patterns, pattern hierarchies or temporal features management in standard/commercial proposals) to a lack of manipulation and processing operations and tools (no manipulation of heterogeneous patterns, no support for similarity, pattern combination and synchronization in standard/commercial proposals). More generally, the analysis has shown that, even if several proposals exist, an overall framework, in terms of the current standards, to represent and manipulate patterns is still missing. In particular, aspects related to the physical management of patterns have not been considered at all.

On the other hand, the diffusion of knowledge intensive applications that may benefit from pattern technology is increasing. A combined effort of the academic community with industries is therefore required for establishing the real need of such features and the extension of existing standards in these directions. We however remark that the support of pattern combination in the last PMML version seems to answer this question positively.

Acknowledgment

The authors would like to thank Maurizio Mazza for his valuable contribution to this chapter.

References

Agrawal, R., & Srikant, R. (1994). Fast algorithms for mining association rules in large databases. In *Proceedings of VLDB'94* (pp. 487-499). Morgan Kaufmann.

Baralis, E., & Psaila, G. (1999). Incremental refinement of mining queries. In *Proceedings of DaWaK'99 (LNCS)* (Vol. 1676, pp. 173-182). Springer-Verlag.

Bartolini, I., Ciaccia, P., Ntoutsi, I., Patella, M., & Theodoridiss, Y. (2004) A unified and flexible framework for comparing simple and complex patterns. In *Proceedings of ECML-PKDD'04 (LNAI)* (Vol. 3202, pp. 496-499). Springer-Verlag.

Braga, D., Campi, A., Ceri, S., Klemettinen, M., & Lanzi, P. L. (2002). A tool for extracting XML association rules from XML documents. In *Proceedings of ICTAI '02* (p. 57). IEEE Computer Society.

Catania, B. et al. (2004). A framework for data mining pattern management. In *Proceedings of ECML-PKDD'04 (LNAI)* (Vol. 3202, pp. 87-98). Springer-Verlag.

Cattell, R. G. G., & Barry, D. K. (2000). *The object data standard:ODMG 3.0.* San Francisco: Morgan Kaufmann.

CINQ. (2001). *The CINQ project.* http://www.cinq-project.org

Conklin, D. (2002). Representation and discovery of vertical patterns in music. In *Proceedings of Second International Conference on Music and Artificial Intelligence'04 (LNAI)* (Vol. 2445, pp. 32-42). Springer-Verlag.

CWM. (2001). *Common warehouse metamodel.* Retrievable from http://www.omg.org/cwm

DB2. (2005). *DB2 intelligent miner.* Retrievable from http://www-306.ibm.com/software/data/iminer/

DCMI. (2005). *Dublin core metadata initiative.* Retrievable from http://dublincore.org/

De Raedt, L. (2002). A perspective on inductive databases. *ACM SIGKDD Explorations Newsletter, 4*(2), 69-77.

De Raedt, L. et al. (2002). A theory on inductive query answering. In *Proceedings of ICDM'02* (pp. 123-130). IEEE Computer Society.

Elfeky, M. G. et al. (2001). ODMQL: Object data mining query language. In *Proceedings of Objects and Databases: International Symposium (LNCS)* (Vol. 1944, pp. 128-140). Springer-Verlag.

Farkas, C., & Jajodia, S. (2002). The inference problem: A survey. *ACM SIGKDD Explorations, 4*(2), 6-11.

Han, J. et al. (1995). Knowledge mining in databases: An integration of machine learning methodologies with database technologies. *Canadian Artificial Intelligence*.

Han, J. et al. (1996). DMQL: A data mining query language for relational databases. In *Proceedings of SIGMOD'96 Workshop on Research Issues in Data Mining and Knowledge Discovery (DMKD'96)*.

Imielinski, T., & Mannila, H. (1996). A database perspective on knowledge discovery. *Communications of the ACM, 39*(11), 58-64.

Imielinski, T., & Virmani, A. (1999). MSQL: A query language for database mining. *Data Mining and Knowledge Discovery, 2*(4), 373-408.

ISO SQL/MM Part 6. (2001). Retrievable from http://www.sql-99.org/SC32/WG4/Progression Documents/FCD/fcd-datamining-2001-05.pdf

JDM (2003). *Java data mining API.* Retrievable from http://www.jcp.org/jsr/detail/73.prt

Johnson, S. et al. (2000). The 3W model and algebra for unified data mining. In *Proceedings of VLDB'00* (pp. 21-32). Morgan Kauffman.

KSE (1997). *Knowledge sharing effort.* Retrievable from http://www.cs.umbc.edu/kse/

Meo, R., Lanzi, P. L., & Klemettinen, M. (2003). *Database support for data mining applications (LNCS)* (Vol. 2682). New York: Springer-Verlag.

Meo, R., Psaila, G., & Ceri, S. (1998). An extension to SQL for mining association rules. *Data Mining and Knowledge Discovery, 2*(2), 195-224.

Minerule System. (2004). *Minerule mining system* (demo version). Retrievable from http://kdd.di.unito.it/minerule2/demo.html

Mitchell, T. M. (1997). *Machine learning.* McGraw Hill.

MOF. (2003). *Meta-object facility (MOF) specification, vers. 1.4.* Retrievable from http://www.omg.org/technology/documents/formal/mof.htm

MOLFEA. (2004). *The molecular feature miner based on the LVS algorithm* (demo version). Retrievable from http://www.predictive-toxicology.org/cgi-bin/molfea.cgi

MS SQL. (2005). *Microsoft SQL server analysis server.* Retrievable from http://www.microsoft.com/sql/evaluation/bi/bianalysis.asp

Nakajima, C. et al. (2000). People recognition and pose estimation in image sequences. In *Proceedings of IJCNN* (Vol. 4, pp. 189-194). IEEE Computer Society.

Ng, R. et al. (1998). Exploratory mining and pruning optimizations of constrained associations rules. In *Proceedings of SIGMOD'98* (pp. 13-24). ACM Press.

OLEDB. (2005). *OLE DB for data mining specification.* Retrievable from http://www.microsoft.com/data/oledb

Oracle DM. (2005). *Oracle data mining tools.* Retrievable from http://www.oracle.com/technology/products/bi/odm/

OWL. (2004). *Web ontology language.* Retrievable from http://www.w3.org/2001/sw/WebOnt

PANDA. (2001). *The PANDA project.* Retrievable from http://dke.cti.gr/panda/

PMML. (2003). *Predictive model markup language.* Retrievable from http://www.dmg.org/pmml-v2-0.html

RDF. (2004). *Resource description framework.* Retrievable from http://www.w3.org/RDF/

Rizzi, S. et al. (2003). Towards a logical model for patterns. In *Proceedings of ER'03 (LNCS)* (pp. 77-90). Springer-Verlag.

SIGKDD. (2002). *SIGKDD Explorations* - Special Issue on Constraint-Based Mining.

Silberschatz, A., & Tuzhilin, A. (1996). What makes patterns interesting in knowledge discovery systems. *IEEE Transactions on Knowledge and Data Engineering,* 8(6), 970-974.

UML. (2003). *UML specification, vers. 1.5.* Retrievable from http://www.omg.org/technology/documents/formal/uml.htm

XMI. (2003). *XML metadata interchange specifications vers.2.0.* Retrievable from http://www.omg.org/technology/documents/formal/xmi.htm

Xquery. (2001). *Xquery 1.0: An XML query language* (W3C working draft). Retrievable from http://www.w3.org/TR/2001/WD-xquery-20011220

Chapter XI

VRMiner:
A Tool for Multimedia
Database Mining with
Virtual Reality

H. Azzag, Université François-Rabelais de Tours,
Laboratoire d'Informatique (EA 2101), France

F. Picarougne, Université François-Rabelais de Tours,
Laboratoire d'Informatique (EA 2101), France

C. Guinot, CE.R.I.E.S., Unité Biométrie et Epidémiologie, and
Université François-Rabelais de Tours,
Laboratoire d'Informatique (EA 2101), France

G. Venturini, Université François-Rabelais de Tours,
Laboratoire d'Informatique (EA 2101), France

Abstract

We present in this chapter a new 3D interactive method for visualizing multimedia data with virtual reality named VRMiner. We consider that an expert in a specific domain has collected a set of examples described with numeric and symbolic attributes but also with sounds, images, videos and Web sites or 3D models, and that this expert wishes to explore these data to understand their structure. We use a 3D stereoscopic display in order to let the expert easily visualize and observe the data. We add to this display contextual information such as texts and small images, voice synthesis and sound. Larger images, videos and Web sites are displayed on a second computer in order to ensure real time display. Navigating through the data is done in a very intuitive and precise way with a 3D sensor that simulates a virtual camera. Interactive requests can be formulated by the expert with a data glove that recognizes the hand gestures. We show how this tool has been successfully applied to several real world applications.

Introduction

Since Fisher's work on Iris database (Fisher, 1936), and thanks to possibilities given by computers, data representations have evolved and become much more complex. In many domains, databases are not only compounded of numeric or symbolic attributes but may also be enriched, for instance, by sounds, images, videos, texts, Web sites or 3D models. The main focus of this chapter is on helping the domain expert to intuitively analyze such data sets.

In our opinion, intuitive analysis of a multimedia database implies the use of visualization and virtual reality techniques, a subset of the visual data mining (VDM) domain. VDM is a growing field of research in data mining (DM) and knowledge discovery in databases (KDD). VDM relies on the fact that the human brain efficiently deals with visual perception and can quickly extract a lot of information and knowledge from a scene. Visualization of data is an important step in DM and KDD, either at the beginning, during or end of the knowledge discovery process (Fayyad et al., 1996); before knowledge extraction, visualization may be useful as a preprocessing step which helps the user to better understand the data set. Visualization can also be used during the KDD process for discovering an efficient classifier. Once knowledge has been discovered, the expert often needs to interpret it in order to take a decision, and visualization techniques can help to represent this knowledge as well. Therefore, most of the DM/KDD tools and applications can be concerned with VDM.

Virtual reality (VR) proposes significant advances in the domain of data visualization as well as user interaction. Virtual worlds can be built by combining an advanced display, sensors and actuators. VR displays are 3D and stereoscopic; sensors may detect the user's moves. Actuators with feedback forces may simulate more efficiently the effects of actions. VR makes the human-computer interaction very intuitive, and this is our motivation for integrating VR in VDM. The remainder of this chapter is organized as follows: the *State of the*

Art section presents a survey of VDM and VR; *Exploring/Understanding Multimedia Data* describes our approach for interactive exploration of multimedia data; *Results* presents the results obtained on benchmark and real data; and the *Conclusion* section concludes on the perspectives which can be derived from this work.

State of the Art

Data Visualization

Data visualization techniques are numerous. They may be classified according to several criteria. One common criterion is the data type that is visualized (Schneiderman, 1996) as documents in the domain of information retrieval (Zamir, 1998), numerical data (Wong & Bergeron, 1997), hierarchical data (Lamping et al., 1995) or geographical data (Schumann & Urban, 1997). Visualization techniques may also be grouped according to the type of display they use: 1D, 2D, 2.5D or 3D (Cugini et al., 2000), and on how they draw the users attention (Wises & Carr, 1998). These techniques may also use metaphors, such as a book or a room (Card et al., 1996), a map (Wise et al., 1995) or a city (Sparacino et al., 1999).

We focus in this chapter on 3D representations (Wises & Carr, 1998). The use of a 3D display may greatly improve the comprehension of the data (Ware & Franck, 1994), but it also has drawbacks (see *Guidelines* section).

Visual Data Mining

As mentioned in Wong and Bergeron (1997), the exploratory analysis of data and VDM are not just a set of tools but rather a philosophical way of solving KDD problems. Two important points can be highlighted in VDM: the perception of the data and the interaction with the data representation. These two points have been studied for many years in domains which are included in or very close to VDM (Cleveland, 1993; Kim & Kriegel, 1996; Larkin et al., 1997; Wong & Bergeron, 1997; Friendly, 2000; Unwin, 2000). A historical example can be found in Chernoff (1973) where data are represented with faces. The values of a given example in the database determine the characteristics of its corresponding face (for instance, the type of eyes or nose, the position of the face in the representation, etc). In this way, similarities between the data are made directly understandable for the human brain, for which recognizing faces is a very common task. The same principles are used in Pickett and Grinstein (1988), where the data are represented by stick icons. Another important example is the scatter plot that displays the data through several points clouds. The user may interact with the data representation with a technique called "brushing" (Becker & Cleveland, 1987): He or she selects points in one cloud and these points are also selected in the other clouds.

More recently, MineSet (Brunk et al., 1997) proposes other 3D visualizations. This system may display data directly coming from the original database, but it may also display the results of a learning process like decision trees, rules, etc. (Thearling et al., 1998). Visage (Derthick et al., 1997) is another example of a VDM system where an important focus has been made on the interaction between the user and the data representation: The user may formulate a request graphically in a geographical domain. Several works present other applications of VDM in various domains, such as medicine (Symanzik et al., 1999), spatial databases (Schumann & Urban, 1997) or atmospheric science (Macedo et al., 2000). These systems also represent complex VDM and visualization tools, but they have the drawback of often being specific to a given domain, and even to a given database. Graphic displays are not systematically in 3D and rarely use a stereoscopic display as well as advanced interactive devices. Commercial products exist, such as IBM's OpenDX or NAG's IRIS Explorer, which can be used for visual data mining applications (and more generally, several kinds of 3D visualizations). However, those tools are better suited for advanced computer scientists and may not use VR devices.

Virtual Reality

Virtual reality may greatly enhance VDM (Baker & Wickens, 1995; Wegman et al., 1998), but only a few VDM systems really use VR. One famous example is the CAVE system which has been used to visualize a database (Symanzik et al., 1996). The user is facing a large screen (video projectors) and observes the data in stereoscopy. He or she may use a data glove for making requests. This tool sounds very promising because of all the possibilities of interaction that it proposes or will propose in the future. However, its main drawback is its cost, which is definitely too high for the numerous domains in which VDM is required.

As will be seen in the following, we study how to propose multimedia data visualizations that would have the same quality as in the best VDM tools with the use of all the interactive possibilities offered by VR but at a lower cost than the CAVE, for instance. Our approach also attempts to be as generic as possible rather than being specific to a given database with the aim to make it useful to as many domains as possible.

Guidelines

One of the key points in VDM is how to encode the attributes that describe the data into visual attributes in the graphical representation. Several guidelines have been studied in papers dealing with human perception. Those guidelines suggest that some visual cues are better perceived than others, and that some cues are better suited than others for encoding different types of data attributes (Mackinlay, 1986; Keller & Keller, 1993). One must also be aware of other facts, like preattentive perception, or the resulting perception that is obtained when two visual cues are combined together (Healey, 1996).

As far as the user (domain expert) aims are concerned, researchers also have highlighted the typical goals that VDM should be able to encompass (Nocket & Schuman, 2004). Specific goals we are interested in are to identify/locate data, to examine the data distribution and to detect correlation between several data dimensions.

Another point to consider is the specific requirements for 3D displays (Wiss & Carr, 1998). Using the third dimension raises specific problems, such as the user's navigation (the user should not be lost and his moves should be intuitive) and the user interaction (properties of 3D objects should be related to the real world, and visualizations must be refreshed at a high rate).

Within the next section, we will detail how we have used those guidelines for the conception of VRMiner.

Exploring/Understanding
Multimedia Data

Principles

Figures 1 and 2 give an overview of VRMiner. We consider that the domain expert has collected many examples which are described with attributes. Those attributes can be numeric or symbolic, but they may also be of "multimedia types." We use herein a broad definition of "multimedia." Such attributes can be sounds, images, videos, Web sites, 3D models (a 3D representation of a data) and, more generally, as will be seen in the following, any file which can be opened by the operating system VRminer is running under.

This database is displayed with 3D views on a main screen and other views on a second computer for large media. Liquid crystal display (LCD) glasses allow

Figure 1. Schematic view of VRMiner

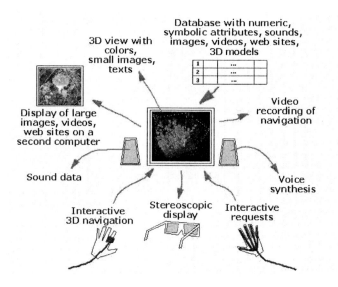

Figure 2. Real view of VRMiner

the user to perceive the data in stereoscopy. Navigation through the data is done with a 3D sensor located on the user's left hand (see Figures 1 and 2). The user formulates interactive requests with a data glove located on the right hand. He or she may select an example and dynamically obtain contextual information (texts, voice synthesis, sounds, etc.). Images of small size can be mapped as textures; each datum can also be represented by a specific 3D model. Images of large size, as well as videos, Web sites or other files are displayed/opened on a second screen and may thus be observed with more detail. The user's

Table 1. Encoding a single datum into the visual representation

Attributes	Role in Visualization/perception
3 numeric attributes	Coordinates of a 3D object
1 symbolic attribute	3D object shape (cube, sphere, pyramid, others)
1 or 2 numeric attributes	Variation in object shape (height, size)
1 symbolic/numeric attribute	Object color
1 small image attribute	Textures mapped to 3D shape
1 textual attribute	Value pronounced with voice synthesis
1 textual attribute	Contextual display
1 sound attribute	Played on speakers
1 to N large image attributes	Displayed in sequence on second computer
1 to N video attributes	Displayed in sequence on second computer
1 to N web site attributes	Displayed in sequence on second computer
Any file which can be opened by the operating system	Opened in sequence on second computer

navigation and actions, as well as the displayed information, can be exported to a video file.

The user interface is simple, and the user does not need to be an advanced computer scientist to use VRMiner (see the discussion in section *Results and Users' Feedback*: VRMiner provides help for selecting the position-based visual cues, but not yet for the others). Moreover, we have tried to minimize the cost of the system hardware. We have also kept a high genericity for this system in order to be able to apply it to numerous databases in many domains.

Visualization of a Single Datum

Figure 3(a) gives an overview of the basic 3D display. A wired frame represents the virtual cube into which the data will be represented. A blue surface represents the bottom of the visualization. These two elements are landmarks that help the user to perceive the orientation of the scene during navigation.

Table 1 sums up how we deal with each type of attribute to facilitate their perception by the user. Special attention has been devoted to multimedia attributes and to all techniques that may increase the volume of simultaneously perceived information. The "heart" of the representation is a cloud of 3D objects where each object represents one example/datum of the database.

The coordinates of the objects are determined according to three numeric attributes. Since position is one of the most important visual cues, these axes must be chosen carefully. These three attributes can come directly from the

Figure 3. Overview of the basic visualization (here the Fisher's Iris database) (a); and with a zoom on textured images (b)

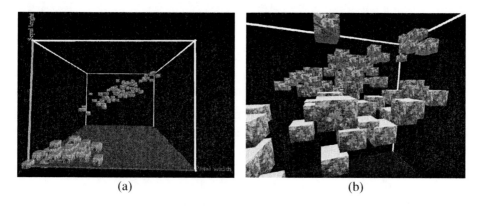

(a)   (b)

Figure 4. Examples of 3D shapes which can be used to represent the data

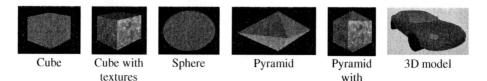

Cube   Cube with   Sphere   Pyramid   Pyramid   3D model
            textures   with
                                                       textures

original data or can be computed with a multivariate data analysis method (see *Results* section). They can be selected by the user among all the numeric attributes of the database, but the three attributes can also be suggested to the user if a class attribute exists in the database. In this case, the proposed algorithm consists in finding the triple of numeric attributes which will maximize a data separability measure and thus improve the visibility. For three given numeric attributes, this separability measure equals the performances of the 1-nearest neighbor algorithm using an Euclidean measure and evaluated with the "leave one out" technique. The higher the performance, the more separable are the classes and the more understandable is the displayed cloud. The values of a symbolic/numeric attribute can be converted into colors which are assigned to 3D objects. For instance, if a class attribute exists in the database, then colors can be determined according to this attribute (see Figure 3(a)). It has been shown that color is well suited for encoding nominal attributes (Mackinlay, 1986).

To this color information may be added a small image attribute: The system reads each image file name indicated by the attribute and maps those images onto the corresponding object (see Figure 3(b) where flower images are mapped onto the examples of the Fisher's Iris database). Images are very informative for a human expert. VRMiner will allow the expert to detect correlations between images and, for instance, the position (axis) or color (class) of the data. This greatly improves the amount of information present in the visualization but is limited to small images because the cube sizes are limited and 3D graphics can not handle too many large images. This is one of the reasons why we propose an architecture with two machines (see next section) for exploring larger images.

A different 3D shape can be assigned to each example. Figure 4 sums up the different shapes which have been defined in VRMiner. A given shape (for instance "pyramid2") has its own parameters (texture, 2 colors, "bottom" and "top" heights parameters). These parameters may depend on the data. We highlight here the motivations for defining the different shapes. Cubes, and more generally boxes, are standard shapes onto which textures can be mapped and which dimensions may depend on the data. Spheres are also standard and have a variable radius but do not allow a representative mapping of textures (unless the original data really look like spheres). One should notice, however, that variable volume of 3D objects (like cubes or spheres) should be used with great care, because volume also plays an important role in the perception of perspective. Thus, we prefer to use different representations based, for instance, on a pyramid. The square basis of the pyramid is fixed and identical for all data, but the "bottom" and "top" heights are variable and depend on two numerical attributes. In this way, the objects will have an invariant property which will not disturb the perception of perspective, and which still allows the system to visualize two additional dimensions and to increase the possibilities of detecting correlations between displayed dimensions. Finally, VRMiner may represent each datum with a user defined 3D shape, which is supposed to be previously designed. In this way, each example can be closely related to the real world or to the application domain. This makes the 3D view even more informative.

Representation of Larger Files on a Second Computer

A second computer is used for the representation of additional dimensions. This was initially motivated by the need to display large images (see sections *Real World Applications: Encoding Databases* and *Results and Users' Feedback*); in our application domain, for example, the expert would like to select an individual and to see all the related images of his skin.

Those large data cannot be included in the 3D representation, either because they are too large to be handled by graphic cards or because they would slow down the navigation. Using a second computer allows VRMiner to quickly open these files without any drawbacks for the first computer.

The displays are triggered when the user selects an object in the 3D representation of the first computer (see next section). We have generalized this technique to any other files types which can be opened by the OS. For instance, one may view videos or Web sites: When selecting an object in the first computer (assume that each object represents a Web page), then the page is currently opened in a Web browser on the second computer. The same principle can be applied to any document types or files. VRMiner could thus be used as a kind of files advanced browser.

Data Selection and Additional Contextual Information

The user may select an object in the representation and ask for additional information. This is the well-known "detail-on-demand" method (see *Guidelines* section). Two possibilities of object selection are offered by VRMiner. The first one is when the user uses the data glove (see *Intuitive Commands With a Data Glove* section). A virtual pointer is located at the center of the screen, and each time this pointer moves over a displayed example, actions can be automatically or manually triggered according to the user's requests. These requests are formulated with the data glove, but if the user does not use the glove, then he may simply select the objects with the mouse.

VRMiner highlights a selected object by rotating it (see Figure 5), because movement is known to be a good way to draw the human brain's attention. Once

Figure 5. Selection of an example triggers the display of typical contextual information, in this case, a text

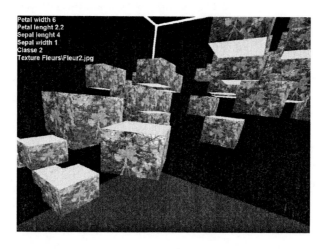

an object is selected, and according to the gesture detected with the data glove (or the mouse's clicks), the following actions can be triggered:

- the display of a text which can give, for instance, all the attribute values of the selected example (see Figure 5), but also any other kind of text label. The user may scroll down or up this display with the data glove (or with the keyboard if too many lines are present). He may check the value of a given attribute for the selected example and move to another example for a comparison;

- the pronunciation of a numeric/symbolic/text attribute value with voice synthesis, as in the CAVE system (Symanzik et al., 1996). This allows the user to easily gain additional information while keeping his visual attention on the data;

- playing the sound file given by the sound attribute; and

- the display of a large image (or other files) on the second computer, which is locally connected to the main computer. This second display does not take any resource from the main computer, and thus allows a visualization in real time (or very close to real time). In addition, the user may freeze the visualization on the main screen and explore with more attention the displayed image/file. Furthermore, the user may use several such attributes, and a list of images can thus be assigned to an object. Each time the user clicks/selects the object, the next image/file in the list is displayed on the second computer. This was especially needed in our real world application (see *Results* section); and

- the opening of any files on the second computer. This may include videos, Web sites, documents and any domain specific files which may require a specific application to be opened. The same list principle is used here again. This allows the user to integrate his own domain-dependent application in our tool.

Stereoscopic Display

Stereoscopic display of information is a very important point for the domain expert because he or she may be able perceive the third dimension in a data set and may thus analyze the data in a more reliable way. In a previous prototype of this system, we have performed tests with a head mounted device (HMD). We have preferred the use of LCD glasses for the following reasons, some of which are common with the analysis found in Wegman et al. (1998): the HMD is heavier than the glasses, it is more tiring and works for a single user only; LCD glasses

(Nuvision 60 GX) are light, they do not make the user feel sick and they may use a high screen resolution at a lower cost; the glasses allow several people to simultaneously view the data, which is a very important feature for VDM application where several experts often need to compare their analysis; and the display is fast enough and flickering is not perceived.

Interactive Navigation

We use a simple and user-intuitive navigation mode. A sensor is fixed to the user's hand and allows him or her to easily define a virtual camera in the 3D space. This sensor has six degrees of freedom and can define a position and an orientation in 3D (Ascension Flock of Birds). The miniature sensor can be placed on a finger just like a ring (see Figures 1 and 2), then everything takes place as if the objects cloud was present in a virtual cube located close to the user. The position of the virtual cube is initially defined by the user; he or she may thus place the cube on the right, left, in front,etc. He or she may thus explore the data while sitting or standing up in front of the display.

When moving his or her hand forward in the direction of the cube or backward, the user may zoom in or out. He or she may place the camera above, beneath or inside the objects cloud; the camera can be oriented in any direction. This sensor also allows the user to point to an example and to select it; this may result in contextual actions (see section *Representation of Larger Files on a Second Computer*).

In order to facilitate the cognitive representation of the scene in the user's mind, we have used a wired frame to materialize the cube where the data are represented, as well as a virtual ground which is useful to give an orientation to the scene and prevent the user from feeling lost (see Figure 3(a)). The basic representation also includes the name of the three axes.

Finally, we mention that it is possible to videorecord all the user's navigation and exploration, all contextual displays and sounds.

Intuitive Commands with a Data Glove

During the visualization, the user is often engaged in a complex process for understanding the structure of the data. During this exploration, using the keyboard can be difficult, at least for the two following reasons: 1) the user concentrates his or her visual attention toward the screen; 2) he or she may be far away from the keyboard. It was necessary to make use of a data glove, a device which can be light and which has a low cost (Fifth Dimension Tech. 5DT).

This glove detects the curvature of each finger and it also detects the orientation of the hand along two axis. All frequent commands used in this system are performed with the glove. The detected gestures are very easy to learn and do not require any special attention from the user. Typical commands are, for instance "freeze the display," "scroll up or down" and "display on second computer."

Results

Evaluation on Benchmarks

We selected several databases from the machine learning repository (Blake & Merz, 1998). We have presented in this chapter how the Iris database could be represented and improved with images. In Figure 6, we show two additional databases, namely the Wine and Pima Indians Diabetes databases.

First, VRMiner uses a simple input file format, namely the Microsoft Excel file format. The user is requested to add three lines, one to give a name to each attribute, one to give the type of the attribute (numeric, symbolic, file name, etc.) and one to define the role of the attribute in the visualization (coordinates, 3D shape, texture, image, color, object size parameters, text label, value pronounced with voice synthesis and file to be opened on second computer). VRminer performs the analysis of the data format (which may include, for instance, the

Figure 6. Typical visualizations of standard databases: Wine database (a) and Pima Indians Diabetes database (b)

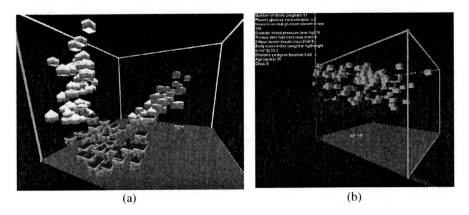

(a)   (b)

normalization of numeric attributes, the generation of the axis with their names in the 3D representation, etc.).

In this example, our 1-NN method suggests to use axes 7, 10 and 13 for the Wine database, and axes 1, 2 and 8 for the Pima Indians database. We have added to the Wine database's fictive images for each class. Those images could be photographs of grapes or of the region where the grapes are produced. As will be shown in the next sections, the intuitive navigation combined with the interactive visualization allows the user to perceive a great deal of information. For instance, it is obvious that the second database is much more complex than the first. In the case of the Wine database, a structure clearly appears in the data, which is not the case for the Pima Indians database. Isolated cases (outliers) can be clearly identified, as well as individuals located at the center of the classes (parangons).

Real World Applications: Encoding Databases

We have applied this system to 15 real world databases in collaboration with the Biometrics and Epidemiology unit of CE.R.I.E.S., a research centre on human skin funded by CHANEL. The number of examples in the databases handled by VRMiner was up to 500. Each database was described with numeric and symbolic attributes, but also with large images. We focus here on two specific databases, one dealing with a healthy human skin clustering task, and one with the definition of typology of behavior related to sun exposure.

The first database consists of 259 examples, where each example represents the description of the visual and tactile facial skin characteristics of a Caucasian

Figure 7. Views of two real databases: human facial healthy skin (a), and sun exposure typology (b) (see text for more explanation)

(a)   (b)

woman between 20 and 50 years old. Thirty skin characteristics, i.e., attributes, were evaluated on the right cheek or on the forehead. Photographs of the skin areas were also taken. The initial aim of the study was to establish a typology of healthy facial skin based on defined skin characteristics, using a multivariate data analysis approach: an ascending hierarchical clustering method (Everitt, 1993) applied on principal components, resulting of multiple correspondence analysis. Finally, a strengthened proposal of a six clusters-classification was obtained, which was mainly characterized by skin color, oiliness, roughness and features associated with the vascular system of the skin. The interested reader may refer, for instance, to Guinot et al. (2005) for more details.

VRMiner is used here to let the expert of the domain explore and visually analyze the resulting clustering (see Figure 7(a)). From the four principal components obtained using multiple correspondence analysis, we select three in order to define the basic cubes cloud used in the 3D visualization. Then, each cube is colored according to the class previously attributed by the clustering method. Small images of faces are mapped onto the cubes. On selection, a larger image is opened on the second computer, and the age of the person is pronounced with voice synthesis.

The second database (Guinot et al., 2004) has been extracted from the SU.VI.MAX. cohort (Hercberg et al., 1998). It consists of 4825 examples (we consider women only) where each example represents the answers given by a woman to a questionnaire dealing with her sun exposure behavior. Each woman is described with 70 numerical/symbolic attributes and six large images of her skin. Multivariate data analysis methods were used to summarize the information (as in the previous study), followed by an ascending hierarchical clustering method to define a behavioral typology (Everitt, 1993). Eventually, to assign a new individual to a given behavioral type, a tree-structured method was applied. Using this method, a decision tree based on the smallest number of the most relevant questions was obtained (Breiman et al., 1984).

Then, the database and the behavior typology have been visualized with VRMiner. The three axes were selected among the variables available according to the expert's wishes. Each datum was represented by a cube with the woman's face as texture. The list of six images was attached to each cube. Each time the user clicked on an object, the next large image was displayed on the second computer. However, the display of nearly 5000 points was not possible due to the number of textures to display. The user interaction was too slow. Therefore, we decided to visualize only 10% of the data with a well-controlled sampling strategy calibrated to respect the initial frequency of each class. VRMiner was used here to analyze/confirm the obtained behavior typology.

Results and Users' Feedback

We present here the main results achieved by VRMiner users. VRMiner main sources of success and users' satisfaction come from its ability to solve at least three problems: detecting correlations between skin photographs and the other data dimensions, checking the quality of discovered clusters and presenting the data to a panel of experts.

Detecting correlations between skin images and the other displayed dimensions is a crucial point for the success of VRMiner in this application. From the practical experience, we have noticed that this point is uniformly appreciated by all users, either bio-statisticians or dermatologists. In this real world application, data dimensions are usually extracted using various means, either with manual (expert based) or automatic (image processing or other measurements) analysis of the skin, and using other sources of information such as age, weight, habits of the person, etc. As a consequence, all data may not be directly derived from the visual aspects of the skin, but correlations between visual aspects and the other data may often exist. In this context, VRMiner greatly facilitates the detection of such correlations thanks to the skin images, which are used as textures, or which are displayed on the second computer. As an example, users can compare the real age of an individual with the age perceived from the photographs.

VRMiner users are also concerned with the confirmation/evaluation of clusters found by standard clustering methods (see previous section). This is especially important because the data are truly unsupervised and no real (and pre-defined) classes exist. The definition of a partition of the data set is thus an important step in this application and must be confirmed by other methods. So, when visualizing such clusters with VRMiner, the expert can analyze the shape of the found classes, and, more precisely, their density, isolated cases (outliers detection), the relative distance between clusters, the examples at the frontier between two clusters, etc. In this context, the stereoscopic display plays a crucial role, as well as the intuitive navigation, which allows the user to easily select the interesting viewpoint. According to the users, this seems to make the use of the VRMiner 3D displays and navigation methods much easier and more efficient than the standard displays of statistical software.

Finally, VRMiner is used to present the results to a panel of experts in dermatology and epidemiology (20 people on average). For this purpose, we have used two large screens with two video projectors. These experts were truly satisfied by these kinds of presentations. They were able to ask specific questions about the data to obtain more details about a given individual or a given cluster.

If one analyzes the main drawbacks of VRMiner from the users' point of view, we can mention the fact that there is no actual help for suggesting how to encode

Figure 8. The data types which can be visualized by VRMiner are being currently extended to rules in (a) (in this example, we have used the Wine database), and to trees such as (b) and (c), where we visualize a hierarchy of Web pages)

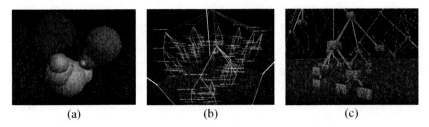

(a)   (b)   (c)

the data attributes into visual cues (except for the selection of the three axes, see *Visualization of a Single Datum* section). This is certainly an important area of research for the future, which is general to VDM (Healey et al., 1999). Another drawback that we have tried to minimize, is the fact that the VR equipment takes several minutes to be set (wearing the glove, setting up the flock of birds, etc). We are currently improving this point by using optical sensors: any real object (like a wand for instance) could be used to define the position/ orientation of the virtual camera, and to give commands to VRMiner.

Our system was successfully used in several applications where visual data mining was involved. This confirms that it is operational and that the choices (software and hardware) that we made were satisfactory. The interactive visualization techniques that we introduce with multimedia data seem to be relevant for an industrial application. Furthermore, this system is easy to use and has a low cost.

As initially stated in the *Virtual Reality* section, we may compare VRMiner to other systems, such as found in Nagel et al. (2003). In this system by Nagel and colleagues, the VR equipment has a much higher cost and the data is multivariate only and thus less complex (no images or other such media). Also, the emphasis is not on the user interaction but rather on the user immersion. We could also mention also the Webpath system because it makes use of textures mapped on small cubes for visualizing the history of a user navigation on the Web. However, this system is devoted to Web history mining and not to the data mining problems we deal with.

Conclusion and Perspectives

We presented in this chapter a system called VRMiner which enlarges the possibilities of visual data mining with the handling of multimedia attributes and the use of virtual reality. We proposed different means in order to perceive small/ large images, sounds, videos, Web sites, 3D models and other domain-specific files. The use of virtual reality is one of the key points in this system because it allows the domain expert to easily perceive the data and to directly interact with them. We have shown how this system can be applied to several real world databases in the context of skin analysis. Part of our future work consists in showing that the genericity of this tool makes it applicable to many other domains.

We wish to extend this work in several directions. We would like to use VRMiner for visualizing other kinds of data and to make this tool even more general. For instance, we can represent not only data, but also knowledge learned from the data, as shown in Figure 8(a), where simple spherical decision rules can be displayed (here for instance the Wine database). We have also started to represent hierarchical data such as a tree of Web pages (a portal site for instance), as represented in Figures 8(b) and (c). The navigation and interaction abilities of VRMiner could be very useful in this domain too. For instance, VRMiner could be used as an advanced browser (each time an object representing a Web page is clicked on, the corresponding Web page is opened on the second computer). We would also like to extend the dynamic properties of the visualization. We are currently developing a simple script language, as for instance Java script in VRML 2.0, based on messages between the represented objects. One object could give commands to other objects (turn, move, hide or show, for instance) through messages. These scripts would be automatically produced by VRMiner and attached to each object. This would allow us to introduce abstraction mechanisms where data are progressively shown with more details as the users move closer in order to deal with larger databases, for example. From the hardware point of view, we wish to study with more depth the use of a larger displays based on video projectors, as shown in the *Results* section. This increases the user immersion into the data and allows multi-expert analysis.

Acknowledgments

We greatly thank Meng Vang, Johann Barbe and Delphine Sénéchal (EPU-DI, University of Tours) for their useful help on this work, and other CE.R.I.E.S. teams for their contribution to the data.

References

Baker, P. M., & Wickens, C. D. (1995). Human factors in virtual environments for the visual analysis of scientific data (Tech. Rep. ARL-95-08/PNL-95-2). University of Illinois Aviation Research Lab.

Becker, R. A., & Cleveland, W. S. (1987). Brushing scatterplots. *Technometrics, 29*, 127-142.

Blake, C. L., & Merz, C. J. (1998). *UCI repository of machine learning databases.*

Breiman, L., Friedman, J. H., Olshen, R. A., & Stone, C. J. (1984). *Classification and regression trees*. New York: Chapman & Hall.

Brunk, C., Kelly, J., & Kohavi, R. (1997). MineSet: an integrated system for data mining. *International Conference on Knowledge Discovery and Data Mining (KDD'97)*. AAAI Press.

Card, S. K., Robertson, G. G., & York, W. (1996). The webbook and the web forager: An information workspace for the world-wide web. In *Human factors in computing systems: Proceedings of the CHI '96 Conference*. New York: ACM.

Chernoff, H. (1973). The use of faces to represent points in k-dimensional space graphically. *Journal of the American Statistical Association, 68*(342), 361-368.

Cleveland, W. S. (1993). *Visualizing data*. Summit, NJ: Hobart Press.

Cugini, J., Laskowski, S., & Sebrechts, M. (2000). Design of 3D visualization of search results: Evolution and evaluation. In *Proceedings of IST/SPIE's 12th Annual International Symposium: Electronic Imaging 2000: Visual Data Exploration and Analysis (SPIE 2000)*. San Jose, CA.

Derthick, M., Kolojejchick, J., & Roth, S. F. (1997). An interactive visualization environment for data exploration. In *Proceedings of Knowledge Discovery in Databases* (pp. 2-9). AAAI Press.

Everitt, B. S. (1993). *Cluster analysis*. London: Arnold.

Fayyad, U., Piatetsky-Shapiro, G., & Smyth, P. (1996). The KDD process for extracting useful knowledge from volumes of data. *Communications of the ACM, 39*(11).

Fisher, R. A. (1936). The use of multiple measurements in taxonomic problems. *Annals of Eugenics, 7*, 179-188.

Frécon, E., & Smith, G. (1998). WebPath: A three-dimensional web history. *IEEE Symp. Information Visualization (Info-Vis 98)*. Piscataway, NJ: IEEE Press.

Friendly, M. (2000). *Visualizing categorical data*. SAS Press, SAS Institute.

Guinot, C., Malvy, D., Mauger, E., Latreille, J., Ambroisine, L., Galan, P. et al. (2004, October 10-12). Study of sun-exposure and sun-protection behaviour in 8,084 French adults. In *Proceedings of the International Congress on Epidemiology Causes and Prevention of Skin Diseases, EDEN-IDEA*, Venice (p. 26).

Guinot, C., Malvy, D., Morizot, F., Tenenhaus, M., Latreille, J., Lopez, S. et al. (2005). Classification of healthy human facial skin. In R. Baran & H. I. Maibach (Eds.). *Textbook of cosmetic dermatology* (3rd ed.) (pp. 27-39). London: Taylor & Francis.

Healey, C. G. (1996). *Effective visualization of large, multidimensional datasets*. Unpublished doctoral dissertation. Department of Computer Science, University of British Columbia.

Healey, C. G., St. Amant, R., & Elhaddad, M. (1999). ViA: A perceptual visualization sssistant. In *Proceedings 28th Applied Imagery Pattern Recognition Workshop*, Washington, DC (pp. 1-11).

Hercberg, S., Preziosi, P., Briançon, S., Galan, P., Triol, I., Malvy et al. (1998). A primary prevention trial using nutritional doses of antioxidant vitamins and minerals in cardio-vascular diseases and cancers in a general population: "The SU.VI.MAX study". Design, methods and participants characteristics. *Control Clin Trials, 19*, 336-51.

Keim, D. A., & Kriegel, H.-P. (1996). Visualization techniques for mining large databases: A comparison. *IEEE Transactions on Knowledge and Data Engineering, 8*(6).

Keller, P. R., & Keller, M. M. (1993). *Visual cues: Practical data visualization*. Los Alamitos: IEEE Computer Society Press.

Lamping, J., Rao, R., & Pirolli, P. (1995). A focus + context technique based on hyperbolic geometry for visualizing large hierarchies. In *Proceedings of ACM Human Factors in Computing Systems (CHI'95)* (pp. 401-408).

Larkin, S., Grant, A., & Hewitt, W. T. (1997). Libraries to support distributed processing of visualization data. *Future Generation Computer Systems* (Special Issue HPCN 96), *12*(5), 431-440.

Macedo, M., Cook, D., & Brown, T. J. (2000). Visual data mining in atmospheric science data. *Data Mining and Knowledge Discovery, 4*(1), 69-80.

Mackinlay, J. D. (1986). Automating the design of graphical presentations of relational information. *ACM Transaction on graphics, 5*(2), 110-141.

Nagel, H. R., Vittrup, M., Granum, E., & Bovbjerg, S. (2003, November). Exploring non-linear data relationships in VR using the 3D visual data mining system. In *Proceedings of the International Workshop on Visual*

Data Mining, in Conjunction With The Third IEEE International Conference on Data Mining, Melbourne, Florida.

Nocke, T., & Schumann, H. (2004, March 29-31). *Goals of analysis for visualization and visual data mining tasks.* CODATA Prague Workshop, Information Visualization, Presentation, and Design.

Pickett, R. M., & Grinstein, G. G. (1988). Iconographics displays for visualizing multidimensional data. In *Proceedings of the IEEE Conference on System, Man, and Cybernetics* (pp 514-519).

Proctor, G., & Winter, C. (1998). Information flocking: Data visualisation in virtual world using emergent behaviours, *Virtual Worlds '98*, 1-9.

Schneiderman, B. (1996). The eyes have it: A task by data type taxonomy for information visualizations. In *Proceedings of IEEE Symposium on Visual Languages 96* (pp 336-343). IEEE Computer Soc. Press.

Schumann, H., & Urban, B. (1997). Evaluation of marine data by visual means. In *Proceedings of the 8th Eurographics Workshop on Visualization in Scientific Computing* (pp. 87-95).

Sparacino, F., DeVaul, R., Wren, C., MacNeil, G., Daveport, G., & Pentland, A. (1999). City of news. In *SIGGRAPH 99, Visual Proceedings, Emerging Technologies.* Los Angeles, CA.

Symanzik, J., Ascoli, G. A., Washington, S. S., & Krichmar, J. L. (1999). Visual data mining of brain cells. *Computing Science and Statistics, 31*, 445-449.

Symanzik, J., Cook, D., Kohlmeyer, B.D., & Cruz-Neira, C. (1996). Dynamic statistical graphics in the CAVE virtual reality environment. *Dynamic Statistical Graphics Workshop*, Sydney, Australia.

Thearling, K, Becker, B., DeCoste, D., Mawby, B., Pilote, M., & Sommerfield, D. (1998). Visualizing data mining models. In *Proceedings of the Integration of Data Mining and Data Visualization Workshop.* Springer Verlag.

Unwin, A. (2000). Visualisation for data mining. *International Conference on Data Mining, Visualization and Statistical System*, Seoul.

Ware, C., & Glenn, F. (1994). Viewing a graph in a virtual reality display is three times as good as a 2d diagram. In *Proceedings of 1994 IEEE Visual Languages* (pp. 182-183). IEEE.

Wegman, E. J., Luo, Q., & Chen, J. X. (1998). Immersive methods for exploratory analysis, *Computing Science and Statistics, 29*(1), 206-214.

Wise, J. A., Thomas, J., Pennock, K., Lantrip, D., Pottier, M., Schur, A., & Crow, V. (1995). Visualizing the Nonvisual: Spatial Analysis and Interaction with Information From Text Documents. In *Proceedings of IEEE Information Visualization 1995* (pp. 51-58). IEEE Computer Soc. Press.

Wiss, U., & Carr, D. (1998). *A cognitive classification framework for 3-Dimensional information visualization* (Research report LTU-TR-1998/4-SE). Lulea University of Technology, 1998.

Wong, P. C., & Bergeron, R. D. (1997). 30 years of multidimensional multivariate visualization. *Scientific Visualization: Overview, Methodologies, Techniques.* IEEE Computer Society Press.

Zamir, O. (1998, September). *Visualization of search results in document retrieval systems: General examination.* Department of Computer Science and Engineering, University of Washington.

Chapter XII

Mining in Music Databases

Ioannis Karydis, Aristotle University of Thessaloniki, Greece

Alexandros Nanopoulos, Aristotle University of Thessaloniki, Greece

Yannis Manolopoulos, Aristotle University of Thessaloniki, Greece

Abstract

This chapter provides a broad survey of music data mining, including clustering, classification and pattern discovery in music. The data studied is mainly symbolic encodings of musical scores, although digital audio (acoustic data) is also addressed. Throughout the chapter, practical applications of music data mining are presented. Music data mining addresses the discovery of knowledge from music corpora. This chapter encapsulates the theory and methods required in order to discover knowledge in the form of patterns for music analysis and retrieval, or statistical models for music classification and generation. Music data, with their temporal, highly structured and polyphonic character, introduce new challenges for data mining. Additionally, due to their complex structure and their subjectivity to inaccuracies caused by perceptual effects, music data present challenges in knowledge representation as well.

Introduction

Musical analysis is recognised as a significant part of the study of musical cognition. The analysis of music data has the objective of determining the fundamental point of contact between mind and musical sound (musical perception) (Bent, 1980). Musical analysis is the activity musicologists are engaged in and is conducted on a single piece of music, on a portion or element of a piece or on a collection of pieces. This research area embays the field of *music data mining* (henceforth called *music mining*), which deals with the theory and methods of discovering knowledge from music pieces and can be considered as a collection of (semi-) automated methods for analysing music data.

Following music-mining methodologies, music analysts extract[1] recurring structures and their organisation in music pieces, trying to understand the style and techniques of composers (Rolland & Ganascia, 2002). However, the size and peculiarities of music data may become prohibitive factors for the aforementioned task. This represents an analogy to the difficulties faced by data analysts when trying to discover patterns from databases, i.e., the huge database sizes and the large number of dimensions, which are the very reasons that paved the way for the development of *database mining,* a.k.a. *data mining* or *knowledge discovery from databases (KDD)*. Despite the previously mentioned analogy between music mining and database mining, the nature of music data requires the development of radically different approaches. In the sequel to this section we will summarise the particular challenges that music mining presents.

Another key issue in which music mining differs from other related areas (for instance, database mining or Web mining) is the applications it finds. Discovered patterns from relational or other types of databases are usually *actionable*, in the sense that they may suggest an action to be taken. For instance, association rules from market-basket data may indicate an improvement in selling policy, or user-access patterns extracted from a Web-log file may help in redesigning the Web site. Such kinds of "actionability" are related to a form of "profit" and stem from the involved industry field (e.g., retail, insurance, telecommunications, etc.). The question, therefore, emerges: "Which is the usability of patterns extracted from music data?" In order to answer this question, one has to consider the current status of the involved industry, that is, the "music industry." The influence that music has always had on people is reflected in music commodities and services that are offered today.[2] The annual gains of the music industry are estimated to reach up to several billion dollars (Leman, 2002). Within this context, the music content is a source of economical activity. This is intensified by the ease that the Web has brought in the delivery of music content; a prominent example of this case is Napster. What is, thus, becoming of significant interest is the need for content-based searching within music collections, e.g., by using a Karaoke machine to retrieve similar songs over a Web site or by humming over a mobile phone to download a song. The corresponding research field that has been developed is called *content-based music information retrieval* (CBMIR) (Lippincott, 2002; Pfeiffer, Fischer, & Effelsberg, 1996).

It is natural, therefore, to anticipate that music mining finds applications in designing effective CBMIR systems. In fact, CBMIR has considerably biased the directions that research in music mining is now following by stating the objectives to be achieved. The contribution of music mining in CBMIR is better understood by considering that the extracted patterns describe and represent music content at different abstraction levels (e.g., by producing concept taxonomies). The description of music content with such representations helps users in posing queries using content descriptors (rational or emotional), which drastically improve the effectiveness of retrieval in CBMIR systems (Leman, 2002), compared to simplistic search using plain text descriptors like song titles or the composers' names. Additionally, searching times are decreased, since the extracted patterns constitute a more compact representation of music content. The advantages from both the aforementioned directions are evident in a broad range of commercial domains, from music libraries to consumer oriented e-commerce of music (Rolland & Ganascia, 2002).

The Challenges of Music Data Mining

Byrd and Crawford (2002) list several reasons for which it is difficult to manage music data. Since most of these issues are inherent in music data due to their nature, they also affect the process of music data mining. In particular, among the most significant problems and difficulties that arise in data mining, are:

(a)   the identification of meaningful musical units;

(b)   the simultaneity of independent voices (denoted as polyphony);

(c)   the fact that patterns are repeated approximately and not exactly (due to variations and ornamentation posed by composers);

(d)   discrepancies (denoted as "errors") caused by differences between performances;

(e)   the large size of music data, which burdens scalability; and

(f)   the non-existence of trivial ways to incorporate background knowledge.

The aforesaid issues, along with references to solutions provided for them, are detailed in the following.

The most basic difficulty stems from the fact that it has not been clear so far how to automatically segment music data into meaningful units, like music *phrases* or *motives*. In order to be able to extract patterns, it is reasonable to desire the representation of music in such units, in the way that text mining considers words as units of text data that are used for pattern searching[3]. Although the difficulty is larger for acoustic representations of music, it is not easy to detect basic units in symbolic representation as well (for representation types, see the following section on music databases). The problem is further intensified by considering that there exists an amount of overlap between music units; one such case is due to polyphony. A number of research works (Chai & Vercoe, 2003; Temperley, 2001; Meredith, 2003) have diversely addressed this issue.

Polyphony is an additional source of difficulties. For simplicity, initial attempts in music mining focused on symbolic representation of monophonic music. Polyphony, however, is present in almost all real works of music. The difficulty arises from the fact that it is required to separate simultaneous independent voices in order to distinguish them, in the same way that one separately recognises the lines of each character in a play. This problem is considered as the most intractable and can significantly impact the quality of the analysis (Byrd & Crawford, 2002), as music phrases may appear audibly only few times while occuring frequently in the music score (e.g., buried within repeated chords). Different approaches (Pickens, 2001; Liu, Wu, & Chen, 2003) have been proposed in literature in order to address polyphony.

Repetition of occurrence signals a pattern in almost all mining fields (database, web, or text mining). However, in all these fields, patterns are repeated *exactly*. In music mining, one should not focus on exact repetition of patterns, due to *variation* and *ornamentation* that are present in music data (Rolland & Ganascia, 2002). Therefore, algorithms searching for music patterns such as Cambouropoulos et al. (1999) and Clifford and Iliopoulos (2004, see section *Methods for MIDI Representation*) should take into account this peculiarity as well.

Data quality is a factor that is taken into account by all mining fields. Data cleansing methods are used to avoid the discovery of patterns that will lead to pitfalls. Therefore it comes at no surprise that music data are very prone to errors, since there is very little quality control publicly available (Byrd & Crawford, 2002). However, music data have an additional source of "error," which is the result of differences in performance-related characteristics; differences in key, tempo, or style cause different instantiations of an identical musical score. These factors have to be additionally taken into account when searching for patterns.

All the aforementioned issues concern the effectiveness of the music mining process. Another important aspect is efficiency. Music databases tend to be large, both due to the large number of music pieces they contain and the large size of each piece. The objective is, therefore, to develop scalable algorithms for music mining. It is worth noticing that many existing approaches are influenced from *soft-computing* methodologies. Soft computing methodologies involve fuzzy sets, neural networks, genetic algorithms, rough sets and hybridizations. These methodologies opt for providing approximate solutions at low cost, thereby speeding up the process (Mitra, Pal, & Mitra, 2004). Although there have been attempts to provide solutions for very large databases (e.g., in the field of neural networks), in general, the problem of scalability to extremely large database sizes is still a challenging issue (Mitra, Pal, & Mitra, 2004). Moreover, algorithms for finding repeating patterns are confined to main-memory resident data. Hence, another challenge is to develop algorithms for disk-resident data.

Finally, it must be argued that although the incorporation of background knowledge in the mining process is considered important, it is generally a vague issue. It seems that domain-specific knowledge in music mining is *sine qua non*. What is, therefore, required is the systematic development of methods to incorporate this knowledge in the music mining process, a task that is very hard to consider.

Chapter Outline

In what follows this chapter, we summarise existing work on music mining. First, we give the necessary background on music databases. Next, we examine the task of similarity searching, which has attracted significant attention in research related to CBMIR. Similarity searching in music mining is of high importance, as it serves as a primitive for more complex undertakings. In the two sections that follow, we study methods for clustering and classification of music data. Clustering methods are for unsupervised learning, whereas supervised learning methods have been mainly used for tasks such as genre classification. Next, we move on to examine algorithms for detecting repeating patterns, and we also discuss the special issue of theme finding. In the final section, we conclude this chapter and present the perspective of music mining.

Music Databases

It is only in the last decade that large scale computer-based storage of sound and music has been possible. Additionally, the increasing ease of distribution of music in computer files over the Internet gave further impulse to the development of digitised music databases as well as to new methods for music information retrieval (MIR) in these collections.

Initial efforts for information retrieval (IR) in music databases relied on the well-studied text IR, that is, on the metadata of the music objects (title, composer, performer, genre, date, etc. — see the extension of the mp3 format, called ID3-Tag, for an example). Although abundantly used, even nowadays, the traditional metadata of a music object give rather minimal information about the actual content of the music object itself. Moreover, metadata in most cases are manually maintained, therefore this process is notoriously time consuming. On the other hand, queries based on humming (using a microphone) or on a small piece of a musical file, are a more natural approach to MIR. These types of queries lie within the CBMIR. In CBMIR, an actual music piece is required in order to compare its content with the content of the music pieces already available in the database.

Music Data Representation and Format Conversion

Music is available in two basic representations: the symbolic representation (MIDI, humdrum format) and the acoustic representation (audio format — wav, mp3, wma, etc.). Their key difference lies in the fact that the family of symbolic representations carries in their objects information of what a musical player should perform, whereas the acoustic representations comprise a specific recorded performance of a music piece. In other words, the term "music" encompasses both performance directions as well as resulting sounds.

The symbolic representation can further be separated into two classes, according to the targeted performer. Thus, there exist symbolic representations aimed at digital devices such as the MIDI and humdrum formats as well as human-oriented symbolic representations that are collectively referred to as conventional music notation (CMN).

A MIDI (MIDI is the musical instrument digital interface specification) object consists of predefined "events" that are quantified factors that define a musical performance (Owen, 2000). Typical events include the notes to be played, the time instance and the force these notes should be played and the type of instrument playing them, just to name a few. Following the high detail an event may contain, a MIDI object can quite accurately describe a music performance and thus its use is rather popular, especially for classical music playback. Additionally, the MIDI format is also used in order to communicate music between digital devices since it is codified[4] and has wide acceptance, thus offering interoperability between different types of music-aware devices.

CMN commonly includes numerous features that are not defined in the MIDI protocol, such as rests, slurs, barlines, triplets and chromatisms. O'Maidin and Cahill (2001) propose a complex object framework that serves as a container for a collection of objects modelled for music scores as well as iterators for use with

Figure 1. Time domain representation of a signal

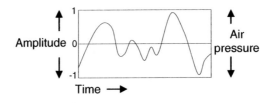

the algorithms available, the C.P.N.View (common practice notation view). C.P.N.View is a class library for representing musical scores in a form suitable for arbitrary processing. Another approach for a score-based music representation is presented by Hoos et al. (1998), which utilises the GUIDO Music notation. The GUIDO music notation format is a novel, general purpose formal language for representing score level music in human-readable way.

Music in the acoustic representation consists of a time-series of sampled signal amplitude values. These values represent the air pressure changes created by the music source that propagate from the source (e.g., loudspeaker or violin) to the listener's ears as air pressure fluctuations. A very simple method of illustration of acoustical signals is to draw these signals as a graph of air pressure versus time (Figure 1). In that case, the representation of the acoustical signal is called time-domain representation and the amplitude of the waveform is the amount of air pressure change (Roads, 1996)

Since the conversion of symbolic music to and from CMN is generally admitted to be easy, in this section interest is focuses on the process of analysing music in the acoustic representation, so as to identify the elements that constitute the piece of music in question (Klapuri, 2004). This process is known as music transcription. The notation utilised for the symbolic representation of the acoustic format can be any symbolic representation offering sufficient information for the transcribed piece to be performed.

Although skilled musicians are able to perform music transcription with high success (Klapuri, 2004), computer music transcription is generally admitted to be very difficult and poorly performing (Yang, 2002; Pickens, 2004). The performance of the computer systems degrades even more when the transcribed music piece is polyphonic. A polyphonic music piece (see Figure 2), for the purposes of this work, refers to a music piece wherein at any time instance, more than one sound may occur — that is, more than one voice, or, in simple terms, more than one note, at a time. In contrast, in a monophonic score only one voice/note is playing at any time (see Figure 2).

Figure 2. An example of a monophonic, homophonic and polyphonic music piece.

The last 10 years of research in polyphonic music transcription brought a great deal of knowledge to the area, though no generally applicable all-purpose system exists. The latest proposals presented a certain degree of accuracy in limited complexity polyphonic music transcription (Davy & Godsill, 2003; Bello, 2003). Their common limitations include as prerequisites, for acceptable performance, a specific number of concurrent sounds and absence of percussive instruments.

Despite the unfavourable research template, a small number of commercial approaches to a music transcription system have been available (AKoff, 2001; Arakisoftware 2003, Innovative 2004; Seventh, 2004)[5], though their performance is rather poor as far as accuracy is concerned (Klapuri, 2004).

Synopsis of the Process for Knowledge Extraction in Music Databases

Having described how music databases are being organized, we now move on to examine the whole process of knowledge extraction. In general, the process of knowledge discovery in databases (KDD process) refers to the broad process of finding knowledge in data, while connoting the "high-level" application of particular data mining methods. Analogously, in music databases, the unifying goal of the KDD process is to extract knowledge from music data in the context of large music databases. This objective is achieved by using music data mining algorithms that extract what is deemed knowledge, according to the specifications of measures and thresholds and using a database along with any required pre-processing, sub-sampling and transformations of that database. The overall KDD process has been established during previous years to contain the stages that are illustrated in Figure 3. In summary, we can identify three main parts in the process: the pre-processing of music data, the core-mining step and the post-processing of mined knowledge.

In the context of music data mining, the aforesaid three main parts are instantiated as follows. Regarding pre-processing, in related research most of

Figure 3. Overview of steps constituting the KDD process (Fayyad, Piatetsky-Shapiro & Smyth,1996)

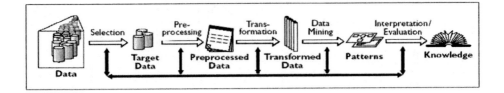

the effort has been attracted by methods for feature extraction and selection. Also related to this part is the research on music database indexing, which can improve the effectiveness and efficiency of the selection stage (see Figure 3). The core-mining part involves several methods that have been adapted from other data mining areas. But, due to peculiarities of music data, several other, novel methods have been developed as well. Finally, although the post-processing part is inextricable in the KDD process, in music data mining it has received relatively less attention compared to other data mining areas. In the remainder of this chapter we elaborate further on the first two parts, and give examples and methods for the problems that have been examined in recent research.

Concluding this discussion, it is useful to contemplate a sample scenario on the KDD process in music databases. Assume a music analyst who has a database of pop, rock and heavy metal songs from the years 1970 to 2000. As an initial step, the analyst performs a selection of all songs from the 1980s decade. Next, he or she selects as features the timbre, pitch and rhythm. For the core-mining, he or she selects a classification algorithm that has been adapted for genre classification. The outcome of this process seeks to characterize the selected songs according to their genre.

Music Features

Music consists of numerous features. Among them, pitch, rhythm, timbre and dynamics are considered to be the most semantically important ones (Byrd & Crawford, 2002). For western music in particular, pitch carries the highest relative weight of information followed by rhythm (Byrd & Crawford, 2002).

For the MIR process to perform matching algorithms on the music data, descriptions of these features for the music data are necessary. Thus, the previously mentioned representations require a conversion from their original format to the format defined by each MIR system. The conversion process is also known as feature extraction. The selection of features to be conversed by

Figure 4. Feature extraction process for (a) acoustic and (b) symbolic music pieces

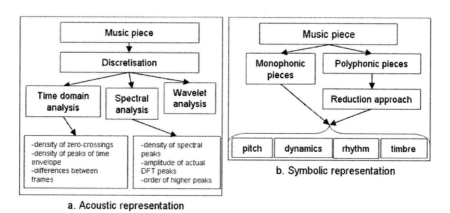

a. Acoustic representation

the feature extraction process is implementation dependent. That is, a variety of alternatives exist with respect to the music characteristics that should be included in the final format.

The feature selection and extraction process can be separated based on the representation of the music piece in symbolic and acoustic feature extraction, while the former can also be divided into monophonic, homophonic and polyphonic (see Figure 4).

Music in the form of acoustic representation requires special analysis in order to extract features such as pitch and rhythm, while the non-triviality of the problem is reflected by the number of methods developed. The key idea in this case is audio transcription to feature events. The most common features (Wieczorkowska & Ras, 2001) are the coefficients of time-domain analysis (Papaodysseus et al., 2001; Paraskevas & Mourjopoulos,1996), spectral analysis (Papaodysseus et al.; Paraskevas & Mourjopoulos, 1996; Kostek & Wieczorkowska, 1997) and wavelet analysis (Wieczorkowska, 2001).

Pitch detection[6] is dealt with via time-domain fundamental period pitch detection, autocorrelation pitch detection (see Figure 5a), adaptive filter pitch detection (see Figure 5b), cepstrum analysis and frequency-domain pitch detection. It should be noted that no pitch detection algorithm is totally accurate and some that appear to be, utilise music inputs that follow specific constraints or show increased computational requirements (non real-time). Key difficulties in pitch detection include attack transients, low and high frequency identification, myopic pitch tracking and acoustical ambience.

Figure 5. Pitch detection process with (a) autocorrelation and (b) adaptive filter

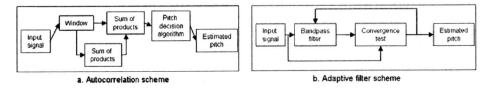

a. Autocorrelation scheme   b. Adaptive filter scheme

In the case of polyphonic acoustic signals, the complexity rises additionally, while attempts towards this direction usually apply frequency-domain analysis techniques within a fundamental pitch or strong harmonics selective mechanism.

Rhythm detection can be divided into three levels: low-level (event detection), mid-level (transcription into notation) and high-level (style analysis). As with pitch detection, rhythm detection is also inherently difficult due to inaccurate human performance of musical scores as well as the ambiguity of the music notation[7].

Moving on to music in the form of symbolic representation, feature extraction from MIDI-like music files is rather easier. The results of the transcription, the step of the acoustic representation feature extraction, are apparently already available in some form.

In monophonic music no note may sound until those currently sounding have finished; in homophonic music, simultaneous notes may start and finish sounding together, while in polyphonic music, a note may sound before a previous one has finished. Addressing homophonic and polyphonic music is achieved by reduction to monophonic and homophonic, respectively, and by modification of the methods utilised for monophonic music.

The problem of monophonic music symbolic feature extraction can be reduced to n-dimension by retaining only n different features of information described in the music file. Additional approaches include N-grams (e.g., sliding windows and repeating patterns) and shallow structure methods (Pickens, 2001) (e.g., statistical measures, lightweight computation and music theory analysis).

Monophonic reduction is an initial attempt to solve the problem of simultaneous notes sounding by selection of only one of the notes sounding in any discrete time. Accordingly, monophonic methods can be utilised for feature extraction from the received monophonic music. The key issue in monophonic reduction is the "representative" note selection method.

In homophonic reduction, instead of selecting only one note at each time step, all notes at each time step are retained and the reduction that occurs is assuming independence of overlapping duration notes (Pickens, 2001).

Finally, as a means of features that can be indexed, clustered and matched for similarity, research has used hidden Markov models (HMM). An HMM is a Markov chain, where each state generates an observation. One can only see the observations, and the goal is to infer the hidden state sequence. From the observable sequence of outputs, one infers the most likely dynamical system. The result is a model for the underlying process. Alternatively, given a sequence of outputs, the user infers the most likely sequence of states.

Hidden Markov models (HMM) have been extensively used in MIR. Numerous approaches (Pikrakis, Theodoridis, & Kamarotos, 2002; Shifrin, Pardo, Meek, & Birmingham, 2002; Velivelli, Zhai, & Huang, 2003) have utilised HMMs in order to represent music pieces in a database and the queries posed. In Pikrakis, Theodoridis, and Kamarotos (2002), a method for automated search of pre-defined sound patterns within a large number of sound files is presented, using HMMs. In Shifrin, Pardo, Meek, and Birmingham (2002), the authors use a stochastic representation of both music sequences in the system and the queries, with hidden Markov models in order to handle queries that contain errors or key and tempo changes. Velivelli et al. (2003) utilise HMMs that can model predefined patterns and simultaneously identify and match an audio segment for a given query.

Indices for Music Data

The selection of appropriate features is considered very important in multimedia information retrieval. Meaningful features not only help in the effective representation of objects but also enable the use of indexing schemes for efficient query processing.

As far as the symbolic representation is concerned, recent research proposed that features could be represented in string format and accordingly presented string indices (Hsu, Liu, & Chen, 1998; Lee & Chen, 2000; Chen & Chen, 1998; Liu, Hsu, & Chen, 1999). These approaches are not easily adopted for multiple features, lack data scalability for large music data (Lee & Chen, 2000) and generally their string matching proves slower than numeric matching (Lo & Chen, 2003). In order to address these inefficiencies, Lo and Chen (2003) proposed a multi-feature numeric indexing structure that transforms music feature strings into numeric values.

As already mentioned, the most common features of acoustic music are produced by time, spectral and wavelet analyses. The coefficients collected from each of these analyses can be indexed in TV-Trees (Lin, Jagadish, & Faloutsos, 1994), locality-sensitive hashing schemes (Yang, 2002) and S-Indexes (Dervos, Linardis, & Manolopoulos, 1997). In addition, Reiss, Aucouturier, and Sandler (2001) compare four different multidimensional indexing schemes for music data, the KD-Tree, the K-Tree, the multidimensional quick-sort and the box assisted method. The authors conclude that KD-Tree is significantly more efficient than the other methods, especially for high-dimensional data. Finally, the authors in Won, Lee, Ku, Park and Kim (2004) utilise an M-Tree in which a selection of features is stored, claiming thus a 65% gain in space requirements.

Difference from Other Database types

This section summarizes the differences of music databases from other structured or semi-structured ones. The term "semi-structured databases" has emerged to describe databases that have some structure but neither regular, nor known *a priori* (Abiteboul, 1997). It is precisely for this reason that most semi-structured data models are self-describing. Following this structure, musical data contain, apart from the main data corpus, textual metadata. A standard such protocol is the ID3-tag for mp3 files. Another emerging standardization effort in this direction is mpeg-7 (ISO/IEC, 2003), formally named "Multimedia Content Description Interface," which describes multimedia content. Nevertheless, we focus on research methods oriented towards the content, which refers to the unstructured data in music databases (for this reason, we use the term music database to refer to this unstructured part).

The aforementioned differences reflect also the methods that have been employed for data management. In particular, for indexing and querying semi-structured databases. Abiteboul (1997) describes several solutions which are very much different from the requirements and solutions that were presented in the previous section.

Relational databases could be involved in the process of managing music data, but only when abstract data types (ADT) are provided. This corresponds to an object-relational DBMS. In fact, such a system for managing sequences has been developed (Seshadri, Livny & Ramakrishnan, 1996). Although one may consider the option of storing MIDI sequences (or even acoustic ones) within such a system, the peculiarities of music data present very different challenges (for instance, as mentioned, very specialized indexing solutions have been developed for music query processing in contrast to the standard ones used by object-relational systems). For this reason, this direction has not been followed in related work.

Similarity Searching

As a result of the rapid developments in WWW, users are able to search for music information among various and large amounts of music data (this is especially popular within P2P systems). This reveals the need for development of effective similarity-searching methods for music data. Additionally, another significant area where similarity-searching is applied is CBMIR systems. Similarity searching in music data differs from searching other types of data in the following:

(a)   users may perceive in different ways the notion of similarity between music pieces;

(b)   the possibility of ad hoc nature in similarity-searching query posing (e.g., querying by humming), which brings the need for high tolerance against inconsistencies; and

(c)   the influence of data representation (symbolic or acoustic) on the designation of similarity-searching algorithms. The importance of similarity searching stems from its special role as primitive for other data mining tasks, like information retrieval, clustering and classification.

Perception of Similarity in Music Data

The stimuli received by a human observer lead to the experience of the event that produced these stimuli, through the interpretation process of the brain. The reception made through the five senses available to humans is the sole contributing channel of information. The final representation of the event that produced the stimuli in the human brain has little direct relevance with what the sensory transducers received, as it is subject to extended further processing by the brain (Shepard, 1999). Accordingly, cognitive psychology studies the final representation corresponding to the perceived stimuli.

Music, being a physical stimulus as well, is amenable to the very same extended-brain processing after being received by the acoustical[8] system. Thus, musical cognition is up to a certain degree subjective (perception ambiguity) while numerous preferred or habitual ways of music cognition/listening do exist.

Based on the Gestalt Laws of Grouping, a number of principles exist by which people organise isolated parts of a visual or acoustic stimulus into groups or whole objects. There are five main laws of grouping: *proximity*, *similarity*, *continuity*, *closure* and *common fate*. All of these laws fall under a sixth law, that of *simplicity*. Although Gestalt laws are usually applied to visual stimuli, their appliance in other senses, such as the auditory, is well known. According to the Gestalt laws, during the experience of music listening, humans do not hear a series of disconnected or random tones. Music is perceived as a whole by means of sound relation-based pitch similarity, time proximity and other factors. Music perception can lead to the identification of melodies, patterns and forms.

Recent work by McAdams et al. (2004) suggested that music similarity is determined based on surface features of the musical material. These findings are also supported by numerous previous works in the field. Additionally, the listener sensitivity to these features is not related to musical education, apart from the terminology used in order to express the similarity or difference. The work considers as surface features duration/rhythm, pitch/melody, timbre, gesture, texture, articulation and, to a lesser degree, dynamics and harmony, although, some of these features may be more or less overlapping.

Additionally, based on studies that have been conducted on what people attend to while detecting similarity, musicians initially observed dynamics, art, texture and then noticed pitch height and contour; non-musicians' attention was firstly drawn to dynamics and art, while texture and pace were subsequently noticed (Lamont & Dibben, 2001).

Musical recognition is greatly affected by the ability of the listener to detect different levels of similarity in different musical elements. Studies on response times in dissonant and consonant differentiation proved that distinguishing dissonant rather than consonant chords is faster, while musical training had a great effect in the number of correct responses (Bigand, Madurell, Tillmann, & Pineau, 1999). However, in experimentation in chord similarity perception, experience did not seem to have an effect on perception (Hubbard, 1996).

The mood or emotional atmosphere evoked when listening to a musical piece was revealed by McAdams et al. (2004) to be relative to musical similarity.

In the perception of musical emotion, timbre, tempo, pitch and rhythm are of critical importance. Fast tempos are regarded as happy and joyful, while slow tempos tend to be considered as sad or gloomy (White, 2004). A more or less similar effect appears with pitch, with high and simple pitches (melodies) producing a feeling of happiness, and lower and more complex pitches (melodies) sadness. The combination of rhythm and pitch is known to affect the degree a musical piece is scarring (Schellenburg, Krysciak, & Campbell, 2001; White, 2004).

Similarity Searching for Symbolic Data

Methods for MIDI Representation

In symbolic music data, the features of music are available in some form, as already previously mentioned, while their extraction reduces in n-dimensional strings of the desired n features. Accordingly, the current literature has long used string processing techniques and indices for similarity searching in symbolic music data. Research is oriented in both monophonic and polyphonic symbolic data.

A number of approximate string matching techniques for musical data, both monophonic and polyphonic, have been extensively studied (Clifford & Iliopoulos, 2004; Cambouropoulos et al., 1999; Crawford, Iliopoulos, & Raman, 1998). Despite the fact that approximate string matching has widely been utilised in various fields of computer science, the approximation methods were not devised for the peculiarities of musical data.

Optimal solutions for exact matching proposed by Crawford, Iliopoulos and Raman (1998) are the Knuth-Morris-Pratt and variants of the Boyer-Moore algorithms. As far as approximate matching is concerned, Clifford and Iliopoulos (2004) and Cambouropoulos et al. (1999) propose as optional the δ-, γ- and (δ,γ)-approximation. In δ-approximation "two strings p and t are δ-approximate if and only if they have the same length, and each value of p is within δ of its corresponding value in t" (Clifford & Iliopoulos, 2004). In γ-approximation, p and t must have equal length and additionally have a sum of absolute differences for corresponding values less or equal to γ. Finally, for p and t to be (δ,γ)-approximate, they must be both δ- and γ-approximate. The best complexity of these algorithms, in general, is $O(nm/w)$, with w being a computer word.

Another approach for approximate matching is δ-, γ-matching using fast Fourier transforms with respective complexities of $O(\delta n \, logm)$ and $O(\sigma n \, logm)$, σ being the size of alphabet. Additionally, δ-matching can also reduce into two instances of the problem known as *less-than matching* (Amir & Farach, 1995) with complexity $O(\sqrt{mn} \log m)$. In this case, for p and t we require all the values of p to be less than or equal to the corresponding ones in t.

String matching techniques have also been proposed for a number of other musicological problems, such as approximate matching with gaps, approximate repetitions and evolutionary chains detection (Iliopoulos, Lemstrom, Niyad, & Pinzon, 2002). In musical patterns, reinstatement with a certain degree of spontaneity or differentiation is rather common. Thus, searching for notes that do not appear successively is in some cases required. A gap size-bounded solution can be solved in $O(nm)$ time (Clifford & Iliopoulos, 2004). The problem of approximate repetitions is formulated as "Given a music sequence S, an approximate repeating pattern P is an approximate subsequence of S that appears at least twice in S." The exact repetition problem has $O(n \ logm)$ complexity and approximate δ-, γ- and (δ, γ)-matching solutions requires $O(n^2)$ time.

In order to address the issue of similarity in polyphony, two main approaches exist. The first method consists of polyphonic reduction to monophony or homophony and accordingly applies monophonic similarity algorithms, while in the second special design similarity algorithms are directly implemented on polyphonic data (Liu et al., 2003).

In the special design similarity algorithms for polyphonic data direction, the authors Clifford and Iliopoulos (2004), opting for exact match of a pattern occurring distributed horizontally in a sequence of notes, proposed the use of a modified shift-or algorithm with $O(|\Sigma| + m) + O(N)$ complexity, with $|\Sigma|$ being the number of distinct pitches, m the size of the pattern and N the length of original score. For the case of approximate matching, the same work suggests the modified Wu-Mamber algorithm, with approximate distance, defined using the edit distance for each character.

Research by Szeto et al. (2003) suggest the extraction of streams based on the musical perception theory that music is perceived in groupings. The proposed methodology separates each musical note according to pitch value and timing into event vectors and, following clusters, these vectors-producing streams. Thus polyphony reduces to the problem of clustering. In Doraisamy and Ruger (2004), the authors propose an n-gram construction with the use of sliding windows that include events made of pitches with the same or similar onset times. Pickens et al. (2003) deal with polyphony by ignoring all duration information for every note in the score, and then retaining at each new note onset all the notes that also begin at that onset.

Methods for CMN Representation

Most of the up-to-date research in MIR is concerned with music in acoustic and symbolic MIDI file representation. However, the symbolic representation, as already mentioned, includes music in the form of notation, especially CMN. The use of CMN is of great importance to music libraries and those musically trained. The number of musical pieces in music notation included solely in the U.S. Library of Congress is believed to be exceeding six million pieces (Byrd, 2001). Thus, the use of mechanical assistance in IR in these collections can be invaluable.

Of the many evolution-impeding reasons for the CMN MIR, its complexity, and consequently the complexity of the tools required to be built in order to process

CMN, as well as the unavailability of a standardised format of CMN are the most hampering.

Initial work on the field could only handle simple monophonic music (Maidín, 1998), while in some cases the query had to be in the acoustic format (Bainbridge,1998). Commercial applications have been available, such as Finale (www.finalemusic.com), that can perform searchs by content in CMN (though searching is limited in a single score at each time), as well as in finding the next match for certain Boolean criteria. The latest developments in commercial packages, such as Nightingalesearch (Byrd, 2001), have overcome the previously mentioned impediments, while offering matching based on pitch and/or duration with approximate matches under certain tolerance conditions. However, Nightingalesearch has numerous shortcomings, the most important of which is that the supported music files are proprietary of the Nightingale (AMNS, 2000) software.

Similarity Searching for Acoustic Data

In similarity searching in acoustic musical data, feature extraction from the music signal produces the required mapping in which similarity functions as well as speed-up indexing schemes operate.

Up-to-date related work on acoustic data-acoustic query, content-based MIR systems is limited. Yang (2002) proposes a spectral indexing algorithm for CBMIR. Its feature-extraction process attempts to identify distinctive notes or rhythmic patterns. The features are used to construct "characteristic sequences," which in the next step are indexed in a probabilistic scheme, the locality-sensitive hashing (LSH). The LSH scheme allows both false positive and negative matches, which are compensated in a later step based on the uniformity in time of music tempo changes. Experimental results indicate high retrieval accuracy for different similarity types. In Won et al. (2004), the authors propose a CBMIR system that is mainly oriented towards servicing different types of queries. The acceptable query types include audio files, common music notation as well as Query-By-Humming (QBH). The MIDI format is used as an intermediate music object representation. The selection of features is called "representative melody" and is registered into an M-tree structure, in which melodies are inserted based on their average length and pitch variation together with melody signatures representing the variation pattern. The used distance is a time-warping function. Preliminary results indicate a 65% gain in space requirements when using the collection of features instead of the whole melodies.

As far as the work in Won et al. (2004) is concerned, its main disadvantage is the assumption that the users' query must include at least one of the parts that they gather in order to create the "representative melodies." And as this might work for QBH, it might not for a random piece of music file included in the index, especially for a small one. In addition, polyphonic music transcription is known to be very difficult and poor performing (Yang, 2002; Pickens, 2004). Regarding the work in Yang (2002), its feature selection mechanism is oriented towards identifying different types of similarity in music pairs. Additionally, the selected features can lead to false negatives, which have to be addressed in a post-processing step. Finally, Yang (2002) uses a specialised indexing mechanism.

The approach proposed by Karydis et al. (2004) presents a feature extraction method based on the first few DFT coefficients of the audio file (sequence). The extracted features are grouped by minimum bounding rectangles (MBRs) and indexed by means of a spatial access method. Given a range query and some results, the authors present a false alarm resolution method that utilises a reverse order schema while calculating the Euclidean distance of the query and results in order to avoid costly calculations. Comparative evaluation to an already existing algorithm shows significant reduction in execution times. The proposed scheme does not introduce false negatives, according to the used similarity model, and, more importantly, it uses general purpose indexes (R-trees), which allow for a direct implementation in existing RDBMSs.

Similarity Searching Methods in P2P Networks

P2P systems are a rapidly developing area. Searching therein for music information[9] presents additional requirements in comparison to the customary client-server model. The size of the transferred data to propagate and resolve a query, the CPU burden produced at each peer to resolve a query as well as the underlying structure of the P2P network and the searching scheme adopted are some the most important facts that need be taken into consideration. In particular, even for compressed acoustic data (e.g., mp3 and wma) the traffic produced to solely propagate the query by a simple flooding algorithm is prohibitive. Thus, similarity searching in P2P networks preferably develops in more than one step, using various granularity samples. That is, when a coarse-grain (small size) representation of the query returns a match, only then does the querying peer send a more fine-grained (and larger in size) query. Additionally, acoustic data also require increased CPU processing in order to perform similarity functions. Since P2P networks typically consist of computers that are utilised otherwise than the P2P application alone, a CPU resource protection must exist in order to ensure that a queried computer is primarily allocating CPU according to its user's needs (Yang, 2003).

P2P networks can be classified based on the control over data location and network topology as *unstructured*, *loosely structured* and *highly structured*

(Li & Wu, 2004). Unstructured P2P networks follow no rule regarding where data is stored while the network topology is arbitrary (Gnutella). Loosely structured P2P networks do not have precisely determined data location and network architecture (Freenet). Finally, in highly structured networks, data storage and network topology are explicitly defined (Chord). What is more, P2P networks can also be classified according to the number of central directories of document locations: *centralised*, *hybrid* and *decentralised*. Centralised networks maintain a central directory in a single location (Napster), hybrid networks maintain more than directories in super-peers (Kazaa) while for the decentralised (Chord), no central directory is kept.

Karydis et al. (2005) study several similarity searching algorithms for acoustic data in unstructured P2P networks. The searching schemes that are being imposed include brute-force flooding BFS, quantitative probabilistic >RES (Yang & Garcial-Molina, 2002), qualitative ISM (Kalogeraki, Gunopulos, & Zeinalipour-Yazti, 2002) and numerous others (Li & Wu, 2004). In the case of the >RES algorithm, the query peer Q propagates the query q to a subset k of its neighbour peers, all of which returned the most results during the last m queries. Thus, searching for similarity initiates from the most probably larger parts of the networks and is followed by the algorithms discussed in the previous section according to the format of the music file. In the ISM approach for each query, a peer propagates the query q to the peers that are more likely to reply to the query based on a profile mechanism and a relevance rank. The profile is built and maintained by each peer for each of its neighbouring peers. The information included in this profile consists of the t most recent queries with matches, their matches as well as the number of matches the neighbouring peer reported. The relevance rank function is computed by comparison of the query q to all the queries for which there is a match in each profile.

In structured P2P networks, the common scenario of searching scheme is based on distributed hash tables (DHT). In such systems, each node is assigned with a region in a virtual address space, while each shared document is associated with a value (id) of this address space. Since in highly structured networks data storage and network topology are explicitly defined, a shared document is stored in the node with address space that the document's id falls within. Thus, locating a document requires only a key lookup of the node responsible for the key. Despite the great acceptance of DHT P2P networks (Chord, Pasty, Can, Koorde, Viceroy, etc.), hashing does not support range queries.

Clustering

Clustering in music data has contributed techniques to automatically organise collections of music recordings in order to lessen human documentation efforts. Therefore, clustering algorithms are used to detect groups between music pieces in cases where further information (e.g., genre, style, etc.) is not available or not required to be predefined, that is, data-driven categorisation of music styles.

Hierarchical Clustering

Hierarchical clustering is renowned for its usage in multidimensional dataset pattern detection. Analysis based on hierarchical clustering is a statistical method for identification of groups of data (clusters), which indicate relative homogeneity, on the basis of measured characteristics. The analysis begins with one piece of data put in a separate cluster and develops by iteratively combining clusters into broader ones, aiming at reduction of their number and finishing, should a desired quantity of clusters be reached.

There are two types of hierarchical clustering algorithms in order to build a tree from an input set S: the *agglomerative* approach (bottom-up) and the *divisive* approach (top-down). The former is the most common approach and the process begins with sets of one element that are subsequently merged until S is achieved as the root. In the latter, a recursive partitioning of S occurs until sets of one element are reached.

Recent work on hierarchical clustering for music databases by Lampropoulos et al. (2004) utilises acoustic data, while the extracted features are based on spectral analysis and tempo. In detail, the spectral features extracted are the mean centroid, mean roll-off, mean flux, zero-crossing and short-time energy. The metrics used therein are Euclidean distance and cosine distance. The clustering algorithm for n data points develops in four steps:

1. initially, each data point occupies a cluster of its own;

2. then, for a desired number of k clusters if the number of available clusters is k stop, else find the pair of clusters with the highest similarity value;

3. merge these clusters, decrease cluster number by one and re-compute the distances between the new cluster and all existing clusters; and finally,

4. repeat procedure from step 2, until all items are clustered into a single cluster of size n.

A variation of the hierarchical clustering approach is utilised in Hoos, Renz, & Gorg, 2001) in order to reduce search effort by purging some of the data that do not match the query, and more importantly, by identifying promising candidate data. This approach utilises a modified hierarchical clustering, resulting in a balanced tree where each node has up to 32 children. In order to additionally speed up the search within this tree, each node stored is assigned with three bit matrices, the entries of which indicate whether the transition probabilities in the probabilistic model for the cluster corresponding to that node exceed a specific value. The use of these matrices supports rapid selection of the most promising sub-cluster at each step at the internal nodes during the search. The introduction of the previously mentioned mechanisms serve in pruning large sections that cannot include an exact match (since the occurrence of transition probabilities are null) as well as guiding searches to promising candidate pieces as fast as possible.

Other Types of Clustering

The remaining categories of clustering, apart from hierarchical, consist of *k*-clustering (partitioning), self-organizing maps (SOM) as well as hybrid solutions. The target of *k*-clustering is the identification of the best set of k cluster centroids, assigning each instance to its nearest centroid, a process that additionally determines the structure of the partition. A SOM is a group of several connected nodes mapped into a *k*-dimensional space following some specific geometrical topology (grids, rings, lines, etc). The nodes are initially placed at random, while subsequent iterative adjustment occurs based on the distribution of input along the *k*-dimensional space.

The following are some prominent research works that fall within hybrid category previously mentioned.In work by Pienimäki et al. (2004) polyphonic music is segmented into phrases using initially a monophonic reduction that retains only the highest pitch notes and subsequently an existing melodic phrase algorithm. The hierarchical structure proposed therein is an amalgamation of *paradigmatic* (Cambouropoulos & Widmer, 2000) and *collection* (Eerola, Järvinen, Louhivuori, & Toiviainen, 2001) clustering. In paradigmatic clustering, each single document inserted is analysed in order to identify inner structure, while collection clustering attempts to cluster a given collection of documents. Initial clustering occurs at the pragmatic level, where variants of a common phrase are clustered together based on a similarity matrix, in which distances are measured by harmonic and melodic edit distances. Each document is described using adjacency lists, while each such list is associated with a document and stores results of paradigmatic and surface level analyses of the corresponding document. At the final step, clustering of the whole collection occurs using the adjacency lists.

Another interesting approach in music clustering is proposed by Cooper et al. (2003). The approach suggested therein is based on methods developed for segmenting still images. Initial time-domain analysis transforms the musical data into features, while similarity is based on the cosine distance. The pairwise similarity of all permutations of features for each music file is computed leading to a "partial time-indexed similarity matrix" (Cooper & Foote, 2003) for the detection of audio segment boundaries. The following step includes clustering of the calculated segments by means of similarity analysis, which consists of identification of time-separated repeated segments as well as cases of over-segmentation errors. Based on the segmentation boundaries, the full similarity matrix can be estimated. Then, segment clustering occurs based on singular value decomposition. The proposed scheme, instead of computing the full sample-indexed similarity matrix, orientates towards segment-level clustering, achieving CPU load gain.

Finally, Cilibrasi et al. (2003) propose a clustering scheme based on musical feature compression. The features utilised in Cilibrasi, de Wolf, and Vitanyi (2003) are note-on, note-off, average volume and modal note extracted from MIDI files. The average volume result stems from the average value of note velocity in each track, while modal note refers to the most often occurring pitch in each track. The similarity measure used (Li, Badger, Chen, Kwong, Kearney, & Zhang, 2001; Li & Vitanyi, 2001/2002; Li, Chen, Li, Ma, & Vitanyi, 2003) is based on Kolmogorov's complexity. In order to cluster the music data, the proposed method consists of computing a phylogeny tree based on the previously mentioned distance between any two music files. The sub-trees of the phylogeny tree constitute the clusters that are created based on closeness of objects stored therein.

Classification

Similar to clustering, classification aims at the purpose of grouping similar documents together. The main difference between clustering and classification is that clustering is a fully automated process requiring no preparation steps or maintenance; classification, on the other hand, generally requires manual, before execution specification of categories and updating these categories as new documents which are added to the collection.

Many different features can be used for music classification, e.g., reference features (title and composer), content-based acoustic features (tonality, pitch and beat), symbolic features extracted from the scores and text-based features extracted from the song lyrics. In this section we focus on content-based features and music genre classification. The latter concerns the classification of music from different sources with respect to genres in general, and styles in particular.

Classification with Content-Based Features

In content-based classification, physical features, such as pitch, duration, loudness and time/spectral domain features as well as perceptual features, such as timbre, its salient components and music properties humans perceive in sound are provided to the classification process. The output of a common classification engine may include retrieved music data similar to one or more of the supplied features, based on previous training of the engine on feature classes or by general similarity. Following are two cases of recent research on the area.

The proposed system by Wold et al. (1996) utilises as features loudness, pitch, brightness, bandwidth and harmonicity. Initially, n features are extracted from the music file producing an n-dimensional vector. The training of the system can either be done by directly defining constraints to the values of the feature vector, i.e., a specific value for pitch, or by supplying feature vectors and assigning them to a specific class manually. For each manually defined set of class, the proposed methodology calculates the mean vector and covariance matrix. Should a new audio file need be classified, its feature vector is calculated; while using the Euclidean distance, it is compared to the class's threshold in order to ensure the degree of similarity. In case of mutually exclusive classes, the newly inserted file is inserted to the class with which its distance is the smallest. In order to define the quality measure of the class, the magnitude of the covariance matrix can be used.

An alternative approach by Li (2000) is based on a classification method called the nearest feature line (NFL). The NFL utilises information provided by multiple prototypes per class explored, in contrast to the nearest neighbour (NN) classification in which the prototype is compared to each query individually. As far as the features used to represent the musical data, Li considers perceptual, cepstral as well as their combinations as features. The NFL's key steps are interpolation or extrapolation of each pair of prototypes belonging to the same class by a linear model and, subsequently, generalisation of the prototypes by the feature line passing through the two points. The feature line's role is to provide information about variants of the two sounds. Thus, the prototype's set capacity is expanded. The classification is achieved using the minimum distance between the query's feature point and feature lines.

Musical Genre Classification

Music can be divided into genres in many different ways, while a genre may contain myriad different styles. These classifications are often arbitrary and controversial, and, furthermore, closely related styles often overlap. Herein we present issues related to genres with respect to classification. In order to categorically describe music, one can use musical genres. Their ability in structuring vast amounts of music available in digital form is rather popular on the Web as well as on non-online collections, thus become important for MIR.

As previously mentioned, the process of genre categorisation in music can be divided into two steps: *feature extraction* and *multi-class classification*. During feature extraction, the system develops a representation of the music data to be classified that it will base on in order to perform the subsequent classification. The extracted features need to be musically coherent, *compact* in terms of size and *effective* in order to facilitate the classification.

Research reported on music genre classification is rather limited. Li et al. (2003) proposed the use of DWCHs as features (based on wavelet histograms) to represent music and classified them using the *one-versus-the-other* method. Tzanetakis and Cook (2001) proposed a comprehensive set of features for direct modelling of music signals and used them for musical genre classification using *k*-nearest neighbours and Gaussian mixture models.

In work by Deshpande et al. (2001), Gaussian mixtures, support vector machines and nearest neighbours are used to classify, based on timbral features, music into rock, piano and jazz. Finally, Soltau et al. (1998) proposed a music classification system using a set of abstract features utilising temporal structures, as well as their classification based on artificial neural networks.

Pattern Discovery

The discovery of a repeated structure in music data is a pivotal step in music analysis. Such structures play a crucial role in the understanding of the construction of a musical piece in terms of musical motifs and themes. A theme (especially in classical music) is a melody that the composer uses as a starting point for development, which may be repeated in the form of variations. Repeating patterns have been considered as *characteristic signatures* of music objects, which have the notion of a quantitative measure for music similarity (Crawford, Iliopoulos, & Raman, 1998).

Algorithms for Repeating Patterns Discovery

A motif is a minimum pattern that is meaningfully independent and complete within a piece of music. The variation extent within and the repetition frequency of a theme can differ depending on the composer and the type of music. Recent research has focused on searching motifs using methods that find repeating patterns in symbolic representations of music data (where the pitch information is selected as the main music feature). Given a music object S, a repeating pattern P is a subsequence of consecutive elements of S that appears at least twice in S (Hsu, Liu & Chen, 2001).

The mining of repeating patterns is described in Hsu et al. (2001), where two algorithms are proposed for the discovery of non-trivial repeating patterns and feature melody string. The first algorithm uses a correlative matrix for the extraction of repeating patterns (Hsu et al., 1998), while the second is based on a repeating string-join operation. Experimental results in Hsu et al. (2001) indicate the superiority of the latter algorithm towards the correlative matrix approach. Koh and Yu (2001) presented a means of mining the maximum repeating patterns from the melody of a music object using a bit index sequence as well as an extension for extraction of frequent note sequences from a set of music objects. Rolland et al. (2002) described an algorithm for the mining of sequential patterns in music data, which considers several peculiarities of music objects.

Nevertheless, the number of repeating patterns may be very large, a fact that burdens their examination by human analysts. Existing research has identified that among the collection of repeating patterns, the longest ones are those that can be characterised as feature melody strings and are typically those that can yield to themes. Karydis et al. (2005) proposed an efficient algorithm for finding the longest repeating patterns, which discovers them by using a fast ascending searching procedure, as far as the length of the patterns is concerned, so as to quickly reach the required patterns. Thus, this algorithm avoids the examination of a large number of intermediate patterns and only considers those patterns that are necessary in order to reach the maximum-length patterns.

Algorithms for Music Theme Discovery

Having argued in the previous section the efficiency and semantic quality of the repeating patterns as far as content-based music data retrieval is concerned, their use in indexing music sequences for the purposes of MIR (Hsu et al., 2001) comes as no surprise. Most importantly though, they provide a reference point for the discovery of music *themes* (Liu, Hsu, & Chen, A. L. P., 1999; Smith &

Medina, 2001). Themes, being the musical phrases most likely to be remembered by listeners, make a theme-index focus the search on the parts of the database most apt to match a query. Although, a theme should be identified by the previous section, the difficulty that arises is how to distinguish the theme of all repeating patterns discovered. To address this issue a number of theme-discovering algorithms that have been proposed and are subsequently presented.

Thus, as far as the use of repeating patterns in theme discovery is concerned, Smith and Medina (2001) proposed a pattern matching technique leading to theme discovery that is based on a collection of previously found longest repeating patterns. Meek and Birmingham (2001) identify numerous features that need to be extracted from each music object for the discovery of themes. Among them, they considered as most important the position of the theme (favouring the themes appearing earlier in the music object). As described, such features can be used for the discovery of themes from the repeating patterns found. In addition, an interesting web-based system for theme discovery is presented in Kornstadt (1998). Patterns may not only be in one voice (the case of polyphonic music), but as a pattern may be distributed across several simultaneously sounding voices. Iliopoulos and Kurokawa (2002) and Iliopoulos, Niyad, Lenstrom, and Pinzon (2002) present a number of different algorithms for the discovery of such patterns, including distributed pattern matching with at most, k-differences (motif evolution).

Summary and Perspectives

We have presented the most significant trends in recent research in the field of music mining. Similarity searching has attracted a lot of attention because it is related to CBMIR, the most prominent application of music mining. Due to peculiarities of music data, we paid special attention to issues regarding the perception of music. Next, we examined how well-known functionalities like clustering, classification and detection of repeating patterns have been applied in music mining. As described, music mining presents unique challenges; thus, the developed methods are quite dissimilar to existing ones from other mining fields.

The prospects of music mining, both in terms of research and applications, seem to be encouraging. Since it is relatively new a research field, it contains several open research issues. To name some important ones: methods for detecting meaningful music units, scalable algorithms (which will also consider disk resident music data) and tools for visualisation *and* audition (which are not required in other mining fields) of the extracted patterns. Music mining can and should expand to new application areas as well. To name some few:

(a)   Tracing of plagiarism and copyright protection, by using clever similarity searching that will disclose hidden reproduction of original music.

(b)   E-commerce of music. Attempts like iTune or iMusic may change the paradigm of how music is merchandised. We can envisage environments in which users can interactively search for individual music pieces and create their own compilations. For this task, a user can be assisted by music mining, which will help in finding the desired pieces and others pieces as well, which may be previously unknown to the user and different in terms of genre and style.

(c)   The relation with industrial standards. MPEG-7 is an example of an emerging standard, which tries to define a description of audio-based musical content. This can have an impact on the hardware industry as well, since manufacturers of recording devices (video cameras and DVD recorders) may want to include the functionality of automatic indexing of recorded music content (Leman, 2002). For all the above reasons, we believe that music mining will grow significantly in the forthcoming years.

References

Abiteboul, S. (1997). Querying semi-structured data. In *Proceedings of Conference on Database Theory* (pp. 1-18).

AKoff. (2001). AKoff sound labs, *AKoff Music Composer*. Retrieved from http://www.akoff.com/

Amir, A., & Farach, M. (1995). Efficient 2-dimensional approximate matching of half-rectangular figures. *Information and Computation, 118*, 1-11.

AMNS. (2000). *Nightingale*. Retrieved from http://www.ngale.com

Arakisoftware. (2003). *Arakisoftware AmazingMIDI*. Retrievable from http://www.pluto.dti.ne.jp/~araki/amazingmidi/

Bainbridge, D. (1998). MELDEX: A web-based melodic index service. In Melodic similarity: concepts, procedures, and applications, *Computing in Musicology*, 11, ch. 12, 223-230.

Bello, J. P. (2003). *Towards the automated analysis of simple polyphonic music: A knowledge-based approach*. Unpublished doctoral dissertation, Univ. of London.

Bent, I. (1980). Analysis. *Grove's Dictionary of Music*. London: Macmillan.

Bigand, E., Madurell, F., Tillmann, B., & Pineau, M. (1999). Effect of global structure and temporal organization on chord processing. *Journal of*

Experimental Psychology: Human Perception and Performance, 25, 184-197.

Byrd, D., & Crawford, T. (2002). Problems of music information retrieval in the real world. *Information Processing and Management, 38*(2), 249-272.

Byrd, D. (2001). Music-notation searching and digital libraries. In *Proceedings of ACM/ IEEE - CS Joint Conference on Digital Libraries* (pp. 239-246).

Cambouropoulos, E., & Widmer, G. (2000). Automatic motivic analysis via melodic clustering. *Journal of New Music Research, 29*(4), 303-317.

Cambouropoulos, E., Crochemore, M., Iliopoulos, C. S., Mouchard, L., & Pinzon Y. J. (1999). Algorithms for computing approximate repetitions in musical sequences. In *Proceedings of Australasian Workshop on Combinatorial Algorithms* (Vol. 3, pp. 114-128).

Chai, W., & Vercoe, B. (2003). Structural analysis of musical signals for indexing and thumbnailing. In *Proceedings of ACM/IEEE-CS Joint Conference on Digital Libraries* (pp. 27-34).

Chen, J. C. C., & Chen, A. L. P. (1998). Query by rhythm: An approach for song retrieval in music databases. In *Proceedings of Workshop Research Issues in Data Engineering* (pp. 139-146).

Cilibrasi, R., de Wolf, R., & Vitanyi, P. (2003). Algorithmic clustering of music. *The Computing Research Repository*.

Clifford, R., & Iliopoulos, C. S. (2004). Approximate string matching for music analysis. *Soft Computing*.

Cooper, M., & Foote, J. (2003). Summarizing popular music via structural similarity Analysis. In *Proceedings of IEEE Workshop on Applications of Signal Processing to Audio and Acoustics*.

Crawford, T., Iliopoulos, C. S., & Raman, R. (1998). String matching techniques for musical similarity and melodic recognition. *Computing in Musicology, 11*, 73-100.

Davy, M., & Godsill, S. (2003). Bayesian harmonic models for musical signal analysis. *Valencia International meeting* (Bayesian Statistics 7), Oxford University Press.

Dervos, D., Linardis, P., & Manolopoulos, Y. (1997). S-index: A hybrid structure for text retrieval. In *Proceedings of East-European Conference on Advances in Databases and Information Systems* (pp. 204-209).

Deshpande, H., Singh, R., & Nam, U. (2001). Classification of music signals in the visual domain. In *Proceedings of the COST-G6 Conference on Digital Audio Effects*.

Doraisamy, S., & Ruger, S. (2004). A polyphonic music retrieval system using N-Gram. In *Proceedings of International Symposium in Music Information Retrieval.*

Eerola, T., Järvinen, T., Louhivuori, J., & Toiviainen, P. (2001). Statistical features and perceived similarity of folk melodies. *Music Perception, 18,* 275-296.

Fayyad, U. M., Piatetsky-Shapiro, G., & Smyth, P. (1996). The KDD process for extracting useful knowledge from volumes of data. *Communications of the ACM, 39*(11), 27-34.

Hoos, H. H., Hamel, K. A., Renz, K., & Kilian, J. (1998). The GUIDO music notation format - A novel approach for adequately representing score-level music. In *Proceedings of International Computer Music Conference* (pp. 451-454).

Hoos, H. H., Renz, K., & Gorg, M. (2001). GUIDO/MIR: An experimental musical information retrieval system based on GUIDO music notation. In *Proceedings of International Symposium on Music Information Retrieval* (pp. 41-50).

Hsu, J., Liu, C., & Chen, A. L. P. (1998). Efficient repeating pattern finding in music databases. In *Proceedings of International Conference on Information and Knowledge Management* (pp. 281-288).

Hsu, J., Liu, C., & Chen, A. L. P. (2001). Discovering non-trivial repeating patterns in music data. *IEEE Transactions on Multimedia, 3*(3), 311-325.

Hubbard, T. L. (1996). Synesthesia-like mappings of lightness, pitch, and melodic interval. *American Journal of Psychology, 109,* 219-238.

Iliopoulos, C. S., & Kurokawa, M. (2002). Exact & approximate distributed matching for musical melodic recognition. In *Proceedings of Convention on Artificial Intelligence and the Simulation of Behaviour* (pp. 49-56).

Iliopoulos, C. S., Lemstrom, K., Niyad, M., & Pinzon, Y. J. (2002). Evolution of musical motifs in polyphonic passages. In *Proceedings of Symposium on AI and Creativity in Arts and Science* (pp. 67-76).

Iliopoulos, C. S., Niyad, M., Lenstrom, K., & Pinzon, Y. J. (2002). Evolution of musical motifs in polyphonic passages. In *Proceedings of Convention on Artificial Intelligence and the Simulation of Behaviour* (pp. 67-75).

Innovative (2004). *Innovative music systems intelliScore.* Retrievable from http://www.intelliscore.net/

ISO/IEC. (2003). *MPEG-7 overview* (version 9). Retrievable from http://www.chiariglione.org/mpeg/standards/ mpeg-7/mpeg-7.htm

Kalogeraki, V., Gunopulos, D., & Zeinalipour-Yazti, D. (2002). A local search mechanism for peer-to-peer networks. In *Proceedings of Conference on Information and Knowledge Management* (pp. 300-307).

Karydis, I., Nanopoulos, A., & Manolopoulos, Y. (2005). Mining maximum-length repeating patterns in music databases. *Multimedia Tools & Applications*. Manuscript submitted for publication.

Karydis, I., Nanopoulos, A., Papadopoulos, A., & Manolopoulos, Y. (2005). Audio indexing for efficient music information retrieval. In *Proceedings of International Multimedia Modelling Conference* (pp. 22-29).

Karydis, I., Nanopoulos, A., Papadopoulos, A., & Manolopoulos, Y. (2005). Evaluation of similarity searching methods for music data in peer-to-peer networks. *International Journal of Business Intelligence and Data Mining*. Manuscript submitted for publication.

Lin, K., Jagadish, H., & Faloutsos, C. (1994). The TV-Tree: An index structure for high-dimensional data. *The VLDB Journal, 3*(4), 517-542.

Klapuri, A. (2004). *Signal processing methods for the automatic transcription of music.* Unpublished doctoral dissertation. Tampere University of Technology, Finland.

Koh, J. L., & Yu, W. D. C. (2001). Efficient feature mining in music objects. In *Proceedings of Database and Expert Systems Applications* (pp. 221-231).

Kornstadt, A. (1998). Themefinder: A web-based melodic search tool. *Computing in Musicology, 11*, 231-236.

Kostek, B., & Wieczorkowska, A. (1997). Parametric representation of musical sounds. *Archive of Acoustics*, 3-26.

Lambropoulos, A. S., & Tsihrintzis, G. A. (2004). Agglomerative hierarchical clustering for musical database visualization and browsing. In *Proceedings of Hellenic Conference on Artificial Intelligence* (pp. 177-186).

Lamont, A., & Dibben, N. (2001). Motivic structure and the perception of similarity. *Music Perception, 18*, 245-274.

Lee, W., & Chen, A. L. P. (2000). Efficient multi-feature index structures for music information retrieval. In *Proceedings of Annual International Symposium Electronic Imaging 2000 Science & Technology* (pp. 177-188).

Leman, M. (2002). *Musical audio mining. Dealing with the data flood: Mining data, text and multimedia.* Rotterdam: STT Netherlands Study Centre for Technology Trends.

Li, M., Badger, J. H., Chen, X., Kwong, S., Kearney, P., & Zhang, H. (2001). An information-based sequence distance and its application to whole mitochondrial genome phylogeny. *Bioinformatics, 17*(2), 149-154.

Li, M., Chen, X., Li, X., Ma, B. & Vitanyi, P. (2003). The similarity metric. In *Proceedings of ACM-SIAM Symposium on Discrete Algorithms* (pp. 863-872).

Li, M., & Vitanyi, P. M. B. (2002). Algorithmic complexity. *International Encyclopedia of the Social & Behavioural Sciences* (pp. 376-382).

Li, S. Z. (2000). Content-based classification and retrieval of audio using the nearest feature line method. *IEEE Transactions on Speech and Audio Processing, 8*(5), 619-625.

Li, T., Ogihara, M, & Li, Q. (2003). A comparative study on content-based music genre classification. In *Proceedings of Conference on Research and Development in Information Retrieval* (pp. 282-289).

Li, X., & Wu, J. (2004). Searching techniques in peer-to-peer networks. In *Handbook of theoretical and algorithmic aspects of ad hoc, sensor, and peer-to-peer networks.* Boca Raton, Florida: CRC Press.

Lippincott, A. (2002). Issues in content-based music information retrieval. *Journal of Information Science,* 137-142.

Liu, C. C., Hsu, J. L., & Chen, A. L. P. (1999). An approximate string matching algorithm for content-based music data retrieval. In *Proceedings of IEEE Multimedia Computing and Systems* (pp. 451-456).

Liu, C. C., Hsu, J. L., & Chen, A. L. P. (1999). Efficient theme and non-trivial repeating pattern discovering in music databases. In *Proceedings of IEEE International Conference on Data Engineering* (pp. 14-21).

Liu, N.-H., Wu, Y.-H., & Chen, A. L. P. (2003). Efficient K-NN search in polyphonic music databases using a lower bounding mechanism. In *Proceedings of International Workshop on Multimedia Information Retrieval* (pp. 163-170).

Lo, Y. L., & Chen, S. J. (2003). The multi-featured indexing for music data. *Journal of Chaoyang University of Technology, 1,* 355-374.

Maidín, D. Ó. (1998). A geometrical difference algorithm. *Computing in Musicology, 11,* 65-72.

Maidín, D. Ó, & Cahill, M. (2001). Score processing for MIR. In *Proceedings of International Symposium on Music Information Retrieval.*

McAdams, S., Vieillard, S., Houix, O., & Reynolds, R. (2004). Perception of musical similarity among contemporary thematic materials in two instrumentations. *Music Perception, 22,* 207-237.

Meek, C., & Birmingham, W. P. (2001). Thematic extractor. In *Proceedings of International Symposium on Music Information Retrieval* (pp. 119-128).

Meredith, D. (2003). Musical grouping structure. *Lectures on Music Perception and Cognition*, Part II Module BMus/BSc in Music Department of Music, City University, London.

Mitra, S., Pal, S., & Mitra, P. (2004). Data mining is soft computing framework: A survey. *IEEE Transactions on Neural Networks, 13*(1), 3-14.

Owen, S.R. (2000). *On the similarity of MIDI documents*. Harvard University.

Papaodysseus, C., Roussopoulos, G., Fragoulis, D., Panagopoulos, Th., & Alexiou, C. (2001). A new approach to the automatic recognition of musical recordings. *Journal of Acoustical Engineering Society, 49*(1/2), 23-35.

Paraskevas, M., & Mourjopoulos, J. (1996). A statistical study of the variability and features of audio signals. *Audio Engineering Society*.

Pfeiffer, S., Fischer, S., & Effelsberg, W. (1996). Automatic audio content analysis. In *Proceedings of ACM International Conference on Multimedia* (pp. 21-30).

Pickens, J. (2001). *A survey of feature selection techniques for music information retrieval*. Technical report, Center for Intelligent Information Retrieval, Department of Computer Science, University of Massachussetts.

Pickens, J. (2004). *Harmonic modeling for polyphonic music retrieval*. Unpublished doctoral dissertation. University of Massachusetts at Amherst.

Pickens, J., Bello, J. P., Monti, G., Crawford, T., Dovey, M., Sandler, M., & Byrd, D. (2003). Polyphonic score retrieval using polyphonic audio queries: A harmonic modeling approach. *Journal of New Music Research, 32*(2), 223-236.

Pienimäki, A., & Lemström, K. (2004). Clustering symbolic music using paradigmatic and surface level analyses. In *Proceedings of International Conference on Music Information Retrieval* (pp. 262-265).

Pikrakis, A., Theodoridis, S., & Kamarotos, D. (2002). Recognition of isolated musical patterns using hidden markov models. In *Proceedings of International Conference on Music and Artificial Intelligence* (pp. 133-143).

Pickens, J. (2001). A survey of feature selection techniques for music information retrieval. In *Proceedings of International Symposium on Music Information Retrieval*.

Reiss, J., Aucouturier, J.-J., & Sandler, M. (2001). Efficient multidimensional searching routines for music information retrieval. In *Proceedings of International Conference on Music Information Retrieval* (pp. 163-171).

Roads, C. (1996). *The computer music tutorial*. MIT Press.

Rolland, P.-R., & Ganascia, J.-G. (2002). Pattern detection and discovery: The case of music data mining. In *Proceedings of ESF Exploratory Workshop on Pattern Detection and Discovery* (pp. 190-198).

Schellenburg, E. G., Krysciak, A. M., & Campbell, R. J. (2001). Perceiving emotion in melody: Interactive effects of pitch and rhythm. *Music Perception, 18*, 155-171.

Seventh (2004). *Seventh String Software, Transcribe!* Retrievable from http://www.seventhstring. demon.co.uk/

Shepard, R. (1999). *Music, cognition, and computerized sound: An introduction to psychoacoustics.* Cambridge, MA: MIT Press.

Shifrin, J., Pardo, B., Meek, C., & Birmingham, W. (2002). HMM-based musical query retrieval. In *Proceedings of ACM/IEEE-CS Conference on Digital libraries* (pp. 295-300).

Smith, L., & Medina, R. (2001). Discovering themes by exact pattern patching. In *Proceedings of International Symposium on Music Information Retrieval* (pp. 31-32).

Soltau, H., Schultz, T., & Westphal, M. (1998). Recognition of music types. In *Proceedings of the IEEE International Conference on Acoustics, Speech and Signal Processing.*

Subrahmanian, V. S. (1998). *Multimedia database systems.* San Francisco: Morgan Kaufmann Publishers.

Szeto, W. M., & Wong, M. H. (2003). A stream segregation algorithm for polyphonic music databases. In *Proceedings of International Database Engineering and Applications Symposium* (pp. 130-138).

Temperley, D. (2001). *The cognition of basic musical structures.* MIT Press.

Tzanetakis, G., Essl, G., & Cook, P. (2001). Automatic musical genre classification of audio signals. In *Proceedings of International Symposium on Music Information Retrieval.*

Velivelli, A., Zhai, C., & Huang, T. S. (2003). Audio segment retrieval using a synthesized HMM. In *Proceedings of ACM SIGIR Workshop on Multimedia Information Retrieval.*

White, R. E. (2004). Recognition and perception of whole-tone, natural minor, harmonic minor, and melodic minor scales. In *Proceedings of Southwestern Psychological Association.*

Wieczorkowska, A. (2001). Musical sound classification based on wavelet analysis. *Fundamenta Informaticae, 47*(1/2), 175-188.

Wieczorkowska, A., & Ras, Z. (2001). Audio content description in sound databases. *Web Intelligence: Research and Development* (pp. 175-183).

374 Karydis, Nanopoulos & Manolopoulos

Wold, E., Blum, T., Keislar, D., & Wheaton, J. (1996). Content-based classification, search and retrieval of audio. *IEEE Trans. Multimedia, 3*(3), 27-36.

Won, J.-Y., Lee, J.-H., Ku, K., Park, J., & Kim, Y.-S. (2004). A content-based music retrieval system using representative melody index from music databases. In *Proceedings of East-European Conference on Advances in Databases and Information Systems*.

Yang, B., & Garcial-Molina, H. (2002). Improving search in peer-to-peer networks. In *Proceedings of International Conference of Distributed Computer Systems*, 5-15.

Yang, C. (2002). Efficient acoustic index for music retrieval with various degrees of similarity. In *Proceedings of ACM Multimedia Conference*, 584-591.

Endnotes

[1] Rolland & Ganascia (2002) makes an interesting distinction between *pattern discovery* and *pattern extraction*. The former refers to the detection of local regularities in data. The latter also refers to such kind of detection, but is additionally concerned with the explicit availability of the patterns in some language, at the end of the mining process.

[2] To name just few: music sold as CDs, concerts, broadcasting of video-clips in mass media, advertised products related to music and music performers and, more recently, online sales of music in electronic format.

[3] Notice that when mining from relational or other highly structured data, this problem is not present at all, since units of information are well defined by the schema of the database.

[4] See: "The Complete Detailed MIDI 1.0 Specification," MIDI Manufactures Association, 1996.

[5] This list is by no means exhaustive. It merely presents a few of the latest systems.

[6] For a broader analysis readers are referred to Roads (1996).

[7] For a broader analysis readers are referred to Roads (1996).

[8] Acoustical pertains to the objective physics of a sound. For example, frequency is a physical or acoustical property, whereas pitch is a subjective or auditory property.

[9] Music information exchanged in P2P networks is customarily in acoustic format.

Chapter XII

Data Mining in Gene Expression Data Analysis: A Survey

Jilin Han, University of Oklahoma, USA

Le Gruenwald, University of Oklahoma, USA

Tyrrell Conway, University of Oklahoma, USA

Abstract

The study of gene expression levels under defined experimental conditions is an important approach to understand how a living cell works. High-throughput microarray technology is a very powerful tool for simultaneously studying thousands of genes in a single experiment. This revolutionary technology results in an extensive amount of data, which raises an important question: how to extract meaningful biological information from these data? In this chapter, we survey data mining techniques that have been used for clustering, classification and association rules for gene expression data analysis. In addition, we provide a comprehensive list of currently available commercial and academic data mining software together with their features. Lastly, we suggest future research directions.

Introduction

Recently, bioinformatics has attracted a lot of attention from biologists and computer scientists. One of the most important aspects of bioinformatics is the application of data mining tools to extract meaningful biological information from gene expression data. The study of gene expression levels at a given time or under established conditions is an important approach to understand how a living cell works (Vingron & Hoheisel, 1999). High-throughput microarray technology (Ramsay, 1998; Harrington, Rosenow, & Retief, 2000; Lipshutz et al., 2000; Jordan, 2001) is a powerful tool for simultaneously studying thousands of genes in a single experiment. This revolutionary technology results in an extensive amount of data, which raises a challenging question: how can meaningful biological information be extracted from these data? Important biological information associated with these data may not be discovered or may be misinterpreted due to lack of appropriate and effective data analysis tools and techniques.

Data mining is one of the most important and difficult tasks in gene expression data analysis. Data mining typically includes clustering, classification, and association rule discovery (Lin & Johnson, 2002; Wei, 2002; Johnson & Wichern, 1998; Mirkin, 1996). With extensive microarray data available, clustering can be used to identify genes that are co-regulated in a similar manner under different experimental conditions. Classification provides a way to identify the differences between tissue types such as between normal cells and cancer cells, which facilitates diagnosis of diseases. Discovery of association rules can help biologists to identify genes that govern the expression of other genes in regulatory pathways.

This chapter is organized as follows. First, a background on biology and microarray technology is presented. Then, we discuss the gene expression data characteristics and presentation. Following are reviews of the existing clustering, classification and association rules mining algorithms that have been applied to gene expression analysis. A comprehensive list of available commercial and open source data mining software with their features is then presented. Lastly, we suggest directions for future work.

Biology Background
and Microarray Technology

It is a challenging task for biologists to understand how genes and their products function, interact, and most importantly, cause an organism to function the way it does. Functional genomics plays an important role in accomplishing this task. The goal of functional genomics is to reveal the biological functions of an individual gene and its cooperative roles on a genome-wide scale. Microarray technology, such as the cDNA (Schena et al., 1995) and oligonucleotide microarray (Lipshutz et al., 1999) has emerged as a powerful tool to provide meaningful information about gene expression levels for entire genomes. To help users understand microarray experiments, in this section, we briefly introduce a background of basic molecular biology.

A deoxyribonucleic acid molecule (DNA) is a double-stranded polymer composed of four component "building blocks", called nucleotides. Each nucleotide consists of a phosphate group, a deoxyribose sugar, and a purine or pyrimidine base. The four different bases found in a DNA molecule are the purines, adenine (A) and guanine (G), and the pyrimidines, cytosine (C) and thymine (T). The two DNA strands are linked together by hydrogen bonds between purine and pyrimidine bases, with G always pairing with C, and A always pairing with T. A ribonucleic acid molecule (RNA) has the same general structure as DNA, except that uracil (U) replaces thymine (T), ribose replaces deoxyribose, and the RNA molecule is single stranded with extensive secondary structure, i.e., folds and loops.

A gene is a sequence of DNA containing genetic information that codes for a particular protein. A protein is polymer of twenty different types of amino acids in a sequence that is unique to the particular gene. The construction of the amino acid sequence of a protein comes from the genetic information stored in a DNA molecule (more precisely, a gene) and occurs in three stages (see Figure 1): (1) transcription, in which a section of DNA is transcribed into a single-stranded complementary copy of the DNA termed messenger ribonucleic acid (mRNA); (2) splicing, which occurs only in eukaryotes and removes certain stretches of the mRNA, called introns, leaving the remaining parts, called exons, that are then linked together to form the mature mRNA, and (3) translation, in which the nucleotide sequence of mRNA is translated on intracellular particles called ribosomes to produce a protein. The process of transcribing the genomic DNA sequences into mRNA, which serves as a template for protein production, is called gene expression.

Microarray technology makes use of genomic sequence information to determine what genes are expressed in a particular cell type, at a specific time, under

Figure 1. Transcription process

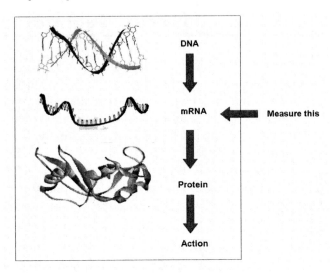

defined conditions. Typically, a microarray is a glass slide on which DNA molecules encoding genes are attached at fixed locations (spots). A microarray experiment (see Figure 2) includes the following five steps: (1) extracting mRNA from two biological samples, one is an experimental (target) sample and the other is a reference (control) sample; (2) labeling the experimental and reference samples with two different fluorescent dyes (Cy3 and Cy5); (3) hybridizing (through complementary base-pairing) a combination of target and reference samples to the DNA probes fixed on the microarray slide; (4) scanning the microarray slide with lasers that excite the dyes bound to each gene, causing fluorescent emissions which are captured by photomultipliers to generate an image of the microarray (see Figure 3); (5) imaging analysis, in which the image is processed with software that locates the probe spots and digitizes the pixel intensity data from the microarray image.

cDNA microarrays (Schena et al., 1995) and oligonucleotide microarrays (Lipshutz et al, 1999) are the two main technologies used to generate large-scale gene expression data. In cDNA microarrays, thousands of individual, gene-specific DNA sequences are printed in a high density array on a glass microscope slide, while in oligonucleotide microarrays, each gene is represented on the array by a set of oligonucleotides, typically 25 bases long. These oligonucleotides are designed to hybridize to unique regions of the genome. This approach greatly improves reproducibility, accuracy, and reduces the rate of false-positives and miscalls.

Figure 2. A typical microarray experiment

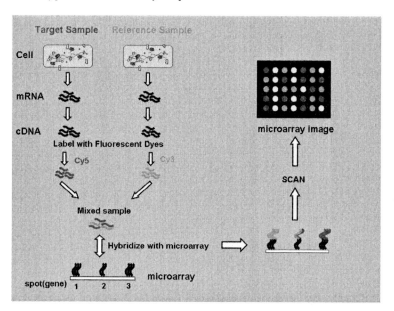

Figure 3. A microarray image

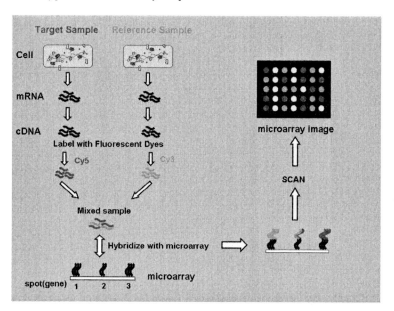

Gene Expression Data Characteristics and Presentation

In functional genomics research, microarray experiments may be carried out under different conditions such as different temperatures and pH values. Under different conditions, the gene expression levels may be different. Table 1 shows a typical example of microarray gene expression data with the transformation of

Table 1. Gene expression data for E.Coli

Gene name	condition 1 5°C	Condition 2 10°C	condition 3 15°C	condition 4 25°C	condition 5 30°C	condition 6 45°C	condition 7 50°C
htgA	-0.848	-0.901	-0.89	-0.514	-0.535	-0.713	-0.404
ykgD	-0.108	-0.057	-0.277	-0.01	0.3497	0.1664	0.2633
yahC	0.1353	-0.351	0.0877	0.3475	0.2842	0.1727	0.3075
caiD	2.4795	1.3399	0.6201	-2.371	-2.003	-2.091	-2.299
yahO	1.4965	0.9468	0.3781	0.0928	2.0444	2.9471	2.2334
folA	0.3958	0.874	-0.164	0.6942	0.9376	0.9048	0.5403
cynX	0.0409	-0.232	0.0219	-0.081	0.3363	0.3081	-0.03
polB	0.1473	0.0839	-0.027	0.3843	-0.073	-0.286	-0.199
mhpT	0.6821	0.7458	0.8537	-0.001	-1.021	-1.054	-0.615
leuC	0.3597	0.4084	0.2441	0.4791	0.3837	0.2013	0.2549

Table 2. Gene expression data for different cell types

Gene name	sample 1 normal cell	sample 2 cancer cell
htgA	-0.848	-0.901
ykgD	-0.108	-0.057
yahC	0.1353	-0.351
caiD	2.4795	1.3399
yahO	1.4965	0.9468
folA	0.3958	0.874
cynX	0.0409	-0.232
polB	0.1473	0.0839
mhpT	0.6821	0.7458
leuC	0.3597	0.4084

the logarithm of the ratio of red channel intensity (i.e., experimental sample) to green channel intensity (i.e., control sample). There are 10 genes listed in the first column. For each gene, the expression level may be different at different temperature. For example, the expression levels of a gene named *caiD* are 2.4795 at 5°C and -2.371 at 25 °C, respectively. In this case, we say that each column corresponds to a condition. Researchers may also conduct microarray experiments for samples of different cell types, let us say, normal cell sample and cancer cell sample. In this case, the gene expression data may look like those in Table 2. Each column represents a sample. These two cases can be abstracted to the form shown in Table 3.

Table 3. Gene expression data presentation for clustering and classification analysis

	Sample 1(Condition 1)	Sample 2(Condition 2)	....	Sample n(Condition n)
Gene $_1$	X_{11}	X_{12}		X_{1n}
Gene $_2$	X_{21}	X_{22}		X_{2n}
:				
Gene $_m$	X_{m1}	X_{m2}		X_{mn}

As shown above, even though the gene expression data essentially are numbers, they do have their own characteristics (described below) that need to be taken into consideration when data mining techniques are applied to them.

Characteristics of Gene Expression Data

1. Gene expression data may have many variances such as random errors (biosample variances due to different experiment conditions…) and systematic errors (efficiency of dye incorporation, variability in hybridization…) because they come from various sources. In order to remove these variances, the preprocessing step (transformation and normalization) has to be taken. This area has been a topic of continuing interest, but is beyond the scope of this chapter. Interested readers may refer to Quackenbush (2002) and Yang et al. (2002) for more information.

2. A high percentage of genes, termed constitutive (noise) genes, are unregulated.

3. Under different experimental conditions, the expression levels of noise genes have similar values.

4. Gene expression data can be analyzed in two ways. With n samples (conditions) and m genes, the expression profiles of the m genes can be analyzed as objects to be mined, with the n samples (conditions) considered as features. Alternatively, the n samples (conditions) can be analyzed as objects to be mined, with the expression profiles of the m genes considered as features.

5. Usually, the number of genes, m, is much larger than the number of samples (conditions), n.

Figure 4. The matrix of gene expression data

	condition 1	....					condition 7
htgA	-0.848	-0.901	-0.89	-0.514	-0.535	-0.713	-0.404
ykgD	-0.108	-0.057	-0.277	-0.01	0.3497	0.1664	0.2633
yahC	0.1353	-0.351	0.0877	0.3475	0.2842	0.1727	0.3075
caiD	2.4795	1.3399	0.6201	-2.371	-2.003	-2.091	-2.299
yahO	1.4965	0.9468	0.3781	0.0928	2.0444	2.9471	2.2334
folA	0.3958	0.874	-0.164	0.6942	0.9376	0.9048	0.5403
cynX	0.0409	-0.232	0.0219	-0.081	0.3363	0.3081	-0.03
polB	0.1473	0.0839	-0.027	0.3843	-0.073	-0.286	-0.199

Gene Expression Data Presentation

Formally, a set of genes can be viewed as a set of vectors $V = \{v_1, v_2, v_3, \ldots, v_m\}^T$, with each expression level of a given condition, x_i, being the components in the vector $v_i = \{x_1, x_2, x_3, \ldots x_n\}$, where m is the number of genes, and n is the number of conditions. Alternatively, a matrix (Figure 4) can represent gene expression data, with rows corresponding to genes and columns corresponding to conditions (Table 1). In a typical microarray experiment, the number of genes is in the range of several thousands to 100, 000, but the number of conditions/samples is much smaller than the number of genes, in the range of 10 to 100. The content of the matrix is the expression levels of each gene under each condition. These levels can be represented as absolute, relative or normalized.

Each column represents the results of different genes under the same condition, and each row represents the results of a particular gene under different conditions. Each measurement (X_{mn}) represents the log of $red_{mn}/green_{mn}$, where red is the test expression level, and green is the reference level for gene m in the n-th experiment. This data representation is often used for the clustering and classification analysis. But a transformation of this data presentation is usually used for association rules discovery such that rows correspond to conditions and columns correspond to genes.

Clustering Analysis

Clustering analysis is used to identify new subgroups or classes of biological entities. In clustering analysis, entities are partitioned into groups according to the features of each entity so that the groups are homogeneous (entities in the same cluster are highly similar to each other) and well separated (entities from different clusters have low similarity to each other) (Sharan et al., 2001). Similarity/dissimilarity is fundamental to the definition of a cluster; a measure of the similarity/dissimilarity between two patterns drawn from the same feature space is essential to most clustering procedures. It is most common to calculate the dissimilarity between two patterns using a distance measure defined on the feature space. There are many ways to compute the similarity/dissimilarity such as Euclidean distance and spearman correlation rank. To the best of our knowledge, there is no final conclusion about which one is the best choice. The most popular metric is the Euclidean distance.

With respect to gene expression data, clustering analysis can be divided into two categories: one-way and two-way clustering. In a DNA microarray experiment, expression levels of thousands of genes are recorded under a certain number of conditions or with a certain number of samples (see Table 1). Gene expression data can be used to perform clustering analysis in two different ways. Assume there are N samples (or conditions) and M genes. For one way, the N samples are considered as the objects to be clustered, while the M genes are considered as the features. For the other way, the M genes are considered as the objects to be clustered, each represented by its expression profile, while samples are considered as features. *One-way clustering* groups either genes or samples separately, while *two-way clustering* groups genes by taking the relationship between the genes and samples into consideration.

One-Way Clustering

Hierarchical Clustering

The hierarchical clustering algorithm (Johnson & Wichern, 1998; Mirkin, 1996) builds a dendrogram tree by computing distances of data elements, and then working from the ground up, the final clusters are obtained by cutting off the tree at different similarity levels based on biological knowledge. There are different methods to calculate the distance between clusters: the single-linkage, complete-linkage, and average-linkage. This distance is measured as the minimum, maximum, and average distance between all pairs of gene vectors drawn from the two clusters in the first, second, and third methods, respectively. These different ways of measuring the similarity between gene vectors will give different results. Currently, average-linkage is most commonly used.

Eisen et al. (1998) was the first to apply hierarchical clustering to gene expression data analysis. Similarly, hierarchical clustering was used to conduct the comprehensive identification of cell cycle–regulated genes of *S. cerevisiae* (Spellman et al., 1998). Iyer et al. (1999) analyzed the response of human fibroblasts to serum by using cDNA microarrays representing about 8600 distinct human genes. Zou et al. (2002) applied this technique to a novel large-scale profile of gene expression in the lung in allergen-induced pulmonary inflammation in non-human primates.

K-ary Clustering

K-ary (Bar-Joseph et al., 2003) clustering is a hierarchical clustering algorithm in which a K-ary tree is built. Every node in a K-ary tree contains at most K children. K clusters are grouped together if they are similar to one another. K-ary algorithm can handle noise and missing data.

K-ary clustering was used for the dataset from Neiman et al. (2001) and Eisen et al. (1998).

Self-Organizing Maps

The self-organizing map (SOM) (Kohonen, 1990, 2001; Jain et al., 1999) is an unsupervised clustering algorithm based on the neural network model. The SOM usually consists of a regular two-dimensional grid of map nodes. Each node of the SOM is associated with a d-dimensional weight vector that has the same dimension as an input vector. SOM was applied to the analysis of a subset of transcriptional profile of primary keratinocytes after UVB irradiation (Sesto et al., 2002), hematopoietic differentiation in four well studied models (HL-60, U937, Jurkat, and NB4 cells) (Tamayo et al., 1999), and the gene expression profiles of 144 primary tumors through the use of oligonucleotide microarrays (Ramaswamy et al., 2001).

Self-Organizing Tree Algorithm (SOTA)

Dopazo and Carazo (1997) and Herrero et al. (2001) introduced a new unsupervised growing and tree-structured SOM called the self-organizing tree algorithm (SOTA). The topology of SOTA is that of a binary tree. The principal advantages of SOTA (Dopazo & Carazo ,1997; Herrero et al., 2001) include: (1) clustering in a hierarchical structure with the capability of evaluating the relationships between clusters; (2) being the fastest hierarchical clustering algorithm; (3) having the ability to adjust the number of clusters; (4) not being sensitive to noise; (5) being scalable to handle huge amounts of data; (6) having linear time complexity with respect to the number of genes; and (7) clustering of both genes and conditions (samples).

The limitation of only two children for each node of SOTA causes the incorrect capture of the hierarchical relationship (Luo, 2003). This algorithm was applied to expression data of the yeast cell cycle (Herrero, 2001).

Hierarchical Growing Self-Organizing Tree (HGSOT)

To overcome the limitations of SOTA, Luo et al. (2002) proposed a new hierarchical growing self-organizing tree algorithm (HGSOT). HGSOT grows both vertically and horizontally. Vertically, HGSOT adds descendents, and horizontally, HGSOT adds siblings. This algorithm was applied to an existing 112 gene expression data set of the rat central nervous system (CNS) (Luo et al., 2003; Wen et al., 1998).

Dynamically Growing Self-Organization Tree (DGSOT)

DGSOT (Luo, 2004) algorithm has several important characteristics. First, DGSOT grows vertically and horizontally where after each vertical growth, a horizontal growth is followed. Second, a new cluster validation criterion, Cluster Separation (CS) based on the geometric characteristics of the clusters, is included. This cluster validation is carried out at each hierarchical level, which makes the DGSOT algorithm practically useful for larger datasets. Third, K-level up distribution (KLD) mechanism is used to correct the errors caused by improperly clustered in the early stage. DGSOT was applied to the yeast gene cell cycle gene expression profiles published by Cho et al. (1998).

Self-Organization Latent Lattice (SOLL)

SOLL "combines the topographic mapping capability of self-organization maps and the generative property of probabilistic latent-variable models" (Zhang et al., 2003). It analyzes the temporal patterns of multiple correlated genes by learning probabilistic lattice maps of the gene expressions, which can be used to find the patterns of temporal expression of multiple correlated genes. SOLL was applied to Spellman (1998) et al.'s microarray data sets consisting amplified genomic DNA of *S. cerevisiae* ORFs for cell cycle analysis.

K-Means Clustering

The K-means algorithm (Alsabti & Ranka, 1998; Faber, 1994; Kaufman & Rousseeuw, 1990) is a top-down clustering that starts with a pre-defined number of clusters and initial values for the centers of these clusters. It is based on the partition model. It divides a data set into predefined K clusters by minimizing the error which is defined by:

$$\sum_{j=1}^{K}\sum_{i=1}^{nj} \| x_i^{(j)} - c_j \|^2$$

where $x_i^{(j)}$ is the i-th gene vector belonging to the j-th cluster, and c_j is the centroid of the j-th cluster. The drawback of K-means clustering is that the resulting clusters are dependent on the initial value of K, and in practice, it is difficult to select the K value. Therefore, it is recommended to first run a principal component analysis to find an acceptable approximate K value for K-means clustering (Quackenbush, 2001).

Lo et al. (2003) generated approximately 3100 unique zebrafish cDNA clusters by applying K-means clustering to a cDNA microarray generated data set. Likewise, Ishida et al. (2002) applied K-means clustering to a large-scale microarray gene expression data set of an *in vitro* osteoclastogenesis system that consists of recombinant RANKL and mouse RAW264 cells. Also, Aronow et al. (2001) used K-means clustering to analyze microarray data that were obtained from gene expression profiles of four transgenic mouse models of cardiac hypertrophy.

Fuzzy K-Means Clustering

The K-means algorithm is "unable to identify genes whose expression is similar to multiple, distinct gene groups, thereby masking the relationships between genes that are co-regulated with different groups of genes in response to different conditions" (Gasch & Eisen, 2002). Gasch and Eisen (2002) used fuzzy K-means clustering to address this issue by implementing a heuristically modified version of fuzzy K-means. Unlike K-means clustering, where genes can belong to only one single group (cluster), with fuzzy K-means clustering, each gene may belong to every cluster, but with a variable degree of membership.

Gasch and Eisen (2002) implemented a heuristically modified version of fuzzy K-means clustering and applied it to published yeast gene expression data representing the response of yeast cells to environmental changes.

Fuzzy C-Means

Fuzzy C-means is proposed by Bezdek (1981). This algorithm requires the input of the number of the clusters, k, and the fuzziness parameter, m. Dembèlè and Kastner (2003) developed a method that allows the computation of the upper bound of the value of m, such that the m value can be chosen independent of the value of k. Fuzzy C-means was applied to serum data (Iyer et al., 1999), Yeast data (Cho et al., 1998) and human cancer data (downloaded from http://discover.nci.nih.gov/nature2000/).

Fuzzy J-Means Embedded Variable Neighborhood Search (VNS)

Belacel et al. (2004) developed an approach to embed the Fuzzy J-Means (Belacel et al. 2002) into VNS (Hansen & Mladenovic, 1977) whose basic goal is to proceed to a systematic change of neighborhood within a local search algorithm. VNS thus alleviates the problem of obtaining only the closest solution instead of the global one when fuzzy methods are applied to large datasets like microarray datasets. This approach was applied to human breast cancer data (Sorlie et al., 2001) and human blood data (Whitney et al., 2003).

GNG

Growing neural gas (GNG) (Fritzke, 1995, 1997) is a growing neural network clustering algorithm. GNG starts with two nodes that have random positions in the input space and a new node is inserted halfway between the two nodes that have the longest distance. The newly inserted node is connected with these two nodes by two edges, and the initial edge between the two nodes is removed. Wei (2003) applied this technique to analyze the gene expression data of *E. coli*'s 4,290 genes under eight conditions for the purpose of identifying unknown genes involved in the acid tolerance response (ATR) of *E. coli*, which is regulated by the protein product of gene *yhiX*.

CLICK

Cluster identification via connectivity kernels (CLICK) (Sharan & Shamir, 2000; Sharan, Elkon & Shamir, 2001; Sharmir & Sharan, 2001) gives statistical meaning to edge weights in the similarity graph and to the stopping criterion. CLICK uses the graph model and the statistical method to identify tight groups of highly similar elements. It makes the following assumptions: 1) similarity values between mates are normally distributed with mean m_T and variance s_T^2, and 2) similarity values between non-mates are normally distributed with mean m_F and variance s_F^2 and 3) $m_T > m_F$. CLICK was applied to the dataset that monitor the expression level of 6,216 putative gene transcripts of the yeast cell, *S. cerevisiae* (Cho et al., 1998). Additionally, Wei et al. (2003) applied this technique to analyze the gene expression data of *E.coli*'s 4,290 genes under eight conditions for the purpose of identifying unknown genes involved in the ATR of *E. coli*, which is regulated by the protein product of gene *yhiX*.

FLVQ

Fuzzy learning vector quantization (FLVQ) (Karayiannis & Bezdek, 1997; Hofmann & Buhmann, 1998) is a clustering algorithm applying a fuzzy membership function. During the process of updating the cluster centroids, FLVQ takes into consideration the relative distances of the cluster nodes with respect to the current input data elements. FLVQ requires the predefined values for the number of clusters, and the initial and final weighting exponents that control the amount of fuzziness of the fuzzy membership function. Wei et al. (2003) applied this technique to analyze the gene expression data of *E. coli*'s 4,290 genes under eight conditions for the purpose of identifying unknown genes involved in the acid tolerance response (ATR) of *E. coli*, which is regulated by the protein product of gene *yhiX*.

CAST and E-CAST

The cluster affinity search technique (CAST) (Ben-Dor, Shamir, & Yakhini, 1999) and enhanced Cluster Affinity Search Technique (E-CAST) (Bellaachia et al., 2002) are based on graph theory. They rely on the concept of a clique graph and employ a divisive clustering approach. The difference between the CAST and E-CAST is that CAST relies on the affinity threshold, T, which is a fixed input variable defined by users before starting the clustering process, while in E-CAST, the threshold is calculated dynamically, based only on the objects that have yet to be assigned a cluster before each cluster is created. This allows for fine-tuning while clusters are formed.

Ben-Dor et al. (2000) compared three classification techniques, nearest neighbor, support vector machines (SVM), and AdaBoost with CAST in the classification of two sets of tumor and normal clinical samples, which consist of 62 colon samples and 32 ovarian samples. Their results indicated that clustering with CAST could be very useful in the classification of cancers. Bellaachia et al. (2003) used three datasets, melanoma, Thanhall and brain to compare CAST, average linkage hierarchical cluster and E-CAST analyses. The results indicated that E-CAST performs better than both CAST and Eisen's hierarchical algorithm.

Superparamagnetic Clustering (SPC)

Superparamagnetic clustering algorithm (SPC) is a hierarchical clustering method introduced by Blatt, Wiseman and Domany (1996a, 1997) and Getz et al. (2000). SPC generalizes Fukunaga's method by introducing a finite temperature at which the division into clusters is stable and completely insensitive to the initial conditions and complements other graph based algorithms by providing a clustering criterion that is sensitive to collective features of the data set. Gaze et al. (2000) applied this algorithm to yeast gene expression analysis.

CLIFF (Clustering via Iterative Feature Filtering)

CLIFF (Xing et al., 2001) combines a clustering process and a feature selection process in a bootstrap-like iterative way, where each process uses the output of the other as an approximate input, and the outputs of the two processes improve over the process of iterations. It employs approximate normalized cut to generate a dichotomy of the samples during each iteration. A mixture of feature evaluation experts based on independent feature modeling, information gain ranking, and Markov blanket filtering is used to remove non-discriminative, irrelevant and redundant genes from the original gene set.

Xing et al. (2001) applied CLIFF to the dataset of 72 Leukemia patient samples. Each sample is measured over 7,130 genes. They found that CLIFF is capable of capturing the partition that characterizes the samples, but is masked in the original high-dimensional feature space.

MATOM (Multilayer Adjusted Tree Organizing Map)

MATOM (Wei, 2002; Wei, Gruenwald, & Conway, 2003) is a semi-supervised clustering algorithm based on the neural network model. Instead of using a single layer of self-organization maps (SOM), the network used in MATOM consists of multiple layers of maps. MATOM builds a multi-layer neural network as well as a relation tree of the resulting clusters. MATOM tracks the selected target gene and deletes the map nodes that contain only noise genes such that it saves training time spent on clustering noise data.

Wei et al. (2003) applied this technique to analyze the gene expression data of *E. coli*'s 4,290 genes under eight conditions for the purpose of identifying unknown genes involved in the acid tolerance response (ATR) of *E. coli*, which is regulated by the protein product of gene *yhiX*. Also, they compared the results obtained by MATOM with other clustering methods.

Two-Way Clustering

Gene Shaving

The goal of gene shaving is to extract coherent and typically small clusters of genes that vary as much as possible across samples (Tibshirani et al., 1999; Hastie et al., 2000). Gene shaving first finds the linear combination of genes that has maximal variation among the samples or conditions. This linear combination is considered as a super gene. The genes having the lowest correlation with the super gene are then removed from the data and the process is repeated until the subset of genes contains only one gene. This process generates a sequence of gene blocks. Genes in each gene block are similar to one another, but have a large variance across samples or conditions. This approach was used to analyze a dataset that consists of 4,673 gene expression measurements taken from 48 patients with diffuse large B-cell lymphoma (DLCL) (Hastie et al., 2000; Tibshirani et al., 1999).

Block Clustering

Block clustering (Tibshirani et al., 1999) is a top down row and column clustering of a data matrix. It reorders the rows and columns to produce a matrix with homogeneous blocks of the gene expression data. Based on the basic algorithm for forward block splitting, there is an added backward pruning procedure and a permutation-based method developed for deciding on the optimal number of blocks. Tibshirani et al. (1999) applied this technique to a dataset that has expression measurements of 6,830 genes from a set of 64 human cancer tumors.

Plaid Models

The plaid model (Lazzeroni & Owen, 2002) is designed to identify gene groups in which similarity extends across only a subset of the experimental samples because a biological process may involve only a relatively small subset of genes in the whole dataset. Likewise, the process may also happen only in a small number of samples. Hence, the biological information of this process may not be discovered by the negative effect of the noise generated by the vast majority of unrelated data. Within a cluster, the model allows a distinct regulatory effect for each gene and each sample. A set of genes, which is called a "layer", behaves similarly in a set of samples. Genes can belong to more than one layer, or to none of them. This algorithm was applied to yeast gene expression data analysis (Eisen et al., 1998).

Coupled Two-Way Clustering (CTWC)

The idea behind this algorithm is to narrow down both the features that are used and the data points that are clustered. Getz, Levine and Domany (2000) believe that only a small subset of genes participates in any cellular process of interest, which takes place only in a subset of the samples. By focusing on small subsets, therefore, the result of all these processes is mixed together. They aimed to separate and identify these processes and to extract as much information as possible from them. It is impossible to implement in a straightforward way which takes all possible sub-matrices of the original data and applies the uncoupled two-way clustering procedure to every one of them. This is because the number of such sub-matrices grows exponentially with the size of the problem. CTWC provides an efficient heuristic to generate such pairs of object and feature subsets by an iterative process that severely restricts the possible candidates for such subsets (Getz et al., 2003).

This algorithm was used successfully to mine expression data from experiments on colon cancer (Alon et al., 1999), leukemia (Golub et al., 1999), breast cancer (Kela, 2002; Sorlie et al., 2001) and colon cancer patients (Notterman et al., 2001).

Interrelated Two-Way Clustering

This approach iteratively clusters through both gene- and sample-dimensions to extract important genes and classify samples simultaneously by using the relationships between the groups of genes and samples. During iterative clustering, the accuracy of class discovery will be improved by reducing the gene-dimension (Tang et al., 2001). This approach was tested with two data sets from multiple sclerosis patients (Tang et al., 2001). The MS IFN group contains 28 samples, while the CONTROL MS group contains 30 samples. Each sample consists of 4,132 genes. This approach was able to simultaneously find important gene patterns and perform class discovery.

Multidimensional Clustering (MDCLUST)

MDCLUST (Dugas, 2004) identifies sets of sample clusters and associated genes, which is suitable for discovering the gene-phenotype association. The identification of clusters and associated genes consists of the following steps:

1.   build two clusters of samples in the dataset by k-means clustering;
2.   select the gene that is most differential for this cluster set based on a t-statistic score; and
3.   remove this gene from the dataset.

This method was applied to Golub's leukemia data (Golub et al., 1999), lymphoma data (Alizadeh et al., 2000) and colon cancer data (Alon et al., 1999).

Biclustering by Gibbs Sampling

Unlike the conventional clustering methods that discover groups of genes sharing similar expression patterns over all conditions, biclustering can group genes over only a subset of conditions under which those grouped genes have a sharp probability distribution. Sheng et al. (2003) developed a biclustering strategy by adopting the Gibbs sampling that is a method for discovering statistically overrepresented subsequences in DNA and protein sequences data. This algorithm was applied to a leukemia microarray data set (Armstrong et al., 2002).

Unsupervised Feature Selection via Two-Way Ordering (UFS-2way)

This algorithm (Ding, 2003) aims at unsupervised feature selection, i.e., selecting genes without any prior knowledge of the phenotype. This approach identifies and discards the 'irrelevant' or non-discriminant features, instead of selecting 'relevant' features. It depends on a two-way ordering of the gene expression profiles base on an optimal similarity criterion: genes and samples are simultaneously re-ordered such that genes or samples adjacent in the order are similar and genes or samples far-away from each other are dissimilar. UFS-2 way was used to study the expression profile of colon tumor tissues (Alon et al., 1999).

Spectral Biclustering

Spectral bioclustering (Kluger, 2003) is based on the checkerboard structures in matrices of expression data which can be found in eigenvectors corresponding to characteristic expression patterns across genes or conditions (samples). It simultaneously clusters the genes and conditions (samples) to find distinctive checkerboard structures. This algorithm was applied to five groups of cancer microarray datasets, that is, lymphoma (Klein et al., 2001), leukemia (Golub et al., 1999), breast cancer (Kluger et al., 2001), and central nervous system embryonal tumors (Pomeroy et al., 2002).

Table 4. Features of clustering algorithms

	Algorithms	Models	Robust to noise data	Prior information about clusters
One-way	Hierarchical clustering	Hierarchical	No	No
	K-ary	Hierarchical	Yes	No
	K-means	Partition	No	Yes
	Fuzzy K-means	Fuzzy/Partition	Not available	Yes
	Fuzzy C-means	Fuzzy/Partition	Not available	Yes
	Fuzzy J-means embedded VNS	Fuzzy	Not available	Yes
	SOM	Neural Network	Yes	Yes
	SOTA	Hierarchical, Neural Network	Yes	Yes
	HGSOT	Hierarchical, Neural Network	Yes	No
	DGSOT	Hierarchical/Neural Network	Yes	No
	SOLL	Neural Network / Probability	Yes	No
	GNG	Neural Network	Yes	Yes
	CLICK	Graph	No	No
	FLVQ	Fuzzy	Yes	Yes
	CAST	Graph	Not available	Yes
	E-CAST	Graph	Not available	No
	SPC	Hierarchical	Yes	No
	CLIFF	Graph/Markv Blanket Filtering	Yes	No
	MATOM	Neural Network	Yes	No
Two-way	Gene shaving	Singular Value Decomposition	Yes	No
	Block clustering	Forward Block Splitting / Backward Pruning	Yes	No
	Plaid models	Plaid Models	No	No
	CTWC	Framework	Yes	No
	Interrelated two-way	Framework	Yes	Yes
	MDCLUST	Partition	Yes	Yes
	Biclustering by Gibbs sampling	Simple Frequency /Gibbs Sampling	Yes	No
	UFS-2way	Graph	Yes	No
	Spectral biclustering	Partition	No	No

Features of Clustering Algorithms

Table 4 list some features of the algorithms that we discussed in this section. The information of each feature in this table is colleted from the literatures, if it is not found, it is marked as not available.

Classification

Currently, most approaches to the analysis of gene expression data attempt to learn functionally significant groups of genes in an unsupervised mode as discussed in the previous section, which means that genes are grouped without prior knowledge of their true functional classes. Supervised learning techniques use the opposite approach, that is, they classify entities into known classes. In classification analysis, one builds a classifier that is capable of discriminating between members and non-members of a given class which are classified by biological function, and uses the classifier to predict the class of genes of unknown functions. The classifier is built from training data, that is, observations that are known to belong to certain given classes.

Support Vector Machine (SVM)

A support vector machine (Brown et al., 2000; Furey, 2000) finds an optimal separating hyperplane between members and non-members of a given class in an abstract space. When SVM is applied to gene expression data, it begins with a set of known classifications of genes; a classifier, which is capable of discriminating between members and non-members of a given class, is built. Such a classifier would be used to find new members of the class from genes of unknown function. The built classifier also can be applied to the original training data set to identify outliers that may have not been recognized previously.

Brown et al. (2000) analyzed expression data from 79 different DNA microarray hybridization experiments involving 2,467 genes from the budding yeast, *S. cerevisiae*. In Furey et al. (2000), the first dataset involves expression experiments on samples taken from patients with human acute leukemia. The second dataset is comprised of expression data measuring levels of expression of genes in human tumor and normal colon tissues.

K-Nearest Neighbor

The nearest neighbor algorithm (Duda & Hart, 1973; Fukunaga, 1990) is a very simple, yet relatively powerful technique. First, find the k closest members of the training dataset for each gene vector in the input dataset. Then, examine the k nearest neighbors to check to which classification or category most of them belong. Assign this category to the gene vectors (features) being examined. Repeat this procedure for the remaining gene vectors (features) in the input set. Theilhaber et al. (2002) applied this technique for finding genes in the osteogenic differentiation pathway of the mouse C2C12 cell line, which is a pathway of direct relevance to disease processes, such as osteoporosis.

Decision Tree

Decision tree represents a learned function for classification of discrete-valued target functions. Each internal node in a decision tree represents a test, and each branch corresponds to a particular value for the attribute that is represented by the node from which the branch descends. Decision trees classify novel items by traversing the tree from the root to a leaf node, which assigns a classification to the item. Algorithms for learning a decision tree generally employ a top-down and divide-and-conquer strategy. C5.0 (or C4.5) (Quinlan & Quinlan, 1997) and CART (Breiman, 1984) are two of the most popular and widely used decision tree algorithms. The three main differences between these two decision tree algorithms are (Dubitzky, 2001):

1. C5.0 uses a measure of information gain to select the candidate attribute for splitting, while CART uses a measure of diversity;

2. C5.0 produces trees with varying numbers of branches per node, while the CART algorithm performs a binary split at each node and constructs a binary tree; and

3. CART makes reference to unseen data in order to prune the tree, while C5.0 does not consult data beyond the training set.

Dubitzky et al. (2000, 2001) applied the decision tree algorithm C5.0 and the well-known backpropagation algorithm for neural networks in a comparative study based on the previously mentioned work by Golub et al. (1999).

Voted Classification

Small changes in the training dataset may lead to large changes in the prediction accuracy, which is referred to as the instability of the prediction model. A solution to this instability problem is to build multiple models and combine them to form the final model. This process is often called voting. Boosting and bagging are two commonly used methods for voting algorithms. They both create and combine multiple classifiers, but they differ in how the classifiers are trained and in how their outputs are combined. Boosting is an algorithm that generates several different models and combines their predictions by using a weighted voting scheme. Bagging (bootstrap aggregating) was introduced by Breiman (1996) to reduce the variance of a predictor. It is very useful for large, high dimensional data set problems. Usually, finding a good classifier for large, high dimensional datasets in one step is very difficult due to the complexity and scale of the problem to be solved (Bühlmann & Yu, 2002). Dudoit et al. (2002) applied bagging and boosting to three recently published datasets: the leukemia (ALL/AML) dataset, the lymphoma dataset, and the 60 cancer cell line (NCI 60) dataset.

Weighted Gene Voting

Golub et al. (1999) proposed a weighted voting scheme for gene expression analysis. In this approach, the prediction of a single gene presented by a gene expression vector is based on weighted votes from the genes. This algorithm was applied to classify leukemia samples (Golub et al., 1999).

Bayesian Classification

The naïve Bayes (Keller et al., 2000; Moler et al., 2000) approach uses the training data to estimate the probability of each class given the gene expression vector of a new sample. It was based upon the following probability assumption: $p(y_1, y_2, ..., y_n \mid c_k) = \Pi\, p(y_j \mid c_k)$, where k is the number of classes and n is the number of features in each example. To classify a novel item, $y = (y_1, y_2, ..., y_n)$, using a naive Bayes approach, it further assumes that the values for each element (y) are conditionally independent.

Keller et al. (2000) applied this approach on three different data sets: the colon dataset, the ovary dataset and the leukemia data set. The naïve Bayes model was applied to 78 published transcription profiling experiments that monitored 5,687 *S. cerevisiae* genes from studies examining cell cycle, responses to stress, and diauxic shift (Moler et al., 2000).

Sliced Average Variance Estimation (SAVE) and Sliced Inverse Regression (SIR)

SAVE and SIR (Bura & Pfeiffer, 2003) are two sufficient dimension reduction methods. These two methods take the correlations among genes into consideration when they are used to identify a small number of linear combinations of subsets of genes. These methods were applied to the microarray data on BRCA1 and BRCA2 mutant carriers and sporadic tumors (Hedenfalk et al., 2001).

Emerging Patterns (EPs)

Emerging patterns are "item sets whose support increase significantly from one data set D_1 to another, D_2" (Dong & Li, 1999). Boulesteix et al (2003) introduced an approach based on the CART algorithm combined with a statistical procedure to discover the EPs in microarray data. This approach improves the classification accuracy by taking the interdependence among the investigated genes into account. This algorithm was used to classify colon cancer samples (Alon et al., 1999) and leukemia cancer samples (Golub et al., 1999).

Maximum Difference Subset (MDSS)

MDSS (Lyons-Weiler, 2003) is an algorithm that combines classification, classical statistics, and elements of machine learning. It learns the critical threshold of statistical significance, instead of setting an arbitrary threshold value. MDSS also employs a jackknife step to reduce the false positive rate and increase the external validity of the predictive gene set. This approach can be used in both ways of partially supervised and completely unsupervised. MDSS was applied to the dataset from Golub et al. (1999) for cancer classification.

Prediction by Collective Likelihoods (PCL)

PCL (Li et al., 2003) is an algorithm based on the concept of emerging patterns (Dong & Li, 1999) described above. Unlike the traditional classification methods such as neural networks and support vector machines with high accuracy but lack of the capability of finding rules, PCL can perform multiple parallel classifications and provide valid and useful rules. This algorithm was applied to the data from Yeoh et al. (2002) and discovered novel rules for the gene expression profile of more than six subtypes of acute lymphoblastic leukemia (ALL) patients.

Simultaneous Gene Clustering and Subset Selection for Classification

Jornsten and Yu (2003) proposed an algorithm for simultaneous gene clustering and subset selection for classification. A new model selection criterion was developed based on the Rissanen's minimum description length (MDL) principle. This algorithm does not conduct gene clustering and sample classification separately or in a directional way. This algorithm was applied to the acute leukemia data (Golub et al., 1999), NCI60 data (Ross et al., 2000) and colon data (Alon, 1999).

Features of Classification Algorithms

Table 5 lists some features of the algorithms that we have discussed in this section. It should be noted that one of the characteristics of gene expression data

Table 5. Features of classification algorithms

Algorithms	Models	Two/Multiple class case	Robust to noise data	Remove noise data by
Support vector machine	Machine Learning	Multiple	No	Modifying The Matrix Of Kernel Values
K-nearest neighbor	Memory Reasoning	Multiple	No	Pre-Filtering
C4.0/C5.0	Decision Tree	Multiple	No	Discretisation Method
CART	Decision Tree	Multiple	No	Discretisation Method
Boosting/bagging	Voted Classification	Multiple	No	Discretisation Method
Bayesian classification	Statistics	Multiple	Yes	None
Sliced average variance estimation (SAVE)	Graphical	Multiple	Yes	None
Sliced inverse regression (SIR)	Graphical	Multiple	Yes	None
Emerging patterns (EPs)	Decision Tree/ Statistics	Two	Yes	None
Maximum difference subset (MDSS)	Statistics/ Machine Learning	Multiple		None
Prediction by collective likelihoods (PCL)	Decision Tree/ Statistics/Rule Finding	Multiple	Yes	None
Simultaneous gene clustering and subset selection for classification	Statistical	Multiple	Yes	None

discussed before is that the number of the genes is much larger than the number of samples/conditions. Preprocessing is needed before applying most classification algorithms listed in the table.

Association Rules Discovery

An association rule (Agrawal et al., 1996) is an expression of the form X => Y, where X and Y are sets of data items (itemsets). The meaning of such a rule is that in the rows of the database, where the attributes in X have a value of true, the attributes Y also have a value of true with high probability. In order to apply association rules discovery to gene expression data, a discretization process, i.e., transforming gene expression data to binary data, is crucial. Interested readers may refer to Pensa et al. (2004) for more information. Recently, Agier et al. (2005) extended the notion of association rules to many different semantics of rules (like functional dependencies) in the setting of gene expression data based on Amstrong's axiom system.

It should be noted that one of characteristics for the gene expression data mentioned before is that the number of genes is greater than the number of conditions. In a microarray experiment, each slide can be considered as a transaction and each gene can be considered as an item. Considering a 5000-gene microarray slide experiment, in order to find 10-item candidates there will be 5000!/(10!*4990!) itemsets, theoretically. For the human genome, there are approximately 35,000 genes. Hence, for an algorithm to work effectively, it must be able to deal robustly with the dimensionality of this feature space.

Apriori

Apriori (Agrawal & Srikant, 1994) is one of the most popular association rules discovery algorithms. This algorithm is based on the property of frequent itemsets (Doddi, 2001), that is, each subset of a frequent itemset must also be a frequent itemset. It first identifies frequent itemsets containing only one item, and then the identified frequent itemsets found in the first step are extended with one more item, and proceeds iteratively. However, one characteristic of the microarray data is that they contain a large number of variables (thousands) which is the number of genes measured in a microarray experiment. By using the standard Apriori algorithm, a large number of rules will be generated. Creighton and Hanash (2003) implemented a version of Apriori in which more criteria are specified in addition to a minimum support in selecting frequent itemsets.

Because the rules that they were interested in is the ones where itemsets contain only one item.

Berrar et al. (2001) applied Apriori to discover the association rules from microarray data which consist of 1376 gene expression profiles of 60 cell lines and the growth inhibition power of 1400 chemical compounds.

Distance-Based Association Rule Mining (DARM)

Icev et al. (2003) proposed a novel algorithm to discover the association rules from gene expression data. They focused on the rules which involve the expression patterns of genes based on their promoter regions. DARM enhances the association rules with biological information about the distances among the motifs. It uses the coefficient of variation of distance (cvd) to determine the distance representing similar clustering among promoters. Then, the frequent itemsets that satisfy the max-cvd (a user defined threshold) are found. Association rules with the required confidence are generated from those itemsets (cvd-frequent itemsets).

The C. *briggsae* datasets (Icev et al., 2003) containing the promoter regions of 31 genes, and 5 cell types are explored to discover the distance-based association rules which have the higher classification performance than standard association rules.

Finding Interesting Association Rule Groups by Enumeration of Rows (FARMER)

The FARMER (Cong et al, 2004) algorithm has the following characteristics:

1. instead of generating all rules, it only discovers the interesting rule groups (IRGs);

2. IRGs are identified by a unique upper bound and a set of lower bounds;

3. row enumeration is performed, instead of column enumeration; and

4. pruning is performed for the efficiency.

The clinical data on lung cancer, breast cancer, prostate cancer, ALL-AML leukemia (ALL) and colon tumor (Cong et al, 2004) were used to illustrate the efficiency and usefulness of discovering biological Interesting Rule groups. Based on FARMER, Xu et al (2004) developed a prototype system which integrates the FARMER with the visualization techniques to help biologists find certain number of significant rules instead of numerous numbers of redundant rules.

Closed Pattern Discovery by Transposing Tables that are Extremely Long (CARPENTER)

CARPENTER (Pan et al, 2003) is the first algorithm that uses the row-wise enumeration for frequent pattern mining. In order to assure the efficiency of the CARPENTER, three pruning strategies are applied: (1) remove search branches that can never generate closed patterns that satisfy the minsup threshold; (2) the rows that appear in all tuples of the X conditional transposed table $(TT'|_x)$ are removed from $TT'|_x$; and (3) prune off any further search down the branch of node X if it is found that the itemset $F(X)$ is already discovered previously in the enumeration tree.

Three gene expression datasets (Pan et al, 2003) were chosen to analyze the performance of the algorithm:

1. Lung cancer datasets that represent 181 tissue samples (with each sample there are 12533 genes);
2. Acute lymphoblastic leukemia (ALL) datasets containing 215 tissue samples (each sample with 12533 genes); and
3. Ovarian cancer (OC) datasets that have 253 tissue samples (15154 genes for each sample).

Closed Association Rule Mining (CHARM)

Zaki and Hsiao (2002) introduced the CHARM algorithm for enumeration of the set of all frequent closed itemsets to address the long pattern problems, which are very common in gene expression data mining. The following innovations have been claimed for CHARM: 1) both the itemset space and transaction space were explored over a novel itemset-tidset tree (IT-tree); 2) a hybrid search method that skips many levels of the IT-tree is used to quickly find the frequent closed itemsets; 3) a hash-based approach is employed to eliminate non-closed itemsets during subsumption checking; and 4) diffset, a novel vertical data representation which cuts down the memory requirement for the storage of intermediate results, is used for fast frequency computation.

This algorithm was compared with **FARMER** (Cong et al., 2004) by using clinical data on lung cancer, breast cancer, prostate cancer, ALL-AML leukemia (ALL) and colon tumor.

CLOSET and CLOSET+

After having done a systematic study on the search strategies such as CLOSET (Pei, Han, & Mao, 2000) and CHARM (Zaki & Hsiao, 2002) for mining frequent closed itemsets, Wang et al. (2003) devised a new algorithm, CLOSET+, in which some verified winners of search strategies were adopted and some new approaches were developed: 1) it uses FP-tree as the compression technique; 2) the horizontal data format and depth-first search are employed; 3) in order to improve the space efficiency, a hybrid tree-projection method was developed to build a conditional projected database; 4) in addition to the adoption of the item emerging and sub-itemset pruning methods, the item skipping technique was also developed to further prune the search space and speed up the mining process; and 5) for the closure checking, it employes the two-level hash-indexed result tree method for dense datasets, and the pseudo-projection based upward checking method for sparse datasets.

Wang et al. (2003) tested the performance of CLOSET+ and showed that CLOSET+ is several times faster than the CHARM (Zaki & Hsiao, 2002). But it was reported in (Cong et al, 2004) that CHARM is always orders of magnitude faster than CLOSET+ on the microarray datasets with which they tested.

Combining Row and Column Enumeration (COBBLER)

COBBLER (Pan et al., 2004) is an algorithm that can be used to discover association rules from the datasets which have a larger number of features and rows. The main idea of the COBBLER algorithm is to build a dynamic enumeration tree by switching between row enumeration and feature enumeration based on the characteristic of the subset. Whether to switch from row enumeration to feature enumeration or vice versa is decided by estimating the enumeration cost for the subtree at a node. The less cost one will be selected.

COBBLER was tested using the datasets (Pan et al., 2004) with 1316 rows and row length of 29745 which represent the compounds binding ability to a target site on thrombin which is a key receptor in blood clotting. Unfortunately, this algorithm has not been applied to microarray gene expression data analysis. It will be interesting to see the output of the microarray expression data.

Min-EX

The Min-Ex (Becquet et al., 2002) association rule algorithm is based on the concept of δ-free itemsets (Boulicaut et al., 2003) and the attempt to eliminate the redundant association rules in the standard association-rule mining technique (Zaki et al., 2000). Becquet et al. (2002) used the ac-miner-close implementation to do the association rule mining. This approach provides every frequent 0-free item set with its frequency and closure.

Becquet et al. (2002) analyzed the data of gene expression (SAGE) in human cells (Lash et al., 2004). They found the expected co-regulation of genes encoded by mitochondrial DNA. They were also able to extract several rules involving signal transduction proteins, some of which were confirmed by published results. They also compared the Ex-min with the SOM approach.

LIS-Growth Tree (Large-Itemsets Growth Tree)

Jiang and Gruenwald (2003) proposed a new algorithm for association rule data mining for gene expression data. This algorithm includes two core parts: a new data structure, JXR-tree and a new data partition format for gene expression data. Any of gene expression levels can be represented as a fraction part and an exponent part. The fraction part can be represented as one bit for ± sign, followed by n bits for fraction, and the exponent part can be represented as one bit for ± sign, followed by m bits for exponent. JXR-tree is a bits string compression tree as well as a lossless tree, which is built for each gene.

Jiang et al. (2003) applied this approach to the dataset from Stanford University (DeRisi, 2005) by evaluating the execution time vs. k-itemsets, and execution time vs. support as the performance measurements, in comparison to the Apriori approach (Apriori et al., 1996).

Features of the Association Rules Discovery

Table 6 lists some of the features the algorithms discussed in this section. It should be noted that not all algorithms are good for interactive and incremental mining. Also, not all algorithms deal with the issue of noise in the data, which is one of the characteristics of the gene expression measurements.

Table 6. Features of association rules discovery algorithms

Algorithms	Data Structures	Row/Column Enumeration	Search modes	Goodness for datasets with larger number of genes
Apriori	Hashtree	Column	Breadth First	Good
Distance-based association rule mining (DARM)	Hashtree	Column	Breadth First	Good
Finding interesting association rule groups by enumeration of rows (FARMER)	Conditional Pointer List	Row	Depth First	Very good
Closed pattern discover by transposing tables that are extremely long (CARPENTER)	Conditional Pointer List	Row	Depth First	Very good
Closed association rule mining(CHARM)	Itemset-Tidset Tree	Column	Depth First	Good
CLOSET	FP-Trees	Column	Depth First	Good
CLOSET+	FP-Trees	Column	Depth First	Good
Combining row and column enumeration (COBBLER)	Conditional Pointer List	Row/Column	Depth First	Very good
Min-EX	Prefix-Tree	Column		Very good
LIS-growth tree (Large-itemsets growth tree)	JG-Tree	Column	Depth First	Very good

Data Mining Software

Recently, the microarray technology has increasingly been applied to gene expression studies, and tremendous data have been generated. Consequently, more and more data mining tools and software packages become available either from commercial vendors or from academic institutions. In Tables 7 and 8, we list the available data mining software for gene expression data together with their features.

Table 7. Commercial data mining software list

	Software Name	Company / Institute	Features
Web-based	Affymate	Array Genetics	"Affymate is designed to rapidly analyze multiple pairs of DNA microarray data."
	ArrayAnalyzer	Insightful	"ArrayAnalyzer provides a structured and guided analysis of Affymetrix and custom cDNA microarray data …"
	Spotfire DecisionSite Statistics	Spotfire	"Web-enabled data mining and statistical methods allow end-users to identify significant variables and patterns using methods that quickly and automatically generate the most meaningful visualizations for further analysis …"
platform independent (in JAVA)	ExpressionSieve	BioSieve	"…strong in linking biological significance to expression patterns, by allowing the user to examine expression data along with data from other domains, such as gene ontology, pathway, biochemical assay, clinical data, mass spectrometry data, etc."
	GeneSpring 5.1	Silicon Genetics	"GeneSpring 5.1 comes with comprehensive script building and editing capabilities. Researchers can create custom scripts to automate repetitive analytical tasks, ensure consistency in the analysis process and simplify data analysis management. "
	Genowiz	Ocimum Biosolutions	"… a powerful gene expression analysis program that has been designed to efficiently store, process and visualize gene expression data."
Windows	Acuity 3.0	Axon Instruments	"Acuity® 3.0 is the complete enterprise microarray informatics platform for microarray data storage, data filtering and data analysis."
	ArrayMiner	Optimal Design	"…a set of analysis tools using advanced algorithms to reveal the true structure of your gene expression data. Its unique graphical interface gives you an intimate understanding of the analysis and an easy publishing of its results."
	AIDA Array Evaluation	raytest GmbH	"Provides data from the comparison of one master array with client arrays."
	BioMine	Gene Network Sciences	"It features flexible data import, normalization and replicate-handling, with specialized Affymetrix® GeneChip® data handling capabilities …"

Table 8. Open source data mining software list

	Software Name	Company / Institute	Features
Web-based	Classification of Expression Arrays (CLEAVER)	Stanford Biomedical Informatics	"CLEAVER allows iterative estimation of performance accuracy allowing for experimentation via the addition or removal of measurements and examples to optimize performance. CLEAVER also provides methods for clustering, visualization, and data reduction."
	CTWC	Weizmann Institute of Science	"The novelty of our method is that we perform the clustering operations in an iterative and coupled fashion."
	ENGENE	Computer Architecture Department, Universidad de Malaga (Spain)	"The clustering algorithms included in the system range from the classical partitional and hierarchical methods to the complex fuzzy ones, ... Novel strategies for data pre-processing, gene and sample clustering and feature selection are also incorporated."
	Expression Profiler	European Bioinformatics Institute	"... allow to perform cluster analysis, pattern discovery, pattern visualization, study and search Gene Ontology categories, generate sequence logos, extract regulatory sequences, study protein interactions, as well as to link analysis results to external tools and databases."
	INCLUSive	http://www.esat.k uleuven.ac.be/incl usive/index.jsp.	"...suite of web-based tools and is aimed at the automatic multistep analysis of microarray data."
	SAM	Tibshirani Lab, Stanford University	"Correlates gene expression data to a wide variety of clinical parameters including treatment, diagnosis categories, survival time and time trends...Provides estimate of False Discovery Rate for multiple testing."
platform independent (in JAVA)	Gene Cluster	Whitehead Institute Center for Genome Research	"It includes algorithms for building and testing supervised models using weighted voting (WV) and k-nearest neighbors (KNN) algorithms."
	J-Express Pro	MolMine	"J-Express Pro is a comprehensive portable software package for analysis and visualization of microarray data ..."
	MeV	The Institute for Genomic Research	"... generates informative and interrelated displays of expression and annotation data from single or multiple experiments."

Future Work

Considerable effort has been put into the analysis of gene expression data, either in developing new data mining techniques, or in developing new software packages by integrating new features. We believe that the application of data mining techniques to the analysis of gene expression data is still in its infancy, but a very promising stage of development. Though existing data mining techniques can be adapted to gene expression data analysis, the unique characteristics of gene expression data always need to be taken into consideration. Below are some possible future research directions.

Development of Novel Algorithms

Development of novel algorithms will always be important. Recently, many efforts have been put into developing clustering algorithms. Association rule mining might be useful in gene expression data analysis, but not much work has been done in this field.

Systematic Comparative Study of Available Data Mining Algorithms

Even though we gave the summary tables for clustering, classification, and association rule discovery, a complete systematic comparative study has not been done. It will be interesting and useful to conduct a systematic comparative study of currently available data mining algorithms, applied to a common set of gene expression data. This study would evaluate the algorithms based on some distinct attributes such as robustness to noisy data, efficiency with respect to large numbers of genes and conditions (samples), biological accuracy of the clusters, classifiers/prediction, rules, and the efficiency /speed.

Multiple Experiments and Time Series Analysis

Usually, comparisons among multiple experiments or time series studies are the interest of biologists. But it should be noted that some genes may have similar expression patterns under certain conditions or within some samples, but not across all conditions or samples. Certain mechanisms should be developed to prevent this information from being missed.

Visualization

Presentation of data analysis results is as important as the choice of a data mining technique. A good algorithm allows one to extract correct and meaningful biological information from a large data set, while a good presentation or visualization allows biologists to intuitively gather biological information from the displayed data. Even though more and more attention has been paid to this area (Bajcsy & Liu, 2002; Yang, Chen, & Kim, 2003), improvement is still needed. The main difficulty may be due to the large amount of data. Presenting the analysis results from a data set, which contains thousands of data items in 2-D or 3-D fashion, is a challenging task, indeed. Presenting the analysis results from a series of data sets, in which each corresponds to a condition or a time point in a time series experiment, is even more challenging.

Acceptance

Though many generic mining algorithms have been developed, it will be important to make new algorithms and techniques suitable for the gene expression data analysis by considering the characteristics of the expression data. More cooperation between computer scientists and biologists is required. Specifically, bioinformatics scientists who are expert in both informatic techniques and biology are needed.

Noise Data

There is a high percentage of unregulated genes, called noise genes, which have similar expression levels. The presence of noise data adds time overhead to mining and usually has a negative influence on data analysis results. Some algorithms have been developed to try to resolve this issue, but more efforts are needed.

References

Agier, M., Petit, J., & Suzuki, E. (2005). *Towards ad-hoc rule semantics for gene expression data.* Paper presented at the 15th International Symposium on Methodologies for Intelligent Systems, Saratoga Springs, New York.

Agrawal, R., Mannila, H., Srikant, R., Toivonen, H., Verkamo, A.I. (1996). Fast discovery of association rules. In U. M. Fayyad, G. Piatetsky-Shapiro, P., Smyth & R. Uthurusamy (Ed.), *Advances in knowledge discovery and data mining* (pp. 307-328). Cambridge, CA: American Association for Artificial Intelligence/MIT press.

Alizadeh, A. A., Eisen, M. B., Davis, R. E., Ma, C., Lossos, I. S., Rosenwald, A. et al. (2000). Distinct types of diffuse large B-cell lymphoma identified by gene expression profiling. *Nature, 403*(6769), 503-511.

Armstrong, S. A., Hsieh, J. J., & Korsmeyer, S. J. (2002). Genomic approaches to the pathogenesis and treatment of acute lymphoblastic leukemias. *Curr Opin Hematol, 9*(4), 339-344.

Aronow, B. J., Toyokawa, T., Canning, A., Haghighi, K., Delling, U., Kranias, E. et al. (2001). Divergent transcriptional responses to independent genetic causes of cardiac hypertrophy. *Physiol Genomics, 6*(1), 19-28.

Bajcsy, P., & Liu, L. (2002). An image-based visualization of microarray features and classification results. In *Proceedings of the 10th Intelligent Systems for Molecular Biology* (p. 59). Edmonton, Alberta, Canada.

Bar-Joseph, Z., Demaine, E. D., Gifford, D. K., Srebro N., Hamel, A. M., & Jaakkola, T. S. (2003). K-ary clustering with optimal leaf ordering for gene expression data. *Bioinformatics, 19*(9), 1070-1078.

Becquet, C., Blachon, S., Jeudy, B., Boulicaut, J-F., & Gandrillon, O. (2002). Strong-association-rule mining for large-scale gene-expression data analysis: A case study on human SAGE data. *Genome Biology, 3*(12), research0067.0061-0067.0016.

Bellaachia, A., Portnoy, D., Chen,Y., & Elkahloun, A. G. (2002). E-CAST: *A data mining algorithm for gene expression data.* Paper presented at the BIOKDD02: Workshop on Data Mining in Bioinformatics (with SIGKDD02 Conference).

Ben-Dor, A., Bruhn, L., Friedman, N., Nachman, I., Schummer, M., & Yakhini, Z. (2000). Tissue classification with gene expression profiles. *Journal of Computational Biology, 7*(3-4), 559-583.

Ben-Dor, A., Shamir, R. & Yakhini, Z. (1999). Clustering gene expression patterns. *Journal of Computational Biology, 6*(3-4), 281-297.

Berrar, D., Dubitzky, W., Granzow, M., & Eils, R. (2001). Analysis of gene expression and drug activity data by knowledge-based association mining. In *Proceedings of Critical Assessment of Microarray Data Analysis Techniques(CAMDA'01)* (pp. 25-28).

Bezdek, J. C. (1981). *Pattern recognitionwith fuzzy objective function algorithms.* New York: Plenum Press.

Blatt, M., Wiseman, S., & Domany, E. (1996a). Super-paramagnetic clustering of data. Physical *Review Letters, 76*, 3251-3255.

Blatt, M., Wiseman, S., & Domany, E. (1997). Data clustering using a model granular. *Neural Computation, 9*, 1805-1842.

Boulesteix, A., Tutz, G., & Strimmer K. (2003). A CART-based approach to discover emerging patterns in microarray data. *Bioinformatics, 19*(18), 2465-2472.

Boulicaut, J.-F., Bykowski, A., & Rigotti, C. (2003). Free-sets: a condensed representation of boolean data for frequency query approximation. *Data Mining and Knowledge Discovery Journal, 7*(1), 5-22.

Breiman, L. (1996). Bagging predictors. *Machine Learning, 24*, 123-140.

Breiman, L., Friedman, J. H., Olshen, R.A., & Stone, C. J. (1984). *Classification and regression trees*. Belmont, CA: Wadsworth.

Brown, M., Grundy, W., Lin, D., Cristianini, N., Sugnet, C., Furey, T., Ares, M., & Haussler, D. (2000). Knowledge-based analysis of microarray gene expression data by using support vector machines. In *Proceedings of the National Academy of Science of the United States of America* (Vol. 97 pp. 262-267).

Bühlmann, P., & Yu, B. (2002). Analyzing bagging. *Annals of Statistics, 30*, 927-961.

Bura, E., & Pfeiffer, R. M. (2003). Graphical methods for classs prediction using dimension reduction techniques on DNA microarray data. *Bioinfomatics, 19*(10), 1252-1258.

Cho, R. J., Campbell, M. J., Winzeler, E. A., Steinmetz, L., Conway, A., Wodicka, L. et al. (1998). A genome-wide transcriptional analysis of the mitotic cell cycle. *Mol Cell, 2*(1), 65-73.

Cong, G., Tung, A. K. H., Xu, T. X., Pan, F., & Yang, J. (2004, June 13-18). FARMER: Finding interesting rule groups in microarray datasets. In A. C. K. G. Weikum & S. Deßloch (Ed.), *Proceedings of the ACM SIGMOD International Conference on Management of Data*, Paris (pp. 143-154). ACM.

Creighton, C., & Hanash, S. (2003). Mining gene expression database for association rules. *Bioinformatics, 19*(1), 79-86.

Dembèlè, D., & Kastner, P. (2003). Fuzzy C-means method for clustering microarray data. *Bioinformatics, 19*(8), 973-980.

DeRisi, J. L., Iyer, V. R., & Brown, P. O. (2005). *Exporing the metabolic and genetic control of gene expression on a genomic scale*. Retrievable from http://cmgm.stanford.edu/pbrown/explore/

Ding, C. H. Q. (2003). Unsupervised feature selection via two-way ordering in gene expression analysis. *Bioinformatics, 19*(10), 1259-1266.

Ding, Q., Ding,Q., & Perrizo, W. (2002). Association rule mining on remotely sensed images using P-trees. In *Proceedings of the 6th Pacific-Asia Conference on Advances in Knowledge Discovery and Data Mining* (pp. 66-79).

Dong, G., & Li, J. (1999, August 15-18). Efficient mining of emerging patterns: Discovering trends and differences. In *Proceedings of the Fifth ACM SIGKDD International Conference on Knowledge Discovery and Data Mining*, San Diego, CA (pp. 43-52). ACM.

Dopazo, J., & Carazo, J. M. (1997). Phylogenetic reconstruction using an unsupervised growing neural network that adopts the topology of a phylogenetic tree. *Journal of Molecular Evolution, 44*, 226-233.

Dubitzky, W., Granzow, M., & Berrar, D. (2001). Data mining and machine learning methods for microarray analysis. In S. M. Lin & K. F. Johnson (Eds.), *Methods of microarray data analysis* (pp. 5-22). Kluwer Academic Publishers.

Dubitzky, W., Granzow, M., Berrar, D., Bulashevska, S., Conrad, C., Gerlich, D., & Eils, R. (2000). *A comparison of symbolic and subsymbolic machine learning approaches to molecular classification of cancer and gene identification*. Paper presented at the Proceedings of Critical Assessment of Techniques for Microarray Data Mining (CAMDA-2000).

Duda, R. O., & Hart, P. E. (1973). *Nonparametric techniques in pattern classification and scene analysis* (pp. 98-105). New York: John-Wiley.

Dudoit, S., Fridlyand, J., & Speed, T. P. (2002). Comparison of discrimination methods for the classification of tumors using gene expression data. *Journal of the American Statistical Association, 97*(457), 77-87.

Dugas, M., Merk, S., Breit, S., & Dirsched, P. (2004). Mdclust-exploratory microarray analysis by multidimensional clustering. *Bioinformatics, 20*(6), 931-936.

Eisen, M. B., Spellman, P. T., Brown, P. O., & Botstein, D. (1998). Cluster analysis and display of genome-wide expression patterns. In *Proceedings of the National Academy of Science of the United States of America, 95* (pp. 14863-14868).

Faber, V. (1994). Clustering and the continuous K-means algorithm. *Los Alamos Science, 22*, 138-144.

Feng Luo, K. T. a. L. K. (2003). Hierarchical clustering of gene expression data. In *Proceedings of Third IEEE Symposium on BioInformatics and BioEngineering (BIBE'03)* (pp. 328-335).

Fritzke, B. (1994). Growing cell structures-A self-organizing network for unsupervised and supervised learning. In Neural Networks (Vol. 7, pp. 1441-1460). Elsevier Science Ltd.

Fritzke, B. (1995). A growing neural gas network learns topologies. In G. Tasauro, D. Tourestzky, & T. Leen (Ed.), *Advances in neural information processing systems* (Vol. 7, pp. 625-632). Cambridge MA: MIT Press.

Fukunaga, K. (1990). Nonparametric classification and error estimation. In *Introduction to statistical pattern recognition* (2nd ed., pp. 303-322). San Diego, CA: Academic Press Professional, Inc.

Furey, T., Cristianini, N., Duffy,N., Bednarski, D., Schummer, M., & Haussler, D. (2000). Support vector machine classification and validation of cancer tissue samples using microarray expressioin data. *Bioinformatics, 16*(10), 906-914.

Gasch, A. P., & Eisen, M. B. (2002). Exploring the conditional coregulation of yeast gene expression through fuzzy k-means clustering. *Genome Biology, 3*(11), research0059.0051-0059.0022.

Getz, G., Gal, H., Notterman, D. A., & Domany, E. (2003). Coupled two-way clustering analysis of breast cancer and colon cancer gene expression data. *Bioinformatics, 19*(9), 1079-1089.

Getz, G., Levine, E., & Domany, E. (2000). Coupled two-way clustering analysis of gene microarray data. In *Proceedings of the National Academy of Science of the United States of America, 97*(22), 12079-12084.

Getz, G., Levinea, E., Domany, E., & Zhang, M. Q. (2000). Super-paramagnetic clustering of yeast gene expression profiles. *Physica A, 279*, 457-464.

Golub, T. R., Slonim, D. K., Tamayo, P., Huard, C., Gaasenbeek, M., Mesirov, J. P., Coller, H., Loh, M. L., Downing, J. R., Caligiuri, M. A., Bloomfield, C. D., & Lander, E. S. (1999). Molecular classification of cancer: Class discovery and class prediction by gene expression monitoring. *Science, 286*, 531-537.

Harrington, C. A., Rosenow, C., & Retief, J. (2000). Monitoring gene expression using DNA Microarrays. *Current Opinions in Microbiology, 3*(3), 285-291.

Hastie, T., Tibshirani, R., Eisen, M, Ash, A., Levy, R., Staudt, L., Chan, W. C, Botstein, D., Brown, P. (2000). 'Gene shaving' as a method for identifying distinct sets of genes with similar expression patterns. *Genome Biology, 1*(2), research0003.0001-0003.0021.

Herrero, J., Valencia, A., & Dopazo, J. (2001). A hierarchical unsupervised growing neural network for clustering gene expression patterns. *Bioinformatics, 17*(2), 126-136.

Hofmann, T., & Buhmann, J.M. (1998). Competitive learning algorithms for robust vector quantization. *IEEE Transaction on Signal Processing, 46*, 1665-1675.

Icev, A., Ruiz, C., & Ryder, E. F. (2003). *Distance-enhanced association rules for gene expression*. Paper presented at the BIOKDD03: 3rd ACM SIGKDD Workshop on Data Mining in Bioinformatics.

Ishida, N., Hayashi, K., Hoshijima, M., Ogawa, T., Koga, S., Miyatake, Y. et al. (2002). Large scale gene expression analysis of osteoclastogenesis in vitro and elucidation of NFAT2 as a key regulator. *J Biol Chem, 277*(43), 41147-41156.

Iyer, V. R., Eisen, M. B., Ross, D. T., Schuler, G., Moore, T., Lee, J. C. et al. (1999). The transcriptional program in the response of human fibroblasts to serum. *Science, 283*(5398), 83-87.

Jain, A. M., Murty, M. N., & Flynn, P. J. (1999). Data clustering. In *ACM Computing Surveys* (Vol. 31, pp. 264 - 323). New York: ACM Press.

Javier Herrero, A. V., & Joaquín Dopazo. (2001). A hierarchical unsupervised growing neural network for clustering gene expression patterns. *Bioinformatics, 17*(2), 126-136.

Jiang, X.-R., & Gruenwald, L. (2003). *Microarray gene expression data association rules mining based on JXR-tree*. Paper presented at the 1st International Workshop on Database and Expert Systems Applications (DEXA'03), Prague, Czech Republic.

Johnson, R. W., & Wichern, D.W. (1998). *Applied multivariate statistical analysis*. Upper Saddle River, NJ: Prentice Hall.

Jordan, B. (2001). *DNA microarrays: Gene expression applications*. New York: Springer-Verlag.

Jornsten, R., & Yu, B. (2003). Simultaneous gene clustering and subset selection for sample classification via MDL. *Bioinformatics, 19*(9), 1100-1109.

Karayiannis, N. B., & Bezdek, J. C. (1997). An integrated approach to fuzzy learning vector quantization and fuzzy c-means clustering. *IEEE Transactions on Fuzzy Systems, 5*(4), 622-628.

Kaufman, L., & Rousseeuw, P. J. (1990). *Finding groups in data: An introduction to cluster analysis*. New York: John Wiley & Sons.

Keller, A. D., Schummer, M., Hood, L., & Ruzzo, W. L. (2000). Bayesian classification of DNA array expression data (Tech. Report No. UW-CSE-2000-08-01), University of Washington.

Kela, I. (2002) *Clustering of gene expression data*. M.Sc. Thesis, Weizmann Institute.

Klein, U., Tu, Y., Stolovitzky, G. A., Mattioli, M., Cattoretti, G., Husson, H. et al. (2001). Gene expression profiling of B cell chronic lymphocytic leukemia reveals a homogeneous phenotype related to memory B cells. *J Exp Med, 194*(11), 1625-1638.

Kluger, H., Kacinski, B., Kluger, Y., Mironenko, O., Gilmore-Hebert, M., Chang, J., Perkins, A.S., and Sapi, E., (2001). Microarry analysis of invasive and metastatic phenotypes in a breast cancer model. In *Poster presented at the Gordon Conference on Cancer,* Newport, RI.

Kluger, Y., Basri, R., Chang, J. T., & Gerstein, M. (2003). Spectral bioclustering of microarray data: coclustering genes and conditions. *Genome Research, 13,* 703-716.

Kohonen, T. (1990). The self-organizing map. In *Proceedings of the IEEE* (Vol. 9, pp. 1464-1479).

Kohonen, T. (2001). *The self-organizing map* (3rd ed.). Springer.

Kotala, P., Perera, A., Zhou, J. K., Mudivarthy, S., Perrizo, W., Deckard, E. (2001). Gene expression profiling of DNA microarray data using peano count trees (P-Trees). In *Proceedings of the First Virtual Conference on Genomics and Bioinformatics.*

Lash, A. E., Tolstoshev, C. M., Wagner, L., Schuler, G. D., Strausberg, R. L., Riggins, G. J. et al. (2000). SAGEmap: A public gene expression resource. *Genome Res, 10*(7), 1051-1060.

Lazzeroni, L., & Owen, A. (2002). Plaid models for gene expression data. *Statistica Sinica, 12*(1), 61-86.

Li, J., Liu, H., Downing, J. R., Yeoh, A. E., & Wong, L. (2003). Simple rules underlying gene expression profiles of more than six subtypes odf acute lymphoblastic leukemia (ALL) patients. *Bioinformatics, 19*(1), 71-78.

Lin, S. M., Johnson, K. F. (2002). *Methods of microarray data analysis.* Boston: Kluwer Academic.

Lipshutz, R. J., Fodor, S. P. A., Gingeras, T. R., & Lockhart, D. J. (2000). High density synthetic oligonucleotide arrays. *Nature Genetics, Supplement 21,* 20-24.

Lo, J., Lee, S., Xu, M., Liu, F., Ruan, H., Eun, A. et al. (2003). 15000 unique zebrafish EST clusters and their future use in microarray for profiling gene expression patterns during embryogenesis. *Genome Research, 13*(3), 455-466.

Luo, F. K. L. (2002). *Ontology construction for information selection.* Dallas: University of Texas at Dallas.

Luo, F., Khan, L., Bastani, F., Yen, I., & Zhou J. (2004). A dynamically growing self-organization tree (DGSOT) for hierarchical clustering gene expression profiles. *Bioinformatics, 20*(16), 2605-2617.

Luo, F., Tang, K. & Khan, L. (2003). *Hierarchical clustering of gene expression data*. Paper presented at the Proceedings of the Third IEEE Symposium on BioInformatics and BioEngineering (BIBE'03).

Lyons-Weiler, J., Patel, S., & Bhattacharya, S. (2003). A classification-based machine learning approach for the analysis of genome-wide expression data. *Genome Research, 13*, 503-512.

Mirkin, B. (1996). *Mathematical classification and clustering*. Boston: Kluwer Academic.

Moler, E. J., Radisky, D. C., & Mian, I. S. (2000). Integrating naive Bayes models and external knowledge to examine copper and iron homeostasis in S. cerevisiae. *Physiol Genomics, 4*(2), 127-135.

Neiman, P. E., Ruddell, A., Jasoni, C., Loring, G., Thomas, S. J., Brandvold, K. A. et al. (2001). Analysis of gene expression during myconcogene-induced lymphomagenesis in the bursa of Fabricius. In *Proceedings of the Nationall Acadamy Science USA, 98*(11), 6378-6383.

Notterman, D. A., Alon, U., Sierk, A. J., & Levine, A. J. (2001). Transcriptional gene expression profiles of colorectal adenoma, adenocarcinoma, and normal tissue examined by oligonucleotide arrays. *Cancer Research, 61*(7), 3124-3130.

Pan, F., Cong, G., & Tung, A. K. H. (2003). Carpenter: Finding closed patterns in long biological datasets and data mining. In *Proceedings of the Ninth ACM SIGKDD International Conference on Knowledge Discovery and Data Mining* (pp. 637-642). New York: ACM Press.

Pan, F., Cong, G., Xin, X., & Tung, A. K. H. (2004, June 21-23). COBBLER: Combining column and row enumeration for closed pattern discovery. In *Proceedings of the 16th International Conference on Scientific and Statistical Database Management (SSDBM 2004),* Santorini Island, Greece (pp. 21-30). IEEE Computer Society.

Pei, J., Han, J., & Mao, R. (2000, May 14). CLOSET: An efficient algorithm for mining frequent closed itemsets. In R. R. D. Gunopulos (Ed.), *Proceedings of 2000 ACM SIGMOD Workshop on Research Issues in Data Mining and Knowledge Discovery,* Dallas, Texas (pp. 21-30).

Pensa, R. G., Leschi, C., Besson, J., & Boulicaut, J. (2004). *Assessment of discretization techniques for relevant pattern discovery from gene expression data*. Paper presented at the 4th ACM SIGKDD Workshop on Data Mining in Bioinformatics, Seattle, WA.

Pomeroy, S. L., Tamayo, P., Gaasenbeek, M., Sturla, L. M., Angelo, M., McLaughlin, M. E. et al. (2002). Prediction of central nervous system embryonal tumour outcome based on gene expression. *Nature, 415*(6870), 436-442.

Quackenbush, J. (2001). Computational Analysis of Microarray data. *Nature Reviews Genetics, 2*(6), 418-427.

Quackenbush, J. (2002). Microarray data normalization and transformation. *Nature Genetics, 32*(suppliment), 496-501.

Quinlan, J. R., & Quinlan, R. (1993). *C4.5: Programs for machine learning.* Morgan Kaufmann.

Ramaswamy, S., Tamayo, P., Rifkin, R., Mukherjee, S., Yeang, C. H., Angelo, M. et al. (2001). Multiclass cancer diagnosis using tumor gene expression signatures. In *Proc Natl Acad Sci USA, 98*(26), 15149-15154.

Ramsay, G. (1998). DNA chips: State-of-the art. *Nature Biotechnology, 16*, 40-44.

Ross, D. T., Scherf, U., Eisen, M. B., Perou, C. M., Rees, C., Spellman, P. et al. (2000). Systematic variation in gene expression patterns in human cancer cell lines. *Nat Genet, 24*(3), 227-235.

Schena, M., Shalon, D, Davis, R. W., & Brown, P. O. (1995). Quantitative monitoring of gene expression patterns with a complementary DNA microarray. *Science, 270*, 467-470.

Sesto, A., Navarro, M., Burslem, F., & Jorcano, J. L. (2002). Analysis of the ultraviolet B response in primary human keratinocytes using oligonucle-otide microarrays. In *Proc Natl Acad Sci USA, 99*(5), 2965-2970.

Shamir, R., & Sharan, R. (2001). Algorithmic approaches to clustering gene expression data. In T. S. T. Jiang, Y. Xu, & M.Q. Zhang (Ed.), *Current topics in computational biology.* Cambridge, MA: MIT Press.

Sharan, R., Elkon,R., & Shamir,R. (2001). *Cluster analysis and its applications to gene expression data.* Paper presented at the Ernst Schering workshop on Bioinformatics and Genome Analysis, Springer Verlag.

Sharan, R., & Shamir, R. (2000). CLICK: A clustering algorithm with applications to gene expression analysis. In *Proceedings of 8th International Conference of Intelligent System Molecular Biology* (Vol. 8, 307-316).

Sheng, Q., Moreau, Y., & Moor, B.D. (2003). Biclustering microarray data by Gibbs sampling. *Bioinformatics, 19*(Supplement 2), ii196-ii205.

Singh, K. A. S. R. V. (1998). An efficient K-means clustering algorithm. In *Proceedings of First Workshop on High Performance Data Mining.*

Spellman, P. T., Sherlock, G., Zhang, M. Q., Iyer, V. R., Anders, K., Eisen, M. B. et al. (1998). Comprehensive identification of cell cycle-regulated genes of the yeast Saccharomyces cerevisiae by microarray hybridization. *Mol Biol Cell, 9*(12), 3273-3297.

Sorlie, T., Perou, C. M., Tibshirani, R., Aas, T., Geisler, S., Johnsen, H. et al. (2001). Gene expression patterns of breast carcinomas distinguish tumor subclasses with clinical implications. In *Proc Natl Acad Sci USA, 98*(19), 10869-10874.

Tamayo, P., Slonim, D., Mesirov, J., Zhu, Q., Kitareewan, S., Dmitrovsky, E. et al. (1999). Interpreting patterns of gene expression with self-organizing maps: methods and application to hematopoietic differentiation. In *Proc Natl Acad Sci USA, 96*(6), 2907-2912.

Tang, C., Zhang, L., Zhang, A., & Ramanathan, M. (2001). *Interrelated two-way clustering: An unsupervised approach for gene expression data analysis.* Paper presented at the 2nd IEEE Symposium on BioInformatics and BioEngineering (BIBE'01), Bethesda, MD.

Theilhaber, J., Connolly, T., Roman-Roman, S., Bushnell, S., Jackson, A., Call, K. et al. (2002). Finding genes in the C2C12 osteogenic pathway by k-nearest-neighbor classification of expression data. *Genome Res, 12*(1), 165-176.

Tibshirani, R., Hastie,T.,Eisen,M., Ross,D., Botstein,D., & Brown,P. (1999). *Clustering methods for the analysis of DNA microarray data* (Technical Report): Stanford University.

Valdivia-Granda, W. A., Perrizo, W., Larson, F., & Deckard, E.L. (2002). *Peano count trees (P-trees) and association rule mining for gene expression profiling of DNA microarray data.* Paper presented at the The International Conference on Bioinformatics, Bangkok, Thailand.

Vingron, M., & Hoheisel, J. (1999). Computational aspects of expression data. *Journal of Molecular Medicine, 77*, 3-7.

Wang, J., Han, J., & Pei, J. (2003). Closet+: Searching for the best strategies for mining frequent closed itemsets. In *Proceedings of the ninth ACM SIGKDD International Conference on Knowledge Discovery and Data Mining* (pp. 236-245). New York: ACM Press.

Wei, N. (2002). Mining for escherichia coli gene expression data analysis. Unpublished master, University of Oklahoma, Norman.

Wei, N., Gruenwald, L., & Conway, T. (2003). *Analyzing the escherichia coli gene expression data by a multilayer adjusted tree organizing map.* Paper presented at the Third IEEE Symposium on BioInformatics and BioEngineering (BIBE'03).

Wen, X., Fuhrman, S., Michaels, G. S., Carr, D. B., Smith, S., Barker, J. L. et al. (1998). Large-scale temporal gene expression mapping of central nervous system development. In *Proc Natl Acad Sci USA, 95*(1), 334-339.

Whitney, A. R., Diehn, M., Popper, S. J., Alizadeh, A. A., Boldrick, J. C., Relman, D. A. et al. (2003). Individuality and variation in gene expression patterns in human blood. . In *Proc Natl Acad Sci USA, 100*(4), 1896-1901.

Xing, E. P., & Karp, R. M. (2001). CLIFF: Clustering of high-dimensionaln microarray data via iterative feature filtering using normalized cuts. *Bioinformatics, 1*(1), 1-9.

Xu, X., Cong, G., Ooi, B. C., Tan, K., & Tung, A. K. H. (2004, August 31-September 3). Semantic mining and anlysis of gene expression data. In M. T. Ö. Mario, A. Nascimento, Donald Kossmann, Renée J. Miller, José A. Blakeley & K. Bernhard Schiefer (Eds.), *Proceedings of the Thirtieth International Conference on Very Large Data Bases,* Toronto, Canada (pp. 1261-1264). Morgan Kaufmann.

Yang, Y., Chen, J.X., & Kim, W. (2003). Gene expression clustering and 3D visualization. *Computing in Science and Engineering, 5*(5), 37-43.

Yang, Y. H., Dudoit, S., Luu, P., Lin, D. M., Peng, V., Ngai, J. and Speed, T. P. (2002). Normalization for cDNA microarray data: A robust composite method addressing single and multiple slide systematic variation. *Nucleic Acids Research, 30*(4), e15.

Yeoh, E. J., Ross, M. E., Shurtleff, S. A., Williams, W. K., Patel, D., Mahfouz, R., Behm, F. G., Raimondi, S. C., Relling, M. V., Patel, A., Cheng, C., Campana, D., Wilkins, D., Zhou, X., Li, J., Liu, H., Pui, C. H., Evans, W. E., Naeve, C., Wong, L., & Downing, J. R. (2002). Classification, subtype discovery, and prediction of outcome in pediatric acute lymphoblastic leukemia by gene expression profiling. *Cancer Cell, 1*(2), 133-143.

Zaki, M. (2000). Generating non-redundant association rules. In *Proceedings of the Sixth ACM SIGKDD International Conference on Knowledge Discovery and Data Mining* (pp. 34-43). New York: ACM Press.

Zaki, M. J., & Hsiao, C.-J. (2002, April 11-13). Charm: An efficient algorithm for closed itemsets mining. In J. H. Robert, L. Grossman, Vipin Kumar, Heikki Mannila & Rajeev Motwani (Eds.), *Proceedings of the Second SIAM International Conference on Data Mining,* Arlington, VA. SIAM.

Zhang, B., Yang, J., & Chi, S. W. (2003). Self-organization latent lattice models for temporal gene expression profile. *Machine Learning, 52*(1-2), 67-89.

Zou, J., Young, S., Zhu, F., Gheyas, F., Skeans, S., Wan, Y. et al. (2002). Microarray profile of differentially expressed genes in a monkey model of allergic asthma. *Genome Biol, 3*(5), research0020.

About the Authors

Jérôme Darmont received his PhD in computer science from the University of Clermont-Ferrand II, France (1999). Since then, he has been an associate professor at the University of Lyon 2, France and head of the Decision Support Databases research group within the ERIC laboratory. His current research interests mainly relate to the evaluation and optimization of database management systems and data warehouses (benchmarking, auto-administration, optimization techniques…), but also include XML and complex data warehousing and mining and medical or health-related applications.

Omar Boussaïd is an associate professor in computer science at the School of Economics and Management, University of Lyon 2, France. He received his PhD in computer science from the University of Lyon 1, France (1988). Since 1995, he has been the director of the Master Computer Science Engineering for Decision and Economic Evaluation of the University of Lyon 2. He is a member of the decision support databases research group within the ERIC Laboratory. His main research subjects are data warehousing, multidimensional databases and OLAP. His current research concerns complex data warehousing, XML warehousing, data mining-based multidimensional modelling, OLAP and data mining combining and mining metadata in RDF form.

* * *

Serge Abiteboul is associated with Telecom Paris and earned PhDs in computer science from USC Los Angeles and Thèse d'Etat University of Paris. Abiteboul has 20 years of experience in research in databases, electronic commerce, document management, digital libraries and Web systems. He is head of the INRIA GEMO Research Group and has hlep professor positions at Stanford and Ecole Polytechnique. He received the 1998 ACM SIGMOD Innovation Award.

H. Azzag has a degree of engineering in computer science from the University of Houari Boumédienne, Algers, Algeria (2001). After obtaining a Master in Computer Science from the University of Tours, France, she started a PhD in computer science, at the University of Tours, that will be defended by the end of 2005. Her research interests are centered on visualization, clustering and data mining with artificial ants, especially when these methods are applied to the Web.

Antonio Badia received a degree in philosophy from the University of Barcelona and studied computer science at the Universitat Politecnica de Catalunya. He holds a PhD in computer science from Indiana University. He is currently as associate professor in the Computer Engineering and Computer Science Department, University of Louisville (USA), where he created and directs the Database Lab. His research focuses on query languages, data models, text processing and data mining, and has been funded by the National Science Foundation (including a CAREER award), the U.S. Navy and industry.

Elisa Bertino is a professor in the Department of Computer Sciences at Purdue University (USA) and research director at CERIAS. She has been a visiting researcher at the IBM Research Laboratory (now Almaden) in San Jose, at the Microelectronics and Computer Technology Corporation, at Rutgers University, and at Telcordia Technologies. Her main research interests include security, privacy, database systems, object-oriented technology, and multimedia systems. In those areas, she has published more than 300 papers and she has co-authored several books. She is a co-editor-in-chief of the *VLDB Journal* and a member of the advisory board of the IEEE TKDE. She serves on the editorial boards of several scientific journals, as a PC member of several international conferences, such as ACM SIGMOD, VLDB, ACM OOPSLA, as program co-chair of the IEEE ICDE 1998, ECOOP 2000, SACMAT 2002, EDBT 2004 conferences. She is a fellow of the IEEE and the ACM, and has been named a Golden Core Member for her service to the IEEE Computer Society.

Barbara Catania is an associate professor at the Department of Computer and Information Sciences of the University of Genova, Italy. In 1993, she graduated from the University of Genoa, Italy, in information sciences. She received her PhD in computer science from the University of Milan, Italy (1998). She has been a visiting researcher at the European Computer-Industry Research Center of Bull, ICL, and Siemens in Munich, Germany, and at the National University of Singapore. Her main research interests include: deductive and constraint databases, spatial databases, XML and Web databases, pattern management, indexing techniques, and database security.

Tao Cheng received his BE in computer science and engineering from Zhejiang University, China (2003). After a short detour in the Computer Science Department at the University of California, Santa Barbara, he joined the Computer Science Department at the University of Illinois, Urbana-Champaign (USA), where he is currently a PhD student. He developed interest in hierarchical structure management during his stay at National Technical University of Athens, where he worked as an intern under the supervision of Professor Timos Sellis. His recent research interest lies in Web search and Web mining.

Tyrrell Conway is a professor of microbiology and co-director of the Advanced Center for Genome Technology, University of Oklahoma (USA). Dr. Conway has published in many scientific journals, including the *Proceedings of the National Academy of Sciences*, *Molecular Microbiology*, *Journal of Bacteriology*. He is co-inventor of several U.S. patents, including Patent No. 5,000,000. Funding for his research has been provided by the National Science Foundation, U.S. Department of Energy, and the National Institutes of Health. Dr. Conway's current research interests involve bacterial metabolism, ecology and pathogenesis, as well as bioinformatics and functional genomics of *E. coli*.

Theodore Dalamagas received his degree in electrical engineering in 1996 from the National Technical University of Athens (NTUA), Greece. In 1997 he received an MSc from Glasgow University and in 2005 a PhD from the NTUA. He is currently a postdoc researcher in the Knowledge and Database Systems Lab of NTUA. His research interests include tree-structured data management, schema integration, integration of Web and databases and information retrieval.

Maria Luisa Damiani graduated in computer science (cum laude) from the University of Pisa (Italy). She is currently an assistant professor at DICO, Dipartimento di Informatica e Comunicazione of the University of Milan (Italy). She has been a researcher at the labs of public and private Italian software companies for several years. As technical leader and project manager she has been involved in several EU-funded research projects. Since 1995 her main research interest is in geographical information management and applications. In 2003 she joined the University of Milan. Current research specifically focuses on geographical data security & privacy and spatial data warehousing.

Tharam S. Dillon is the dean of the Faculty of Information Technology at University of Technology, Sydney (UTS), Australia. His research interests include data mining, Internet computing, e-commerce, hybrid neuro-symbolic systems, neural nets, software engineering, database systems and computer networks. He has also worked with industry and commerce in developing systems in telecommunications, health care systems, e-commerce, logistics, power systems, and banking and finance. He is editor-in-chief of the *International Journal of Computer Systems Science and Engineering* and the *International Journal of Engineering Intelligent Systems*, as well as co-editor of the *Journal of Electric Power and Energy Systems*. He is on the advisory editorial board of *Applied Intelligence* published by Kluwer in the U.S. and *Computer Communications* published by Elsevier in the UK. He has published more than 400 papers in international and national journals and conferences and has written four books and edited five other books. He is a fellow of the IEEE, fellow of the Institution of Engineers (Australia), and fellow of the Australian Computer Society.

Adir Even is a doctoral student at the Boston University School of Management (USA). He received his MBA from the Tel-Aviv University School of Management and his MSc in computer engineering from the Technion of Israel. His research interests include business valuation of information systems, data and metadata, studying implications for system architecture, data quality management, data warehousing, and knowledge management. Prior to pursuing a doctoral degree, he has worked as a senior software development manager, responsible for large-scale data warehousing and DSS implementations.

Georges Gardarin was born in Riom, France on February 19, 1947. He entered Ecole Normale Superieure de l'Enseignement Technique in 1968. From 1971 to 1978, he was an assistant professor at Paris VI University. During that period, he was also a consultant at Ordoprocessor where he built a computer system, and at Renault, where he designed a new distributed information system. He did his PhD thesis in 1978 on concurrency control in distributed databases at the University of Paris VI. From 1978 to 1980, he was visiting professor at UCLA, California. He published several papers on concurrency control and database integrity, notably with Professor W. Chu and M. Melkanoff. From 1980 to 1990, he was a professor at Paris VI University, teaching databases and distributed systems. He was also chief scientist at INRIA where he headed the Sabre project, which was developing an object-relational parallel DBMS. From 1990 to 2000, he created and developed the PRiSM Research Laboratory at the new University of Versailles Saint-Quentin. He is heading the PRiSM research laboratory, the computer science research laboratory specialized in parallelism, networking, DBMSs and performance modeling. The laboratory now has 40 permanent researchers and more than 60 PHD students. Georges Gardarin has written more than 120 papers in international journal and conferences, and several books in French, some of them being translated in English and Spanish. Georges Gardarin is currently working on federated databases (MIRO-Web project) based on XML and the XMLQL query language, and also on data mining.

Le Gruenwald is a professor in the School of Computer Science at the University of Oklahoma (USA). She received her PhD in computer science from Southern Methodist University (1990). She was a member of the technical staff in the Database Management Group at the Advanced Switching Laboratory of NEC, America, a lecturer in the Computer Science and Engineering Department at Southern Methodist University and a software engineer at White River Technologies, Inc. Her major research interests include mobile and distributed databases, data mining, bioinformatics, Web-enabled databases, real-time databases, multimedia databases and data warehouse. She is a member of ACM, SIGMOD, and IEEE Computer Society.

Giovanna Guerrini is an associate professor at the Department of Computer Science of the University of Pisa, Italy. She received the MS and PhD degrees in computer science from the University of Genova, Italy (1993 and 1998, respectively). Before joining the University of Pisa in 2001 she had been an assistant professor at the Department of Computer and Information Sciences, University of Genova. Her research interests include object-oriented, active, and temporal databases as well as semi-structured and XML data handling. She has served as Program Committee member of international conferences, like EDBT, ECOOP, ACM OOPSLA, ACM CIKM.

C. Guinot, PhD, DSc, took two post-doctoral positions from 1982 to 1986 in medical statistics at Gustave-Roussy Institute in France and at Showa University School of Medicine in Japan. In 1986, she started working for an international pharmaceutical group to head biostatistical departments. Then in 1991, she took part in the creation of the C.E.R.I.E.S., a research centre on human skin. Since this date, she is in charge of the Biometrics and Epidemiology Department, CERIES. In addition, she was elected president of the French Association of Statisticians (SFdS) in 2005. She also was elected a member of the International Statistical Institute in 2002.

Jilin Han, PhD, is currently working for the Bioinformatics Core Facility/ dvanced Center for Genome Technology at the University of Oklahoma (USA). He has published more than 20 papers in scientific journals and in national and international conference proceedings. His current interests include data mining for gene expression data analysis, as well as database modeling, design, and management.

Ioannis Karydis was born in Athens, Greece in 1979. He received his BEng (2000) in engineering science and technology from Brunel University, UK and an MSc (2001) in advanced methods in computer science from Queen Mary University, UK. Currently he is researching for a PhD in music databases. His research interests include music databases, music information retrieval (indexing & searching) and music object representation.

Anna Maddalena is a PhD student in computer science at the Department of Computer and Information Sciences of the University of Genova, Italy. In 2001, she graduated from the University of Genova, Italy, in computer science. Her main research interests include: pattern management and data mining, data warehousing, XML query processing.

Yannis Manolopoulos was born in Thessaloniki, Greece in 1957. He received a BEng (1981) in electrical eng. and a PhD (1986) in computer eng., both from the Aristotle University of Thessaloniki (Greece). Currently, he is professor at the Department of Informatics of the latter university. He has been with the Department of Computer Science of the University of Toronto, the Department of Computer Science of the University of Maryland at College Park and the University of Cyprus. He has published over 150 papers in refereed scientific journals and conference proceedings. He is co-author of the following books *Advanced Database Indexing* and *Advanced Signature Indexing for Multimedia and Web Applications* (Kluwer), as well as *Nearest Neighbor Search: A Database Perspective* and *R-trees: Theory and Applications* (Springer). He served/serves as PC co-chair of the 8th National Computer Conference (2001), the 6th ADBIS Conference (2002) the 5th WDAS Workshop (2003), the 8th SSTD Symposium (2003), the 1st Balkan Conference in Informatics (2003) and the 16th SSDBM Conference (2004). Also, currently he is vice-chairman of the Greek Computer Society and chair of the Greek SIGKDD Section. His research interests include databases, data mining, Web and geographical information systems, Performance evaluation of storage subsystems. Further information can be found at http://delab.csd.auth.gr.

Marco Mesiti is an assistant professor at University of Milan, Italy. He received MS and PhD degrees in computer science from the University of Genova, Italy (1998 and 2003, respectively). His main research interests include management of semi-structured data, querying and classification of XML documents, access control mechanisms for XML, database technology for telecommunication applications and data age on temporal databases. He has been a visiting researcher at the applied research center of Telcordia Technologies, Morristown, NJ. He was co-organizer of the 1st EDBT Workshop DataX 2004 and served as PC member of IEEE SAINT'2005, IEEE SAINT'2006, EDBT'2004 Workshop ClustWeb, and as reviewer for international conferences and journals.

Bernhard Mitschang is a professor for database and information systems at Stuttgart University, Germany. He received a PhD (Dr.-Ing.) in computer science from the University of Kaiserslautern (1988). From 1994 to 1998 he was a professor at the Technische Universität München. From 1989 to 1990 he was on leave to IBM Almaden Research Center, San Jose, CA as a visiting scientist. His research interests are database management systems, including object-oriented support, semantic modelling, query languages, optimizations and parallelism, and application-oriented areas like middleware and component technology, engineering information systems, and knowledge base management systems.

Rodrigo Salvador Monteiro is a PhD student at the Federal University of Rio de Janeiro (Brazil). His area of specialization is databases, and he is involved in research in fields such spatial databases, data mining, data warehouse and GIS. Mr. Monteiro received his bachelor's degree in computer science (2000) and his master's degree (2001) in computer science from the Federal University of Rio de Janeiro (Brazil). From April/2004 to June/2005 Mr. Monteiro was a visitor PhD student at the University of Stuttgart (Germany).

Jano Moreira de Souza is a professor of computer science at the Graduate School of Engineering (COPPE) and Mathematics Institute of the Federal University of Rio de Janeiro (UFRJ) (Brazil). His area of specialization is databases, and he is involved in research in fields such as CSCW, decision support systems, knowledge management and GIS. Professor de Souza received his bachelor's degree in mechanical engineering (1974) and his master's degree (1978) in system engineering from the Federal University of Rio de Janeiro (Brazil), and his PhD in information systems (1986) from the University of East Anglia (England).

Alexandros Nanopoulos was born in Craiova, Romania, in 1974. He graduated from the Department of Informatics, Aristotle University of Thessaloniki, Greece (1996), and obtained a PhD from the same institute (2003). The subject of his dissertation was "Techniques for Non Relational Data Mining". He is co-author of more than 30 articles in international journals and conferences, also co-author of the monographs "Advanced Signature Techniques for Multimedia and Web Applications" and "R-trees: Theory and Applications". His research interests include spatial and Web mining, integration of data mining with DBMSs, and spatial database indexing.

Vicky Nassis received her Bachelor of Information Systems and Bachelor of Business from La Trobe University, Australia and is currently a PhD student within the school of Computer Science and Computer Engineering at the same university. Her research interests include object-oriented conceptual models, XML and data warehousing. Her thesis is concerned with the conceptual design of data warehouses in integration with XML. She has been examining techniques to overcome some of the problems encountered during the conceptual design process. She has also been involved in exploring the issues of XML and its use in handling publications over the Web. She has had publications in the proceedings of several international conferences, in the field of data warehousing and knowledge discovery, Web systems and intelligence as well as a journal publication in the subject of data warehousing and mining.

Benjamin Nguyen studied at the Ecole Normale Supérieure de Cachan, and received his PhD from the University of Paris XI (2003). He is an assistant professor in the database group at the University of Versailles and St-Quentin-En-Yvelines, and member of the World Wide Web Consortium Working Group on Semantic Web Best Practices. His research interests include XML applications and Web warehousing.

F. Picarougne, PhD, has been an assistant professor since September 2005 in the University of Nantes, France. After obtaining a Master in Computer Science from the University of Tours, France (2001), he has defended his PhD in computer science in October 2004. His research interests are centered on Web search engines.

Wenny Rahayu is an associate professor at the Department of Computer Science and Computer Engineering LaTrobe University, Australia. She has been actively working in the areas of database design and implementation covering object-relational databases, Web and e-commerce databases, semi-structured databases and XML, Semantic Web and ontology, data warehousing, and parallel databases. She has worked with industry and expertise from other disciplines in a number of projects including bioinformatics databases, parallel data mining, and e-commerce catalogues. She has been invited to give seminars in the area of e-commerce databases in a number of international institutions. She has edited three books, which form a series in Web applications, including Web databases, Web information systems and Web semantics. She has also published over 70 papers in international journals and conferences.

R Rajugan holds a bachelor's degree in information systems from La Trobe University, Australia. He has worked in the industry as chief application/database programmer in developing sports planing and sports fitness & injury management software and as database administrator. He was also involved in developing an e-commerce solution for a global logistics (logistics, cold-storage and warehousing) company as a software engineer/architect. He is currently a PhD student at University of Technology, Sydney (UTS) Australia. He has published research articles, which have appeared in international refereed conference and journal proceedings. His research interests include object-oriented conceptual models, XML, data warehousing, software engineering, database and e-commerce systems. He is an Associate member of Australian Computer Society (AACS), member of ACM and student member of IEEE.

Jörg Rech received the BS (Vordiplom) and the MS (Diplom) in computer science with a minor in electrical science from the University of Kaiserslautern, Germany. He was a research assistant at the software engineering research group (AGSE) by Prof. Dieter Rombach at the University of Kaiserslautern. Currently, he is a researcher and project manager at the Fraunhofer Institute for Experimental Software Engineering, Germany. His research mainly concerns knowledge discovery in software repositories, defect discovery, code mining, code retrieval, software analysis, software measurement, and knowledge management.

Gabriela Ruberg works as a system analyst at Central Bank of Brazil, the Financial Regulatory Agency and Federal Reserve System of the Brazilian government. She has a Master degree in database systems by the Federal University of Rio de Janeiro (COPPE/UFRJ), with emphasis on cost-based performance analysis of query processing in partitioned object databases. She is currently a PhD candidate at COPPE/UFRJ, and her recent works address query optimization techniques for distributed XML repositories. Her research interests include distributed data management, XML, Web services, and P2P computing.

Holger Schwarz received his PhD in computer science from the University of Stuttgart (Germany) in 2002 where he currently works as senior researcher and lecturer. His main scientific interests cover data warehousing and data mining as well as technologies supporting data-intensive applications.

Timos Sellis received his degree in electrical engineering in 1982 from the National Technical University of Athens (NTUA), Greece. In 1983 he received an MSc from Harvard University and in 1986 a PhD from the University of California at Berkeley. In 1986, he joined the Department of Computer Science of the University of Maryland, College Park, and in 1992 the Computer Science Division of NTUA, where he is currently a full professor. His research interests include peer-to-peer database systems, data warehouses, the integration of Web and databases, and spatial database systems. He has published over 120 articles in journals and conferences and has been an invited speaker in major international events.

G. Shankaranarayanan obtained his PhD in management information systems from The University of Arizona. He is an assistant professor of Information Systems in Boston University School of Management (USA). His research interests include schema evolution in databases, data modeling requirements and methods, and structures for and the management of metadata. Specific topics in metadata include metadata implications for data warehouses, metadata management for knowledge management systems, metadata management for data quality, metadata models for mobile data services.

Stefano Spaccapietra is a full professor. Since 1998 he is heading the Database Laboratory at the Ecole Polytechnique Fédérale in Lausanne, Switzerland. His PhD is from University of Paris VI, in 1978. His research focus has always been on semantic issues. In particular, he significantly contributed to the areas of conceptual data modelling and distributed data management. He developed

R&D activities on visual user interfaces, semantic interoperability, spatio-temporal data modelling, multimedia databases and various other modelling issues. He currently serves as editor-in-chief for the Journal on Semantics of Data, for LNCS Springer.

G. Venturini is a professor in computer science at the University of Tours, France, since 1998. He is at the head of the Networks and New ITs research group of the Computer Science Lab. His research interests are located at the crossroads between the Web/Internet, biomimetic algorithms, and visual data mining techniques. He is co-editor of the French New ITs journal.

Geraldo Zimbrão is an assistant professor of computer science at the Graduate School of Engineering (COPPE) and Mathematics Institute of the Federal University of Rio de Janeiro (UFRJ) (Brazil). His area of specialization is databases, and he is involved in research in fields such as spatial databases, GIS, query optimization and database cluster. Professor Zimbrao received his bachelor's degree in computer science (1992), his master's degree in Applied Mathematics (1993) and his PhD in computer science (1998) from the Federal University of Rio de Janeiro (Brazil).

Index

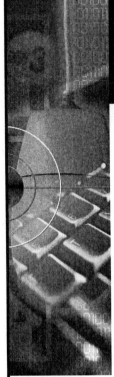

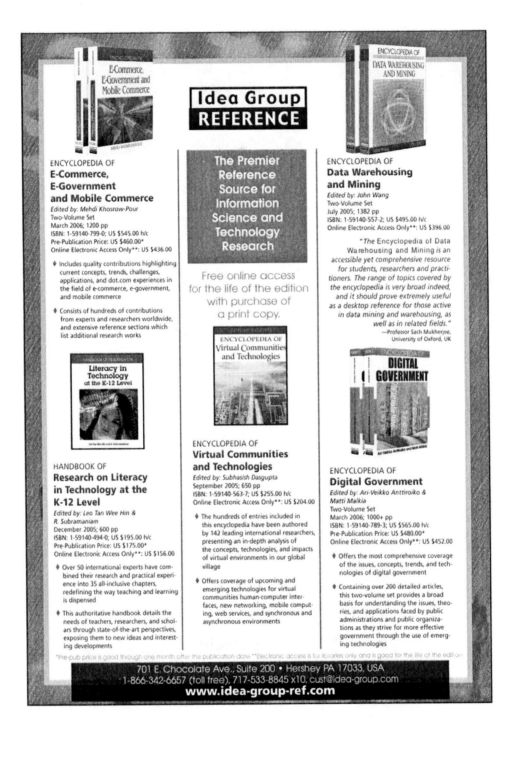